Granada & Monarch Automotive Repair Manual

by Larry Warren and John H Haynes
Member of the Guild of Motoring Writers

Models covered

1975 thru 1980 Ford Granada and Mercury Monarch 2-door
and 4-door sedans with in-line 6-cyl and V8 engines

ISBN 0 85696 359 3

THE BOOK

AUTOMOTIVE
PARTS &
ACCESSORIES
ASSOCIATION   MEMBER

Haynes Publishing Group
Sparkford Nr Yeovil
Somerset BA22 7JJ England

Haynes Publications, Inc
861 Lawrence Drive
Newbury Park
California 91320 USA

Acknowledgements

We wish to thank the Ford Motor Company for the supply of technical manuals and information as well as some of the illustrations which were used in the production of this manual.

The Champion Spark Plug Company supplied the illustrations showing the various spark plug conditions. The bodywork repair photographs used in this manual were provided by Holt Lloyd Ltd who supply 'Turtle Wax', 'Dupli-Color Holts', and other Holts range products.

About this manual

Its purpose

The purpose of this manual is to help you get the best value from your vehicle. It can do so in several ways. It can help you decide what work must be done even if you choose to get it done by a dealer service department or a repair shop; it provides information and procedures for routine maintenance and servicing; and it offers diagnostic and repair procedures to follow when trouble occurs.

It is hoped that you will use the manual to tackle the work yourself. For many simpler jobs, doing it yourself may be quicker than arranging an appointment to get the vehicle into a shop and making the trips to leave it and pick it up. More importantly, a lot of money can be saved by avoiding the expense the shop must pass on to you to cover its labor and overhead costs. An added benefit is the sense of satisfaction and accomplishment that you feel after having done the job yourself.

Using the manual

The manual is divided into Chapters. Each Chapter is divided into numbered Sections, which are headed in bold type between horizontal lines. Each Section consists of consecutively numbered paragraphs.

The two types of illustrations used (figures and photographs) are referenced by a number preceding their captions. Figure reference numbers denote Chapter and numerical sequence in the Chapter; i.e. Fig. 12.4 means Chapter 12, figure number 4. Figure captions are followed by a Section number which ties the figure to a specific portion of the text. All photographs apply to the Chapter in which they appear, and the reference number pinpoints the pertinent Section and paragraph.

Procedures, once described in the text, are not normally repeated. When it is necessary to refer to another Chapter, the reference will be given as Chapter and Section number; i.e. Chapter 1/16. Cross reference given without use of the word 'Chapter' apply to Sections and/or paragraphs in the same Chapter. For example, 'see Section 8' means in the same Chapter.

Reference to the left or right of the vehicle is based on the assumption that one is sitting in the driver's seat facing forward.

Even though extreme care has been taken during the preparation of this manual, neither the publisher nor the author can accept responsibility for any errors in, or omissions from, the information given.

Introduction to the Ford Granada and Mercury Monarch

The Ford Granada and Mercury Monarch are available as 2- and 4-door sedans in a variety of trim options.

Engine options include the 200 (3.3 liter) and 250 (4.1 liter) cubic inch in-line cylinder engine and V8 engines of 255 (4.2 liter), 302 (5.0 liter) and 351 (5.8 liter) cubic inch displacement.

Chassis layout is conventional with the engine mounted at the front and the power being transmitted through either a manual or automatic transmission by a driveshaft to the solid rear axle.

Front suspension is an independent coil spring design and rear suspension is by leaf spring and shock absorber. Steering is the recirculating ball type.

Brakes are disc at front with self-adjusting drum at the rear with vacuum assist as an option.

Contents

Top **Lincoln Mercury Monarch 4-door sedan** *Bottom* **1975 Ford Granada 2-door Coupe**

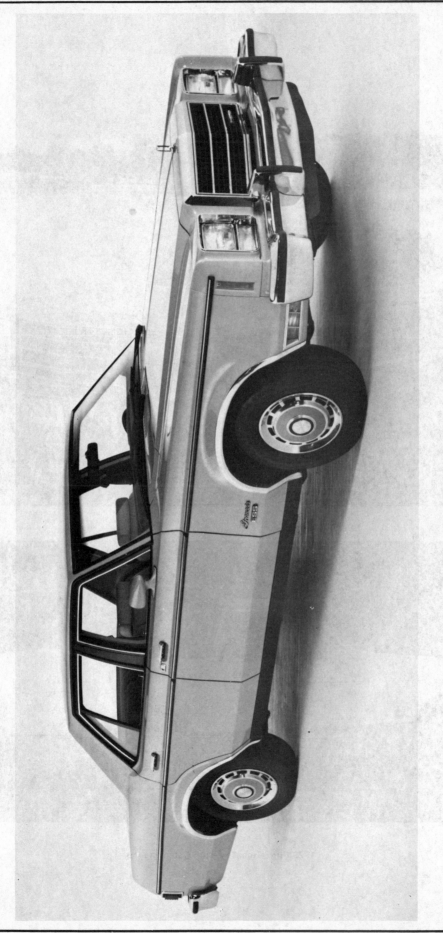

1978 Ford Granada ESS

1978 Ford Granada 2-door Coupe models

1980 Ford Granada Ghia 4-door sedan

1980 Lincoln Mercury Monarch 2-door Coupe

General dimensions, capacities and weights

Dimensions
Overall length	197.8 in
Overall height	53.3 in
Overall width	74.5 in
Wheelbase	109.9 in

Capacities

Engine oil .... 4.0 US qts (Add 1 quart extra if the filter is replaced)

Coolant

	Air conditioning US qts	Standard US qts
1975 thru 1977		
3.3L six-cylinder	–	9.9
4.1L six-cylinder	10.7	10.5
5.0L V8	14.6	14.4
5.8L V8	16.7	15.7
1978 thru 1980		
4.1L six-cylinder	10.6	10.5
4.2L V8	14.3	14.2
5.0L V8	14.3	14.2

Fuel tank (approximate)

1975 thru 1977	19.2 US gal
1978 thru 1980	18.0 US gal

Manual transmission lubricant

3-speed	3.5 US pints
4-speed	4.5 US pints

Automatic transmission fluid

1975 and 1976	
C4 (3.3L. 4.1L and 5.0L)	8.75 US pints
C4 (5.8L)	10.25 US pints
1977	
C4 (4.1L and 5.0L)	8.25 US pints
C4 (5.8L)	10.25 US pints
1978	
JATCO (4.1L)	8.5 US pints
C4 (4.1L)	8.25 US pints
C4 (5.0L)	10.0 US pints
1979	
JATCO (4.1L)	8.5 US pints
C4 (4.1L and 5.0L)	10.0 US pints
1980	
JATCO (4.1L)	8.6 US pints
C4 (4.1, 4.2 and 5.0L)	9.6 US pints

Rear axle

8-in ring gear	4.5 US pints
8.7-in ring gear	4.0 US pints
9-in ring gear	5.0 US pints

Curb weight (approximate)
2-door	3207 lbs
4-door	3250 lbs

Buying parts and vehicle identification numbers

Buying spare parts

Spare parts are available from many sources, which generally fall into one of two categories – authorized dealer parts departments and independent retail auto parts stores. Our advice concerning spare parts is as follows:

Authorized dealer parts department: This is the best source for parts which are peculiar to your vehicle and not generally available elsewhere (i.e. major engine parts, transmission parts, trim pieces, etc). It is also the only place you should buy parts if your vehicle is still under warranty, as non-factory parts may invalidate the warranty. To be sure of obtaining the correct parts, have your vehicle's engine and chassis numbers available and, if possible, take the old parts along for positive identification.

Retail auto parts stores: Good auto parts stores will stock frequently needed components which wear out relatively fast (i.e. clutch components, exhaust systems, brake parts, tune-up parts, etc). These stores often supply new or reconditioned parts on an exchange basis, which can save a considerable amount of money. Discount auto stores are often very good places to buy materials and parts needed for general vehicle maintenance (i.e. oil, grease, filters, spark plugs, belts, touch-up, paint, bulbs. etc). They also usually sell tools and general accessories, have convenient hours, charge lower prices, and can often be found not far from your home.

Vehicle identification numbers

Regardless from which source parts are obtained, it is essential to provide correct information concerning the vehicle model and year of manufacture plus the engine serial number and the vehicle identification number (VIN). The accompanying illustrations show where these important numbers can be found.

Typical vehicle identification number location

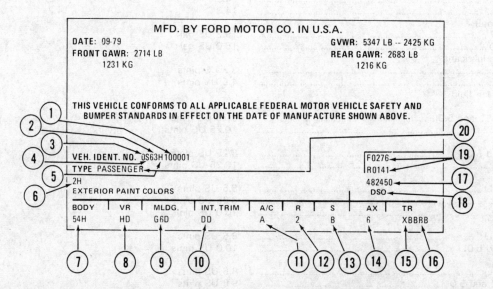

Located on the front left door post, the vehicle certification tag contains the following information:

1 Consecutive unit number	6 Paint	11 Air conditioning	16 Springs – Front L and R, Rear L and R (4 codes)
2 Body serial code	7 Body type code	12 Radio	17 District sales office
3 Model year code	8 Vinyl roof	13 Sun/Moon roof	18 Special order number
4 Assembly plant code	9 Body side moulding	14 Axle ratio	19 Accessories
5 Engine code	10 Trim code	15 Transmission	20 Vehicle type

Maintenance techniques, tools and working facilities

Basic maintenance techniques

There are a number of techniques involved in maintenance and repair that will be referred to throughout this manual. Application of these techniques will enable the home mechanic to be more efficient, better organized and capable of performing the various tasks properly, which will ensure that the repair job is thorough and complete.

Fasteners

Fasteners, basically, are nuts, bolts, studs and screws used to hold two or more parts together. There are a few things to keep in mind when working with fasteners. Almost all of them use a locking device of some type; either a lock washer, locknut, locking tab or thread adhesive. All threaded fasteners should be clean and straight, with undamaged threads and undamaged corners on the hex head where the wrench fits. Develop the habit of replacing damaged nuts and bolts with new ones. Special locknuts with nylon or fiber inserts can only be used once. If they are removed, they lose their locking ability and must be replaced with new ones.

Rusted nuts and bolts should be treated with a penetrating fluid to ease removal and prevent breakage. Some mechanics use turpentine in a spout-type oil can, which works quite well. After applying the rust penetrant, let it "work" for a few minutes before trying to loosen the nut or bolt. Badly rusted fasteners may have to be chiseled or sawed off or removed with a special nut breaker, available at tool stores.

If a bolt or stud breaks off in an assembly, it can be drilled and removed with a special tool commonly available for this purpose. Most automotive machine shops can perform this task, as well as other repair procedures (such as repair of threaded holes that have been stripped out).

Flat washers and lock washers, when removed from an assembly should always be replaced exactly as removed. Replace damaged washers with new ones. Always use a flat washer between a lock washer and any soft metal surface (such as aluminum), thin sheet metal or plastic.

Fastener sizes

For a number of reasons, automobile manufacturers are making wider and wider use of metric fasteners. Therefore, it is important to be able to tell the difference between standard (sometimes called U.S., English or SAE) and metric hardware, since thay cannot be interchanged.

All bolts, whether standard or metric, are sized according to diameter, thread pitch and length. For example, a standard $\frac{1}{2} - 13 \times 1$ bolt is $\frac{1}{2}$ inch in diameter, has 13 threads per inch and is 1 inch long. An M12 − 1.75 x 25 metric bolt is 12 mm in diameter, has a thread pitch of 1.75 mm (the distance between threads) and is 25 mm long. The 2 bolts are nearly identical, and easily confused, but they are not interchangeable.

In addition to the differences in diameter, thread pitch and length, metric and standard bolts can also be distinguished by examining the bolt heads. To begin with, the distance across the flats on a standard bolt head is measured in inches, while the same dimension on a metric bolt is measured in millimeters (the same is true for nuts). As a result, a standard wrench should not be used on a metric bolt and a metric wrench should not be used on a standard bolt. Also, standard bolts have slashes radiating out from the center of the head to denote the grade or strength of the bolt (which is an indication of the amount of

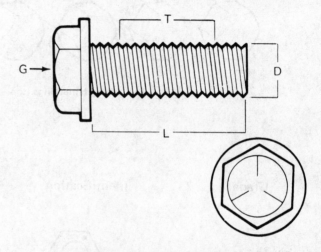

Standard (SAE) bolt dimensions/grade marks

G	−	Grade marks (bolt strength)
L	−	Length (in inches)
T	−	Thread pitch (number of threads per inch)
D	−	Nominal diameter (in inches)

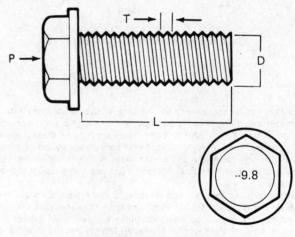

Metric bolt dimensions/grade marks

P	−	Property class (bolt strength)
L	−	Length (in millimeters)
T	−	Thread ptich (distance between threads: in millimeters)
D	−	Nominal diameter (in millimeters)

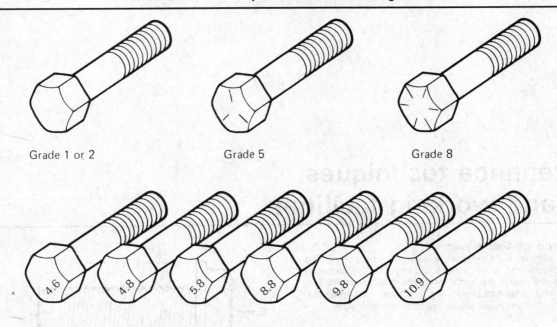

Grade 1 or 2   Grade 5   Grade 8

Bolt strength markings (top – standard/SAE, bottom – metric)

Grade	Identification
Hex Nut Grade 5	3 Dots
Hex Nut Grade 8	6 Dots

Standard hex nut strength markings

Class	Identification
Hex Nut Property Class 9	Arabic 9
Hex Nut Property Class 10	Arabic 10

Metric hex nut strength markings

torque that can be supplied to it). The greater the number of slashes, the greater the strength of the bolt (grades 0 through 5 are commonly used on automobiles). Metric bolts have a property class (grade) number, rather than a slash, molded into their heads to indicate bolt strength. In this case, the higher the number the stronger the bolt (property class numbers 8.8, 9.8 and 10.9 are commonly used on automobiles).

Strength markings can also be used to distinguish standard hex nuts from metric hex nuts. Standard nuts have dots stamped into one side, while metric nuts are marked with a number. The greater the number of dots, or the higher the number, the greater the strength of the nut.

Metric studs are also marked on their ends according to property class (grade). Larger studs are numbered (the same as metric bolts), while smaller studs carry a geometric code to denote grade.

It should be noted that many fasteners, especially Grades 0 through 2, have no distinguishing marks on them. When such is the

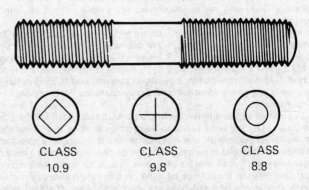

CLASS 10.9   CLASS 9.8   CLASS 8.8

Metric stud strength markings

case, the only way to determine whether it is standard or metric is to measure the thread pitch or compare it to a known fastener of the same size.

Since fasteners of the same size (both standard and metric) may have different strength ratings, be sure to reinstall any bolts, studs or nuts removed from your vehicle in their original locations. Also, when replacing a fastener with a new one, make sure that the new one has a strength rating equal to or greater than the original.

Tightening sequences and procedures

Most threaded fasteners should be tightened to a specific torque value (torque is basically a twisting force). Over-tightening the fastener can weaken it and lead to eventual breakage, while under-tightening can cause it to eventually come loose. Bolts, screws and studs, depending on the materials they are made of and their thread diameters, have specific torque values (many of which are noted in the Specifications Section at the beginning of each Chapter). Be sure to follow the torque recommendations closely. For fasteners not assigned a specific torque, a general torque value chart is presented here as a guide. As was previously mentioned, the sizes and grade of a fastener determine the amount of torque that can safely be applied to it. The figures listed here are approximate for Grade 2 and Grade 3 fasteners (higher grades can tolerate higher torque values).

	ft-lb	Nm
Metric thread sizes		
M-6	6 to 9	9 to 12
M-8	14 to 21	19 to 28
M-10	28 to 40	38 to 54
M-12	50 to 71	68 to 96
M-14	80 to 140	109 to 154
Pipe thread sizes		
$\frac{1}{8}$	5 to 8	7 to 10
$\frac{1}{4}$	12 to 18	17 to 24
$\frac{3}{8}$	22 to 33	30 to 44
$\frac{1}{2}$	25 to 35	34 to 47
U.S. thread sizes		
$\frac{1}{4}$ - 20	6 to 9	9 to 12
$\frac{5}{16}$ - 18	12 to 18	17 to 24
$\frac{5}{16}$ - 24	14 to 20	19 to 27
$\frac{3}{8}$ - 16	22 to 32	30 to 43
$\frac{3}{8}$ - 24	27 to 38	37 to 51
$\frac{7}{16}$ - 14	40 to 55	55 to 74
$\frac{7}{16}$ - 20	40 to 60	55 to 81
$\frac{1}{2}$ - 13	55 to 80	75 to 108

Fasteners laid out in a pattern (i.e. cylinder head bolts, oil pan bolts, differential cover bolts, etc.) must be loosened and tightened in a definite sequence to avoid warping the component. Initially, the bolts or nuts should be assembled finger-tight only. Next, they should be tightened one full turn each, in a criss-cross or diagonal pattern. After each one has been tightened one full turn, return to the first one and tighten them all one half turn, following the same pattern. Finally, tighten each of them one-quarter turn at a time until they all have been tightened to the proper torque value. To loosen and remove them the procedure would be reversed.

Component disassembly

Component disassembly should be done with care and purpose to help ensure that the parts go back together properly. Always keep track of the sequence in which parts are removed. Make note of special characteristics or markings on parts that can be installed more than one way (such as a grooved thrust washer on a shaft). It is a good idea to lay the disassembled parts out on a clean surface in the order that they were removed. It may also be helpful to make simple sketches or take instant photos of components before removal.

When removing fasteners from an assembly, keep track of their locations. Sometimes threading a bolt back in a part, or putting the washers and nut back on a stud, can prevent mixups later. If nuts and bolts cannot be returned to their original locations, they should be kept in a compartment box or a series of small boxes. A cupcake or muffin tin is ideal for this purpose, since each cavity can hold the bolts and nuts from a particular area (i.e. oil pan bolts, valve cover bolts, engine mount bolts, etc.). A pan of this type is especially helpful when working on assemblies with very small parts (such as the carburetor, alternator, valve train or interior dash and trim pieces). The cavities can be marked with paint or tape to identify the contents.

Whenever wiring looms, harnesses or connectors are separated, it's a good idea to identify them with numbered pieces of masking tape so that they can be easily reconnected.

Gasket sealing surfaces

Throughout any vehicle, gaskets are used to seal the mating surfaces between two parts and keep lubricants, fluids, vacuum or pressure contained in an assembly.

Many times these gaskets are coated with a liquid or paste-type gasket sealing compound before assembly. Age, heat and pressure can sometimes cause the two parts to stick together so tightly that they are very difficult to separate. Often the assembly can be loosened by striking it with a soft-faced hammer near the mating surfaces. A regular hammer can be used if a block of wood is placed between the hammer and the part. Do not hammer on cast parts or parts that could be easily damaged. With any particularly stubborn part, always recheck to see that every fastener has been removed.

Avoid using a screwdriver or bar to pry apart an assembly, as they can easily mar the gasket sealing surfaces of the parts (which must remain smooth). If prying is absolutely necessary, use an old broom handle, but keep in mind that extra clean-up will be necessary if the wood splinters.

After the parts are separated, the old gasket must be carefully scraped off and the gasket surfaces cleaned. Stubborn gasket material can be soaked with rust penetrant or treated with a special chemical to soften it so that it can be easily scraped off. A scraper can be fashioned from a piece of copper tubing by flattening and sharpening one end. Copper is recommended because it is usually softer than the surfaces to be scraped, which reduces the chance of gouging the part. Some gaskets can be removed with a wire brush, but regardless of the method used, the mating surfaces must be left clean and smooth. If for some reason the gasket surface is gouged, then a gasket sealer thick enough to fill scratches will have to be used upon reassembly of the components. For most applications, a non-drying (or semi-drying) gasket sealer should be used.

Hose removal tips

Caution: *If equipped with air conditioning, do not ever disconnect any of the a/c hoses without first de-pressurizing the system.*

Hose removal precautions closely parallel gasket removal precautions. Avoid scratching or gouging the surface that the hose mates against or the connection may leak. This is especially true for radiator hoses. Because of various chemical reactions, the rubber in hoses can bond itself to the metal spigot that the hose fits over. To remove a hose, first loosen the hose clamps that secure it to the spigot. Then, with slip joint pliers, grab the hose at the clamp and rotate it around the spigot. Work it back and forth until it is completely free, then pull it off (silicone or other lubricants will ease removal if they can be applied between the hose and the spigot). Apply the same lubricant to the inside of the hose and the outside of the spigot to simplify installation.

If a hose clamp is broken or damaged, do not re-use it. Do not reuse hoses that are cracked, split or torn.

Tools

A selection of good tools is a basic requirement for anyone who plans to maintain and repair his or her own vehicle. For the owner who has few tools, if any, the initial investment might seem high, but when compared to the spiraling costs of professional auto maintenance and repair, it is a wise one.

To help the owner decide which tools are needed to perform the tasks detailed in this manual, the following tool lists are offered: *Maintenance and minor repair, Repair and overhaul* and *Special*. The newcomer to practical mechanics should start off with the *Maintenance and minor repair* tool kit, which is adequate for the simpler jobs performed on a vehicle. Then, as his confidence and experience grow, he can tackle more difficult tasks, buying additional tools as they are needed. Eventually the basic kit will be expanded into the *Repair and overhaul* tool set. Over a period of time, the experienced do-it-yourselfer will assemble a tool set complete enough for most repair and overhaul procedures and will add tools from the *Special* category when he feels the expense is justified by the frequency of use.

Maintenance and minor repair tool kit

The tools in this list should be considered the minimum for performance of routine maintenance, servicing and minor repair work. We recommend the purchase of combination wrenches (box end and open end combined in one wrench); while more expensive than open-ended ones, they offer the advantages of both types of wrench.

Combination wrench set ($\frac{1}{4}$ in to 1 in or 6 mm to 19 mm)
Adjustable wrench – 8 in
Spark plug wrench (with rubber insert)
Spark plug gap adjusting tool
Feeler gauge set
Brake bleeder wrench
Standard screwdriver ($\frac{5}{16}$ in x 6 in)
Phillips screwdriver (No.2 x 6 in)
Combination pliers – 6 in
Hacksaw and assortment of blades
Tire pressure gauge
Grease gun
Oil can
Fine emery cloth
Wire brush
Battery post and cable cleaning tool
Oil filter wrench
Funnel (medium size)
Safety goggles
Jack stands (2)
Drain pan

Note: *If basic tune-ups are going to be a part of routine maintenance, it will be necessary to purchase a good quality stroboscopic timing light and a combination tachometer/dwell meter. Although they are included in the list of Special Tools, they are*

mentioned here because they are absolutely necessary for tuning most vehicles properly.

Repair and overhaul tool set

These tools are essential for anyone who plans to perform major repairs and are in addition to those in the *Maintenance and minor repair tool kit*. Included is a comprehensive set of sockets which, though expensive, will be found invaluable because of their versatility (especially when various extensions and drives are available). We recommend the $\frac{1}{2}$ in drive over the $\frac{3}{8}$ in drive. Although the larger drive is bulky and more expensive, it has the capability of accepting a very wide range of large sockets (ideally, the mechanic would have a $\frac{3}{8}$ in drive set and a $\frac{1}{2}$ in drive set).

Socket set(s)
Reversible ratchet
Extension – 10 in
Universal joint
Torque wrench (same size drive as sockets)
Ball pein hammer – 8 oz
Soft-faced hammer (plastic/rubber)
Standard screwdriver ($\frac{1}{4}$ in x 6 in)
Standard screwdriver (stubby – $\frac{5}{16}$ in)
Phillips screwdriver (No.3 x 8 in)
Phillips screwdriver (stubby – No.2)
Pliers – vise grip
Pliers – lineman's
Pliers – needle nose
Pliers – spring clip (internal and external)
Cold chisel – $\frac{1}{2}$ in
Scriber
Scraper (made from flattened copper tubing)
Center punch
Pin punches ($\frac{1}{16}$, $\frac{1}{8}$, $\frac{3}{16}$ in)
Steel rule/straight edge – 12 in
Allen wrench set ($\frac{1}{8}$ to $\frac{3}{8}$ in or 4 mm to 10 mm)
A selection of files
Wire brush (large)
Jack stands (second set)
Jack (scissor or hydraulic type)

Note: *Another tool which is often useful is an electric drill motor with a chuck capacity of $\frac{3}{8}$ in (and a set of good quality drill bits).*

Special tools

The tools in this list include those which are not used regularly, are expensive to buy, or which need to be used in accordance with their manufacturer's instructions. Unless these tools will be used frequently, it is not very economical to purchase many of them. A consideration would be to split the cost and use between yourself and a friend or friends. In addition, most of these tools can be obtained from a tool rental shop on a temporary basis.

This list contains only those tools and instruments widely available to the public, and not those special tools produced by vehicle manufacturers for distribution to dealer service departments. Occasionally, references to the manufacturer's special tools are included in the text of this manual. Generally, an alternative method of doing the job without the special tool is offered. However, sometimes there is no alternative to their use. Where this is the case, and the tool

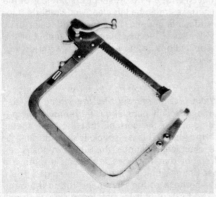

Valve spring compressor

Piston ring groove cleaning tool

Piston ring compressor

Piston ring removal/installation tool

Cylinder ridge reamer

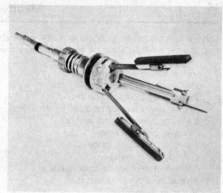

Cylinder surfacing hone

Cylinder bore gauge

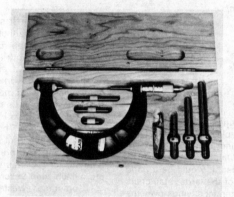

Micrometer set

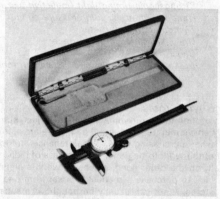

Dial caliper

Hydraulic lifter removal tool

Universal-type puller

Dial indicator set

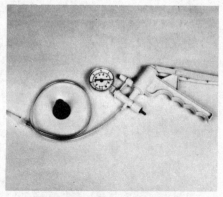

Hand-operated vacuum pump

Brake shoe spring tool

cannot be purchased or borrowed, the work should be turned over to the dealer, a repair shop or an automotive machine shop.

Valve spring compressor
Piston ring groove cleaning tool
Piston ring compressor
Piston ring installation tool
Cylinder compression gauge
Cylinder ridge reamer
Cylinder surfacing hone
Cylinder bore gauge
Micrometer(s) and/or dial calipers
Hydraulic lifter removal tool
Balljoint separator
Universal-type puller
Impact screwdriver
Dial indicator set
Stroboscopic timing light (inductive pickup)
Hand-operated vacuum/pressure pump
Tachometer/dwell meter
Universal electrical multi-meter
Cable hoist
Brake spring removal and installation tools
Floor jack

Buying tools

For the do-it-yourselfer who is just starting to get involved in vehicle maintenance and repair, there are a couple of options available when purchasing tools. If maintenance and minor repair is the extent of the work to be done, the purchase of individual tools is satisfactory. If, on the other hand, extensive work is planned, it would be a good idea to purchase a modest tool set from one of the large retail chain stores. A set can usually be bought at a substantial savings over the individual tool prices (and they often come with a tool box). As additional tools are needed, add-on sets, individual tools and a larger tool box can be purchased to expand the tool selection. Building a tool set gradually allows the cost of the tools to be spread over a longer period of time and gives the mechanic the freedom to choose only those tools that will actually be used.

Tool stores will often be the only source of some of the special tools that are needed, but regardless of where tools are bought, try to avoid cheap ones (especially when buying screwdrivers and sockets) because they won't last very long. The expense involved in replacing cheap tools will eventually be greater than the initial cost of quality tools.

Care and maintenance of tools

Good tools are expensive, so it makes sense to treat them with respect. Keep them in a clean and usable condition and store them properly when not in use. Always wipe off any dirt, grease or metal chips before putting them away. Never leave tools lying around in the work area. Upon completion of a job, always check closely under the hood for tools that may have been left there (so they don't get lost during a test drive).

Some tools, such as screwdrivers, pliers, wrenches and sockets, can be hung on a panel mounted on the garage or workshop wall, while others should be kept in a tool box or tray. Measuring instruments, gauges, meters, etc. must be carefully stored where they cannot be damaged by weather or impact from other tools.

When tools are used with care and stored properly, they will last a very long time. Even with the best of care, tools will wear out if used frequently. When a tool is damaged or worn out, replace it; subsequent jobs will be safer and more enjoyable if you do.

For those who desire to learn more about tools and their uses, a book entitled *How to Choose and Use Car Tools* is available from the publishers of this manual.

Working facilities

Not to be overlooked when discussing tools is the workshop. If anything more than routine maintenance is to be carried out, some sort of suitable work area is essential.

It is understood, and appreciated, that many home mechanics do not have a good workshop or garage available, and end up removing an engine or doing major repairs outside (it is recommended that the overhaul or repair be completed under the cover of a roof).

A clean, flat workbench or table of suitable working height is an absolute necessity. The workshop should be equipped with a vise that has a jaw opening of at least 4 inches.

As mentioned previously, some clean, dry storage space is also required for tools, as well as the lubricants, fluids, cleaning solvents, etc. which soon become necessary.

Sometimes waste oil and fluids, drained from the engine or transmission during normal maintenance or repairs, present a disposal problem. To avoid pouring oil on the ground or into the sewage system, simply pour the used fluids into large containers, seal them with caps and deliver them to a local recycling center or disposal facility. Plastic jugs (such as old anti-freeze containers) are ideal for this purpose.

Always keep a supply of old newspapers and clean rags available. Old towels are excellent for mopping up spills. Many mechanics use rolls of paper towels for most work because they are readily available and disposable. To keep the area under the vehicle clean, a large cardboard box can be cut open and flattened to protect the garage or shop floor.

Whenever working over a painted surface (such as when leaning over a fender to service something under the hood), always cover it with an old blanket or bedspread to protect the finish. Vinyl covered pads, made especially for this purpose, are available at auto parts stores.

Automotive chemicals and lubricants

A number of automotive chemicals and lubricants are available for use in vehicle maintenance and repair. They represent a wide variety of products ranging from cleaning solvents and degreasers to lubricants and protective sprays for rubber, plastic and vinyl.

Contact point/spark plug cleaner is a solvent used to clean oily film and dirt from points, grime from electrical connectors and oil deposits from spark plugs. It is oil free and leaves no residue. It can also be used to remove gum and varnish from carburetor jets and other orifices.

Carburetor cleaner is similar to contact point/spark plug cleaner but it is a stronger solvent and may leave a slight oily residue. It is not recommended for cleaning electrical components or connections.

Brake system cleaner is used to remove grease or brake fluid from brake system components (where clean surfaces are absolutely necessary and petroleum-based solvents cannot be used); it also leaves no residue.

Silicone based lubricants are used to protect rubber parts such as hoses, weatherstripping and grommets, and are used as lubricants for hinges and locks.

Multi-purpose grease is an all purpose lubricant used whenever grease is more practical than a liquid lubricant such as oil. Some multi-purpose grease is colored white and specially formulated to be more resistant to water than ordinary grease.

Bearing grease/wheel bearing grease is a heavy grease used where increased loads and friction are encountered (i.e. wheel bearings, universal joints, etc.).

High temperature wheel bearing grease is designed to withstand the extreme temperatures encountered by wheel bearings in disc brake equipped vehicles. It usually contains molybdenum disulfide, which is a 'dry' type lubricant.

Gear oil (sometimes called gear lube) is a specially designed oil used in differentials, manual transmissions and manual gearboxes, as well as other areas where high friction, high temperature lubrication is required. It is available in a number of viscosities (weights) for various applications.

Motor oil, of course, is the lubricant specially formulated for use in the engine. It normally contains a wide variety of additives to prevent corrosion and reduce foaming and wear. Motor oil comes in various weights (viscosity ratings) of from 5 to 80. The recommended weight of the oil depends on the seasonal temperature and the demands on the engine. Light oil is used in cold climates and under light load conditions; heavy oil is used in hot climates and where high loads are encountered. Multi-viscosity oils are designed to have characteristics of both light and heavy oils and are available in a number of weights from 5W-20 to 20W-50.

Oil additives range from viscosity index improvers to slick chemical treatments that purportedly reduce friction. It should be noted that most oil manufacturers caution against using additives with their oils.

Gas additives perform several functions, depending on their chemical makeup. They usually contain solvents that help dissolve gum and varnish that build up on carburetor and intake parts. They also serve to break down carbon deposits that form on the inside surfaces of the combustion chambers. Some additives contain upper cylinder lubricants for valves and piston rings.

Brake fluid is a specially formulated hydraulic fluid that can withstand the heat and pressure encountered in brake systems. Care must be taken that this fluid does not come in contact with painted surfaces or plastics. An opened container should always be resealed to prevent contamination by water or dirt.

Undercoating is a petroleum-based tar-like substance that is designed to protect metal surfaces on the under-side of a vehicle from corrosion. It also acts as a sound deadening agent by insulating the bottom of the vehicle.

Weatherstrip cement is used to bond weatherstripping around doors, windows and trunk lids. It is sometimes used to attach trim pieces as well.

Degreasers are heavy duty solvents used to remove grease and grime that accumulate on engine and chassis components. They can be sprayed or brushed on and, depending on the type, are rinsed with either water or solvent.

Solvents are used alone or in combination with degreasers to clean parts and assemblies during repair and overhaul. The home mechanic should use only solvents that are non-flammable and that do not produce irritating fumes.

Gasket sealing compounds may be used in conjunction with gaskets, to improve their sealing capabilities, or alone, to seal metal-to-metal joints. Many gaskets can withstand extreme heat, some are impervious to gasoline and lubricants, while others are capable of filling and sealing large cavities. Depending on the intended use, gasket sealers either dry hard or stay relatively soft and pliable. They are usually applied by hand, with a brush, or are sprayed on the gasket sealing surfaces.

Thread cement is an adhesive locking compound that prevents threaded fasteners from loosening because of vibration. It is available in a variety of types for different applications.

Moisture dispersants are usually sprays that can be used to dry out electrical components such as the distributor, fuse block and wiring connectors. Some types can also be used as treatment for rubber and as a lubricant for hinges, cables and locks.

Waxes and polishes are used to help protect painted and plated surfaces from the weather. Different types of paint may require the use of different types of wax or polish. Some polishes utilize a chemical or abrasive cleaner to help remove the top layer of oxidized (dull) paint in older vehicles.

Jacking and towing

Jacking

The jack supplied with the vehicle should only be used for raising the car for changing a tire or placing jackstands under the frame. **Under no circumstances should work be performed beneath the vehicle or the engine started while this jack is being used as the only means of support.**

All vehicles are supplied with a scissors type jack which fits into a notch in the vertical rocker panel flange nearest to the wheel being changed.

The car should be on level ground with the wheels blocked and the transmission in Park (automatic) or Reverse (manual). Pry off the hub cap (if equipped) using the tapered end of the lug wrench. Loosen the wheel nuts one half turn and leave them in place until the wheel is raised off the ground.

Place the jack under the side of the car in the jacking notch. Use the supplied wrench to turn the jackscrew clockwise until the wheel is raised off the ground. Remove the wheel nuts, pull off the wheel and replace it with the spare.

With the beveled side in, replace the wheel nuts and tighten them until snug. Lower the vehicle by turning the jackscrew counterclockwise. Remove the jack and tighten the nuts in a diagonal fashion. Replace the hubcap by placing it into position and using the heel of your hand or a rubber mallet to seat it.

Towing

The vehicle can be towed with all four wheels on the ground provided speeds do not exceed 35 mph and the distance is not over 50 miles, otherwise transmission damage can result.

Towing equipment specifically designed for this purpose should be used and should be attached to the main structural members of the car and not the bumper or brackets.

Safety is a major consideration when towing and all applicable state and local laws must be obeyed. A safety chain system must be used for all towing.

While towing, the parking brake should be fully released and the transmission should be in Neutral. The steering must be unlocked (ignition switch in the Off position). Remember that power steering and power brakes will not work with the engine off.

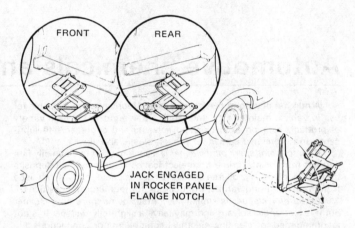

JACK ENGAGED IN ROCKER PANEL FLANGE NOTCH

Typical chassis jacking

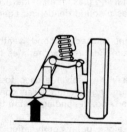

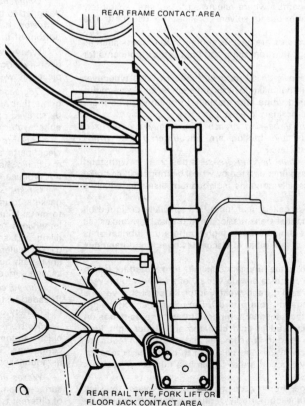

REAR FRAME CONTACT AREA

REAR RAIL TYPE, FORK LIFT OR FLOOR JACK CONTACT AREA

Frame jacking points

Safety first!

Regardless of how enthusiastic you may be about getting on with the job at hand, take the time to ensure that your safety is not jeopardized. A moment's lack of attention can result in an accident, as can failure to observe certain simple safety precautions. The possibility of an accident will always exist, and the following points should not be considered a comprehensive list of all dangers. Rather, they are intended to make you aware of the risks and to encourage a safety conscious approach to all work you carry out on your vehicle.

Essential DOs and DON'Ts

DON'T rely on a jack when working under the vehicle. Always use approved jackstands to support the weight of the vehicle and place them under the recommended lift or support points.

DON'T attempt to loosen extremely tight fasteners (i.e. wheel lug nuts) while the vehicle is on a jack — it may fall.

DON'T start the engine without first making sure that the transmission is in Neutral (or Park where applicable) and the parking brake is set.

DON'T remove the radiator cap from a hot cooling system — let it cool or cover it with a cloth and release the pressure gradually.

DON'T attempt to drain the engine oil until you are sure it has cooled to the point that it will not burn you.

DON'T touch any part of the engine or exhaust system until it has cooled sufficiently to avoid burns.

DON'T siphon toxic liquids such as gasoline, antifreeze and brake fluid by mouth, or allow them to remain on your skin.

DON'T inhale brake lining dust — it is potentially hazardous (see *Asbestos* below)

DON'T allow spilled oil or grease to remain on the floor — wipe it up before someone slips on it.

DON'T use loose fitting wrenches or other tools which may slip and cause injury.

DON'T push on wrenches when loosening or tightening nuts or bolts. Always try to pull the wrench toward you. If the situation calls for pushing the wrench away, push with an open hand to avoid scraped knuckles if the wrench should slip.

DON'T attempt to lift a heavy component alone — get someone to help you.

DON'T rush or take unsafe shortcuts to finish a job.

DON'T allow children or animals in or around the vehicle while you are working on it.

DO wear eye protection when using power tools such as a drill, sander, bench grinder, etc. and when working under a vehicle.

DO keep loose clothing and long hair well out of the way of moving parts.

DO make sure that any hoist used has a safe working load rating adequate for the job.

DO get someone to check on you periodically when working alone on a vehicle.

DO carry out work in a logical sequence and make sure that everything is correctly assembled and tightened.

DO keep chemicals and fluids tightly capped and out of the reach of children and pets.

DO remember that your vehicle's safety affects that of yourself and others. If in doubt on any point, get professional advice.

Asbestos

Certain friction, insulating, sealing, and other products — such as brake linings, brake bands, clutch linings, torque converters, gaskets, etc. — contain asbestos. *Extreme care must be taken to avoid inhalation of dust from such products since it is hazardous to health.* If in doubt, assume that they *do* contain asbestos.

Fire

Remember at all times that gasoline is highly flammable. Never smoke or have any kind of open flame around when working on a vehicle. But the risk does not end there. A spark caused by an electrical short circuit, by two metal surfaces contacting each other, or even by static electricity built up in your body under certain conditions, can ignite gasoline vapors, which in a confined space are highly explosive. Do not, under any circumstances, use gasoline for cleaning parts. Use an approved safety solvent.

Always disconnect the battery ground (–) cable *at the battery* before working on any part of the fuel system or electrical system. Never risk spilling fuel on a hot engine or exhaust component.

It is strongly recommended that a fire extinguisher suitable for use on fuel and electrical fires be kept handy in the garage or workshop at all times. Never try to extinguish a fuel or electrical fire with water.

Fumes

Certain fumes are highly toxic and can quickly cause unconsciousness and even death if inhaled to any extent. Gasoline vapor falls into this category, as do the vapors from some cleaning solvents. Any draining or pouring of such volatile fluids should be done in a well ventilated area.

When using cleaning fluids and solvents, read the instructions on the container carefully. Never use materials from unmarked containers.

Never run the engine in an enclosed space, such as a garage. Exhaust fumes contain carbon monoxide, which is extremely poisonous. If you need to run the engine, always do so in the open air, or at least have the rear of the vehicle outside the work area.

If you are fortunate enough to have the use of an inspection pit, never drain or pour gasoline and never run the engine while the vehicle is over the pit. The fumes, being heavier than air, will concentrate in the pit with possibly lethal results.

The battery

Never create a spark or allow a bare light bulb near the battery. The battery normally gives off a certain amount of hydrogen gas, which is highly explosive.

Always disconnect the battery ground (–) cable *at the battery* before working on the fuel or electrical systems.

If possible, loosen the filler caps or cover when charging the battery from an external source. Do not charge at an excessive rate or the battery may burst.

Take care when adding water and when carrying a battery. The electrolyte, even when diluted, is very corrosive and should not be allowed to contact clothing or skin.

Always wear eye protection when cleaning the battery to prevent the caustic deposits from entering your eyes.

Household current

When using an electric power tool, inspection light, etc., which operates on household current, always make sure that the tool is correctly connected to its plug and that, where necessary, it is properly grounded. Do not use such items in damp conditions and, again, do not create a spark or apply excessive heat in the vicinity of fuel or fuel vapor.

Secondary ignition system voltage

A severe electric shock can result from touching certain parts of the ignition system (such as the spark plug wires) when the engine is running or being cranked, particularly if components are damp or the insulation is defective. In the case of an electronic ignition system, the secondary system voltage is much higher and could prove fatal.

Troubleshooting

Contents

1 Engine will not rotate when attempting to start

1 Battery terminal connection loose or corroded. Check the cable terminals at the battery; tighten or clean corrosion as necessary.
2 Battery discharged or faulty. If the cable connectors are clean and tight on the battery posts, turn the key to the On position and switch on the headlights and/or windshield wipers. If these fail to function, the battery is discharged.
3 Automatic transmission not fully engaged in Park or manual transmission clutch not fully depressed.
4 Broken, loose or disconnected wiring in the starting circuit. Inspect all wiring and connectors at the battery, starter solenoid (at lower right side of engine) and ignition switch (on steering column).
5 Starter motor pinion jammed on flywheel ring gear. If manual transmission, place gearshift in gear and rock the vehicle to manually turn the engine. Remove starter (Chapter 5) and inspect pinion and flywheel (Chapter 5) at earliest convenience.
6 Starter solenoid faulty (Chapter 5).
7 Starter motor faulty (Chapter 5).
8 Ignition switch (Chapter 12).

2 Engine rotates but will not start

1 Fuel tank empty.
2 Battery discharged (engine rotates slowly). Check the operation of electrical components as described in previous Section (see Chapter 1).
3 Battery terminal connections loose or corroded. See previous Section.
4 Carburetor flooded and/or fuel level in carburetor incorrect. This will usually be accompanied by a strong fuel odor from under the hood. Wait a few minutes, depress the accelerator pedal all the way to the floor and attempt to start the engine.
5 Choke control inoperative (Chapter 4).
6 Fuel not reaching carburetor. With ignition switch in Off position, open hood, remove the top plate of air cleaner assembly and observe the top of the carburetor (manually move choke plate back if necessary). Have an assistant depress accelerator pedal fully and check that fuel spurts into carburetor. If not, check fuel filter (Chapters 1 and 4), fuel lines and fuel pump (Chapter 4).
7 Excessive moisture on, or damage to, ignition components (Chapter 5).
8 Worn, faulty or incorrectly adjusted spark plugs (Chapter 5).
9 Broken, loose or disconnected wiring in the starting circuit (see previous Section).
10 Distributor loose, thus changing ignition timing. Turn the distributor as necessary to start the engine, then set ignition timing as soon as possible (Chapter 5).
11 Ignition condenser faulty (Chapter 5).
12 Broken, loose or disconnected wires at the ignition coil, or faulty coil (Chapter 5).

3 Starter motor operates without rotating engine

1 Starter pinion sticking. Remove the starter (Chapter 5) and inspect.
2 Starter pinion or engine flywheel teeth worn or broken. Remove the inspection cover at the rear of the engine and inspect.

4 Engine hard to start when cold

1 Battery discharged or low. Check as described in Section 1.
2 Choke control inoperative or out of adjustment (Chapter 4).
3 Carburetor flooded (see Section 2).
4 Fuel supply not reaching the carburetor (see Section 4).
5 Carburetor worn and in need of overhauling (Chapter 4).

5 Engine hard to start when hot

1 Choke sticking in the closed position (Chapter 4).
2 Carburetor flooded (see Section 2).

3 Air filter in need of replacement (Chapter 4).
4 Fuel not reaching the carburetor (see Section 4).

6 Starter motor noisy or excessively rough in engagement

1 Pinion or flywheel gear teeth worn or broken. Remove the inspection cover at the rear of the engine and inspect.
2 Starter motor retaining bolts loose or missing.

7 Engine starts but stops immediately

1 Loose or faulty electrical connections at distributor, coil or alternator.
2 Insufficient fuel reaching the carburetor. Disconnect the fuel line at the carburetor and remove the filter (Chapter 4). Place a container under the disconnected fuel line. Observe the flow of fuel from the line. If little or none at all, check for blockage in the lines and/or replace the fuel pump (Chapter 4).
3 Vacuum leak at the gasket surfaces or the intake manifold and/or carburetor. Check that all mounting bolts (nuts) are tightened to specifications and all vacuum hoses connected to the carburetor and manifold are positioned properly and are in good condition.

8 Engine 'lopes' while idling or idles erratically

1 Vacuum leakage. Check mounting bolts (nuts) at the carburetor and intake manifold for tightness. Check that all vacuum hoses are connected and are in good condition. Use a doctor's stethoscope or a length of fuel line hose held against your ear to listen for vacuum leaks while the engine is running. A hissing sound will be heard. A soapy water solution will also detect leaks. Check the carburetor and intake manifold gasket surfaces.
2 Leaking EGR valve or plugged PCV valve (see Chapter 6).
3 Air cleaner clogged and in need of replacement (Chapter 4).
4 Fuel pump not delivering sufficient fuel to the carburetor (see Section 7).
5 Carburetor out of adjustment (Chapter 4).
6 Leaking head gasket. If this is suspected, take the vehicle to a repair shop or dealer where this can be pressure checked without the need to remove the heads.
7 Timing chain or gears worn and in need of replacement (Chapter 1).
8 Camshaft lobes worn, necessitating the removal of the camshaft for inspection (Chapter 2).

9 Engine misses at idle speed

1 Spark plugs faulty or not gapped properly (Chapter 5).
2 Faulty spark plug wires (Chapter 5).
3 Carburetor choke not operating properly (Chapter 4).
4 Sticking or faulty emissions systems (see Troubleshooting in Chapter 6).
5 Clogged fuel filter and/or foreign matter in fuel. Remove the fuel filter (Chapter 4) and inspect.
6 Vacuum leaks at carburetor, intake manifold or at hose connections. Check as described in Section 8.
7 Incorrect speed (Chapter 5) or idle mixture (Chapter 4).
8 Incorrect ignition timing (Chapter 5).
9 Uneven or low cylinder compression. Remove plugs and use compression tester as per manufacturer's instructions.

10 Engine misses throughout driving speed range

1 Carburetor fuel filter clogged and/or impurities in the fuel system (Chapter 4). Also check fuel output at the carburetor (see Section 7).
2 Faulty or incorrectly gapped spark plugs (Chapter 5).
3 Incorrectly set ignition timing (Chapter 5).
4 Check for a cracked distributor cap, disconnected distributor wires or damage to the distributor components (Chapter 5).
5 Leaking spark plug wires (Chapter 5).
6 Emission system components faulty (Chapter 6).

7   Low or uneven cylinder compression pressures. Remove spark plugs and test compression with gauge.
8   Weak or faulty EEC ignition system (see Chapter 5).
9   Vacuum leaks at carburetor, intake manifold or vacuum hoses (see Section 8).

11 Engine stalls

1   Carburetor idle speed incorrectly set (Chapter 4).
2   Carburetor fuel filter clogged and/or water and impurities in the fuel system (Chapter 4).
3   Choke improperly adjusted or sticking (Chapter 4).
4   Distributor components damp, points out of adjustment or damage to distributor cap, rotor etc. (Chapter 5).
5   Emission system components faulty (Troubleshooting section, Chapter 6).
6   Faulty or incorrectly gapped spark plugs Chapter 5). Also check spark plug wires (Chapter 5).
7   Vacuum leak at the carburetor, intake manifold or vacuum hoses. Check as described in Section 8.
8   Valve lash incorrectly set (Chapter 2).

12 Engine lacks power

1   Incorrect ignition timing (Chapter 5).
2   Excessive play in distributor shaft. At the same time check for worn or maladjusted contact rotor, faulty distributor cap, wires, etc. (Chapter 5).
3   Faulty or incorrectly gapped spark plugs (Chapter 5).
4   Carburetor not adjusted properly or excessively worn (Chapter 4).
5   Weak coil or condensor (Chapter 5).
6   Faulty EEC system coil (Chapter 5).
7   Brakes binding (Chapter 5).
8   Automatic transmission fluid level incorrect, causing slippage (Chapter 7).
9   Manual transmission clutch slipping (Chapter 8).
10 Fuel filter clogged and/or impurities in the fuel system (Chapter 4).
11 Emission control system not functioning properly (Chapter 6).
12 Use of sub-standard fuel. Fill tank with proper octane fuel.
13 Low or uneven cylinder compression pressures. Test with compression tester, which will detect leaking valves and/or blown head gasket.

13 Engine backfire

1   Emission system not functioning properly (Chapter 6).
2   Ignition timing incorrect (Section 3).
3   Carburetor in need of adjustment or worn excessively (Chapter 4).
4   Vacuum leak at carburetor, intake manifold or vacuum hoses. Check as described in Section 8.
5   Valve lash incorrectly set, and/or valves sticking (Chapter 1).

14 Pinging or knocking engine sounds on hard acceleration or uphill

1   Incorrect grade of fuel. Fill tank with fuel of the proper octane rating.
2   Ignition timing incorrect (Chapter 5).
3   Carburetor in need of adjustment (Chapter 4).
4   Improper spark plugs. Check plug type with that specified on tune-up decal located inside engine compartment. Also check plugs and wires for damage (Chapter 4).
5   Worn or damaged distributor components (Chapter 5).
6   Faulty emission system (Chapter 6).
7   Vacuum leak. (Check as described in Section 8).

15 Engine 'diesels' (continues to run) after switching off

1   Idle speed too fast (Chapter 5).
2   Electrical solenoid at side of carburetor not functioning properly (not all models, see Chapter 4).

3   Ignition timing incorrectly adjusted (Chapter 5).
4   Air cleaner valve not operating properly (Chapter 4).
5   Excessive engine operating temperatures. Probable causes of this are: malfunctioning thermostat, clogged radiator, faulty water pump (see Chapter 3).

Engine electrical

16 Battery will not hold a charge

1   Alternator drivebelt defective or not adjusted properly (Chapter 5).
2   Electrolyte level too low or too weak (Chapter 5).
3   Battery terminals loose or corroded (Chapter 5).
4   Alternator not charging properly (Chapter 5).
5   Loose, broken or faulty wiring in the charging circuit (Chapter 10).
6   Short in vehicle circuitry causing a continual drain on battery.
7   Battery defect internally.

17 Ignition light fails to go out

1   Faulty in alternator or charging circuit (Chapter 5).
2   Alternator drivebelt defective or not properly adjusted (Chapter 5).

18 Ignition light fails to come on when key is turned

1   Ignition light bulb faulty (Chapter 10).
2   Alternator faulty (Chapter 5).
3   Fault in the printed circuit, dash wiring or bulb holder (Chapter 10).

Engine fuel system

19 Excessive fuel consumption

1   Dirty or choked air filter element (Chapter 4).
2   Incorrectly set ignition timing (Chapter 4).
3   Choke sticking or improperly adjusted (Chapter 4).
4   Emission system not functioning properly (not all vehicles, see Chapter 6).
5   Carburetor idle speed and/or mixture not adjusted properly (Chapter 4).
6   Carburetor internal parts excessively worn or damaged (Chapter 4).
7   Low tire pressure or incorrect tire size (Chapter 11).

20 Fuel leakage and/or fuel odor

1   Leak in a fuel feed or vent line (Chapter 4).
2   Tank overfilled. Fill only to automatic shut-off.
3   Emission system filter in need of replacement (Chapter 6).
4   Vapor leaks from system lines (Chapter 4).
5   Carburetor internal parts excessively worn or out of adjustment (Chapter 4).

Engine cooling system

21 Overheating

1   Insufficient coolant in system (Chapter 3).
2   Fan belt defective or not adjusted properly (Chapter 3).
3   Radiator core blocked or radiator grille dirty and restricted (Chapter 2).
4   Thermostat faulty (Chapter 3).
5   Fan blades broken or cracked (Chapter 3).
6   Radiator cap not maintaining proper pressure. Have cap pressure tested by gas station or repair shop.
7   Ignition timing incorrect (Chapter 5).

22 Overcooling

1   Thermostat faulty (Chapter 3).
2   Inaccurate temperature gauge (Chapter 10).

23 External water leakage

1   Deteriorated or damaged hoses. Loosen clamps at hose connections (Chapter 3).
2   Water pump seals defective. If this is the case, water will drip from the 'weep' hole in the water pump body (Chapter 3).
3   Leakage from radiator core or header tank. This will require the radiator to be professionally repaired (see Chapter 3 for removal procedures).
4   Engine drain plugs or water jacket freeze plugs leaking (see Chapters 2 and 3).

24 Internal water leakage

Note: *Internal coolant leaks can usually be detected by examining the oil. Check the dipstick and inside of valve cover for water deposits and an oil consistency like that of a milkshake.*
1   Faulty cylinder head gasket. Have the system pressure-tested professionally or remove the cylinder heads (Chapter 1) and inspect.
2   Cracked cylinder bore or cylinder head. Dismantle engine and inspect (Chapter 2).

25 Water loss

1   Overfilling system (Chapter 3).
2   Coolant boiling away due to overheating (see causes in Section 15).
3   Internal or external leakage (see Sections 22 and 33).
4   Faulty radiator cap. Have the cap pressure tested.

26 Poor coolant circulation

1   Inoperative water pump. A quick test is to pinch the top radiator hose closed with your hand while the engine is idling, then let it loose. You should feel the surge of water if the pump is working properly (Chapter 3).
2   Restriction in cooling system. Drain, flush and refill the system (Chapter 3). If it appears necessary, remove the radiator (Chapter 3) and have it reverse-flushed or professionally cleaned.
3   Fan drivebelt defective or not adjusted properly (Chapter 3).
4   Thermostat sticking (Chapter 3).

Clutch

27 Fails to release (pedal pressed to the floor – shift lever does not move freely in and out of reverse)

1   Improper linkage adjustment (Chapter 8).
2   Clutch fork off ball stud. Look under the car, on the left side of transmission.
3   Clutch disc warped, bent or excessively damaged (Chapter 8).

28 Clutch slips (engine speed increases with no increases in road speed)

1   Linkage in need of adjustment (Chapter 8).
2   Clutch disc oil soaked or facing worn. Remove disc (Chapter 8) and inspect.
3   Clutch disc not seated in. It may take 30 or 40 normal starts for a new disc to seat.

29 Grabbing (juddering) on take-up

1   Oil on clutch disc facings. Remove disc (Chapter 8) and inspect. Correct any leakage source.
2   Worn or loose engine or transmission mounts. These units move slightly when clutch is released. Inspect mounts and bolts.
3   Worn splines on clutch gear. Remove clutch components (Chapter 8) and inspect.
4   Warped pressure plate or flywheel. Remove clutch components and inspect.

30 Squeal or rumble with clutch fully engaged (pedal released)

1   Improper adjustment; no lash (Chapter 8).
2   Release bearing binding on transmission bearing retainer. Remove clutch components (Chapter 8) and check bearing. Remove any burrs or nicks, clean and relubricate before reinstallation.
3   Weak linkage return spring. Replace the spring.

31 Squeal or rumble with clutch fully disengaged (pedal depressed)

1   Worn, faulty or broken release bearing (Chapter 8).
2   Worn or broken pressure plate springs (or diaphragm fingers) (Chapter 8).

32 Clutch pedal stays on floor when disengaged

1   Bind in leakage or release bearing. Inspect linkage or remove clutch components as necessary.
2   Linkage springs being over-traveled. Adjust linkage for proper lash. Make sure proper pedal stop (bumper) is installed.

Manual transmission
Note: *All the following Sections contained within Chapter 7 unless noted.*

33 Noisy in Neutral with engine running

1   Input shaft bearing worn.
2   Damaged main drive drive gear bearing.
3   Worn countergear bearings.
4   Worn or damaged countergear anti-lash plate.

34 Noisy in all gears

1   Any of the above causes, and/or:
2   Insufficient lubricant (see checking procedures in Chapter 7).

35 Noisy in one particular gear

1   Worn, damaged or chipped gear teeth for that particular gear.
2   Worn or damaged synchronizer for that particular gear.

36 Slips out of high gear

1   Transmission loose on clutch housing.
2   Shift rods interfering with engine mounts or clutch lever.
3   Shift rods not working freely.
4   Damaged mainshaft pilot bearing.
5   Dirt between transmission case and clutch housing, or misalignment of transmission (Chapter 7).
6   Worn or improperly adjusted linkage (Chapter 7).

37 Difficulty in engaging gears

1   Clutch not releasing fully (see clutch adjustment, Chapter 8).
2   Loose, damaged or maladjusted shift linkage. Make a thorough inspection, replacing parts as necessary. Adjust as described in Chapter 8.

38 Fluid leakage

1   Excessive amount of lubricant in transmission (see Chapter 7) for correct checking procedures. Drain lubricant as required).
2   Side cover loose or gasket damaged.
3   Rear oil seal or speedometer oil seal in need of replacement (Section 6).

Automatic transmission
Note: *Due to the complexity of the automatic transmission, it is difficult for the home mechanic to properly diagnose and service this component. For problems other than the following, the vehicle should be taken to a reputable mechanic.*

39 Fluid leakage

1   Automatic transmission fluid is a deep red color, and fluid leaks should not be confused with engine oil which can easily be blown by air flow to the transmission.
2   To pinpoint a leak, first remove all built-up dirt and grime from around the transmission. Degreasing agents and/or steam cleaning will achieve this. With the underside clean, drive the vehicle at low speeds so that air flow will not blow the leak far from its source. Raise the vehicle and determine where the leak is coming from. Common areas of leakage are:

a)   Fluid pan: tighten mounting bolts and/or replace pan gasket as necessary (see Chapter 7)
b)   Rear extension: tighten bolts and/or replace oil seal as necessary (Chapter 7)
c)   Filler pipe: replace the rubber seal where pipe enters transmission case
d)   Transmission oil lines: tighten connectors where lines enter transmission case and/or replace lines
e)   Vent pipe: transmission over-filled and/or water in fluid (see checking procedures, Chapter 7)
f)   Speedometer connector: replace the O-ring where speedometer cable enters transmission case

40 General shift mechanism problems

1   Chapter 7 deals with checking and adjusting the shift linkage on automatic transmissions. Common problems which may be attributed to maladjustment linkage are:

a)   Engine starting in gears other than Park or Neutral
b)   Indicator on quadrant pointing to a gear other than the one actually being used
c)   Vehicle will not hold firm when in Park position
Refer to Chapter 7 to adjust the manual linkage.

41 Transmission will not downshift with accelerator pedal pressed to the floor

1   Chapter 7 deals with adjusting the downshift cable or downshift switch to enable the transmission to downshift properly.

42 Engine will not start in gears other than Park or Neutral

Chapter 7 deals with adjusting the Neutral start switches used ^th automatic transmissions.

43 Transmission slips, shifts rough, is noisy or has no drive in forward or reverse gears

1   There are many probable causes for the above problems, but the home mechanic should concern himself only with one possibility: fluid level.
2   Before taking the vehicle to a specialist, check the level of the fluid and condition of the fluid as described in Chapter 7. Correct fluid level as necessary or change the fluid and filter if needed. If problem persists, have a professional diagnose the probable cause.

Driveshaft

44 Leakage of fluid at front of driveshaft

1   Defective transmission rear oil seal. See Chapter 7 for replacing procedures. While this is done, check the splined yoke for burrs or a rough condition which may be damaging the seal. If found, these can be dressed wth crocus cloth or a fine dressing stone.

45 Knock or clunk when transmission is under initial load (just after transmission is put into gear)

1   Loose or disconnected rear suspension components. Check all mounting bolts and bushings (Chapter 11).
2   Loose driveshaft bolts. Inspect all bolts and nuts and tighten to torque specifications (Chapter 8).
3   Worn or damaged universal joint bearings. Test for wear (Chapter 8).

46 Metallic grating sound consistent with road speed

1   Pronounced wear in the universal joint bearings. Test for wear (Chapter 8).

47 Vibration

Note: *Before it can be assumed that the driveshaft is at fault, make sure the tires are perfectly balanced and perform the following test.*
1   Install a tachometer inside the vehicle to monitor engine speed as the vehicle is driven. Drive the vehicle and note the engine speed at which the vibration (roughness) is most pronounced. Now shift the transmission to a different gear and bring the engine speed to the same point.
2   If the vibration occurs at the same engine speed (rpm) regardless of which gear the transmission is in, the driveshaft is NOT at fault since the driveshaft speed varies.
3   If the vibration decreases or is eliminated when the transmission is in a different gear at the same engine speed, refer to the following probable causes.
4   Bent or dented driveshaft. Inspect and replace as necessary (Chapter 8).
5   Undercoating or built-up dirt, etc, on the driveshaft. Clean the shaft throroughly and test.
6   Worn universal bearings. Remove and inspect (Chapter 8).
7   Driveshaft and/or companion flange out of balance. Check for missing weights on the shaft. Remove driveshaft (Chapter 8) and reinstall 180° from original position. Retest. Have driveshaft professionally balanced if problem persists.

Rear axle

48 Noise – same when in drive as when vehicle is coasting

1   Road noise. No corrective procedures available.
2   Tire noise. Inspect tires and tire pressures (Chapter 11).
3   Front wheel bearings loose, worn or damaged (Chapter 11).

49 Vibration

1   See probable causes under *Driveshaft*. Proceed under the guide-

lines listed for the driveshaft. If the problem persists, check the rear wheel bearings by raising the rear of the car and spinning the wheels by hand. Listen for evidence of rough (noisy) bearings. Remove and inspect (Chapter 8).

50 Oil leakage

1 Pinion oil seal damaged (Chapter 8).
2 Axle shaft oil seals damaged (Chapter 8).
3 Differential inspection cover leaking. Tighten mounting bolts or replace the gasket as required (Chapter 8).

Brakes

Note: *Before assuming a brake problem exists, check; that the tires are in good condition and are inflated properly (see Chapter 1); the front end alignment is correct; and that the vehicle is not loaded with weight in an unequal manner.*

51 Vehicle pulls to one side under braking

1 Defective, damaged or oil contaminated disc pad on one side. Inspect as described in Chapter 9.
2 Excessive wear of brake pad material or disc on one side. Inspect and correct as necessary.
3 Loose or disconnected front suspension components. Inspect and tighten all bolts to specifications (Chapter 11).
4 Defective caliper assembly. Remove caliper and inspect for stuck piston or damage (Chapter 8).

52 Noise (high-pitched squeak without brake applied)

1 Front brake pads worn out. This noise comes from the wear sensor rubbing against the disc. Replace pads with new ones immediately (Chapter 9).

53 Excessive brake pedal travel

1 Partial brake system failure. Inspect entire system (Chapter 9) and correct as required.
2 Insufficient fluid in master cylinder. Check (Chapter 9) and add fluid and bleed system if necessary.
3 Rear brakes not adjusting properly. Make a series of starts and stops while the vehicle is in Reverse. If this does not correct the situation remove drums and inspect self-adjusters (Chapter 9).

54 Brake pedal feels spongy when depressed

1 Air in hydraulic lines. Bleed the brake system (Chapter 9).
2 Faulty flexible hoses. Inspect all system hoses and lines. Replace parts as necessary.
3 Master cylinder mountings insecure. Inspect master cylinder (nuts) and torque-tighten to specifications.
4 Master cylinder faulty (Chapter 9).

55 Excessive effort required to stop vehicle

1 Power brake servo not operating properly (Chapter 9).
2 Excessively worn linings or pads Inspect and replace if necessary (Chapter 9).
3 One or more caliper pistons (front wheels) or wheel cylinders (rear wheels) seized or sticking. Inspect and rebuild as required (Chapter 9).
4 Brake linings or pads contaminated with oil or grease. Inspect and replace as required (Chapter 9).
5 New pads or linings fitted and not yet 'bedded in'. It will take awhile for the new material to seat against the drum (or rotor).

56 Pedal travels to floor with little resistance

1 Little or no fluid in the master cylinder reservoir caused by; leaking wheel cylinder(s); leaking caliper piston(s); loose, damaged or disconnected brake lines. Inspect entire system and correct as necessary.

57 Brake pedal pulsates during brake application

1 Wheel bearings not adjusted properly or in need of replacement (Chapter 11).
2 Caliper not sliding properly due to improper installation or obstructions. Remove and inspect (Chapter 9).
3 Rotor not within specifications. Remove the rotor (Chapter 9) and check for excessive lateral run-out and parallelism. Have the rotor professionally machined or replace it with a new one.

Suspension and steering

58 Vehicle pulls to one side

1 Tire pressures uneven (Chapter 11).
2 Defective tire (Chapter 11).
3 Excessive wear in suspension or steering components (Chapter 11).
4 Front end in need of alignment. Take vehicle to a qualified specialist.
5 Front brakes dragging. Inspect braking system as described in Chapter 9.

59 Shimmy, shake or vibration

1 Tire or wheel out of balance or out of round. Have professionally balanced.
2 Loose, worn or out of adjustment wheel bearings (Chapter 11).
3 Shock absorbers and/or suspension components worn or damaged (Chapter 11).

60 Excessive pitching and/or rolling around corners or during braking

1 Defective shock absorbers. Replace as a set (Chapter 11).
2 Broken or weak springs and/or suspension components. Inspect as described in Chapter 11.

61 Excessively stiff steering

1 Lack of lubricant in steering box (manual) or power steering fluid reservoir (Chapter 11).
2 Incorrect tire pressures (Chapter 11).
3 Lack of lubrication at steering joints (Chapter 11).
4 Front end out of alignment.
5 See also Section 62 *Lack of power assistance.*

62 Excessive play in steering

1 Loose wheel bearings (Chapter 11).
2 Excessive wear in suspension or steering components (Chapter 11).
3 Steering gear out of adjustment (Chapter 11).

63 Lack of power assistance

1 Steering pump drivebelt faulty or not adjusted properly (Chapter 11).
2 Fluid level low (Chapter 11).

3   Hoses or pipes restricting the flow. Inspect and replace parts as necessary.
4   Air in power steering system. Bleed system (Chapter 11).

64   Excessive tire wear (not specific to one area)

1   Incorrect tire pressures (Chapter 11).
2   Tires out of balance. Have professionally balanced.
3   Wheels damaged. Inspect and replace as necessary.
4   Suspension or steering components excessively worn (Chapter 11).

65   Excessive tire wear on outside edge

1   Inflation pressures not correct (Chapter 11).
2   Excessive speed on turns.

3   Front end alignment incorrect (excessive toe-in). Have professionally aligned.
4   Suspension arm bent or twisted.

66   Excessive tire wear on inside edge

1   Inflation pressures incorrect (Chapter 11).
2   Front end alignment incorrect (toe-out). Have professionally aligned.
3   Loose or damaged steering components (Chapter 11).

67   Tire tread worn in one place

1   Tires out of balance. Balance tires professionally.
2   Damaged or buckled wheel. Inspect and replace if necessary.
3   Defective tire.

Chapter 1 Tune-up and routine maintenance

Contents

Specifications

Note: *Additional specifications can be found in appropriate Chapters*

Fluid types and capacities

Engine oil type	API classification SE, SF or SD, consult owners manual for viscosity recommendations
Engine oil capacity	4 US qts (5 US qts with new dry filter)
Engine coolant type	50/50 mix of ethylene glycol based coolant
Radiator capacity	See Chapter 3
Automatic transmission fluid	Dexron II, series D
Automatic transmission capacity	See Chapter 7
Manual transmission lubricant	140 weight gear oil
Manual transmission capacity	4.5 US qts
Rear axle lubricant	140 weight gear oil
Brake fluid type	DOT type 3
Power steering fluid	Type F automatic transmission fluid
Power steering pump capacity	3.6 US pts
Suspension and steering component grease	EP type
Wheel bearing grease type	NLGI No. 2

Ignition system

Spark plug type	See emissions decal
Spark plug gap	See emissions decal
Ignition timing	See emissions decal
Spark plug firing order	
3.3L and 4.1L	1-5-3-6-2-4
4.2L & 5.0L	1-5-4-2-6-3-7-8
5.8L	1-3-7-2-6-5-4-8
Distributor direction of rotation	
3.3L & 4.1L	Clockwise
4.2L, 5.0L and 5.8L	Counter-clockwise
Battery electrolyte specific gravity (fully charged)	1.270
Drivebelt (fan belt) tension	90-110 (Ford belt tension gauge tool)

Clutch

Clutch pedal free travel	0.136 in

Brakes

Disc brake lining thickness
　　Replace pads at .... $\frac{1}{8}$ in from back plate
Drum brake lining thickness
　　Replace linings at .... $\frac{1}{32}$ in from rivet head

Recommended lubricants and fluids

Door, trunk and hood hinges .... Polyethylene grease
Brake master cylinder .... DOT type 3 brake fluid
Front suspension and balljoint .... EP type grease
Wheel bearings .... NLGI No. 2 type grease
Automatic transmission .... Dexron II, series D fluid
Manual transmission .... 140 weight gear oil
Power steering pump reservoir .... Type F automatic transmission fluid
Rear axle and differential
　　Standard .... 140 weight gear oil
　　Limited-slip .... 90 weight gear oil
Engine oil .... API type SE, SF or SD
Engine coolant .... Ethylene glycol based
Weatherstripping .... Silicone lubricant
Lock cylinders .... Graphite lock lubricant

1　Introduction

This Chapter was designed to help the home mechanic maintain his (or her) car for peak performance, economy, safety and longevity.

On the following pages you will find a maintenance schedule along with Sections which deal specifically with each item on the schedule. Included are visual checks, adjustments and item replacements.

Servicing your car using the time/mileage maintenance schedule and the sequenced Sections will give you a planned program of maintenance. Keep in mind that it is a full plan, and maintaining only a few items at the specified intervals will not give you the same results.

You will find as you service your car that many of the procedures can, and should, be grouped together, due to the nature of the job at hand. Examples of this are as follows:

If the car is fully raised for a chassis lubrication, for example, this is the ideal time for the following checks: manual transmission fluid, rear axle fluid, exhaust system, suspension, steering and the fuel system.

If the tires and wheels are removed, as during a routine tire rotation, go ahead and check the brakes and wheel bearings at the same time.

If you must borrow or rent a torque wrench, you will do best to service the spark plugs and/or repack (or replace) the wheel bearings all in the same day to save time and money.

The first step of this or any maintenance plan is to prepare yourself before the actual work begins. Read through the appropriate Sections for all work that is to be performed before you begin. Gather together all necessary parts and tools. If it appears you could have a problem during a particular job, don't hesitate to ask advice from your local parts man or dealer service department.

Routine maintenance intervals

The following recommendations are given with the assumption that the vehicle owner will be doing the maintenance or service work (as opposed to a dealer service department). They are based on factory service/maintenance recommendations, but the time and/or mileage intervals have been shortened in most cases, to ensure that the service is thorough and complete.

When the vehicle is new, it should be serviced initially by a factory authorized dealer service department to protect the factory warranty. In most cases the initial maintenance check is done at no cost to the owner.

Every 250 miles (400 km), weekly, and before long trips

Steering

　　Check tire pressures (cold) (Sec 3)
　　Inspect tires for wear and damage (Sec 3)

　　Check power steering reservoir level (Sec 8)
　　Check steering for smooth and accurate operation (Sec 8)

Brakes

　　Check the level in the brake fluid reservoir, if fluid level has dropped noticeably since the last check inspect all brake lines and hoses for leakage (Sec 27)
　　Check for satisfactory brake operation (Sec 27)

Lights, wipers, horns, instruments

　　Check all lights for proper operation
　　Check the operation of the windshield wipers and washers
　　Check the windshield wiper blade element condition (Sec 31)
　　Check the horn operation
　　Check the operation of all instruments

Engine

　　Check the oil level, add oil as required (Sec 2)
　　Check the radiator coolant level and add coolant as required (Sec 2)
　　Check the battery electrolyte level, adding water as necessary (Sec 2)

5000 miles (8000 km) or 5 months

　　Check engine drivebelt condition and tensions (Sec 9)
　　Check engine idle speed (Sec 16)
　　Check engine oil and oil filter (Sec 4)
　　Check and adjust automatic transmission bands as required (Chapter 7)

---

10 000 miles (16 000 km) or 10 months

　　Change engine oil and oil filter (Sec 4)
　　Check and adjust automatic transmission bands as required (Chapter 7)
　　Check engine drivebelt condition and tension (Sec 9)
　　Check clutch pedal free play and adjust as required (Sec 13)
　　Check and adjust engine idle speed as required (Sec 16)
　　Inspect exhaust system and shields (Sec 7)
　　Check and lubricate exhaust control valve (if equipped) (Sec 21)

---

15 000 (24 000 km) or 15 months

　　Check and adjust automatic transmission bands as required (Chapter 7)
　　Change engine oil and oil filter (Sec 4)
　　Replace spark plugs (Sec 22)

Tighten intake manifold bolts and nuts to specification (V8) (Chapter 2)
Check clutch pedal free play and adjust as required (Sec 13)
Check engine drivebelt condition and tension (Sec 9)
Replace carburetor air cleaner filter element (Sec 12)

20 000 miles (32 000 km) or 20 months

Drain and refill automatic transmission fluid (Chapter 7)
Change engine oil and oil filter (Sec 4)
Check and lubricate exhaust control valve (if equipped) (Sec 21)
Check clutch pedal free play and adjust as required (Sec 13)
Inspect exhaust system and shields (Sec 7)
Check engine drivebelt condition and tension (Sec 9)

25 000 miles (40 000 km) or 25 months

Change engine oil and oil filter (Sec 4)
Check and adjust automatic transmission bands as required (Chapter 7)
Replace crankcase air filter in the air cleaner housing (Sec 12)
Check clutch pedal free play and adjust as required (Sec 13)
Check engine drivebelt condition and tension (Sec 9)

30 000 miles (48 000 km) or 30 months

Check the choke system for freedom of movement and adjust and lubricate as necessary (Chapter 4)
Check and lubricate exhaust control valve (if equipped) (Sec 21)
Inspect exhaust system and shields (Sec 7)
Lubricate front suspension and steering linkage (Sec 8)
Check and adjust automatic transmission bands as required (Chapter 7)
Change engine oil and oil filter (Sec 4)
Replace spark plugs (Sec 22)
Check engine drivebelt condition and tension (Sec 9)
Replace PCV valve (Sec 11)
Replace carburetor air cleaner element (Sec 12)
Replace crankcase filter in air cleaner (Sec 12)
Check Thermactor delay valve and replace if necessary (Chapter 6)
Inspect brake lining, lines and hoses (Sec 27)
Inspect front wheel bearing lubrication (Sec 26)
Check master cylinder fluid level (Sec 27)
Check clutch pedal free play (Sec 13)

35 000 miles (56 000 km) or 35 months

Change engine oil and oil filter (Sec 4)
Check and adjust automatic transmission bands as required (Chapter 7)
Check clutch pedal free play and adjust as required (Sec 13)
Check engine drivebelt condition and tension (Sec 9)

40 000 miles (80 000 km) or 40 months

Drain and refill automatic transmission (Sec 28)
Change engine oil and oil filter (Sec 4)
Check and lubricate exhaust control valve (if equipped) (Sec 21)
Check clutch pedal free play and adjust as required (Sec 13)
Check and adjust automatic transmission bands as required (Chapter 7)
Check engine drivebelt tension and condition (Sec 9)

45 000 miles (72 000 km) or 45 months

Change engine oil and oil filter (Sec 4)
Check and adjust automatic transmission bands as required (Chapter 7)
Check clutch pedal free play and adjust as required (Sec 13)

Check engine drivebelt condition and tension (Sec 9)
Replace carburetor air filter element (Sec 12)

50 000 miles (80 000 km) or 50 months

Check and adjust automatic transmission band as required (Chapter 7)
Change engine oil and oil filter (Sec 4)
Replace coolant (Sec 29)
Check cooling system hoses and clamps (Sec 6)
Check clutch pedal free play and adjust as required (Sec 13)
Replace PCV filter (Sec 13)
Replace carburetor air cleaner element (Sec 12)
Check engine drivebelt condition and tension (Sec 13)
Check and lubricate exhaust control valve (if equipped) (Sec 21)

Over 50 000 miles (80 000 km) or 50 months

Return to 10 000 mile (16 000 km) schedule and begin again

Severe operating conditions

Severe operating conditions are defined as follows:

a) Extended periods of idling or low-speed operation
b) Towing any trailers up to 1000 lb (450 kg) for long disntances
c) Operating when the outside temperatures remain below 10°F (-12°C) for 60 days or more and most trips are less than 10 miles 816 km)
d) Operation in severe dust conditions
e) The automatic transmission is also considered to be part of the systems under severe operating conditions and must be serviced at closer intervals on vehicles which accumulate 2000 miles (3200 km) per month

If your vehicle falls into the severe operating conditions category, the maintenance schedule must be amended as follows:

a) Change engine oil and filter every 3 months or 3000 miles (4800 km)
b) Check, clean and regap spark plugs every 6000 miles (9600 km)
c) Service the automatic transmission bands every 5000 miles (8000 km) (Chapter 7) and drain and refill the transmission with fresh fluid every 20 000 miles (32 000 km)

Annual checks

Check coolant levels and coolant protection just prior to the onset of freezing weather. If the coolant appears to be dirty or rusty, the system must be drained and flushed, then filled with new coolant
Check all coolant system hoses and clamps
Change coolant every three years or at the required mileage interval
Change coolant hoses and clamps every three years or at the required mileage interval, whichever occurs first

Additional instructions

Change engine oil and filter every 10 000 miles (16 000 km) or 12 months, whichever occurs first
Checking of all engine idle speeds at 10 000 miles (16 000 km) need only be repeated to correct unusual engine operation thereafter
Checking of engine idle fuel mixture at 30 000 miles (48 000 km) need only be repeated to correct unusual operation thereafter

2 Fluid levels check

1   There are a number of components on a vehicle which rely on the use of fluids to perform their job. Through the normal operation of the

car, these fluids are used up and must be replenished before damage occurs. See the *Recommended Lubricants* Section for the specific fluid to be used when adding is required. When checking fluid levels it is important that the car is on a level surface.

Engine oil

2   The engine oil level is checked with a dipstick which is located at the side of the engine block. This dipstick travels through a tube and into the oil pan at the bottom of the engine.

3   The oil level should be checked preferably before the car has been driven, or about 15 minutes after the engine has been shut off. If the oil is checked immediately after driving the car, some of the oil will remain in the upper engine components, thus giving an inaccurate reading on the dipstick.

4   Pull the dipstick from its tube and wipe all the oil from the end with a clean rag. Insert the clean dipstick all the way back into the oil pan and pull it out again. Observe the oil at the end of the dipstick. At its highest point, the level should be within the 'Safe' range.

5   It takes approximately 1 quart of oil to raise the level from the 'Add' mark to the 'Safe' mark on the dipstick. Do not allow the level to drop below the 'Add' mark as this may cause engine damage due to oil starvation. On the other hand, do not overfill the engine by adding oil above the 'Safe' mark as this may result in oil-fouled spark plugs, oil leaks or oil seal failures.

6   Oil is added to the engine after removing a twist-off cap located either on the rocker arm cover or through a raised tube near the front of the engine. The cap should be duly marked 'Engine oil' or similar wording. An oil can spout or funnel will reduce spills as the oil is poured in.

7   Checking the oil level can also be a step towards preventative maintenance. If you find the oil level dropping abnormally, this is an indication of oil leakage or internal engine wear which should be corrected. If there are water droplets in the oil, or it is milky looking, this also indicates component failure and the engine should be checked immediately. The condition of the oil can also be checked along with the level. With the dipstick removed from the engine, take your thumb and index finger and wipe the oil up the dipstick, looking for small dirt particles or engine filings which will cling to the dipstick. This is an indication that the oil should be drained and fresh oil added (Sec 4).

Engine coolant

8   All vehicles are equipped with a pressurized coolant recovery system which makes coolant level checks very easy. A coolant reservoir attached to the inner fender panel is connected by a hose to the radiator cap. As the engine heats up during operation, coolant is forced from the radiator, through the connecting tube and into the reservoir. As the engine cools, this coolant is automatically drawn back into the radiator to keep the correct level.

9   The coolant level should be checked when the engine is cold. Merely observe the level of fluid in the reservoir, which should be at or near the 'Full cold' mark on the side of the reservoir. If the system is completely cooled, also check the level in the radiator by removing the cap. Some systems also have a 'Full hot' mark to check the level when the engine is hot.

10   If your particular vehicle is not equipped with a coolant recovery system, the level should be checked by removing the radiator cap. However, **the cap should not under any circumstances be removed while the system is hot,** as escaping steam could cause serious injury. Wait until the engine has completely cooled, then wrap a thick cloth around the cap and turn it to its first stop. If any steam escapes from the cap, allow the engine to cool further. Then remove the cap and check the level in the radiator. It should be about 2 to 3 inches below the bottom of the filler neck.

11   If only a small amount of coolant is required to bring the system up to the proper level, regular water can be used. However, to maintain the proper antifreeze/water mixture in the system, both should be mixed together to replenish a low level. High-quality antifreeze offering protection to -20° should be mixed with water in the proportion specified on the container. Do not allow antifreeze to come in contact with your skin or painted surfaces of the car. Flush contacted areas immediately with plenty of water.

12   On systems with a recovery tank, coolant should be added to the reservoir after removing the cap at the top of the reservoir. Coolant should be added directly into the radiator on systems without a coolant recovery tank.

13   As the coolant level is checked, observe the condition of the coolant. It should be relatively clear. If the fluid is brown or a rust color, this is an indication that the system should be drained, flushed and refilled (Section 29).

14   If the cooling system requires repeated additions to keep the proper level, have the pressure radiator cap checked for proper sealing ability. Also check for leaks in the system (cracked hoses, loose hose connections, leaking gaskets, etc).

Windshield washer

15   The fluid for the windshield washer system is located in a plastic reservoir. The level inside the reservoir should be maintained at the 'Full' mark.

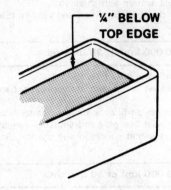

Fig. 1.1 Checking brake fluid in the master cylinder (Sec 2)

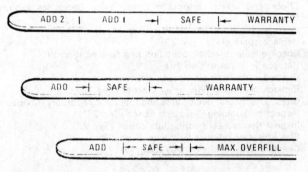

Fig. 1.2 Typical oil dipsticks and markings (Sec 2)

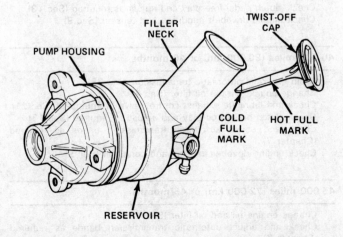

Fig. 1.3 Power steering pump and built-in dipstick (Sec 2)

2.16 Checking the windshield washer fluid level

16 An approved washer solvent should be added through the plastic cap (photo) whenever replenishing is required. Do not use plain water alone in this system, especially in cold climates where the water could freeze.

Battery

Note: *There are certain precautions to be taken when working on or near the battery: (a) Never expose a battery to open flame or spark which could ignite the hydrogen gas given off by the battery; (b) Wear protective clothing and eye protection to reduce the possibility of the corrosive sulfuric acid solution inside the battery harming you (if the fluid is splashed or spilled, flush the contacted area immediately with plenty of water); (c) Remove all metal jewelry which could contact the positive terminal and another grounded metal source, thus causing a short circuit; (d) Always keep batteries and battery acid out of the reach of children.*

17 Vehicles equipped with maintenance-free batteries require no maintenance as the battery case is sealed and has no removal caps for adding water.

18 If a maintenance-type battery is installed, the caps on the top of the battery should be removed periodically to check for a low water level. This check will be more critical during the warm summer months.

19 Remove each of the caps and add distilled water to bring the level of each cell to the split ring in the filler opening.

20 At the same time the battery water level is checked, the overall condition of the battery and its related components should be inspected. If corrosion is found on the cable ends or battery terminals, remove the cables and clean away all corrosion using a baking soda/water solution or a wire brush cleaning tool designed for this purpose. See Chapter 5 for battery care and servicing and jump-starting procedures.

Brake master cylinder

21 The brake master cylinder is located on the left side of the engine compartment firewall and has a cap which must be removed to check the fluid level.

22 Before removing the cap, use a rag to clean all dirt, grease, etc. from around the cap area. If any foreign matter enters the master cylinder with the cap removed, blockage in the brake system lines can occur. Also make sure all painted surfaces around the master cylinder are covered, as brake fluid will ruin paintwork.

23 Release the clip(s) securing the cap to the top of the master cylinder. In most cases, a screwdriver can be used to pry the wire clip(s) free.

24 Carefully lift the cap off the cylinder and observe the fluid level. It should be approximately $\frac{1}{4}$-inch below the top edge of each reservoir.

25 If additional fluid is necessary to bring the level up to the proper height, carefully pour the specified brake fluid into the master cylinder. Be careful not to spill the fluid on painted surfaces. Be sure the specified fluid is used, as mixing different types of brake fluid can

cause damage to the system. See *Recommended Lubricants* or your owner's manual.

26 At this time the fluid and master cylinder can be inspected for contamination. Normally, the braking system will not need periodic draining and refilling, but if rust deposits, dirt particles or water droplets are seen in the fluid, the system should be dismantled, drained and refilled with fresh fluid.

27 Reinstall the master cylinder cap and secure it with the clip(s). Make sure the lid is properly seated to prevent fluid leakage and/or system pressure loss.

28 The brake fluid in the master cylinder will drop slightly as the brake shoes or pads at each wheel wear down during normal operation. If the master cylinder requires repeated replenishing to keep it at the proper level, this is an indication of leakage in the brake system which should be corrected immediately. Check all brake lines and their connections, along with the wheel cylinders and booster (see Chapter 9 for more information).

29 If upon checking the master cylinder fluid level you discover one or both reservoirs empty or nearly empty, the braking system should be bled (Chapter 9). When the fluid level gets low, air can enter the system and should be removed by bleeding the brakes.

Manual transmission

30 Manual shift transmissions do not have a dipstick. The fluid level is checked by removing a plug in the side of the transmission case. Locate this plug and use a rag to clean the plug and the area around it.

31 With the vehicle components cold, remove the plug. If fluid immediately starts leaking out, thread the plug back into the transmission because the fluid level is alright. If there is no fluid leakage, completely remove the plug and place your little finger inside the hold. The fluid level should be just at the bottom of the plug hole.

32 If the transmission needs more fluid, use a syringe to squeeze the appropriate lubricant into the plug hole to bring the fluid up to the proper level.

33 Thread the plug back into the transmission and tighten it securely. Drive the car and check for leaks around the plug.

Automatic transmission

34 The fluid inside the transmission must be at normal operating temperature to get an accurate reading on the dipstick. This is done by driving the car for several miles, making frequent starts and stops to allow the transmission to shift through all gears.

35 Park the car on a level surface, place the selector lever in 'Park' and leave the engine running at an idle.

36 Remove the transmission dipstick (located on the right side, near the rear of the engine) and wipe all the fluid from the end of the dipstick with a clean rag.

37 Push the dipstick back into the transmission until the cap seats firmly on the dipstick tube. Now remove the dipstick again and observe the fluid on the end. The highest point of fluid should be between the 'Full' mark and $\frac{1}{4}$ inch below the 'Full' mark.

38 If the fluid level is at or below the 'Add' mark on the dipstick, add sufficient fluid to raise the level to the 'Full' mark. One pint of fluid will raise the level from 'Add' to 'Full'. Fluid should be added directly into the dipstick guide tube, using a funnel to prevent spills.

39 It is important that the transmission not be overfilled. Under no circumstances should the fluid level be above the 'Full' mark on the dipstick, as this could cause damage to the transmission. The best way to prevent overfilling is to add fluid a little at a time, driving the car and checking the level between additions.

40 Use only transmission fluid specified by the manufacturer. This information can be found in the *Recommended Lubricants* Section.

41 The condition of the fluid should also be checked along with the level. If the level at the end of the dipstick is a dark reddish-brown color, or if the fluid has a 'burnt' smell, the transmission fluid should be changed. If you are in doubt about the condition of the fluid, purchase some new fluid and compare the two for color and smell.

Rear axle

42 Like the manual transmission, the rear axle has an inspection and fill plug which must be removed to check the fluid level.

43 Remove the plug which is located either in the removable cover plate or on the side of the differential carrier. Use your little finger to reach inside the rear axle housing to feel the level of the fluid. It should

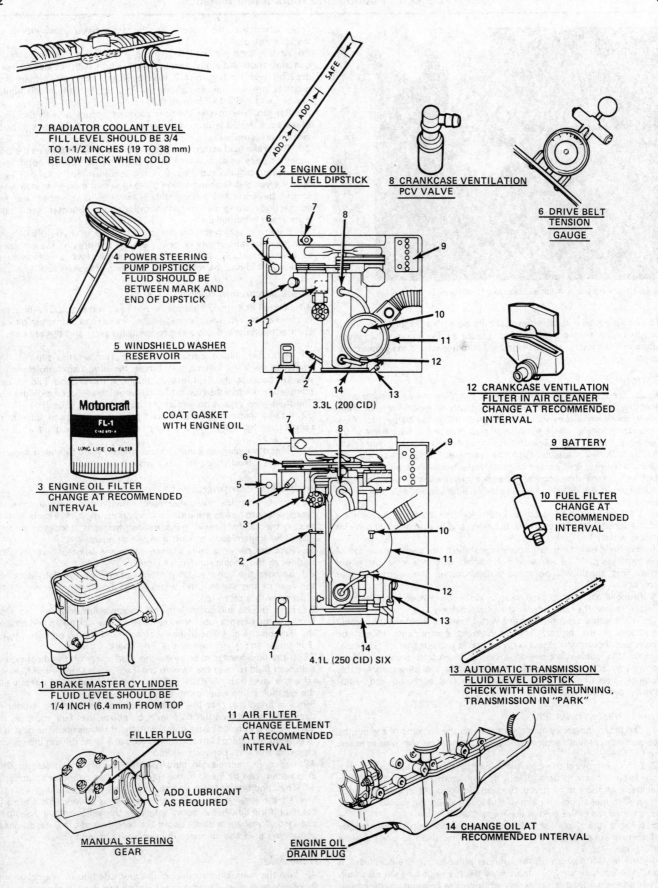

7 RADIATOR COOLANT LEVEL
FILL LEVEL SHOULD BE 3/4
TO 1-1/2 INCHES (19 TO 38 mm)
BELOW NECK WHEN COLD

2 ENGINE OIL
LEVEL DIPSTICK

ADD 2 → ADD 1 → SAFE

8 CRANKCASE VENTILATION
PCV VALVE

6 DRIVE BELT
TENSION
GAUGE

4 POWER STEERING
PUMP DIPSTICK
FLUID SHOULD BE
BETWEEN MARK AND
END OF DIPSTICK

5 WINDSHIELD WASHER
RESERVOIR

Motorcraft
FL-1
LONG LIFE OIL FILTER

3 ENGINE OIL FILTER
CHANGE AT RECOMMENDED
INTERVAL

COAT GASKET
WITH ENGINE OIL

3.3L (200 CID)

12 CRANKCASE VENTILATION
FILTER IN AIR CLEANER
CHANGE AT RECOMMENDED
INTERVAL

9 BATTERY

10 FUEL FILTER
CHANGE AT
RECOMMENDED
INTERVAL

4.1L (250 CID) SIX

13 AUTOMATIC TRANSMISSION
FLUID LEVEL DIPSTICK
CHECK WITH ENGINE RUNNING,
TRANSMISSION IN "PARK"

1 BRAKE MASTER CYLINDER
FLUID LEVEL SHOULD BE
1/4 INCH (6.4 mm) FROM TOP

11 AIR FILTER
CHANGE ELEMENT
AT RECOMMENDED
INTERVAL

FILLER PLUG

ADD LUBRICANT
AS REQUIRED

MANUAL STEERING
GEAR

ENGINE OIL
DRAIN PLUG

14 CHANGE OIL AT
RECOMMENDED INTERVAL

Fig. 1.4 Six cylinder engine service points (Sec 2)

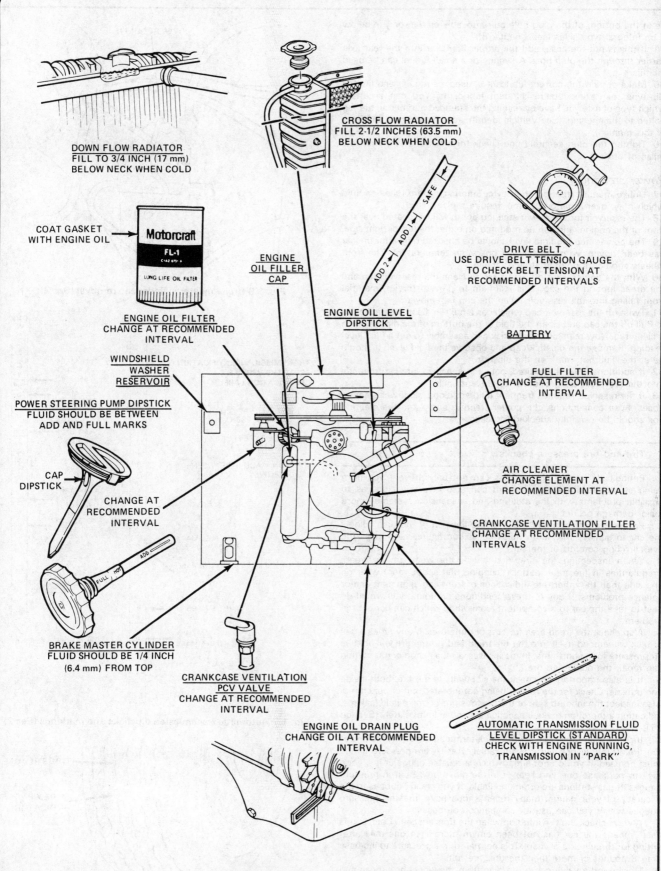

DOWN FLOW RADIATOR
FILL TO 3/4 INCH (17 mm)
BELOW NECK WHEN COLD

CROSS FLOW RADIATOR
FILL 2-1/2 INCHES (63.5 mm)
BELOW NECK WHEN COLD

COAT GASKET
WITH ENGINE OIL

Motorcraft
FL-1
LONG LIFE OIL FILTER

ENGINE
OIL FILLER
CAP

DRIVE BELT
USE DRIVE BELT TENSION GAUGE
TO CHECK BELT TENSION AT
RECOMMENDED INTERVALS

ENGINE OIL FILTER
CHANGE AT RECOMMENDED
INTERVAL

ENGINE OIL LEVEL
DIPSTICK

BATTERY

WINDSHIELD
WASHER
RESERVOIR

FUEL FILTER
CHANGE AT RECOMMENDED
INTERVAL

POWER STEERING PUMP DIPSTICK
FLUID SHOULD BE BETWEEN
ADD AND FULL MARKS

CAP
DIPSTICK

AIR CLEANER
CHANGE ELEMENT AT
RECOMMENDED INTERVAL

CHANGE AT
RECOMMENDED
INTERVAL

CRANKCASE VENTILATION FILTER
CHANGE AT RECOMMENDED
INTERVALS

BRAKE MASTER CYLINDER
FLUID SHOULD BE 1/4 INCH
(6.4 mm) FROM TOP

CRANKCASE VENTILATION
PCV VALVE
CHANGE AT RECOMMENDED
INTERVAL

ENGINE OIL DRAIN PLUG
CHANGE OIL AT RECOMMENDED
INTERVAL

AUTOMATIC TRANSMISSION FLUID
LEVEL DIPSTICK (STANDARD)
CHECK WITH ENGINE RUNNING,
TRANSMISSION IN "PARK"

Fig. 1.5 V8 engine service points (Sec 2)

be at the bottom of the plug hole on removable carrier, or $\frac{1}{2}$ in below it on integral type axles (see Chapter 8).

44 If this is not the case, add the proper lubricant into the rear axle carrier through the plug hole. A syringe or a small funnel can be used for this.

45 Make certain the correct lubricant is used, as regular and limited slip-type rear axles require different lubricants. You can ascertain which type of axle you have by reading the stamped number on the tag bolted to the housing. (See Vehicle Identification Numbers at the front of this manual).

46 Tighten the plug securely and check for leaks after the first few miles of driving.

Power steering

47 Unlike manual steering, the power steering system relies on fluid which may, over a period of time, require replenishing.

48 The reservoir for the power steering pump will be located near the front of the engine, and can be mounted on either the left or right side.

49 The power steering fluid level should be checked only after the car has been driven, with the fluid at operating temperature. The front wheels should be pointed straight ahead.

50 With the engine shut off, use a rag to clean the reservoir cap and the areas around the cap. This will help to prevent foreign material from falling into the reservoir when the cap is removed.

51 Twist off the reservoir cap which has a built-in dipstick attached to it. Pull off the cap and clean the fluid at the bottom of the dipstick with a clean rag. Now reinstall the dipstick/cap assembly to get a fluid level reading. Remove the dipstick/cap and observe the fluid level. It should be at the 'Full hot' mark on the dipstick.

52 If additional fluid is required, pour the specified lubricant directly into the reservoir using a funnel to prevent spills.

53 If the reservoir requires frequent fluid additions, all power steering hoses, hose connections, the power steering pump and the steering box should be carefully checked for leaks.

3 Tire and tire pressure checks

1 Periodically inspecting the tires can not only prevent you from being stranded with a flat tire, but can also give you clues as to possible problems with the steering and suspension systems before major damage occurs.

2 Proper tire inflation add miles to the lifespan of the tires, allows the car to achieve maximum miles per gallon figures, and helps the overall riding comfort of the car.

3 When inspecting the tire, first check the wear on the tread. Irregularities in the tread pattern (cupping, flat spots, more wear on one side than the other) are indications of front end alignment and/or balance problems. If any of these conditions are found you would do best to take the car to a competent repair shop which can correct the problem.

4 Also check the tread area for cuts or punctures. Many times a nail or tack will embed itself into the tire tread and yet the tire will hold its air pressure for a short time. In most cases, a repair shop or gas station can repair the punctured tire.

5 It is also important to check the sidewalls of the tire, both inside and outside. Check for the rubber being deteriorated, cut or punctured. Also inspect the inboard side of the tire for signs of brake fluid leakage, indicating a thorough brake inspection is needed immediately (Section 27).

6 Incorrect tire pressures cannot be determined merely by looking at the tire. This is especially true for radial tyres. A tire pressure gauge must be used. If you do not already have a reliable gauge, it is a good idea to purchase one and keep it in the glove box. Built-in pressure gauges at gas stations are often unreliable. If you are in doubt as to the accuracy of your gauge, many repair shops have 'master' pressure gauges which you can use for comparison purposes.

7 Always check the tire inflation when the tires are cold. Cold, in this case, means the car has not been drawn more than one mile after sitting for three hours or more. It is normal for the pressure to increase 4 to 8 pounds or more then the tires are hot.

8 Unscrew the valve cap protruding from the wheel or hubcap and firmly press the gauge onto the valve stem. Observe the reading on the gauge and check this figure against the recommended tire pressure listed on the tire placard.

9 Check all tires and add air as necessary to bring all tires up to the

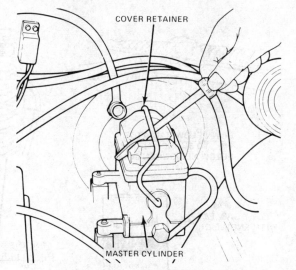

Fig. 1.6 Brake master cylinder cap removal (Sec 2)

COVER RETAINER

MASTER CYLINDER

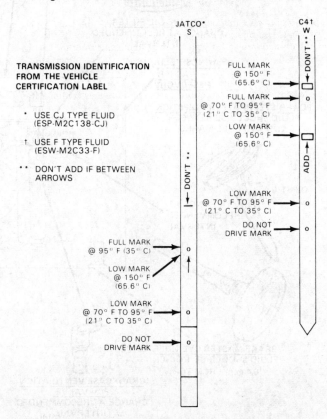

TRANSMISSION IDENTIFICATION FROM THE VEHICLE CERTIFICATION LABEL

JATCO* S

C4† W

- USE CJ TYPE FLUID (ESP-M2C138-CJ)
† USE F TYPE FLUID (ESW-M2C33-F)
** DON'T ADD IF BETWEEN ARROWS

DON'T **

DON'T **

FULL MARK @ 150° F (65.6° C)

FULL MARK @ 70° F TO 95° F (21° C TO 35° C)

LOW MARK @ 150° F (65.6° C)

ADD →

LOW MARK @ 70° F TO 95° F (21° C TO 35° C)

DO NOT DRIVE MARK

FULL MARK @ 95° F (35° C)

LOW MARK @ 150° F (65.6° C)

LOW MARK @ 70° F TO 95° F (21° C TO 35° C)

DO NOT DRIVE MARK

Fig. 1.7 Automatic transmission dipsticks and markings (Sec 2)

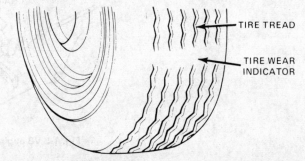

TIRE TREAD

TIRE WEAR INDICATOR

Fig. 1.8 Tread wear indicators which run across the tread when the tire is in need of replacement (Sec 3)

recommended pressure levels. Do not forget the spare tire. Be sure to reinstall the valve caps which will keep dirt and moisture out of the valve stem mechanism.

4 Engine oil and filter change

1 Frequent oil changes may be the best form of preventative maintenance available for the home mechanic. When engine oil ages, it gets diluted and contaminated which ultimately leads to premature parts wear.

2 Although some sources recommend oil filter changes every other oil change, we feel that the minimal cost of an oil filter and the relative ease with which it is installed dictates that a new filter be used whenever the oil is changed.

3 The tools necessary for a normal oil and filter change are: a wrench to fit the drain plug at the bottom of the oil pan; an oil filter wrench to remove the old filter; a container with at least a six-quart capacity to drain the old oil into; and a funnel or oil can spout to help pour fresh oil into the engine.

4 In addition, you should have plenty of clean rags and newspapers handy to mop up any spills. Access to the underside of the car is greatly improved if the car can be lifted on a hoist, driven onto ramps or supported by jack stands. Do not work under a car which is supported only by a bumper, hydraulic or scissors-type jack.

5 If this is your first oil change on the car, it it a good idea to crawl underneath and familiarize yourself with the locations of the oil drain plug and the oil filter. Since the engine and exhaust components will be warm during the actual work, it is best to figure out any potential problems before the car and its accessories are hot.

6 Allow the car to warm up to normal operating temperature. If the new oil or any tools are needed, use this warm-up time to gather everything necessary for the job. The correct type of oil to buy for your application can be found in *Recommended Lubricants* near the front of this Chapter.

7 With the engine oil warm (warm engine oil will drain better and more built-up sludge will be removed with the oil), raise the vehicle for access beneath. Make sure the car is firmly supported. If jack stands are used they should be placed towards the front of the frame rails which run the length of the car.

8 Move all necessary tools, rags and newspaper under the car. Position the drain pan under the drain plug. Keep in mind that the oil will initially flow from the pan with some force, so place the pan accordingly.

9 Being careful not to touch any of the hot exhaust pipe components, use the wrench to remove the drain plug near the bottom of the oil pan. Depending on how hot the oil has become, you may want to wear gloves while unscrewing the plug the final few turns.

10 Allow the old oil to drain into the pan. It may be necessary to move the pan further under the engine as the oil flow reduces to a trickle.

11 After all the oil has drained, clean the drain plug thoroughly with a clean rag. Small metal filings may cling to this plug which could immediately contaminate your new oil.

12 Clean the area around the drain plug opening and reinstall the drain plug. Tighten the plug securely with your wrench.

13 Move the drain pan in position under the oil filter.

14 Now use the filter wrench to loosen the oil filter (photo). Chain or metal band-type filter wrenches may distort the filter canister, but don't worry too much about this as the filter will be discarded anyway.

15 Sometimes the oil filter is on so tight it cannot be loosened, or it is positioned in an area which is inaccessible with a filter wrench. As a last resort, you can punch a metal bar or long screwdriver horizontally through the **bottom** of the canister and use this as a T-bar to turn the filter. If this must be done, be prepared for oil to spurt out of the canister as it is punctured.

16 Completely unscrew the old filter. Be careful, it is full of oil. Empty the old oil inside the filter into the drain pan.

17 Compare the old filter with the new one to make sure they are of the same type.

18 Use a clean rag to remove all oil, dirt and sludge from the area where the oil filter mounts to the engine. Check the old filter to make sure the rubber gasket is not stuck to the engine mounting surface. If this gasket is stuck to the engine (use a flashlight if necessary), remove it.

19 Open one of the cans of new oil and fill the new filter with fresh

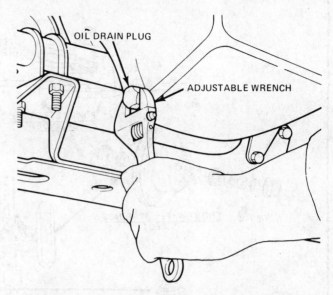

Fig. 1.9 Removing the oil pan drain plug (Sec 4)

oil. Also smear a light coat of this fresh oil onto the rubber gasket of the new oil filter.

20 Screw the new filter to the engine following the tightening directions printed on the filter canister or packing box. Most filter manufacturers recommend against using a filter wrench due to possible overtightening or damage to the canister.

21 Remove all tools, rags, etc. from under the car, being careful not to spill the oil in the drain pan. Lower the car off its support devices.

22 Move to the engine compartment and locate the oil filler cap on the engine.

23 If an oil can spout is used, push the spout into the top of the oil can and pour the fresh oil through the filler opening. A funnel placed into the opening may also be used.

24 Pour about 4 qts of fresh oil into the engine. Wait a few minutes to allow the oil to drain to the pan, the check the level on the oil dipstick (see Section 2 if necessary). If the oil level is at or near the lower 'Add' mark, start the engine and allow the new oil to circulate.

25 Run the engine for only about a minute and then shut it off. Immediately look under the car and check for leaks at the oil pan drain plug and around the oil filter. If either is leaking, tighten with a bit more force.

26 With the new oil circulated and the filter now completely full, recheck the level on the dipstick and add enough oil to bring the level to the 'Full' mark on the dipstick.

27 During the first few trips after an oil change, make a point to check for leaks and also the oil level.

28 The old oil drained from the engine cannot be reused in its present state and should be disposed of. Oil reclamation centers, auto repair shops and gas stations will normally accept the oil which can be refined and used again. After the oil has cooled, it can be drained into a suitable container (capped plastic jugs, topped bottles, milk cartons, etc.) for transport to one of these disposal sites.

5 Chassis lubrication

1 A grease gun and a cartridge filled with the proper grease (see *Recommended Lubricants*) are the only equipment necessary to lubricate the various chassis components.

2 Using the accompanying Figure, locate the various grease fittings.

3 For easier access under the car, raise the vehicle with a jack and place jack stands under the frame. Make sure the car is firmly supported by the stands.

4 Before you do any greasing, force a little of the grease out of the nozzle to remove any dirt from the end of the gun. Wipe the nozzle clean with a rag.

5 Wipe the grease fitting nipple clean and push the nozzle firmly over the fitting nipple. Squeeze the trigger on the grease gun to force grease into the component. Both the balljoints and tie rods should be

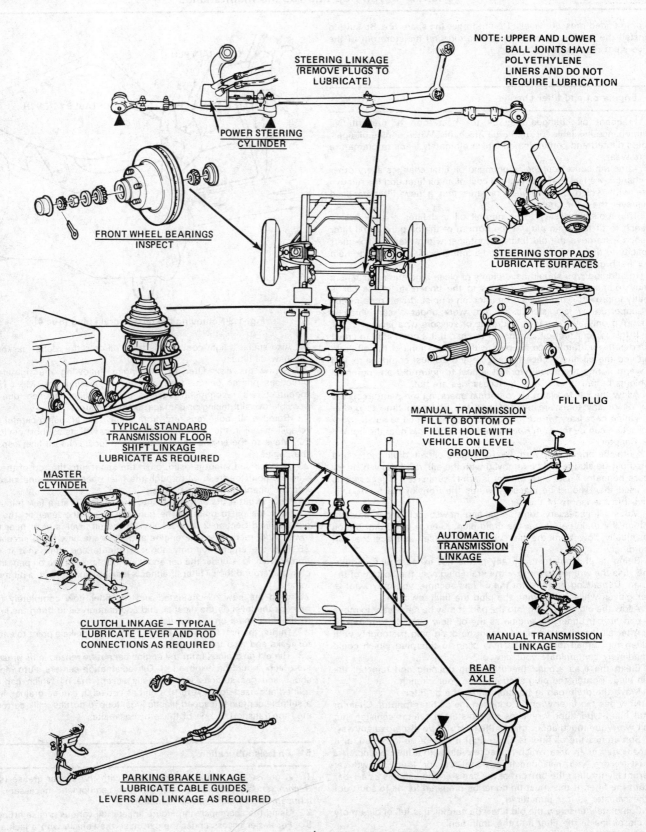

STEERING LINKAGE
(REMOVE PLUGS TO
LUBRICATE)

NOTE: UPPER AND LOWER
BALL JOINTS HAVE
POLYETHYLENE
LINERS AND DO NOT
REQUIRE LUBRICATION

POWER STEERING
CYLINDER

FRONT WHEEL BEARINGS
INSPECT

STEERING STOP PADS
LUBRICATE SURFACES

TYPICAL STANDARD
TRANSMISSION FLOOR
SHIFT LINKAGE
LUBRICATE AS REQUIRED

FILL PLUG

MANUAL TRANSMISSION
FILL TO BOTTOM OF
FILLER HOLE WITH
VEHICLE ON LEVEL
GROUND

MASTER
CLYINDER

CLUTCH LINKAGE – TYPICAL
LUBRICATE LEVER AND ROD
CONNECTIONS AS REQUIRED

AUTOMATIC
TRANSMISSION
LINKAGE

MANUAL TRANSMISSION
LINKAGE

REAR
AXLE

PARKING BRAKE LINKAGE
LUBRICATE CABLE GUIDES,
LEVERS AND LINKAGE AS REQUIRED

▲ LUBRICATION POINT

Fig. 1.10 Chassis lubrication points (Sec 5)

lubricated until the rubber reservoir is firm to the touch. The upper balljoints have polyethylene liners and do not require lubrication. Do not pump too much grease into these fittings as this could rupture the reservoir. If the grease seeps out around the grease gun nozzle, the nipple is clogged or the nozzle is not fully seated around the fitting nipple. Resecure the gun nozzle to the fitting and try again. If necessary, replace the fitting.

6   Wipe any excess grease from the components and the grease fitting.

7   Lubrication of the power steering control valve ball stud can be accomplished only with a special fitting available at your dealer. If this fitting is not available, have the lubrication performed by your dealer. If you can acquire this fitting, remove the plug from the control valve, install the fitting and lubricate the ball stud with specification grease, using a low-pressure hand-operated grease gun.

8   While you are under the car, clean and lubricate the brake cable along with its cable guides and levers. This can be done by smearing some of the chassis grease onto the cable and its related parts with your fingers.

9   Lower the car to the ground for the remaining body lubrication process.

10   Open the hood and smear a little chassis grease on the hood latch mechanism. Have an assistant pull the release knob from inside the car as you lubricate the cable at the latch.

11   Lubricate all the hinges (door, hood, trunk) with a few drops of light engine oil to keep them in proper working order.

12   Finally, the key lock cylinders can be lubricated with spray-on graphite, which is available at auto parts stores.

6   Cooling system check

1   Many major engine failures can be attributed to a faulty cooling system. If equipped with an automatic transmission, the cooling system also plays an integral role in the transmission longevity.

2   The cooling system should be checked with the engine cold. Do this before the car is driven for the day or after it has been shut off for one or two hours.

3   Remove the radiator cap and thoroughly clean the cap (inside and out) with clean water. Also clean the filler neck on the radiator. All traces of corrosion should be removed.

4   Carefully check the upper and lower radiator hoses (photo) along with the smaller diameter heater hoses. Inspect their entire lengths, replacing any hose which is cracked, swollen or shows signs of deterioration. Cracks may become more apparent if the hose is squeezed.

5   Also check that all hose connections are tight. A leak in the cooling system will usually show up as white or rust colored deposits on the areas adjoining the leak.

6   Use compressed air or a soft brush to remove bugs, leaves, etc. from the front of the radiator or air conditioning condensor. Be careful not to damage the delicate cooling fins, or cut yourself on the sharp fins.

7   Finally, have the cap and system tested for proper pressure. If you do not have a pressure tester, most gas stations and repair shops will do this for a minimal charge.

7   Exhaust system check

1   With the exhaust system cold (at least three hours after being driven), check the complete system from its starting point at the engine to the end of the tailpipe. This is best done on a hoist where full access is available.

2   Check the pipes and their connections for signs of leakage and/or corrosion including a potential failure. Check that all brackets and hangers are in good condition and are tight.

3   At the same time, inspect the underside of the body for holes, corrosion, open seams, etc. which may allow exhaust gases to enter the trunk or passenger compartment. Seal all body openings with silicone or body putty.

4   Rattles and other driving noises can often be traced to the exhaust system, especially the mounts and hangers. Try to move the pipes, muffler and catalytic converter (if equipped). If the components can come into contact with the body or driveline parts, secure the exhaust system with new mountings.

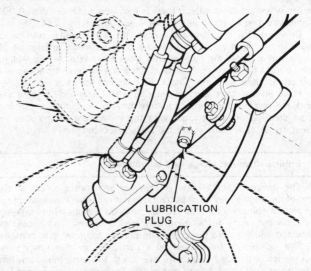

Fig. 1.11 Power steering control valve ball stud lubrication (Sec 5)

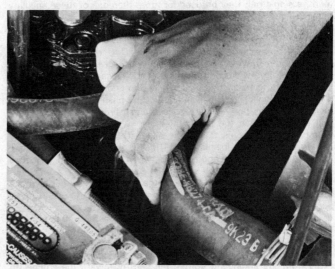

6.4 Squeezing the radiator hose to check for cracks

5   This is also an ideal time to check the running condition of the engine by inspecting the very end of the tailpipe. The exhaust deposits here are an indication of engine tune. If the pipe is black and sooty or bright white deposits are found here, the engine is in need of a tune-up including a thorough carburetor inspection and adjustment.

8   Suspension and steering check

1   Whenever the front of the car is raised for service it is a good idea to visually check the suspension and steering components for wear.

2   Indications of a fault in these systems are: excessive play in the steering wheel before the front wheels react; excessive sway around corners or body movement over rough roads; binding at some point as the steering wheel is turned.

3   Before the car is raised for inspection, test the shock absorbers by pushing downward to rock the car at each corner. If you push the car down and it does not come back to a level position within one or two bounces, the shocks are worn and need to be replaced. As this is done, check for squeaks and strange noises from the suspension components. Information on shock absorber and suspension components can be found in Chapter 11.

4   Now raise the front end of the car and support firmly by jack stands placed under the frame rails. Because of the work to be done, make sure the car cannot fall from the stands.

5   Grab the top and bottom of the front tire with your hands and rock

the tire/wheel on its spindle. If there is movement of more than 0.005 in, the wheel bearings should be serviced (see Section 26).

6   Crawl under the car and check for loose bolts, broken or disconnected parts and deteriorated rubber bushings (photo) on all suspension and steering components. Look for grease or fluid leaking from around the steering box. Check the power steering hoses and their connections for leaks. Check the balljoints for wear.

7   Have an assistant turn the steering wheel from side to side and check the steering components for free movement, chafing or binding. If the steering does not react with the movement of the steering wheel, try to determine where the slack is located.

9   Engine drivebelt check and adjustment

1   The drivebelts, or V-belts as they are sometimes called, at the front of the engine play an important role in the overall operation of the car and its components. Due to their function and material make-up, the belts are prone to failure after a period of time and should be inspected and adjusted periodically to prevent major engine damage.

2   The number of belts used on a particular car depends on the accessories installed. Drivebelts are used to turn: the generator (alternator), AIR smog pump; power steering pump; water pump; fan; and air conditioning compressor. Depending on the pulley arrangement, a single belt may be used for more than one of these ancillary components.

3   With the engine off, open the hood and locate the various belts at the front of the engine. Using your fingers (and a flashlight if necessary), move along the belts checking for cracks or separation. Also check for fraying and for glazing which gives the belt a shiny appearance. Both sides of the belts should be inspected, which means you will have to twist the belt to check the underside.

4   The tension of each belt is checked by pushing on the belt at a distance halfway between the pulleys. Push firmly with your thumb and see how much the belt moves downward (deflects). A rule of thumb, so to speak, is that if the distance (pulley center to pulley center) is between 7 inches and 11 inches the belt should deflect $\frac{1}{4}$ inch. If the belt is longer and travels between pulleys spaced 12 inches to 16 inches apart, the belt should deflect $\frac{3}{8}$ in.

5   If it is found necessary to adjust the belt tension, either to make the belt tighter or looser, this is done by moving the belt-driven accessory on its bracket.

6   For each component there will be an adjustment or strap bolt and a pivot bolt. Both bolts must be loosened slightly to enable you to move the component.

7   After the two bolts have been loosened, move the component away from the engine (to tighten the belt) or toward the engine (to loosen the belt). Hold the accessory in this position and check the belt tension. If it is correct, tighten the two bolts until snug, then recheck the tension. If it is alright, fully tighten the two bolts.

8   It will often be necessary to use some sort of pry bar to move the accessory while the belt is adjusted. If this must be done to gain the proper leverage, be very careful not to damage the component being moved, or the part being pried against.

10   Fuel system check

1   There are certain precautions to take when inspecting or servicing the fuel system components. Work in a well ventilated area and do not allow open flames (cigarettes, appliance pilot lights, etc.) to get near the work area. Mop up spills immediately and do not store fuel-soaked rags where they could ignite.

2   The fuel system is under some amount of pressure, so if any fuel lines are disconnected for servicing, be prepared to catch the fuel as it spurts out. Plug all disconnected fuel lines immediately after disconnection to prevent the tank from emptying itself.

3   The fuel system is most easily checked with the car raised on a hoist where the components under the car are readily visible and accessible.

4   If the smell of gasoline is noticed while driving, or after the car has sat in the sun, the system should be thoroughly inspected immediately.

5   Remove the gas filler cap and check for damage, corrosion and a proper sealing imprint on the gasket. Replace the cap with a new one if necessary.

6   With the car raised, inspect the gas tank and filler neck for

puntures, cracks or any damage. The connection between the filler neck and the tank is especially critical. Sometimes a rubber filler neck will leak due to loose clamps or deteriorated rubber; problems a home mechanic can usually rectify.

7   Do not under any circumstances try to repair a fuel tank yourself (except rubber components) unless you have considerable experience. A welding torch or any open flame can easily cause the fuel vapors to explode if the proper precautions are not taken.

8   Carefully check all rubber hoses and metal lines leading away from the fuel tank. Check for loose connections, deteriorated hose, crimped lines or damage of any kind. Follow these lines up to the front of the car, carefully inspecting them all the way. Repair or replace damaged sections as necessary.

9   If a fuel odor is still evident after the inspection, inspect the evaporative emissions system and Section 16 for carburetor adjustment.

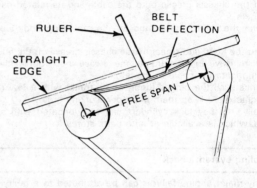

Fig. 1.12 Measuring drivebelt deflection (Sec 9)

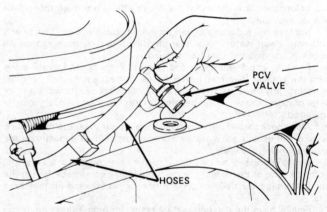

Fig. 1.13 Typical PCV valve replacement (6 cylinders) (Sec 11)

11   Positive Crankcase Ventilation (PCV) valve replacement

1   The PCV valve can usually be found pushed into one of the rocker arm covers at the side of the engine. There will be a hose connected to the valve which runs to either the carburetor or the intake manifold.

2   When purchasing a replacement PCV valve, make sure it is for your particular vehicle, model year and engine size.

3   Pull the valve (with the hose attached) from its rubber grommet in the rocker arm cover.

4   Now pull the PCV valve from the end of the hose, noting its installed position and direction.

5   Compare the old valve with the new one to make sure they are the same.

6   Push the new valve into the end of the hose until it is fully seated.

7   Inspect the rubber grommet in the cover for damage and replace it with a new one if faulty.

8   Push the PCV valve and hose securely into the rocker arm cover.

9   More information on the PCV system can be found in Chapter 6.

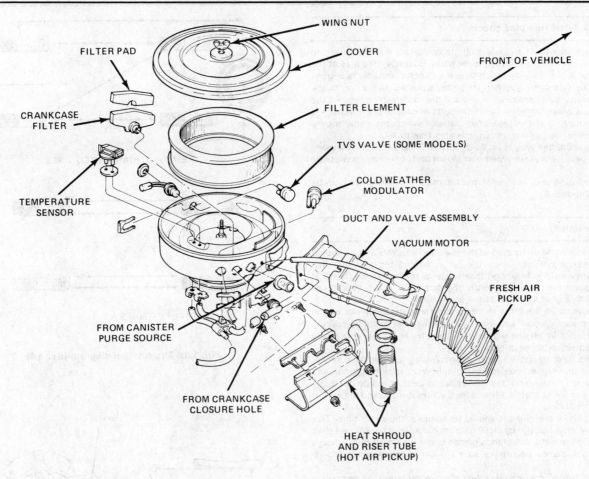

WING NUT

FILTER PAD

COVER

FRONT OF VEHICLE

CRANKCASE FILTER

FILTER ELEMENT

TVS VALVE (SOME MODELS)

COLD WEATHER MODULATOR

TEMPERATURE SENSOR

DUCT AND VALVE ASSEMBLY

VACUUM MOTOR

FRESH AIR PICKUP

FROM CANISTER PURGE SOURCE

FROM CRANKCASE CLOSURE HOLE

HEAT SHROUD AND RISER TUBE (HOT AIR PICKUP)

Fig. 1.14 Typical air cleaner assembly components (Sec 12)

12 Air filter and crankcase filter replacement

1   At the specified intervals, the air filter and crankcase filter should be replaced with new ones. A thorough program of preventative maintenance would call for the two filters to be inspected periodically between changes.

2   The air filter is located inside the air cleaner housing on the top of the engine. To remove the filter, unscrew the wing nut at the top of the air cleaner and lift off the top plate. If there are vacuum hoses connected to this plate, note their positions and disconnect them.

3   While the top plate is off, be careful not to drop anything down into the carburetor.

4   Lift the air filter out of the housing.

5   To check the filter, hold it up to strong sunlight, or place a flashlight or droplight on the inside of the ring-shaped filter. If you can see light coming through the paper element, the filter is alright. Check all the way around the filter.

6   Wipe the inside of the air cleaner clean with a rag.

7   Place the old filter (if in good condition) or the new filter (if specified interval has elapsed) back into the air cleaner housing. Make sure it seats properly in the bottom of the housing.

8   Connect any disconnected vacuum hoses to the top plate and reinstall the top plate with the wing nut.

9   On nearly all cars the crankcase filter is also located inside the air cleaner housing. Remove the top plate as described previously and locate the filter on the side of the housing.

10   Loosen the hose clamp at the end of the crankcase filter hose leading to the filter. Disconnect the hose from the filter.

11   Remove the metal locking clip which secures the filter holder to the air cleaner housing. Pliers can be used for this.

12   Remove the filter and plastic holder from the inside of the air cleaner.

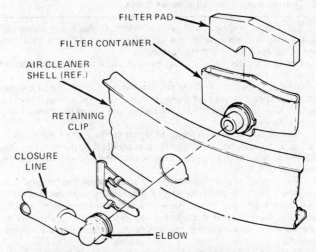

FILTER PAD

FILTER CONTAINER

AIR CLEANER SHELL (REF.)

RETAINING CLIP

CLOSURE LINE

ELBOW

Fig. 1.15 Crankcase filter installation (Sec 12)

13   Remove the old filter pad from the container. Wash the container in a suitable solvent. Lightly oil the new filter pad.

14   Place the new filter assembly into position and install the metal locking clip on the outside of the air cleaner.

15   Connect the filter hose and tighten the clamp around the end of the hose.

16   Reinstall the air cleaner top plate and any vacuum hoses which were disconnected.

17   For more information on these filters and the systems they are a part of, see Chapter 4 and Chapter 6.

13 Clutch pedal free play check

1   If equipped with a manual shift transmission, it is important to have the clutch free play at the proper point. Basically, free play at the clutch pedal is the point at which time the clutch components engage and the car starts moving. When the pedal is pushed all the way to the floor, the clutch parts are disengaged and the car doesn't travel. As the pedal travels away from the floor, the parts engage and the vehicle is set into motion. It is the measured distance which the pedal moves between these two points which indicates free travel.

2   Clutch pedal free play must be periodically measured and adjusted to compensate for wear or when new clutch parts or linkage have been installed.

3   A description of clutch pedal measurement and adjustment can be found in Chapter 8.

14 Tire rotation

1   The tires should be rotated at the specified intervals and whenever uneven wear is noticed. Since the car will be raised and the tires removed anyway, this is a good time to check the brakes (Section 27) and/or repack the wheel bearings (Section 26). Read over these sections if this is to be done at the same time.

2   The location for each tire in the rotation sequence depends on the type of tire used on your car. Tire type can be determined by reading the raised printing on the sidewall of the tire. Fig. 1.16 shows the rotation sequence for each type of tire.

3   See the information in *Jacking and Towing* at the front of this manual for the proper procedures to follow in raising the car and changing a tire; however, if the brakes are to be checked do not apply the parking brake as stated. Make sure the tires are blocked to prevent the car from rolling.

4   Preferably, the entire car should be raised at the same time. This can be done on a hoist or by jacking up each corner of the car and then lowering the car onto jack stands placed under the frame rails. Always use four jack stands and make sure the car is firmly supported all around.

5   After rotation, check and adjust the tire pressures as necessary and be sure to check wheel nut tightness.

15 Thermo controlled air cleaner check

1   All models are equipped with a thermostatically controlled air cleaner which draws air to the carburetor from different locations depending upon engine temperature.

2   This is a simple visual check; however, if access is tight, a small mirror may have to be used.

3   Open the hood and find the vacuum flapper door on the air cleaner assembly. It will be located inside the long 'snorkel' of the metal air cleaner. Check that the flexible air hose(s) are securely attached and are not damaged.

4   If there is a flexible air duct attached to the end of the snorkel, leading to an area behind the grille, disconnect it at the snorkel. This will enable you to look through the end of the snorkel and see the flapper door inside.

5   The testing should preferably be done when the engine and outside air are cold. Start the engine and look through the snorkel at the flapper door which should move to a closed position. With the door closed, air cannot enter through the end of the snorkel, but rather air enters the air cleaner through the flexible duct attached to the exhaust manifold.

6   As the engine warms up to operating temperature, the door should open to allow air through the snorkel end. Depending on ambient temperature, this may take 10 to 15 minutes. To speed up this check you can reconnect the snorkel air duct, drive the car and then check that the door is fully open.

7   If the thermo controlled air cleaner is not operating properly, see Chapter 6 for more information.

16 Engine idle speed adjustment

1   Engine idle speed is the speed at which the engine operates when no accelerator pedal pressure is applied. This speed is critical to the

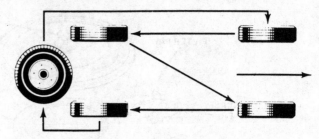

BIAS AND BIAS BELTED TIRES

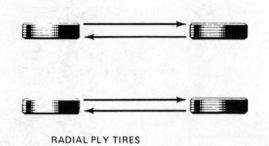

RADIAL PLY TIRES

Fig. 1.16 Tire rotation diagram (Sec 14)

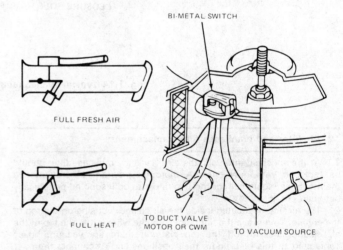

BI-METAL SWITCH

FULL FRESH AIR

FULL HEAT

TO DUCT VALVE
MOTOR OR CWM

TO VACUUM SOURCE

Fig. 1.17 Operation of the thermostatically-controlled air cleaner (Sec 15)

performance of the engine itself, as well as many engine sub-systems.

2   A hand-held tachometer must be used when adjusting the idle speed to get an accurate reading. The exact hook-up for these meters varies with the manufacturer, so follow the particular directions included.

3   Since the manufacturer used many different carburetors for their vehicles in the time period covered by this book, and each has its own peculiarities when setting idle speed, it would be impractical to cover all types in this Section. Chapter 4 contains information on each individual carburetor used. The carburetor used on your particular engine can be found in the Specifications Section of Chapter 4. However, all vehicles covered in this manual should have an emissions decal in the engine compartment. The printed instructions for setting idle speed can be found on this decal, and should be followed since they are for your particular engine.

4   Basically, for most applications, the idle speed is set by turning an adjustment screw located at the side of the carburetor. This screw

changes the linkage, in essence, depressing or letting up on your accelerator pedal. This screw may be on the linkage itself or may be part of the idle stop solenoid. Refer to the emissions decal or Chapter 4.

5   Once you have found the idle screw, experiment with different length screwdrivers until the adjustments can be easily made, without coming into contact with hot or moving engine components.

6   Follow the instructions on the emissions decal or in Chapter 4, which will probably include disconnecting certain vacuum or electrical connections. To plug a vacuum hose after disconnecting it, insert a properly-sized metal rod into the opening, or thoroughly wrap the open end with tape to prevent any vacuum loss through the hose.

7   If the air cleaner is removed, the vacuum hose to the snorkel should be plugged.

8   Make sure the parking brake is firmly set and the wheels blocked to prevent the car from rolling. This is especially true if the transmission is to be in Drive. An assistant inside the car pushing on the brake pedal is the safest method.

9   For all applications, the engine must be completed warmed-up to operating temperature, which will automatically render the choke fast idle inoperative.

17 Underhood hoses – checking and replacement

Caution: *Replacement of air conditioner hoses should be left to a dealer or a/c specialist who can de-pressurize the system and perform the work safely.*

1   The high temperatures present under the hood can cause deterioration of the numerous rubber and plastic hoses.

2   Periodic inspection should be made for cracking, loose clamps and leaking because some of the hoses are part of the emissions system and can affect the engine's running and idling.

3   Remove the air cleaner if necessary and trace the entire length of each hose. Squeeze the hose to check for cracks and look for swelling, discoloration and leaks.

4   If the vehicle has considerable mileage or one or more of the hoses is suspect, it is a good idea to replace all of the hoses at one time.

5   Measure the length and inside diameter of each hose and obtain and cut the replacement to size. As original equipment hose clamps are often good for only one or two uses, it is a good idea to replace them with screw-type clamps.

6   Replace each hose one at a time to eliminate the possibility of confusion. Hoses attached to the heater system, choke or ported vacuum switched contain radiator coolant so newspapers or rags should be kept handy to catch the spillage when they are disconnected.

7   After installation, run the engine until up to operating temperature, shut it off and check for leaks. After the engine has cooled, re-tighten all of the screw-type clamps.

18 Fuel filter replacement

1   Fuel filters are of the paper replacement type and are located either in the fuel line itself or at the screw-in fuel inlet in the carburetor.

2   Filter replacement should be done with the engine cold (after sitting at least 3 hours). You will need the proper replacement filter, screwdriver, pliers, a length of rubber fuel line and an adjustable wrench. Also, gather together some clean rags to catch any spilled fuel.

3   Remove the air cleaner assembly and follow the fuel line from the fuel pump to locate the filter. If any vacuum hoses are disconnected, make sure to note their positions and/or tag them to help during the reassembly process.

4   Place some rags under the filter to catch the fuel which will be spilled when the filter is disconnected.

5   On in-line mounted filters, remove the spring-type clamps, fuel filter and rubber hoses. Discard the hoses and cut new ones to length.

6   Install the clamps on the hoses and push one end of the hose on the filter inlet and the other on the outlet. Push the inlet side on the metal supply line and the other on the carburetor inlet side.

7   Install the spring-type clamps with pliers.

8   On carburetor-mounted filters, release the spring-type clamp from the fuel inlet and remove the fuel line.

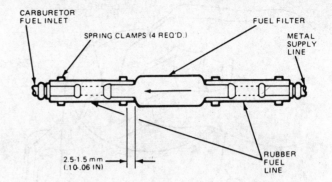

Fig. 1.18 In-line fuel filter installation (Sec 18)

9   Loosen the fuel inlet fitting with the wrench and unscrew the fitting, gasket, spring and filter.

10 Install the new filter along with the fitting, gasket and spring in the carburetor.

11 If the fuel line does not appear serviceable, cut a new one to length and install it.

12 Run the engine to check for leaks and reinstall the air cleaner assembly, connecting all hoses to their proper locations.

19 Carburetor choke check

1   The choke only operates when the engine is cold, and thus this check can only be performed before the car has been started for the day.

2   Open the hood and remove the top plate of the air cleaner assembly. It is held in place by a wing nut at the center. If any vacuum hoses must be disconnected, make sure you tag the hoses for reinstallation to their original positions. Place the top plate and wing nut aside, out of the way of moving engine components.

3   Look at the top of the carburetor at the center of the air cleaner housing. You will notice a flat plate at the carburetor opening.

4   Have an assistant press the accelerator pedal to the floor. The plate should close fully. Start the engine while you observe the plate at the carburetor. Do not position your face directly over the carburetor, as the engine could backfire, causing serious burns. When the engine starts, the choke plate should open slightly.

5   Allow the engine to continue running at an idle speed. As the engine warms up to operating temperature, the plate should slowly open, allowing more cold air to enter through the top of the carburetor.

6   After a few minutes, the choke plate should be fully open to the vertical position.

7   You will notice that the engine speed corresponds with the plate opening. With the plate fully closed, the engine should run at a fast idle speed. As the plate opens, the engine speed will decrease.

8   If during the above checks a fault is detected, refer to Chapter 4 for specific information on adjusting and servicing the choke components.

20 Rear axle fluid change

1   Models are equipped with either removable or integral carrier-type rear axles. Ford does not recommend changing oil in the removable carrier axle, only periodic checking and topping up so that the fluid is just below the plug hole. Chapter 8 contains information on identifying the two types of axles. The fluid changing procedure for the integral-type axle is as follows:

2   To change the fluid in the rear axle it is necessary to remove the cover plate on the differential housing.

3   Move a drain pan of at least 6 pints capacity, a tube of silicone sealant, rags, newspaper and your wrenches under the rear of the car. With the drain plug under the differential cover, loosen all of the cover plate bolts.

4   Remove the bolts on the lower half of the cover, but use the upper bolts to keep the cover loosely attached to the axle housing. Allow the fluid to drain into the drain pan, then completely remove the cover.

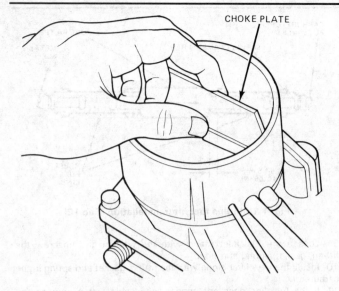

Fig. 1.19 Checking carburetor choke plate (Sec 20)

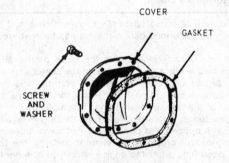

Fig. 1.20 Differential cover and gasket installation (Sec 20)

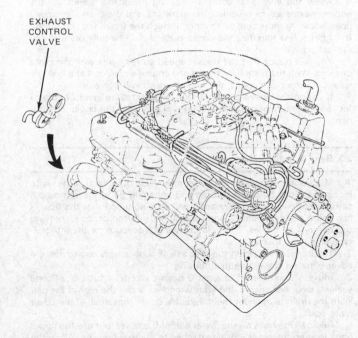

Fig. 1.21 Exhaust control valve location (Sec 21)

5   Using a lint-free rag, clean the inside of the cover and the accessible areas of the differential housing. As this is done, check for chipped gears or metal filings in the fluid, indicating that the differential should be thoroughly inspected and repaired (see Chapter 8 for more information).

6   Thoroughly clean the mating surface of the cover and differential housing of old gasket material, using a gasket scraper or putty knife.

7   Using a thin coat of gasket sealant to hold it in place, install the gasket to the differential housing.

8   Place the cover on the housing and install the securing bolts. Tighten the bolts a little at a time, working across the cover in a diagonal fashion until all of the bolts are tight.

9   Remove the inspection plug on the front side of the differential housing and fill the housing with the proper lubricant to within $\frac{1}{2}$ inch of the plug hole.

10   Install the filler plug securely.

21 Exhaust control valve – checking and lubrication

1   Earlier models (1975-1976) are equipped with an exhaust control valve which is located in the exhaust pipe near the junction of the pipe and the manifold. The valve should be checked every time the chassis is lubricated.

2   With the engine cold, push down gently on the butterfly valve actuator lever several times.

3   If the lever operation is smooth, the lever shaft should be lubricated with lithium grease. Push the lever up and down several times to distribute the lubricant evenly on the shaft.

22 Spark plug wires – inspection and replacement

1   The wires leading from the distributor cap to the spark plugs and the single wire from the center of the cap to the ignition coil are called the secondary or high-tension wires. These wires play an important role in the overall operation of the ignition system and should be periodically inspected and replaced if necessary.

2   These wires are of the radio resistance type designed to filter out electrical impulses which are the source of ignition noise interference. Replacement wires should always be of this type.

3   Any time a high-tension wire is disconnected, silicone grease should be applied in a thin coat to the inside boot surface, distributor cap, ignition coil junction or wherever the connection is made to maintain conductivity.

4   Use a clean rag to wipe each wire clean over its entire length and inspect for cracks, burns or damage.

5   Suspect wires can be checked for short circuits, using an ohmmeter.

6   Disconnect the distributor cap from the top of the distributor.

7   Disconnect one of the spark plug leads from its spark plug by grasping the molded boot, twisting and then pulling the wire from the plug.

8   If the spark plug wire boot is faulty, it hould be cut off and replaced

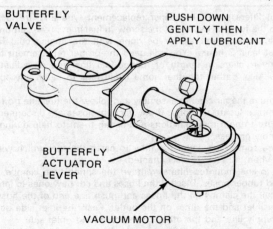

Fig. 1.22 Exhaust control valve lubrication (Sec 21)

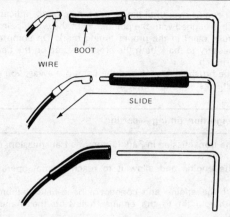

Fig. 1.23 Spark plug boot installation (Sec 22)

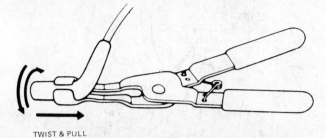

Fig. 1.24 Spark plug wire removal tool (Sec 23)

with a new one. Apply a thin coat of silicone lubricant to the area on the old wire where it will contact the new boot. Guide the boot onto the wire as shown in the accompanying figure.

9 To check the wire with an ohmmeter, place one probe inside the plug boot with the other touching the appropriate terminal inside the distributor cap.

10 If the resistance of the wire exceeds 5000 ohms per inch, the wire should be completely removed from the distributor cap and the resistance measured directly from the wire ends.

11 If the resistance still exceeds 5000 ohms per inch, the wire should be replaced with a new one.

12 All wires should be checked in the same manner.

13 If the wires are in good condition, apply a thin coat of silicone grease to the inside of each disconnected boot and reinstall.

14 When replacing plug wires, remove one at a time to avoid mixing them up. It is a good idea for the home mechanic to purchase replacement plug wire sets which are pre-cut to the proper length and ready to install.

23 Spark plugs – removal, checking and installation

Note: *During this operation, the end of your wrench may be near the battery. To avoid an electrical shock, either cover the top of the battery with a heavy cloth or disconnect the negative cable.*

1 Before removing any spark plug wires, check that they are properly numbered as to their original location. Mark the wires with tape if necessary or remove only one plug at a time so that the wires are always in order.

2 Remove each spark plug by grasping the molded boot, twisting it slightly and then pulling it away from the end of the spark plug. Do not pull on the wire itself because it could separate the connector inside the boot. If this happens, the wire must be replaced with a new one. A special tool, available at your dealer or a parts supply store, makes plug wire removal much easier and eliminates the possibility of separating the boot and connector.

3 Using an insulated spark plug socket, loosen each spark plug about two turns and carefully clean around the plug hole so that no dirt can enter when the plug is removed.

4 Fully remove each of the spark plugs by hand.

5 Inspect the firing ends of the plugs for deposits and electrode condition. Inspect the insulators for cracks and discoloration.

6 If the plug appears useable, clean it with wire brush to remove carbon deposits from the electrodes and threads.

7 Use a small file to clean the electrode surfaces.

8 Set the spark plug electrode gap to the setting on the emission control decal by bending the outer electrode, never the center one.

9 Position each plug into its cylinder head port and thread into the hole by hand.

10 Fully tighten each of the plugs to the proper torque specifications.

11 Using a clean standard screwdriver, apply a thin film of silicone grease on the entire interior surface of the spark plug wire boot.

12 Push each of the spark plug wires into position on the ends of the plugs, again using a twisting motion to fully seat the boots. Make sure that the wires are reinstalled in their original positions.

13 Uncover or re-connect the battery.

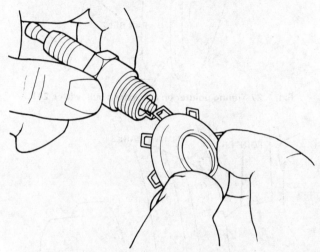

Fig. 1.25 Checking spark plug gap (Sec 23)

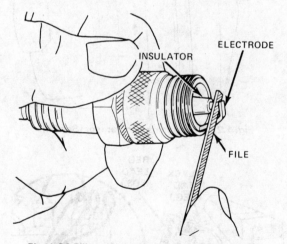

Fig. 1.26 Filing the spark plug electrode (Sec 23)

24 Ignition timing – preparation

1 Before you begin the task of timing the engine or checking the timing, a few special tools must be gathered and some preparatory steps taken.

2 Engine timing requires the following tools:

Induction strobe light or Sun meter pickup probe
Hand-held dwell-tachometer
Proper box end wrench to fit the distributor hold-down bolt
White paint and thin brush
Shop cloths and cleaning solvent

With the items above readily at hand, perform the following:

3 Clean the surface of the front damper and the pointer with the solvent and cloths.

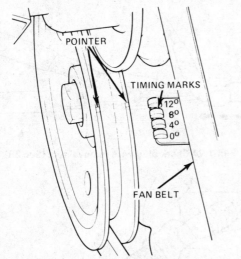

Fig. 1.27 Timing pointer on crankshaft pulley (Sec 24)

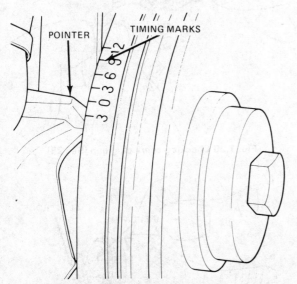

Fig. 1.28 Timing marks on damper (Sec 24)

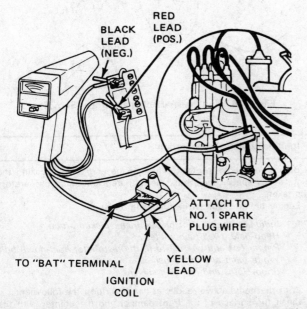

Fig. 1.29 Typical inductive timing light installation (Sec 25)

4   Turn the engine over until the proper timing mark, indicated on the engine decal, is aligned with the pointer. With the white paint and thin brush, carefully paint in the proper timing mark. On some engines it may be necessary to mark both the proper degree on the damper and the damper notch.
5   When the brush is cleaned and the paint put away, you can begin the timing checks and adjustments.

25 Engine ignition timing – setting

1   Place the transmission in Park (automatic transmission) or Neutral (manual).
2   Start the engine and allow it to reach normal operating temperature.
3   Shut off the engine and connect a hand-held tachometer and inductive timing light to the engine, following the manufacturer's instructions.
4   Remove the vacuum hose from the distributor advance connection and plug the hose.
5   With the engine at normal idle (consult emissions decal), shine the beam of the timing light against the timing marks on the front marker and note whether timing mark (marked with paint as described in Section 24) is aligned with the pointer. If the timing mark is not aligned, loosen the hold-down bolt on the distributor and turn the distributor until the marks are in alignment. Tighten the bolt.
6   Shut off the engine and remove the plug from the distributor advance hose and reconnect the hose. Remove all of the timing check equipment.

26 Wheel bearing check and repack

1   In most cases, the front wheel bearings will not need servicing until the brake pads are changed. However, these bearings should be checked whenever the front wheels are raised for any reason.
2   With the vehicle securely supported on jack stands, spin the wheel and check for noise, rolling resistance or free play. Now grab the top of the tire with one hand and the bottom of the tire with the other. Move the tire in and out on the spindle. If it moves more than 0.005 in, the bearings should be checked, then repacked with grease or replaced if necessary.
3   To remove the bearings for replacing or repacking, begin by removing the hub cap and wheel.
4   Remove the brake caliper as described in Chapter 9.
5   Use wire to hang the caliper assembly out of the way. Be careful not to kink or damage the brake hose.
6   Pry the hub grease cap off the hub using a screwdriver. This cap is located at the center of the hub.
7   Use needle-nose pliers to straighten the bent ends of the cotter pin and then pull the cotter pin out of the locking nut. Discard the cotter pin, as a new one should be used on reassembly.
8   Remove the spindle nut and its washer from the end of the spindle.
9   Pull the hub assembly outward slightly and then push it back into its original position. This should force the outer bearing off the spindle enough so that it can be removed with your fingers. Remove the outer bearing, noting how it is installed on the end of the spindle.
10   Now the hub assembly can be pulled off the spindle.
11   On the rear side of the hub, use a screwdriver to pry out the inner bearing lip seal. As this is done, note the direction in which the seal is installed.
12   The inner bearing can now be removed from the hub, again noting now it is installed.
13   Use clean parts solvent to remove all traces of the old grease from the bearings, hub and spindle. A small brush may prove useful; however, make sure no bristles from the brush embed themselves inside the bearing rollers. Allow the parts to air dry.
14   Carefully inspect the bearings for cracks, heat discoloration, bent rollers, etc. Check the bearing races inside the hub for cracks, scoring or uneven surfaces. If the bearing races are in need of replacement, this job is best left to a repair shop which can press the new races into position.
15   Use an approved high temperature front wheel bearing grease to pack the bearings. Work the grease fully into the bearings, forcing the grease between the rollers, cone and cage.

45

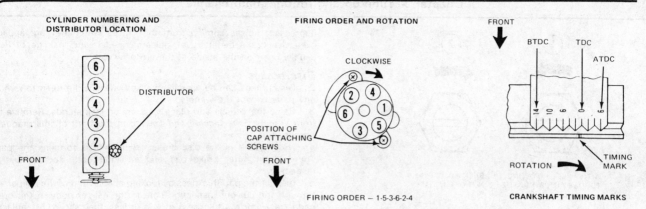

CYLINDER NUMBERING AND DISTRIBUTOR LOCATION

FIRING ORDER AND ROTATION

FRONT

FIRING ORDER — 1-5-3-6-2-4

CRANKSHAFT TIMING MARKS

Fig. 1.30 Six-cylinder engine ignition timing marks and firing order (Sec 25)

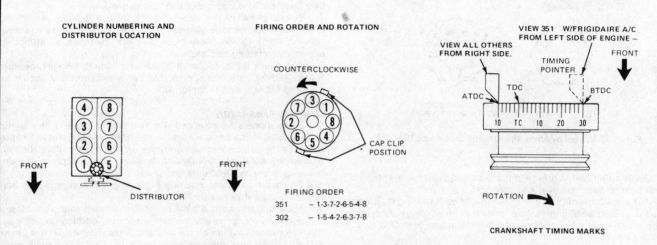

CYLINDER NUMBERING AND DISTRIBUTOR LOCATION

FIRING ORDER AND ROTATION

FIRING ORDER
351 — 1-3-7-2-6-5-4-8
302 — 1-5-4-2-6-3-7-8

CRANKSHAFT TIMING MARKS

Fig. 1.31 V8 engine ignition timing marks and firing order (Sec 25)

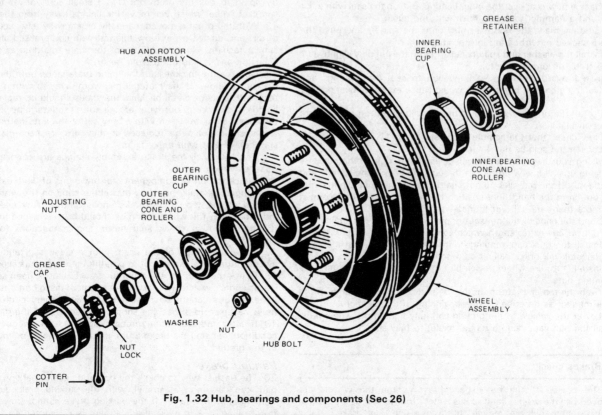

Fig. 1.32 Hub, bearings and components (Sec 26)

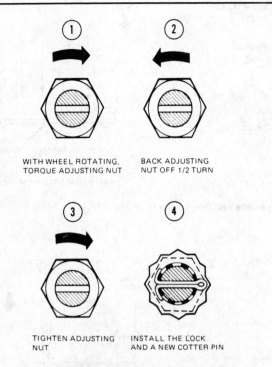

WITH WHEEL ROTATING,   BACK ADJUSTING
TORQUE ADJUSTING NUT   NUT OFF 1/2 TURN

TIGHTEN ADJUSTING   INSTALL THE LOCK
NUT   AND A NEW COTTER PIN

Fig. 1.33 Wheel bearing adjustment procedure (Sec 26)

16 Apply a thin coat of grease to the spindle at the outer bearing seat, inner bearing seat, shoulder and seal seat.
17 Put a small quantity of grease inboard of each bearing race inside the hub. Using your fingers, form a dam at these points to provide extra grease availability and to keep thinned grease from flowing out of the bearing.
18 Place the grease-packed inner bearing into the rear of the hub and put a little more grease outboard of the bearings.
19 Place a new seal over the inner bearing and tap the seal with a flat plate and a hammer until it is flush with the hub.
20 Carefully place the hub assembly onto the spindle and push the grease-packed outer bearing into position.
21 Install the washer and spindle nut. Tighten the nut only slightly (17 to 25 ft-lbs of torque) (photo).
22 In a forward direction, spin the hub to seat the bearings and remove any grease or burrs which would cause excessive bearing play later.
23 Put a little grease outboard of the outer bearing to provide extra grease availability.
24 Now check that the spindle nut is still tight (17 to 25 ft-lbs).
25 Loosen the spindle nut $\frac{1}{2}$ turn.
26 Using your hand (not a wrench of any kind), tighten the nut until it is snug. Install a new cotter pin through the hole in the spindle and spindle nut. If the nut slits do not line up, loosen the nut slightly until they do. From the hand-tight position the nut should not be loosened any more than one-half flat to install the cotter pin.
27 Bend the ends of the new cotter pin until they are flat against the nut. Cut off any extra length which could interfere with the dust cap.
28 Install the dust cap, tapping it into place with a rubber mallet.
29 Reinstall the brake caliper as described in Chapter 9.
30 Install the tire/wheel assembly to the hub and tighten the mounting nuts.
31 Grab the top and bottom of the tire and check the bearings in the same manner as described at the beginning of this Section.
32 Lower the vehicle to the ground and fully tighten the wheel nuts. Install the hub cap, using a rubber mallet to fully seat it.

27 Brakes check

1   The brakes should be inspected every time the wheels are removed or whenever a fault is suspected, Indications of a potential braking system fault are: the car pulls to one side when brake pedal is depressed; noises coming from the brakes when they are applied; excessive brake pedal travel; pulsating pedal; and leakage of fluid, usually seen on the inside of the tire or wheel.

Disc brakes
2   Disc brakes can be visually checked without the need to remove any parts except the wheels.
3   Raise the vehicle and place securely on jack stands. Remove the front wheels (See *Jacking and Towing* at the front of this manual if necessary.)
4   Now visible is the disc brake caliper which contains the pads. There is an outer brake pad and an inner pad. Both should be inspected.
5   Inspect the pad thickness by looking at each end of the caliper and through the cut-out inspection hole in the caliper body. If the brake pads are worn to a thickness of $\frac{1}{8}$ in or less, they should be replaced.
6   Since it will be difficult, if not impossible, to measure the exact thickness of the remaining lining material, if you are in doubt as to the pad quality, remove the pads for further inspection or replacement. See Chapter 9 for disc brake pad replacement.
7   Before installing the wheels, check for any leakage around the brake hose connections leading to the caliper or damage (cracking, splitting, etc.) to the brake hose. Replace the hose or fittings as necessary, referring to Chapter 9.
8   Also check the condition of the disc for scoring, gouging or burnt spots. If these conditions exist, the hub/rotor assembly should be removed for servicing (Chapter 9).

Drum brakes (rear)
9   Some models are equipped with rear disc brakes and they should be inspected in the same manner as the front brakes (refer to Chapter 9). Raise the vehicle and support firmly on jack stands. Block the front tires to prevent the car from rolling; however, do not apply the parking brake as this lock the drums into place.
10 Remove the wheels, referring to *Jacking and Towing* at the front of this manual if necessary.
11 Mark the hub so it can be reinstalled in the same place. Use a scribe, chalk, etc. on drum and center hub and backing plate.
12 Pull the brake drum off the axle and brake assembly. If this proves difficult, make sure the parking brake is released, then squirt some penetrating oil around the center hub area. Allow the oil to soak in and try again to pull the drum off. Use a small screwdriver to turn the sprocket wheel which will move the linings away from the drums.
13 With the drum removed, carefully brush away any accumulations of dirt and dust. Do not blow this out with compressed air or in any similar fashion. Make an effort not to inhale this dust as it contains asbestos and is harmful to your health.
14 Observe the thickness of the lining material on both the front and rear brake shoes. If the material has worn away to within $\frac{1}{32}$ in of the recessed rivets or metal backing, the shoes should be replaced. If the linings look worn, but you are unable to determine their exact thickness, compare them with a new set at the auto parts store. The shoes should also be replaced if they are cracked, glazed (shiny surface), or wet with brake fluid.
15 Check that all the brake assembly springs are connected and in good condition.
16 Check the brake components for any signs of fluid leakage. With your finger, carefully pry back the rubber cups on the wheel cylinder located at the top of the brake shoes (photo). Any leakage is an indication that the wheel cylinders should be overhauled immediately (Chapter 9). Also check fluid hoses and connections for signs of leakage.
17 Wipe the inside of the drum with a clean rag, and denatured alcohol. Again, be careful not to breathe the dangerous asbestos dust.
18 Check the inside of the drum for cracks, scores, deep scratches or 'hard spots' which will appear as small discolorations. If these imperfections cannot be removed with fine emery cloth, the drum must be taken to a machine shop equipped to turn the drums.
19 If after the inspection process all parts are in good working condition, reinstall the brake drum. Install the wheel and lower the car to the ground.

Parking brake
20 The easiest way to check the operation of the parking brake is to park the car on a steep hill, with the parking brake set and the transmission in Neutral. If the parking brake cannot prevent the car from rolling, it is in need of adjustment (see Chapter 9).

28 Automatic transmission fluid change

1   At the specified time intervals, the transmission fluid should be changed and the filter replaced with a new one. Since there is no drain plug, the transmission oil pan must be removed from the bottom of the transmission to drain the fluid.

2   Before any draining, purchase the specified transmission fluid (see *Recommended Lubricants*) and a new filter. The necessary gaskets should be included with the filter; if not, purchase an oil pan gasket and a strainer-to-valve body gasket.

3   Other tools necessary for this job include: jack stands to support the vehicle in a raised position; wrench to remove the oil pan bolts; standard screwdriver; drain pan capable of holding at least 8 pints; newspapers and clean rags.

4   The fluid should be drained immediately after the car has been driven. This will remove any built-up sediment better than if the fluid were cold. Because of this, it may be wise to wear protective gloves (fluid temperature can exceed 350° in a hot transmission).

5   After the car has been driven to warm up the fluid, raise the vehicle and place it on jack stands for access underneath. Make sure it is firmly supported by the four stands placed on the frame rails.

6   Move the necessary equipment under the car, being careful not to touch any of the hot exhaust components.

7   Place the drain pan under the transmission oil pan and remove the oil pan bolts along the rear and sides of the pan. Loosen, but do not remove, the bolts at the front of the pan.

8   Carefully pry the pan downward at the rear, allowing the hot fluid to drain into the drain pan. If necessary, use a screwdriver to break the gasket seal at the rear of the pan; however, do not damage the pan or transmission in the process.

9   Support the pan and remove the remaining bolts at the front of the pan. Lower the pan and drain the remaining fluid into the drain receptacle. As this is done, check the fluid for metal filings which may be an indication of internal failure.

10   Now visible on the bottom of the transmission is the filter/strainer.

11   Remove the retaining screws, the filter and its gasket.

12   Thoroughly clean the transmission oil pan with solvent. Inspect for metal filings or foreign matter. Dry with compressed air if available. It is important that all remaining gasket material be removed from the oil pan mounting flange. Use a gasket scraper or putty knife for this.

13   Clean the filter mounting surface on the valve body. Again, this surface should be smooth and free of any leftover gasket material.

14   Place the new filter into position, with a new gasket between it and the transmission valve body. On JATCO transmissions clean the oil pan screen thoroughly. Install the remaining screws and tighten securely.

15   Apply a bead of gasket sealant around the oil pan mounting surface, with the sealant to the inside of the bolt holes. Press the new gasket into place on the pan, making sure all bolt holes line up.

16   Lift the pan up to the bottom of the transmission and install the mounting bolts. Tighten the bolts in a diagonal fashion, working around the pan. Using a torque wrench, tighten the bolts to specifications.

17   Lower the car off its jack stands.

18   Open the hood and remove the transmission fluid dipstick from its guide tube.

19   Since fluid capacities vary between the various transmission types, it is best to add a little fluid at a time, continually checking the level with the dipstick. Allow the fluid time to drain into the pan. Add fluid until the level just registers on the end of the dipstick. In most cases, a good starting point will be 4 to 5 pints added to the transmission through the filler tube (use a funnel to prevent spills).

20   With the selector lever in Park, apply the parking brake and start the engine without depressing the accelerator pedal (if possible). Do not race the engine at a high speed; run at slow idle only.

21   Depress the brake pedal and shift the transmission through each gear. Place the selector back into Park and check the level on the dipstick (with the engine still idling). Look under the car for leaks around the transmission oil pan mounting surface.

22   Add more fluid through the dipstick tube until the level on the dipstick is $\frac{1}{4}$ inch below the 'Add' mark on the dipstick. Do not allow the fluid level to go above this point, as the transmission would then be overfull, necessitating the removal of the pan to drain the excess fluid.

23   Push the dipstick firmly back into its tube and drive the car to reach normal operating temperature (15 miles of highway driving or its equivalent in the city). Park the car on a level surface and check the fluid level on the dipstick with the engine idling and the transmission in Park. The level should now be at the 'Full Hot' mark on the dipstick. If not, add more fluid as necessary to bring the level up to this point. Again, do not overfill.

29 Cooling system servicing (draining, flushing and refilling

1   Periodically, the cooling system should be drained, flushed and refilled. This is to replenish the antifreeze mixture and prevent rust and corrosion which can impair the performance of the cooling system and ultimately cause engine damage.

2   At the same time the cooling system is serviced, all hoses and the fill cap should be inspected and replaced if faulty (see Section 6).

3   As antifreeze is a poisonous solution, take care not to spill any of the cooling mixture on the vehicle's paint or your own skin. If this happens, rinse immediately with plenty of clear water. Also ,it is advisable to consult your local authorities about the dumping of antifreeze before draining the cooling system. In many areas reclamation centers have been set up to collect automobile oil and drained antifreeze/water mixtures rather than allowing these liquids to be added to the sewage and water facilities.

4   With the engine cold, remove the radiator pressure fill cap.

5   Move a large container under the radiator to catch the water/antifreeze mixture as it is drained.

6   Drain the radiator. Most models are equipped with a drain plug at the bottom of the radiator which can be opened using a wrench to hold the fitting while the petcock is turned to the open position. If this drain has excessive corrosion and cannot be turned easily, or the radiator is not equipped with a drain, disconnect the lower radiator hose to allow the coolant to drain. Be careful that none of the solution is splashed on your skin or in your eyes.

7   If accessible, remove the two engine drain plugs (photo). There is one plug on each side of the engine, about halfway back and on the lower edge near the oil pan rail. These will allow the coolant to drain from the engine itself.

8   On systems with an expansion reservoir, disconnect the overflow pipe and remove the reservoir. Flush it out with clean water.

9   Place a cold water hose (a common garden hose is fine) in the radiator filler neck at the top of the radiator and flush the system until the water runs clean at all drain points.

10   In severe cases of contamination or clogging of the radiator, remove (see Chapter 3) and reverse flush it. This involves simply inserting the cold pressure hose in the bottom radiator outlet to allow the clear water to run against the normal flow, draining through the top. A radiator repair shop should be consulted if further cleaning or repair is necessary.

11   Where the coolant is regularly drained and the system refilled with the correct antifreeze/inhibitor mixture there should be no need to employ chemical cleaners or descalers.

12   To refill the system, reconnect the radiator hoses and install the drain plugs securely in the engine. Special thread sealing tape (available at auto parts stores) should be used on the drain plugs going into the engine block. Install the expansion reservoir and the overflow hose where applicable.

13   On vehicles without an expansion reservoir, refill the system through the radiator filler cap until the water level is about three inches below the filler neck.

14   On vehicles with an expansion reservoir, fill the radiator to the base of the filler neck and then add more coolant to the expansion reservoir so that it reaches the 'FULL COLD' mark.

15   Run the engine until normal operating temperature is reached and with the engine idling, add coolant up to the correct level (see Section 2), then fit the radiator cap so that the arrows are in alignment with the overflow pipe. Install the reservoir cap.

16   Always refill the system with a mixture of high quality antifreeze and water in the proportion called for on the antifreeze container or in your owner's manual. Chapter 3 also contains information on antifreeze mixture.

17   Keep a close watch on the coolant level and the various cooling hoses during the first few miles of driving. Tighten the hose clamps and/or add more coolant mixture as necessary.

30 Windshield wiper element – removal and installation

1   Windshield wiper blade elements should be checked periodically

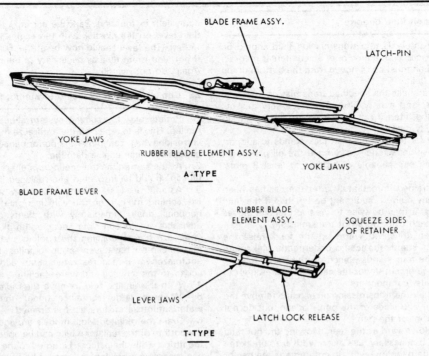

BLADE FRAME ASSY.

LATCH-PIN

YOKE JAWS

RUBBER BLADE ELEMENT ASSY.

YOKE JAWS

A-TYPE

BLADE FRAME LEVER

RUBBER BLADE
ELEMENT ASSY.

SQUEEZE SIDES
OF RETAINER

LEVER JAWS

LATCH LOCK RELEASE

T-TYPE

Fig. 1.34 Windshield wiper element installation (Sec 30)

for signs of cracking and deterioration. Two types of wiper blades are used, A-type and T-type.
2   To remove A-type wiper elements, depress the latch pin and then slide the element out of the yoke jaws. To install, slide the element through the jaws and then insert the blade frame assembly into the jaw slots.
3   The T-type wiper is removed by squeezing the tabs at the end together and then pulling the blade from the frame. Installation is the reverse of removal.

Chapter 2 Part A 6-cylinder engine

Contents

Specifications

Engine – general

Displacement .... 3.3 liters (200 CID) or 4.1 liters (250 CID)

Type .... 6-cylinder in line, overhead valve

Bore and stroke
3.3L .... 3.68 in x 3.13 in
4.1L .... 3.68 in x 3.91 in

Firing order .... 1 – 5 – 3 – 6 – 2 – 4

Oil pressure (hot at 2000 rpm)
3.3L .... 30 to 50 psi
4.1L .... 40 to 60 psi

Compression test .... Lowest cylinder (psi) must be within 75% of highest cylinder pressure

Cylinder head and valve train

Valve guide bore diameter .... 0.3115 in to 0.3125 in

Valve seat width
Intake .... 0.060 in to 0.080 in
Exhaust .... 0.070 in to 0.090 in

Valve face runout limit .... 0.002 in max.

Valve seat angle .... 44°

Valve arrangement (front to rear) .... E–I–I–E–I–E–E–I–E–I–E

Valve stem-to-guide clearance
Intake .... 0.0008 in to 0.0025 in
Exhaust .... 0.0010 in to 0.0027 in
Service clearance limit .... 0.0055 in

Valve head diameter
Intake
    1975 thru 1977 .... 1.642 in to 1.660 in
    1978 thru 1980 .... 1.739 in to 1.763 in
Exhaust
    1975 thru 1977 .... 1.381 in to 1.399 in
    1978 thru 1980 .... 1.378 in to 1.402 in

Valve stem diameter (standard)
Standard
    Intake .... 0.3100 in to 0.3107 in
    Exhaust .... 0.3098 in to 0.3105 in
0.015 in oversize
    Intake .... 0.3250 in to 0.3257 in
    Exhaust .... 0.3248 in to 0.3255 in
0.030 in oversize
    Intake .... 0.3400 in to 0.3407 in
    Exhaust .... 0.3398 in to 0.3405 in

Valve springs
Compression pressure (lb at spec. length)
Intake
    3.3L .... 51 to 57 at 1.59 in
    4.1L .... 61 to 67 at 1.55 in
Exhaust
    3.3L and 4.1L .... 142 to 158 at 1.222 in
Free length (approximate) .... 1.79 in
Service limit .... 10% pressure loss @ spec length
Out-of-square limit .... $\frac{5}{64}$ (0.078) in

Rocker arm
Shaft diameter .... 0.7797 in to 0.7807 in
Bore diameter .... 0.7830 in to 0.7845 in
Ratio 1.52:1
Pushrod runout .... 0.020 in

Valve tappet
Diameter (standard) .... 0.8740 in to 0.8745 in
Clearance-to-bore .... 0.0007 in to 0.0027 in
    Service limit .... 0.005 in max.
Hydraulic leakdown rate .... 10 to 50 sec. time required for plunger to leak down $\frac{1}{8}$ inch with 50 lb load and leakdown fluid in tappet

Allowable collapsed gap
    3.3L .... 0.085 in to 0.209 in
    4.1L .... 0.071 in to 0.209 in
Desired gap
    3.3L .... 0.110 in to 0.184 in
    4.1L .... 0.096 in to 0.184 in

Camshaft

Lobe lift
Intake .... 0.245 in
Exhaust .... 0.245 in
Allowable lobe lift loss .... 0.005 in max.

Endplay .... 0.001 in to 0.007 in
Service limit .... 0.009 in

Journal-to-bearing clearance .... 0.001 in to 0.003 in
Service limit .... 0.006 in

Journal diameter (all) .... 1.8095 in to 1.8105 in

Run-out limit .... 0.005 in

Front bearing location .... 0.110 in to 0.130 in. Distance in inches that front edge of bearing is installed below front face of block

Camshaft bearing inside diameter (all) .... 1.8115 in to 1.8125 in

Cylinder block

Head gasket surface flatness .... 0.003 in in any 6 inches; 0.006 in overall

Cylinder bore
Diameter .... 3.6800 in to 3.6848 in
Out-of-round limit .... 0.0015 in
Out-of-round service limit .... 0.005 in
Taper service limit .... 0.010 in

Tappet bore diameter .... 0.8752 in to 0.8767 in

Main bearing bore diameter
3.3L .... 2.4012 in to 2.4020 in
4.1L .... 2.5902 in to 2.5990 in

Distributor shaft bearing bore diameter .... 0.5155 in to 0.5170 in

Crankshaft and flywheel

Main bearing journal diameter
3.3L .... 2.2482 in to 2.2490 in
4.1L .... 2.3982 in to 2.3990 iin
Out-of-round limit .... 0.0006 in max.
Taper limit .... 0.0006 in per inch
Journal runout limit .... 0.002 in max.
Runout service limit .... 0.005 in

Thrust bearing journal length
3.3L .... 1.275 in to 1.277 in
4.1L .... 1.199 in to 1.201 in

Connecting rod journal

Diameter .... 2.1232 in to 2.1240 in
Out-of-round limit .... 0.0006 in max.
Taper limit .... 0.0006 in max.

Main bearing thrust face

Runout limit .... 0.001 in max.

Flywheel ring gear lateral run-out

Standard transmission .... 0.030 in
Automatic transmission .... 0.060 in

Crankshaft free endplay .... 0.004 in to 0.008 in

Service limit .... 0.012 in

Connecting rod bearings

Clearance to crankshaft
   Desired .... 0.0008 in to 0.0015 in
   Allowable .... 0.0008 in to 0.0024 in
Bearing wall thickness (standard*) .... 0.0569 in to 0.0574
*For 0.002 in undersize, add 0.001 in to standard thickness

Main bearings

Clearance to crankshaft
   Desired .... 0.0008 in to 0.0015 in
   Allowable .... 0.0008 in to 0.0024 in
Bearing wall thickness (standard*)
   1975
      3.3L .... 0.0758 in to 0.0761 in
      4.1L .... 0.0954 in to 0.0957 in
   1976 thru 1978 all .... 0.0954 in to 0.0957 in
   1979 and 1980
      3.3L .... 0.0757 in to 0.0760 in
      4.1L .... No. 1 upper 0.0958 in
                                        0.0961 in all others
                                        0.0951 in to 0.0954 in

*For 0.002 in undersize, add 0.001 in to standard thickness

Connecting rod

Piston pin bore diameter .... 0.9104 in to 0.9112 in
Crankshaft bearing bore diameter .... 2.2390 in to 2.2398 in
Out-of-round limit .... 0.0004 in max.
Taper limit .... 0.0004 in max.
Length (center-to-center)
   3.3L .... 4.7135 in to 4.7166 in
   4.1L .... 5.8785 in to 5.8815 in
Alignment (bore-to-bore max. dif.)
   Twist .... 0.012 in
   Bend .... 0.024 in
Side clearance (assembled to crankshaft)
   Standard .... 0.0035 in to 0.0105 in
   Service limit .... 0.014 in

Piston

Diameter .... Measured at the pin bore centerline at 90° to the pin
   Coded red .... 3.6784 in to 3.6790 in
   Coded blue .... 3.6796 in to 3.6802 in
   0.003 in oversize .... 3.6808 in to 3.6814 in
Piston-to-bore clearance .... 0.0013 in to 0.0021 in
Pin bore diameter .... 0.9124 in to 0.9127 in
Ring groove width
   Compression (top) .... 0.080 in to 0.081 in
   Compression (bottom) .... 0.080 in to 0.081 in
   Oil .... 0.188 in to 0.189 in

Piston pin

Length .... 3.010 in to 3.040 in
Diameter
   Standard .... 0.9119 in to 0.9124 in
   0.001 in oversize .... 0.9130 in to 0.9133 in
   0.002 in oversize .... 0.9140 in to 0.9143 in
Pin-to-piston clearance .... 0.0003 in to 0.0005 in
Pin-to-rod clearance .... Interference fit

Piston rings

Ring width
    Compression (top) .... 0.077 in to 0.078 in
    Compression (bottom) .... 0.077 in to 0.078 in
Side clearance
    Compression (top) .... 0.002 in to 0.004 in
    Compression (bottom) .... 0.002 in to 0.004 in
    Oil ring .... Snug fit
    Service limit .... 0.006 in
Ring gap
    Compression (top) .... 0.008 in to 0.016 in
    Compression (bottom) .... 0.008 in to 0.016 in
    Oil ring (steel rail) .... 0.015 in to 0.055 in

Lubricating system

Oil pump
Relief valve spring tension (lbs at spec. length) .... 9.00 to 10.01 at 1.078 in
Driveshaft-to-housing bearing clearance .... 0.0015 in to 0.0030 in
Relief valve-to-bore clearance .... 0.0015 in to 0.0030 in
Rotor assembly end clearance (assembled) .... 0.004 in. max.
Outer race-to-housing clearance .... 0.001 in to 0.013 in

Oil capacity .... 4 quarts – add one quart with filter change

Fuel pump

Static pressure .... 5.0 to 7.0 psi. On engine at curb idle speed, brakes set, temperature normalized. With pump to tank fuel return line pinched off and a new fuel filter installed in fuel line

Minimum volume flow .... 1 pint in 20 seconds. On engine at curb idle speed, brakes set, temperature normalized. The inside diameter of the smallest passage in the test flow circuit must not be less than 0.220 in

Torque specifications

	ft-lb	Nm
Camshaft sprocket-to-camshaft	35 to 45	48 to 61
Camshaft thrust plate-to-block	12 to 18	16 to 24
Connecting rod nut	21 to 26	29 to 35
Cylinder front cover bolts	6 to 9	8 to 12
Cylinder head bolts – In sequence		
Step 1	50 to 55	68 to 75
Step 2	60 to 65	81 to 88
Damper or pulley-to-crankshaft	85 to 100	115 to 136
Fuel filter-to-carburetor	80 to 100 in-lbs	9 to 11
EGR valve-to-carburetor spacer or intake manifold	12 to 18	16 to 24
Fuel pump-to-cylinder block or front cover	12 to 18	16 to 24
Flywheel-to-crankshaft	75 to 85	102 to 115
Main bearing cap bolts	60 to 70	81 to 85
Manifold-to-cylinder head exhaust	18 to 24	24 to 33
Oil filter insert-to-cylinder block	10 to 15	14 to 20
Oil filter-to-block or adapter	½ turn after gasket contacts sealing surface – with oiled gasket	
Oil inlet tube-to-oil pump	10 to 15	14 to 20
Oil pan drain plug	15 to 25	20 to 34
Oil pan-to-cylinder block	7 to 9	9 to 12
Oil pump-to-cylinder block	10 to 15	14 to 20
Pulley-to-damper (bolt)	35 to 50	47 to 68
Rocker arm support shaft-to-cylinder head	30 to 35	41 to 47
Spark plug-to-cylinder head	10 to 15	13 to 20
Valve rocker arm cover	3 to 5	4 to 7
Alternator bracket-to-cylinder block (bolt)	35 to 50	47 to 68
Alternator adjusting arm-to-cylinder block	15 to 20	20 to 27
Alternator adjusting arm-to-alternator	24 to 34	33 to 46
Thermactor pump bracket-to-cylinder block	12 to 18	16 to 24
Thermactor pump pivot bolt	22 to 32	30 to 43
Thermactor pump adjusting arm-to-pump	24 to 34	33 to 46
Thermactor pump adjusting arm-to-cylinder block	12 to 18	16 to 24
Thermactor pump pulley-to-pump hub	130 to 180 in-lbs	15 to 20
Fan-to-water pump hub (bolt)	12 to 18	16 to 24
Carburetor mounting nuts	12 to 15	16 to 20
Carburetor mounting stud	15 max.	20 max.
Distributor clamp hold-down bolt	17 to 25	23 to 34
Vacuum fitting/plugs-to-intake manifold (with Teflon tape)	6 to 10	8 to 13

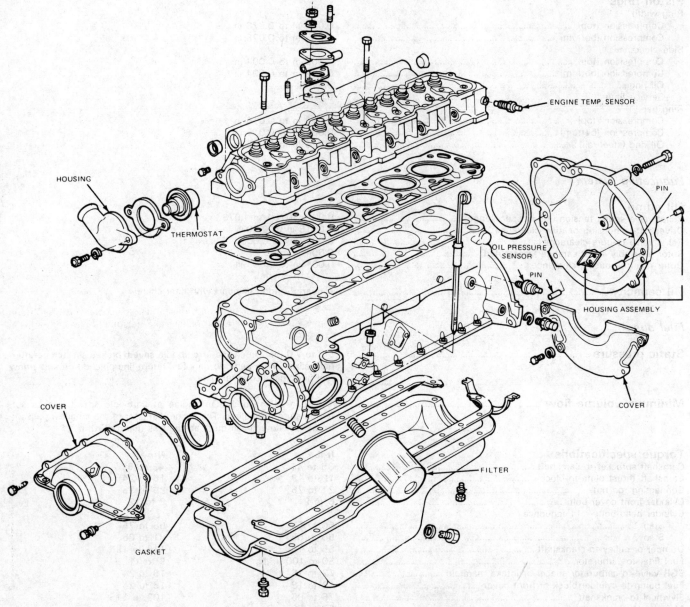

Fig. 2.1 Exploded view of six cylinder engine (Sec 1)

1 General information

Models are equipped with an inline 6-cylinder engine of either 3.3 liter (200 cu in) or 4.1 liter (250 cu in) displacement. The engine is of cast iron construction and uses overhead valves operated by a camshaft in the block by pushrods and hydraulic tappets.

The camshaft is located at the right of the crankshaft and is driven by the crankshaft via a multi-link timing chain. The camshaft rides on four bearings, the inner race of which is a machined part of the shaft while the outer race is a replaceable part fitted into the engine block.

The crankshaft is supported by seven main bearings and the bearing shells are replaceable. To compensate for wear when rebuilding the engine, undersize parts such as bearings and oversize parts such as pistons and valve guides are available.

2 Methods of engine removal

The engine may be lifted out either on its own or in unit with the transmission. On models which have an automatic transmission, it is recommended that the engine be lifted out separate from the

transmission, unless a very substantial engine lift is available. Removing the engine and transmission as a unit means that they must be lifted out at a very steep angle. Be sure sufficient overhead clearance is available before you begin work.

3 Engine – rebuilding alternatives

1 The home mechanic is faced with a number of options for completing an engine overhaul. The decision to replace the cylinder block, piston/rod assemblies and crankshaft depends on a number of factors with the number one consideration being the condition of the cylinder block. Other considerations are: cost, competent machine shop facilities, parts availability, time available to complete the project and experience.

2 Some of the rebuilding alternatives are as follows:

Individual parts – If the inspection procedures prove that the engine block and most engine components are in reusable condition, this may be the most economical alternative. The block, crankshaft and piston/rod assemblies should all be inspected carefully. Even if the block shows little wear, the cylinder bores should receive new camshaft bearings and a finish hone; both jobs for a machine shop.

Master kit (crankshaft kit) – This rebuild package usually consists of a reground crankshaft and a matched set of pistons and connecting rods. The pistons will come already installed with new piston pins to the connecting rods. Piston rings and the necessary bearings may or may not be included in the kit. These kits are commonly available for standard cylinder bores, as well as for engine blocks which have been bored to a regular oversize.

Short block – A short block consists of a cylinder block with a crankshaft and piston/rod assemblies already installed. All new bearings are incorporated and all clearances will be within tolerances. Depending on where the short block is purchased, a guarantee may be included. The existing camshaft, valve mechanism, cylinder heads and ancillary parts can be bolted to this short block with little or no machine shop work necessary for the engine overhaul.

Long block – A long block consists of a short block plus oil pump, oil pan, cylinder heads, valve covers, camshaft and valve mechanism, camshaft gear, timing chain and crankcase front cover. All components are installed with new bearings, seals and gaskets incorporated throughout. The installation of manifolds and ancillary parts is all that is necessary. Some form of guarantee is usually included with purchase.

3   Give careful thought to which method is best for your situation and discuss the alternatives with local machine shop owners, parts dealers or dealership parts men.

4   Engine – work which may be performed without engine removal

1   Before setting about the task of removing the engine from the car, consider quite carefully the work which must be performed. A general rule of thumb in engine work is that the engine need not be removed if the component to be adjusted, repaired, or replaced is mounted ahead of the engine block casting or above the cylinder deck atop the engine block. In these instances, it is a simple matter of removing surrounding components, then removing or adjusting the component in question when sufficient work space has been obtained.

5   Engine – removal (without transmission)

1   Providing a good set of tools and lifting tackle is available, the home mechanic should be able to remove the engine without encountering any major problems. Make sure that a set of metric sockets and wrenches is available in addition to a hydraulic jack and a pair of axle stands. An assistant will make the task easier.
2   First raise the car hood and disconnect the battery leads.
3   Mark the position of the hood hinges with a pencil. Undo the retaining bolts and remove the hood.
4   Remove the air cleaner and exhaust manifold shroud.
5   If air conditioning is fitted remove the compressor unit from the engine mounting bracket but **do not** disconnect the refrigerant hoses. Position the pump out of the way without straining the hoses. **Note:** *If it is necessary to remove the pump from the car the hoses should be disconnected by an air conditioning specialist.*
6   Remove the plug and drain the crankcase oil into a suitable container.
7   Remove the bottom radiator hose and drain the coolant.
8   Remove the top hose and transmission oil cooler hoses (if fitted) from the radiator, undo and remove the mounting bolts and remove the radiator.
9   Undo the four bolts and remove the fan.
10   Jack up the front of the car and support it on axle stands.
11   Where applicable, remove the engine shield.

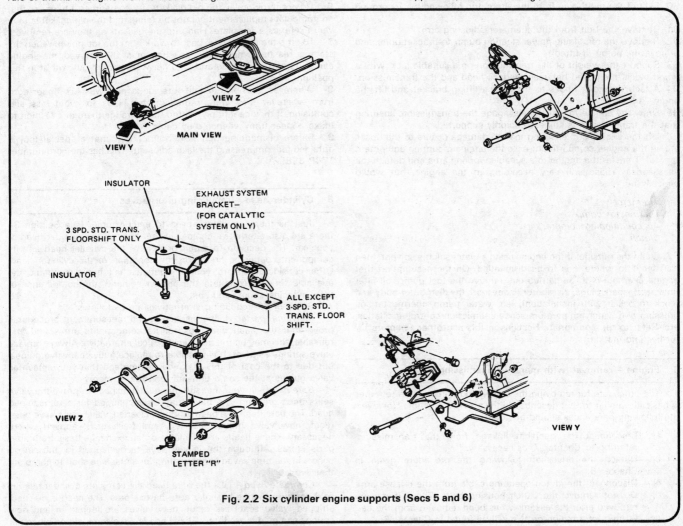

Fig. 2.2 Six cylinder engine supports (Secs 5 and 6)

12 Remove the starter motor. Further details will be found in Chapter 5, if required.

13 *On automatic transmission models* remove the torque converter bolt access plug. Remove the three flywheel-to-converter bolts. Remove the converter housing cover and disconnect the converter from the flywheel.

14 *On manual transmission models* remove the flywheel cover.

15 Remove the flywheel or converter housing cover, as applicable.

16 Detach the exhaust pipe from the exhaust manifold. Remove the packing washer.

17 Remove the nuts from the engine mountings, and remove the nuts and through bolts retaining the rear engine support crossmember.

18 Detach the fuel lines from the fuel pump, plugging the lines to prevent fuel spillage.

19 Where applicable, remove the power steering pump drivebelt and draw off the pulley. The drivebelt arrangement is shown in Chapter 3; refer to Chapter 3 for further information on the pump.

20 Remove the lower bolt securing the power steering pump to the bracket.

21 Lower the car to the ground.

22 Disconnect the heater and vacuum hoses from the engine. It is recommended that a sketch be made showing the various connections to avoid confusion when refitting.

23 Disconnect the power brake hose.

24 Remove the oil pressure union from the connection on the rear left-hand side of the cylinder head.

25 Detach the carburetor cable(s).

26 Disconnect the wire to the throttle solenoid and choke heater.

27 Detach the wire from the water temperature sender on the rear left side of the cylinder block.

28 Disconnect the lines from the vacuum amplifier.

29 From the distributor, disconnect the coil wire and vacuum line.

30 Pull off the multi-plug from the alternator, followed by the ground wire.

31 Remove the bolt from the alternator adjusting arm.

32 Remove the remaining power steering pump-to-bracket bolts, and remove the pump (if fitted).

33 Support the weight of the transmission on a suitable jack, with a wood block interposed between the jack head and the transmission.

34 Attach the hoist hooks to the engine lifting bracket and lift the engine a little.

35 Draw the engine forward to disengage the transmission, ensuring that the transmission is still satisfactorily supported.

36 Lift the engine out, ensuring that no damage occurs to the hoses etc, in the engine compartment or to the engine mounting equipment (photo). Transfer the engine to a suitable working area and detach the accessories. These will vary according to the engine, but would typically be:

> Alternator
> Thermactor pump
> Air conditioning compressor
> Clutch

37 Clean the outside of the engine using a water soluble solvent, then transfer it to where it is to be dismantled. On the assumption that engine overhaul is to be carried out, remove the fuel pump, oil filter (unscrew), spark plugs, distributor (index mark the distributor body and block to assist with installation), fan, water pump, thermostat, oil pressure and water temperature senders, emission control ancillaries, etc. Refer to the appropriate Sections in this and other Chapters for further information.

6 Engine – removal (with manual transmission)

1 The procedure for removing the engine and transmission together is basically similar to that described in the previous Section. However, the following differences should be noted:

  a) Disconnect the gearshift linkage from the transmission, referring to Chapter 7, as necessary.

  b) Detach the driveshaft following the procedure given in Chapter 8.

  c) Disconnect the clutch operating cable from the release arm.

  d) Do not remove the clutch housing bolts. These items are removed after the assembly has been removed from the car. Further information on this will be found in Chapter 8.

  e) Remove the speedometer drive cable, and the transmission electrical connections. If there is any possibility of their being mixed up, suitably label them or make a sketch showing their installed position.

  f) Support the weight of the transmission in a similar manner to that described in the previous Section, paragraph 33, while the rear mounting is being detached.

  g) It is a good idea to do the preliminary cleaning of the engine with the transmission still attached.

7 Engine – dismantling (general)

1 It is best to mount the engine on a dismantling stand, but if this is not available, stand the engine on a strong bench at a comfortable working height. Failing this, it can be stripped down on the floor.

2 During the dismantling process, the greatest care should be taken to keep the exposed parts free from dirt. As an aid to achieving this, thoroughly clean down the outside of the engine, first removing all traces of oil and dirt.

3 A good grease solvent will make the job much easier. for, after the solvent has been applied and allowed to stand for a time, a vigorous jet of water will wash off the solvent and grease with it. If the dirt is thick and deeply embedded, work the solvent into it with a strong stiff brush.

4 Finally wipe down the exterior of the engine with a rag and only then, when it is quite clean, should the dismantling process begin. As the engine is stripped, clean each part in a bath of solvent. Clean oil passages with a small brush or, preferably, air pressure.

5 Re-use of old gaskets is false economy. To avoid the possibility of trouble after the engine has been reassembled always use new gaskets throughout.

6 Do not throw away the old gaskets, for sometimes it happens that an immediate replacement cannot be found and the old gasket is then very useful as a template. Hang up the gaskets as they are removed.

7 To strip the engine, it is best to work from the top down. When the stage is reached where the crankshaft must be removed, the engine can be turned on its side and all other work carried out with it in this position.

8 Wherever possible, install nuts, bolts and washers finger-tight from wherever they were removed; this helps to avoid loss and confusion. If they cannot be refitted then arrange them in a fashion to make it clear from whence they came.

9 Before dismantling begins it is important that a special tool is obtained for compressing the lash adjusters. This has the Ford number T74P-6585-A.

8 Cylinder head – rebuilding alternatives

Just as there are alternatives to engine repair (see Section 3), there are also alternative choices in the repair of the cylinder head of your car. The decision to repair or replace the cylinder head and its components depends, firstly, on the condition of the cylinder head. Other considerations are: your competence as a home mechanic, the available time to complete the project at hand, the competence of local machine shops, and cost.

Some of the rebuilding alternatives are as follows:

Individual parts – If the inspection and measurement procedures prove that the head and most of its components are sound and reusable, this may be the most economical alternative. Always replace valve springs as a set. It is possible to replace individual valve guides, but due to the cost of this task, we recommend that you replace all valve guides at the same time for long-run economy.

Bare head – If your measurements and inspection prove the valve seats need grinding, the head may be exchanged for a remachined head. The bare head has been stripped, cleaned, valve seats have been recut, new valve guides inserted, and fresh paint applied where necessary. These heads are available on an exchange basis from auto parts stores. Although the valves have to be lapped in, the saving occurs in the time saved in not waiting for a machine shop to complete their work.

Complete head – Like the bare head the complete cylinder head is sold on an exchange basis by auto parts stores. The head is cleaned, stripped, valve seats are recut, new valves are lapped in and new springs and guides are fitted. These heads are also repainted wherever necessary and are ready for the addition of rocker arms, pushrods, and a valve cover to be complete.

Remanufactured heads carry the additional bonus of a guarantee, which is usually included at the time of purchase.

Give careful thought and consideration to your circumstances and abilities, then decide which method has the best solution for you. Discuss the alternatives with local shop operators, auto parts dealers, and parts men before you decide.

9 Cylinder head – removal (engine out of car)

1   Remove the carburetor from the intake manifold.
2   Remove the EGR spacer, gaskets, and any other attached items from the carburetor mounting flange on the intake manifold.
3   Remove all other emission control hoses, fittings, and wiring from the intake manifold. We recommend that you sketch the location of the various parts and connections before removing them.
4   Remove the intake manifold mounting bolts and remove the manifold. If the intake manifold is stuck in place with sealant, the manifold may be broken free by tapping on the top and bottom of the manifold with a large rubber mallet. Never use a hard-faced striking tool for this task as damage to the intake manifold may result. Some models have an intake manifold which is part of the cylinder head casting.
5   Loosen the various drivebelts from the front of the engine and remove them. If they are cracked or worn, replace them when you reassemble the engine (Chapter 3).
6   Remove the Thermactor pump (Chapter 6) and the air conditioning pump, if installed. Remember, do not disconnect any portion of the air conditioning system while it is under pressure.
7   Unbolt the exhaust manifold and remove it. If any difficulty is encountered, rapping on the top and bottom of the manifold with a rubber mallet should help break the seal of any gasket sealer used during assembly.
8   Remove the thermostat housing and thermostat from the front of the cylinder head (Chapter 3).
9   Remove the water temperature sensor housing from the rear of the cylinder head (Chapter 3).
10 The rocker arm cover and cylinder head should now be completely clear of obstructing parts and stripped of all extra parts. If this is not

the case, remove any other wires, sensors, fittings, or components which remain, noting their location for ease in assembly.
11 Remove the bolts from the rocker arm cover and remove the cover. If a gasket sealer has been used in previous assembly squeeze the cover tightly and pull upward. Do not insert any object between the rocker arm cover and the cylinder head as damage to the sealing surface may result.
12 Remove the rocker arm shaft support bolts by loosening each in turn, 2 turns until all have been removed. The rocker arm assembly may now be removed by lifting it from the cylinder head.
13 Remove the pushrods, one at a time, labeling each one as you proceed. The Specifications Section will give you the order of the pushrods and valves from front to rear. We recommend you mark each one with a loop of tape and indelible pen, as matching pushrods to their rocker arms is critical to efficient running of your engine.
14 Remove the cylinder head bolts by loosening each one in sequence. Loosen each bolt in turn, going on to the next number in the sequence. Continue until all bolts can be removed.
15 The cylinder head may now be removed. Do not insert any tools between the cylinder head and engine block as damage to the mating surfaces will result. Do not attempt to pry or lever the two components apart in any way. If breaking the seal between the cylinder head and engine block is difficult, rap on either side of the cylinder head with a rubber mallet and rock the cylinder head from side to side while pulling upward. There are locating pins on top of the engine block which will damage the seal surface if the cylinder head is set back down onto them without a proper match.
16 Remove the old gasket from the engine block or cylinder head after the head has been transferred to a workbench for further stripdown.

10 Cylinder head – removal (engine in car)

Removal of the cylinder head with the engine in the car is very similar to the procedure given in Section 9. The following additional points should be noted:

a)   First remove the hood for improved access (Chapter 12).
b)   Disconnect the negative lead from the battery.
c)   Drain all engine coolant and remove all hoses which are connected to the cylinder head (Chapter 3).

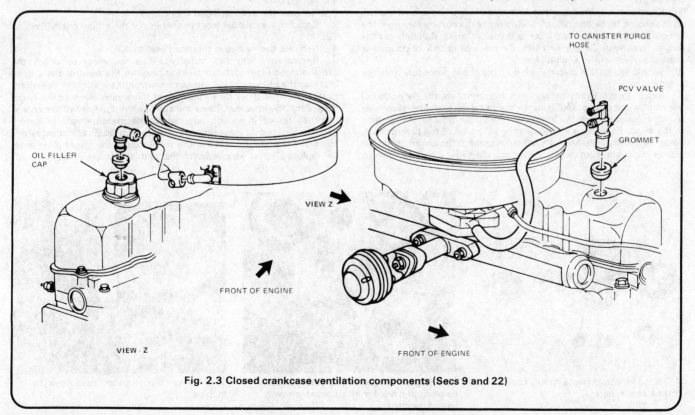

Fig. 2.3 Closed crankcase ventilation components (Secs 9 and 22)

d) Remove the air cleaner, carburetor, and emission controls which are attached to the cylinder head, manifolds, and carburetor. See Chapter 4 for further information, and be sure to make a sketch of all connections before disconnection.

e) Remove whichever drivebelts and accessories are in the way of the removal procedure. In most cases, you will need to remove the thermactor pump and air conditioning pump. If you must evacuate the air conditioning system, have this done by a qualified service specialist before you begin head removal.

f) Detach the spark plug leads and any other connections which are in the way. You may wish to note the location of these components before removal.

11 Cylinder head – disassembly

1   Before the valves can be removed, the carbon deposits should be removed from the combustion chambers and valve heads. This should be done with a wire brush and a scraper, being very careful not to scratch the head gasket surface.
2   Using a valve spring compressor, compress one of the valve springs and then remove the two-piece retainer at the top of the valve.
3   Release the compressor and lift away the sleeve, spring retainer, spring, stem seal and finally the valve. Carefully identifiy each of these parts as to the cylinder they were removed from (photo).
4   Follow these same procedures for the remaining valve assemblies.
5   See Section 51 for valve installation procedures.

12 Cylinder front cover and timing chain – removal

1   Although the following steps are presented for performance with the engine removed from the car, the timing chain and front cover may be removed while the engine is installed. It will be necessary to drain and disconnect the cooling system, remove the cooling fan, drivebelts, ancillary driven components, and the crankshaft and water pump drive pulleys before the following steps can be accomplished.
2   If the engine is removed from the car and you have not yet disconnected the cooling fan, the water pump, and crankshaft pulleys, do so now.
3   Remove the cylinder front cover by removing all bolts on the cover at the engine block and oil pan. Carefully pry the cover away from the engine block at the top and insert a thin blade knife. Carefully cut the gasket flush with the engine block. Be sure not to nick or gouge the mating surface of the engine block.
4   Scrape any gasket material left from the above procedure from the engine block.
5   Before removing the timing chain and sprockets, the deflection of the chain must be checked. Turn the crankshaft in a counter-clockwise direction (as seen from the front) and take up the slack on the left side of the chain. Establish a reference point to the left of the timing chain. Measure the distance from the reference point to the center of the left side of the chain. Turn the crankshaft in a clockwise direction (as seen from the front) and take up the slack on the right side of the timing chain. Press the slack chain on the left side toward the center with your thumb and measure the distance from your reference point to the center of the slack chain on the left side. Subtract the smaller figure from the larger and the difference will be the total deflection. If the deflection of the timing chain is greater than 0.250 in ($\frac{1}{4}$ in) the timing chain and sprockets must be replaced. If you are in doubt on condition at all, replace the timing chain and sprocket. Never replace just the chain or sprockets, replace all at once.
6   Rotate the crankshaft until the two timing marks on the sprockets align. Remove the camshaft sprocket attaching bolt and pull both sprockets evenly from the front of the engine (photo).
7   Clean the chain and sprockets in solvent if you have decided to reuse them. Inspect the teeth of the sprockets for chipping and wear and the chain for any wear pattern showing. If a wear pattern shows on the chain or the sprockets, we recommend that you replace the sprockets and chain.

13 Hydraulic tappets – removal

1   This task may be performed with the engine in or out of the car. Once the cylinder head is removed (Sections 9 and 10), it is a simple matter to perform the following tasks.
2   Using a cylindrical magnet, remove the tappets by inserting it into the tops of the pushrod tubes and contacting the top of a tappet. Work from the front of the engine to the back and keep the tappets in the order of their removal. It is important to match the valve train components for proper performance of the engine (photo).
3   If the tappets are held in place by sludge or gum, it will be necessary to remove the tappets with a plier or claw-type tool. Ford sells one such tool under part number T70L-6500-A. Tool shops and auto parts stores should be able to supply a reasonable alternative.
4   Do not disassemble or mix up the tappets. Disassembly, cleaning, and testing instructions will be found in Section 33.

14 Camshaft – removal

1   Although the camshaft may be removed with the engine installed in the car, we recommend that you perform this task only with the engine removed.
2   Remove the cylinder head (Section 9).
3   Remove the cylinder front cover but not the timing chain (Section 12).
4   Remove the hydraulic tappets (Section 13).
5   Before removing the camshaft, it is necessary to check the camshaft end play. Install a dial indicator on the front of the engine block so the plunger of the indicator rests on the end of the camshaft. Push the camshaft as far to the rear of the engine block as it will go, then 'Zero' the indicator. Press the camshaft to the front of the engine block as far as it will go and record the measurement indicated. Perform this test at least three times to ensure accuracy of measurement. If the end play exceeds the service limit, the thrust plate must be replaced upon assembly. If the end play measurement is ap-

11.3 All valve components for each cylinder must be kept separate

12.6 Align the marks on the timing chain sprocket and crankshaft sprocket (arrows) before removal

13.2 Using a claw-type tool to remove the tappets

proaching the outside limit, we recommend that you replace the thrust plate.
6 Remove the timing chain and sprockets (Section 12).
7 Remove the camshaft thrust plate.
8 Carefully pull the camshaft squarely out of the block. Be especially careful not to damage the camshaft lobes or bearing surfaces.

15 Flywheel and rear cover plate – removal

1 With the clutch removed, as described in Chapter 8, lock the flywheel using a screwdriver in mesh with the starter ring gear and undo the six bolts that secure the flywheel to the crankshaft in a diagonal and progressive manner. Lift away the bolts.
2 Mark the relative position of the flywheel and crankshaft and then lift away the flywheel.
3 Undo the remaining engine rear cover plate securing bolts and ease the rear cover plate from the two dowels. Lift away the rear cover plate.

16 Oil pan, oil pump and strainer – removal

1 Undo and remove the bolts that secure the oil pan to the underside of the crankcase.
2 Lift away the oil pan and its gaskets.
3 Undo the two bolts that secure the oil pump to the underside of the crankcase.
4 Lift away the oil pump and strainer assembly.
5 Carefully lift away the oil pump drive making a special note of which way round it is fitted.

17 Pistons, connecting rods and connecting rod bearings – removal

1 Note that the pistons have a notch marked on the crown showing the forward facing side. Inspect the connecting rod bearing caps and connecting rods to make sure identification marks are visible. This is to ensure that the correct caps are fitted to the correct connecting rods and the connecting rods placed in their respective bores.
2 Undo the connecting rod nuts and place to one side in the order in which they were removed.
3 Remove the connecting rod caps, taking care to keep them in the right order and the correct way round. Also ensure that the shell bearings are kept with their correct connecting rods unless the rods are to be replaced.
4 If the connecting rod caps are difficult to remove, they may be gently tapped free with a rubber mallet.
5 To remove the shell bearings, press the bearing opposite the groove in both the connecting rod and its cap, and the bearing will slide out easily.
6 Withdraw the pistons and connecting rods upwards and ensure they are kept in the correct order for replacement in the same bore as they were originally installed.

18 Crankshaft and main bearings – removal

1 Make sure that identification marks are visible on the main bearing caps, so that they may be installed in their original positions and also the correct way round.
2 If the bearing caps are not already marked, mark them as they are removed to ensure correct installation.
3 Undo by one turn at a time the bolts which hold the seven bearing caps.
4 Lift away each main bearing cap and the bottom half of each bearing shell, taking care to keep the bearing shells in the right caps.
5 When removing the rear main bearing cap note that this also retains the crankshaft rear oil seal.
6 When removing the center main bearing cap, note the bottom semi-circular halves of the thrust washers, one half lying on each side of the cap. Lay them with the main bearing cap on the correct side.
7 As the center and rear bearing caps are accurately located by dowels, it may be necessary to gently tap the caps to release them.
8 Slightly rotate the crankshaft to free the upper halves of the

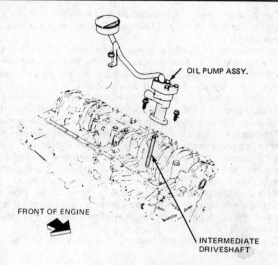

Fig. 2.4 Oil pump and strainer installation (Secs 16 and 4)

bearing shells and thrust washers which can be extracted and placed over the correct bearing caps.
9 Remove the two halves of the rear crankcase oil seal.
10 Remove the crankshaft by lifting it away from the crankcase.

19 Thermostat and water pump – removal

1 If the cylinder head and block are being completely dismantled, the thermostat and housing, and water pump should be removed. Further information on these procedures will be found in Chapter 3.

20 Piston pin – removal

1 A press type piston pin is used and it is important that no damage is caused during removal and installation. Because of this, should it be necessary to fit new pistons, take the parts along to the local Ford dealer or local repair shop who will have the special equipment to do this job.

21 Piston rings – removal

1 To remove the piston rings, slide them carefully over the top of the piston, taking care not to scratch the aluminum alloy; never slide them off the bottom of the piston skirt. It is very easy to break the cast iron piston rings if they are pulled off roughly, so this operation should be done with extreme care. It is helpful to make use of an old 0.020 inch (0.5 mm) feeler gauge.
2 Lift one end of the piston ring to be removed out of its groove and insert under it the end of the feeler gauge.
3 Turn the feeler gauge slowly round the piston and, as the ring comes out of its groove, apply slight upward pressure so that it rests on the land above. It can be eased off the piston with the feeler gauge stopping it from slipping into an empty groove if it is any but the top piston ring that is being removed.

22 Lubrication and crankcase ventilation system – description

1 The pressed steel oil pan is attached to the underside of the crankcase and acts as a reservoir for the engine oil. The oil pump draws oil through a strainer located under the oil surface, passes it along a short passage and into the full-flow oil filter. The freshly filtered oil flows from the center of the filter element and enters the main gallery. Seven small drillings connect the main gallery to the seven main bearings. The connecting rod bearings are supplied with oil by the front and rear main bearings via skew oil bores. When the crankshaft is rotating, oil is thrown from the hole in each connecting rod bearing and splashes the thrust side of the piston.

2   The auxiliary shaft is lubricated directly from the main oil gallery. The distributor shaft is supplied with oil passing along a drilling inside the auxiliary shaft.

3   A further three drillings connect the main oil gallery to the overhead camshaft to provide lubrication for the camshaft bearings and cam followers. Oil then passes back to the oil pan via large drillings in the cylinder head and cylinder block.

4   A semi-enclosed engine ventilation system is used to control crankcase vapor. It is controlled by the amount of air drawn in by the engine when running and the throughput of the regulator valve.

5   The system is known as the PCV (Positive Crankcase Ventilation) system. The advantage of this system is that should the 'blow-by' exceed the capacity of the PCV valve, excess fumes are fed into the engine through the air cleaner. This is effected by the rise in crankcase pressure which creates a reverse flow in the air intake pipe.

6   Periodically pull the valve and hose from the rubber grommet of the oil separator and inspect the valve for free-movement. If it is sticky in action or is clogged with sludge, dismantle it and clean the component parts.

7   Occcasionally check the security and condition of the system connecting hoses.

23 Oil pump – inspection

1   The oil pump cannot be dismantled or repaired in any way. If there is any obvious damage, or in the case of major engine overhaul, a replacement item must be installed.

2   Detach the oil intake pipe and screen (2 screws and spring washers), and clean the parts thoroughly in gasoline.

3   Install the intake pipe and screen, using a new solvent.

24 Oil filter – removal and installation

The oil filter is a complete throw away cartridge screwed into the left-hand side of the cylinder block. Simply unscrew the old unit, clean the seating on the block and lubricate with engine oil. Screw the new one into position taking care not to cross the thread. Continue until the sealing ring just touches the block face, then tighten one half turn by hand only. Always run the engine and check for signs of leaks after installation.

25 Engine components – inspection for wear

When the engine has been stripped down and all parts properly cleaned, decisions have to be made as to what needs replacing and the following Sections tell the mechanic what to look for. In any border-line case, it is always best to decide in favor of a new part. Even if a part may still be serviceable, its life will have been reduced by wear and the degree of trouble needed to replace it in the future must be taken into consideration. However, these things are relative and it depends on whether a 'quick' survival job is being done or whether the car as a whole is being regarded as having many thousands of miles of useful and economical life remaining.

26 Crankshaft – examination and renovation

1   Look at the main bearing journals and the crankpins, and if there are any scratches or score marks then the shaft will need regrinding. Such conditions will nearly always be accompanied by similar deterioration in the matching bearing shells.

2   Each bearing journal should also be round and can be checked with a micrometer or caliper gauge around the periphery at several points. If there is more than 0.001 in of ovality regrinding is necessary (photo).

3   A good way to check for wear and taper of a crankshaft or connecting rod journal is by using Plastigage. Place a piece of Plastigage across the full width of the bearing surface, about $\frac{1}{8}$ in off center, install the bearing cap and tighten to specification. Remove the cap and measure the width of the Plastigage at its widest point to obtain the minimum clearance and the narrowest point for the maximum clearance using the supplied gauge. The difference between

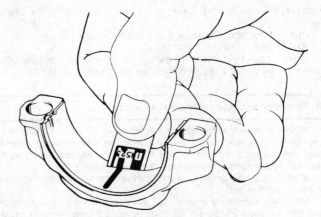

Fig. 2.5 Measuring Plastigage with scale (Sec 26)

26.2 Checking the crankshaft with a micrometer

these two measurements equals the taper. Be sure to remove all traces of the Plastigage from the journal after measurement.

4   A Ford service department or machine shop will be able to decide to what extent regrinding is necessary and also supply the special undersize shell bearings to match whatever may need grinding off.

5   Before taking the crankshaft for regrinding check also the cylinder bores and pistons as it may be advantageous to have the whole engine done at the same time.

6   During any major engine repair, pry out the roller pilot bearing from the rear end of the crankshaft; this may require the use of a hook-ended tool to get behind the bearing. Fit the replacement bearing with the seal outwards (where applicable) so that it is just below the surface of the crankshaft flange. This procedure is described in Chapter 8.

27 Crankshaft, main and connecting rod bearings – inspection and overhaul

1   With careful servicing and regular oil and filter changes, bearings will last for a very long time but they can still fail for unforeseen reasons. With connecting rod bearings, the indication is a regular rhythmic loud knocking from the crankcase. The frequency depends on engine speed and is particularly noticeable when the engine is under load. This symptom is accompanied by a fall in oil pressure although this is not normally noticeable unless an oil pressure gauge is fitted. Main bearing failure is usually indicated by serious vibration, particularly at higher engine revolutions, accompanied by a more significant drop in oil pressure and a 'rumbling' noise.

2   Bearing shells in good condition have bearing surfaces with a

smooth, even matte silver/grey color all over. Worn bearings will show patches of a different color when the bearing metal has worn away and exposed the underlay. Damaged bearings will be pitted or scored. It is always well worthwhile fitting new shells as their cost is relatively low. If the crankshaft is in good condition it is merely a question of obtaining another set of standard size. A reground crankshaft will need new bearing shells as a matter of course.

28 Cylinder bores – inspection and overhaul

1 A new cylinder bore is perfectly round and the walls parallel throughout its length. The action of the piston tends to wear the walls at right angles to the piston pin due to side thrust. This wear takes place principally on that section of the cylinder swept by the piston rings.

2 It is possible to get an indication of bore wear by removing the cylinder head with the engine still in the car. With the piston down in the bore first signs of wear can be seen and felt just below the top of the bore where the top piston ring reaches and there will be a noticeable lip. The lip should be removed as part of cylinder bore overhaul (photo). If there is no lip it is fairly reasonable to expect that bore wear is not severe and any lack of compression or excessive oil consumption is due to worn or broken piston rings or pistons.

3 If it is possible to obtain a bore measuring micrometer measure the bore in the thrust plane below the lip and again at the bottom of the cylinder in the same plane. If the difference is more than 0.003 inch (0.08 mm) then a rebore is necessary. Similarly, a difference of 0.003 inch (0.08 mm) or more across the bore diameter is a sign of ovality calling for rebore (photo).

4 Any bore which is significantly scratched or scored will need reboring. This symptom usually indicates that the piston or rings are damaged also. In the event of only one cylinder being in need of reboring, it will still be necessary for all six to be bored and fitted with new oversize pistons and rings. Your Ford dealer or local machine shop will be able to rebore and obtain the necessary matched pistons. If the crankshaft is undergoing regrinding also, it is a good idea to let the same firm renovate and reassemble the crankshaft and pistons to the block. A reputable firm normally gives a guarantee for such work. In cases where engines have been rebored already to their maximum, new cylinder liners are available which may be fitted. In such cases the same reboring processes have to be followed and the services of a specialist engineering firm are required.

29 Piston and piston rings – inspection and testing

1 Worn pistons and rings can usually be diagnosed when the symptoms of excessive oil consumption and lower compression occur and are sometimes, though not always, associated with worn cylinder bores. Compression testers that fit into the spark plug hole are available and these can indicate where low compression is occurring. Wear usually accelerates the more it is left so when the symptoms occur early action can possibly save the expense of a rebore.

2 Another symptom of piston wear is piston slap – a knocking noise from the crankcase not to be confused with the connecting rod bearing failure. It can be heard clearly at low engine speed when there is no load (idling for example) and is much less audible when the engine speed increases. Piston wear usually occurs in the skirt or lower end of the piston and is indicated by vertical streaks in the worn area which is always on the thrust side. It can also be seen where the skirt thickness is different.

3 Piston ring wear can be checked by first removing the rings from the piston as described in Section 21. Then place the rings in the cylinder bores from the top, pushing them down about 1½ inches (38 mm) with the head of a piston (from which the rings have been removed), so that they rest square in the cylinder bore. Then measure the gap at the ends of the ring with a feeler gauge. If it exceeds that given in the Specifications, they need replacement (photo).

4 The grooves in which the rings locate in the piston can also become enlarged in use. The clearance between ring and piston, in the groove, should not exceed that given in the Specifications.

5 However, it is rare that a piston is only worn in the ring grooves and the need to replace them for this fault alone is hardly ever encountered. Wherever pistons are replaced the weight of the six piston/connecting rod assemblies should be kept within the limit variations of 8 gms to maintain engine balance.

28.2 Removing the lip from the top of the bore with a ridge reamer tool

28.3 Checking cylinder bore for taper and ovality

29.3 Measuring the piston ring end gap inside the cylinder bore

30 Connecting rods and pistons – inspection and overhaul

1   Piston pins are a shrink fit into the connecting rods. Neither of these would normally need replacement unless the pistons were being changed, in which case the new pistons would automatically be supplied with new piston pins.

2   Connecting rods are not subject to wear but in extreme circumstances such as engine seizure they could be distorted. Such conditions may be visually apparent but where doubt exists they should be changed. The bearing caps should also be examined for indications of filing down which may have been attempted in the mistaken idea that bearing slackness could be remedied in this way. If there are such signs then the connecting rods should be replaced.

31 Camshaft and camshaft bearings – inspection and overhaul

1   The camshaft bearings should be examined for signs of scoring and pitting. If they need replacement they will have to be dealt with professionally as, although it may be relatively easy to remove the old bearings, the correct fitting of new ones requires special tools. If they are not fitted evenly and square from the very start they can be distorted, thus causing localized wear in a very short time. See your Ford dealer or local engineering specialist for this work.

2   The camshaft itself may show signs of wear on the bearing journals or cam lobes. The main decision to make is what degree of wear justifies replacement, which is costly. Any signs of scoring or damage to the bearing journals cannot be removed by grinding. Replacement of the whole camshaft is the only solution. **Note:** *Where excessive cam lobe wear is evident, refer to the following Section.*

3   The cam lobes themselves may show signs of ridging or pitting on the high points. If ridging is light then it may be possible to smooth it out with fine emery. The cam lobes, however, are surface hardened and once this is penetrated, wear will be very rapid thereafter.

4   Ensure that the camshaft oilways are unobstructed.

5   To check the thrust plate for wear, position the camshaft into its location in the cylinder head and lift the thrust plate at the rear. Using a dial gauge, check the total shaft endfloat by tapping the camshaft carefully back-and-forth along its length. If the endplay is outside the specified limit, replace the thrust plate.

32 Valves and valve seats – inspection and overhaul

1   With the valves removed from the cylinder head examine the head for signs of cracking, burning away and pitting of the edge where it sits in the port. The valve seats in the cylinder head should also be examined for the same signs (photo). Usually it is the valve that deteriorates first but if a bad valve is not rectified the seat will suffer and this is more difficult to repair.

2   Provided there are no obvious signs of serious pitting the valve should be ground with its seat. This may be done by placing a smear of carborundum paste on the edge of the valve and, using a suction type valve holder, grinding the valve in place. This is done with a semi-rotary action, rotating the handle of the valve holder between the hands and lifting it occasionally to re-distribute the traces of paste. Use a coarse paste to start with. As soon as a matte grey unbroken line appears on both the valve and seat the valve is 'ground in'. All traces of carbon should also be cleaned from the head and neck of the valve stem. A wire brush mounted in a power drill is a quick and effective way of doing this.

3   If the valve requires replacement it should be ground into the seat in the same way as the old valve.

4   Another form of valve wear can occur on the stem where it runs in the guide in the cylinder head. This can be detected by trying to rock the valve from side to side. If there is any movement at all it is an indication that the valve stem or guide is worn. Check the stem first with a micrometer at points along and around its length and if they are not within the specified size new valves will probably solve the problem (photo). If the guides are worn, however, they will need reboring for oversize valves or for fitting guide inserts. The valve seats will also need recutting to ensure they are concentric with the stems. This work should be entrusted to your Ford dealer or local auto-machine shop.

5   When valve seats are badly burned or pitted, requiring replacement, inserts may be fitted – or replaced if already fitted once before

32.1 Measuring the valve seat width

32.4 Measuring the valve stem wear

– again this is a specialist task to be carried out by a suitable rebuilding firm.

6   When all valve grinding is complete it is essential that every trace of grinding paste is removed from the valves and ports in the cylinder head. This should be done by thorough washing in parts solvent and blowing out with a jet of air. If particles of carborundum should work their way into the engine they would seriously damage the bearings or cylinder walls.

33 Hydraulic tappets – disassembly, inspection, assembly

1   All tappet assemblies are matched sets of parts. Do not mix parts or mix the order of the tappets. Keep the various components in their proper sequence for ease of reassembly.

2   Carefully clean the outside surfaces of the tappet. Inspect the surface for chips, scratching, or scoring.

3   Grasp the lock ring at the cup end with needle nose pliers and snap it from its groove. It may be necessary to fully depress the plunger so the lock ring may be removed.

4   Remove the pushrod cup, plunger valve disc, and spring from the tappet body and lay them out in their order of removal.

5   Invert the plunger assembly and locate the check valve retainer. Using a flat blade screwdriver, carefully pry the check valve retainer from the plunger.

6   Clean all tappet assembly components and remove all traces of engine oil. Dry the parts with a lint-free cloth or compressed air.
7   Check all parts for tight fit and make sure all moving parts are free of scoring, scratches, or chipping. If any of these conditions is noted, consult your local dealer or mechanic for further advice. Since any of the conditions above suggests a number of possible engine problems, these people will be able to diagnose the problem most quickly.
8   Reassemble the tappets in the reverse of the reassembly instructions.
9   Tappets may be checked for leakdown rate if they are suspected of being defective. This test requires special equipment and is most economically performed by a dealer or shop.

34 Flywheel – inspection and overhaul

1   If the ring gear is badly worn or has missing teeth it should be replaced. The old ring can be removed from the flywheel by cutting a notch between two teeth with a hacksaw and then splitting it with a cold chisel.
2   To fit a new ring gear requires heating the ring to 400°F (204°C). This can be done by polishing four equally spaced sections of the gear, laying it on a suitable heat resistant surface (such as fire bricks) and heating it evenly with a blow torch until the polished areas turn a light yellow tinge. Do not overheat or the hard wearing properties will be lost. The gear has a chamfered inner edge which should go against the shoulder when put on the flywheel. When hot enough place the gear in position quickly, tapping it home, and let it cool naturally without quenching it.

35 Cylinder head and piston crowns – carbon removal

1   When the cylinder head is removed, either in the course of an overhaul or for inspection of bores or valve condition when the engine is in the car, it is normal to remove all carbon deposits from the piston crowns and head.
2   This is best done with a cup shaped wire brush and an electric drill and is fairly straightforward when the engine is dismantled and the pistons removed. Sometimes hard spots of carbon are not easily removed except by a scraper. When cleaning the pistons with a scraper, take care not to damage the surface of the piston in any way.
3   When the engine is in the car, certain precautions must be taken when cleaning the pistons' crowns in order to prevent dislodged pieces of carbon falling into the interior of the engine which could cause damage to cylinder bores, piston and rings – or if allowed into the water passages – damage to the water pump. Turn the engine so that the piston being worked on is at the top of its stroke and then mask off the adjacent cylinder bores and all surrounding water jacket orifices with paper and adhesive tape. Press grease into the gap all round the piston to keep carbon particles out and then scrape all carbon away by hand carefully. Do not use a power drill and wire brush when the engine is in the car as it will virtually be impossible to keep all the carbon dust clear of the engine. When completed, carefully clear out the grease around the rim of the piston with a matchstick or something similar – bringing any carbon particles with it. Repeat the process on the other piston crown.

36 Valve guides – inspection

Examine the valve guides internally for wear. If the valves are a very loose fit in the guides and there is the slightest suspicion of lateral rocking using a new valve, then the guides will have to be reamed and oversize valves fitted. This is a job best left to the local Ford dealer, or machine shop.

37 Oil pan – inspection

Wash out the oil pan in solvent and wipe dry. Inspect the exterior for signs of damage or excessive rust. If evident, a new oil pan must be obtained. To ensure an oil tight joint scrape away all traces of the old gasket from the cylinder block mating face.

38 Engine reassembly (general)

All components of the engine must be cleaned of oil, sludge and old gasket and the working area should also be cleared and clean. In addition to the normal range of good quality socket wrenches and general tools which are essential, the following must be available before reassembling begins:

Complete set of new gaskets
Supply of clean lint-free cloths
Clean oil can full of clean engine oil
Torque wrench
All new spare parts as necessary

39 Crankshaft – installation

1   Ensure that the crankcase is thoroughly clean and that all oilways are clear. A thin twist drill or a piece of wire is useful for cleaning them out. If possible blow them out with compressed air.
2   Treat the crankshaft in the same fashion, and then inject engine oil in the crankshaft oilways.
3   Commence the work of rebuilding the engine by installing the crankshaft and main bearings.
4   Wipe the bearing shell locations in the crankcase with a lint-free cloth.
5   Wipe the crankshaft journals with a soft lint-free cloth.
6   If the old main bearing shells are to be reused (to do so is false economy unless they are virtually new) fit the seven upper halves of the main bearing shells to their location in the crankcase.
7   Identify each main bearing cap and place in order. The number is cast into the cap and with intermediate caps an arrow indicates that the cap is fitted the correct way round.
8   Lubricate the new crankshaft rear oil seals in engine oil and fit one in the rear crankcase groove and the other in the rear main bearing cap groove making sure the oil seal tabs face towards the rear of the engine.
9   Wipe the cap bearing shell location with a soft lint-free rag.
10 Fit the main bearing lower shells onto each main bearing cap.
11 Apply a little grease to each side of the center bearing so as to retain the thrust washers.
12 Fit the upper halves of the thrust washers into their grooves on either side of the main bearing. The slots must face outwards.
13 Lubricate the crankshaft journals and the upper and lower main bearing shells with engine oil or assembly lube (photo).
14 Carefully lower the crankshaft into the crankcase.
15 Lubricate the crankshaft main bearing journals again and then fit No. 1 bearing cap. Fit the two securing bolts but do not tighten yet.
16 Apply a little non-setting gasket sealant to the crankshaft rear main bearing cap location.
17 Next fit No. 7 cap. Fit the two securing bolts but as before do not tighten yet.

39.13 Lubricating the bearing with assembly lube

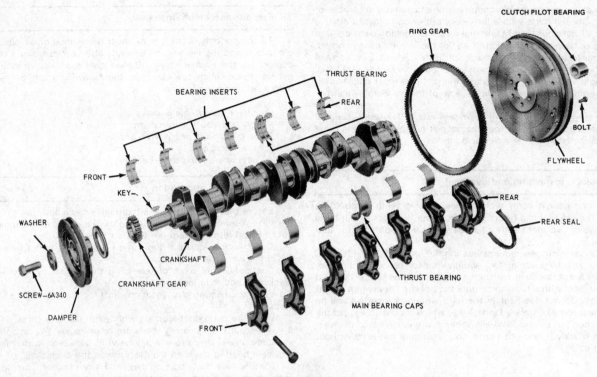

Fig. 2.6 Crankshaft, bearings and components (Sec 39)

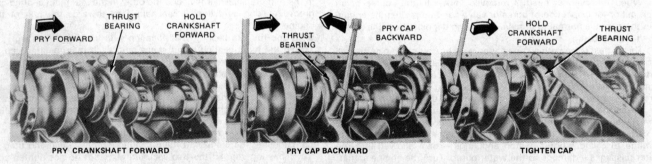

Fig. 2.7 Crankshaft thrust bearing alignment procedure (Sec 39)

18 Apply a little grease to either side of the center main bearing cap so as to retain the thrust washers. Fit the thrust washers with the tag located in the groove and the slots facing outwards.
19 Fit the center main bearing cap and the two securing bolts. Then install the intermediate main bearing caps. Make sure that the arrows always point towards the front of the engine.
20 Lightly tighten all main bearing cap securing bolts and then fully tighten in a progressive manner to the final torque wrench setting as specified (photo).
21 Using a screwdriver, ease the crankshaft fully forward and with feeler gauges check the clearance between the crankshaft journal side and the thrust washers. The clearance must not exceed that given in the Specifications. Oversize thrust washers are available.
22 Test the crankshaft for freedom of rotation. Should it be stiff to turn or possess high spots, a most careful inspection must be made with a micrometer, preferably by a qualified mechanic, to get to the root of the trouble. It is very seldom that any trouble of this nature will be experienced when fitting the crankshaft.

40 Pistons and connecting rods – reassembly

As a press type piston pin is used (see Section 20) this operation must be carried out by the local Ford dealer. Do not forget that the notch in the piston crown must face toward the front of the engine.

41 Piston rings – installation

1 Check that the piston ring grooves and oilways are thoroughly clean and unblocked. Piston rings must always be fitted over the head of the piston and never from the bottom (photos).
2 The easiest method to use when fitting rings is to wrap a 0.20 in (0.5 mm) feeler gauge round the top of the piston and place the rings one at a time, starting with the bottom oil control ring, over the feeler gauge.
3 The feeler gauge, complete with ring, can then be slid down the piston over the other piston ring grooves until the correct groove is reached. The piston ring is then slid gently off the feeler gauge into the groove.
4 An alternative method is to fit the rings by holding them slightly open with the thumbs and both of the index fingers. This method requires a steady hand and great care, as it is easy to open the ring too much and break it.

42 Pistons – installation

1 The pistons, complete with connecting rods, can be fitted to the cylinder bores in the following sequence:
2 With a wad of clean rag wipe the cylinder bores clean.

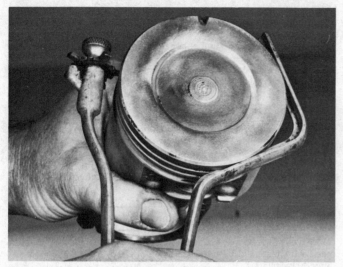

41.1A Cleaning the piston ring groove with tool

41.1B Installing the piston rings with compressor tool

3   The pistons, complete with connecting rods, are fitted to their bores from the top of the block.
4   Locate the piston ring gaps as shown in the accompanying figure.

Note: *The oil control ring segment gaps are to be approximately 80° away from the expander gap and not in the area of the skirt. The piston should be installed in the block so that the expander gap is towards the front and the segment gap is towards the rear.*

5   Well lubricate the piston and rings and cylinder bore (photo) with engine oil and push lengths of rubber hose over the rod bolts. This will protect the cylinder and crankshaft from damage.
6   Fit a universal piston ring compressor and prepare to install the first piston into the bore. Make sure it is the correct piston connecting rod assembly for that particular bore, that the connecting rod is the correct way round and that the front of the piston is towards the front of the bore, ie, towards the front of the engine.
7   Again lubricate the piston skirt and insert into the bore up to the bottom of the piston ring compressor.
8   Gently but firmly tap the piston through the piston ring compressor and into the cylinder bore with a wooden, or plastic faced, hammer (photo).
9   Remove the hose pieces.

43 Connecting rods – installation

1   Wipe clean the connecting rod upper shell bearing location and the underside of the shell bearing, and fit the shell bearing in position with its locating tongue engaged with the corresponding cut-out in the rod.
2   If the old shell bearings are nearly new and are being refitted then

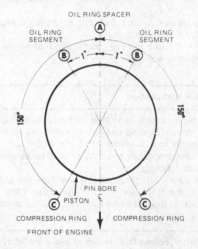

Fig. 2.8 Piston ring gap spacing (Sec 42)

ensure they are installed in their correct locations on the correct rods.
3   Generously lubricate the crankpin journals with engine oil and turn the crankshaft so that the crankpin is in the most advantageous position for the connecting rods to be drawn onto it.
4   Wipe clean the connecting rod cap and back of the shell bearing, and fit the shell bearing in position ensuring that the locating tongue at the back of the bearing engages with the locating groove in the connecting rod cap.
5   Generously lubricate the shell bearing and install the connecting rod cap to the connecting rod (photo).

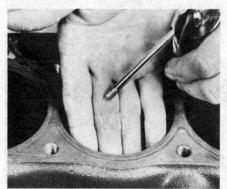

42.5 The cylinder bores should be well lubricated before installing the pistons

42.8 Tapping the piston into the bore through the compressor

43.5 Drawing the connecting rod snugly up to the crankshaft

6 Install the connecting rod nuts and tighten finger-tight.
7 Tighten the nuts with a torque wrench to the specified torque.
8 When all the connecting rods have been installed, rotate the crankshaft to check that everything is free, and that there are no high spots causing binding. The bottom half of the engine is now near completion.

44 Oil pump and strainer – installation

1 Wipe the mating faces of the oil pump and underside of the cylinder block.
2 Insert the hexagonal driveshaft into the end of the oil pump.
3 Install the oil pump and the two bolts. Tighten the two bolts to the specified torque.

45 Oil pan – installation

1 Wipe the mating faces of the underside of the crankcase and the oil pan.
2 Smear some non-setting gasket sealant on the underside of the crankcase.
3 Fit the oil pan gasket and end seals making sure that the bolt holes line up.
4 Install the oil pan taking care not to dislodge the gaskets and secure in position with the bolts.
5 Tighten the oil pan bolts in a progressive manner, to a final torque wrench setting as specified.

46 Camshaft – installation

1 Coat the bearing and cam lobe surfaces with thick coatings of multipurpose grease. Spread the grease evenly on all surfaces.
2 Carefully insert the camshaft into its hole. Do not allow the cam lobes or the bearing surfaces to contact the outer bearing races or the sides of the hole (photo).
3 When the camshaft contacts the rear bearing plug, install the thrust plate on the front and tighten the thrust plate bolts evenly. Torque the bolts to their specified torque (Specifications).

47 Cylinder front cover and timing chain – installation

1 Place the camshaft sprocket and the crankshaft sprocket in place and turn them until the timing marks on the sprockets face one another (photo).
2 Remove the sprockets and place them inside the timing chain. Make sure the timing marks still face each other.
3 Slide the two sprockets, complete with the timing chain on the ends of the crankshaft and camshaft.

4 Install the camshaft sprocket bolt and torque to specification.
5 Before installing the cylinder front cover, check the condition of the oil seal which fits over the crankshaft. If the seal is dried or has shown signs of leaking, it must be replaced. Carefully pry the seal from its groove. Install the new seal with a seal pusher or a socket which has the same outside diameter as the seal.
6 Smear oil resistant sealer on a new front cover gasket and position the gasket on the front cover. Coat all exposed portions of the gasket with sealer. Cut and locate the sections of the gasket which fit the oil pan, on the oil pan. Apply sealer to all exposed surfaces of the gasket.
7 Install the cylinder front cover. To prevent damage to the seal as it contacts with the Woodruff key on the crankshaft, place a thin wall socket over the crankshaft end. Make sure the outside diameter of the socket is less than or equal to the inside diameter of the seal.
8 Torque all mounting bolts to their specified torque.

48 Hydraulic tappets – installation

1 If your tappets were disassembled, but not tested, they must be filled with test fluid before installation. Tested and new tappets will already be filled.
2 Lubricate the outside surfaces of the tappets with engine oil.
3 Place a magnet on the cup end of the tappet and slide it into place in the appropriate pushrod tube. Remember to install each tappet in its proper hole.

46.2 When inserting the camshaft, be careful not to contact the sides of the bores with the lobes

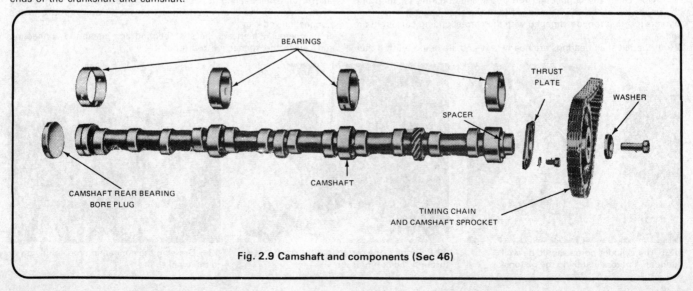

Fig. 2.9 Camshaft and components (Sec 46)

49 Water pump – installation

Install the water pump to the cylinder block (if removed), referring to Chapter 2 as necessary.

50 Rear cover plate (flywheel) and clutch – installation

1 Wipe the mating faces of the rear cover plate and cylinder block and carefully fit the rear cover plate to the two dowels.
2 Wipe the mating faces of the flywheel and crankshaft and install the flywheel to the crankshaft, aligning the previously made marks unless new parts are being used. A reinforcing plate is fitted to the flywheel on automatic models.
3 Fit the six crankshaft securing bolts and lightly tighten.
4 Lock the flywheel using a screwdriver engaged in the starter ring gear and tighten the securing bolts in a diagonal and progressive manner to a final torque wrench setting as specified.
5 Install the clutch disc and pressure plate assembly to the flywheel making sure the disc is the right way round.
6 Secure the pressure plate assembly with the six retaining bolts and spring washers.
7 Center the clutch disc using an old input shaft or piece of wooden dowel, and fully tighten the retaining bolts.

51 Valves – installation

1 With the valves suitably ground in (see Section 32) and kept in their correct order, start with No. 1 cylinder and insert the valve into its guide.
2 Lubricate the valve stem with engine oil and slide on a new oil seal. The spring must be uppermost.
3 Fit the valve spring and retainer.
4 Using a universal valve spring compressor, compress the valve spring, until the keys can be slid into position. Note these keys have serrations which engage in slots in the valve stem. Release the valve spring compressor.
5 Repeat this procedure until all twelve valves and valve springs are installed.

52 Cylinder head – installation

1 Wipe the mating surfaces of the engine block and cylinder head.
2 Coat a new cylinder head gasket with sealer and place it over the locating pegs on the engine block. The gasket is usually marked with a 'front' and 'up' marking for proper installation.
3 Carefully place the cylinder head over the locating pins and set into place.
4 Install the twelve pushrods in their proper order (photo).
5 Install the cylinder head bolts and tighten them evenly in the order shown in the accompanying figure.
6 When all cylinder head bolts are snug, torque them in order, then torque them once again as specified.

52.4 Installing the pushrods. Note the assembly lube where the rod will contact the rocker arm

Fig. 2.10 Cylinder head bolt tightening sequence (Sec 52)

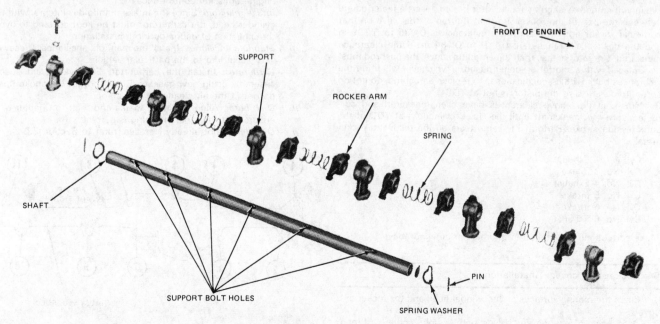

Fig. 2.11 Rocker arms, shafts and components (Sec 52)

52.7A Pushrod properly seated in the rocker arm

52.7B Tightening the rocker arm shaft bolts

7   Install the rocker arm support shaft in its proper location and tighten the bolts two turns each from the innermost bolts outward until snug. Torque the bolts, from the inside outward (see Specifications) (photos).

53 Valves – adjusting

1   Turn the engine until the No. 1 cylinder is at TDC of the compression stroke. With the spark plug removed and your finger over the hole, you can feel the compression.
2   Using Ford tool, number 6513-K, or a similar tool, compress each rocker arm in the following order so the hydraulic lifter's plunger will bottom. Do not press too hard, or the pushrod may be bent. Compress the rocker arms in the following order while checking for clearance:

    Cyl. No. 1 Intake
    Cyl. No. 1 Exhaust
    Cyl. No. 2 Intake
    Cyl. No. 3 Exhaust
    Cyl. No. 4 Intake
    Cyl. No. 5 Exhaust

While you compress each hydraulic lifter in turn, insert a feeler gauge between the pad of the rocker arm and the top of the valve on that particular rocker arm. The allowable clearance is 0.085 to 0.209 in and the desired clearances are 0.110 to 0.184 in. If the clearance measured is greater or less than the amounts above, the pushrod must be replaced with a shorter or longer pushrod, whichever will bring the clearances back within specifications. To replace a pushrod, do not do so until you are sure the piston is hot at TDC.
3   When all the above clearances have been measured and corrected, turn the crankshaft until the No. 6 cylinder is at TDC of the compression stroke. Perform the same tests on the following rocker arms:

    Cyl. No. 2 Exhaust
    Cyl. No. 3 Intake
    Cyl. No. 4 Exhaust
    Cyl. No. 5 Intake
    Cyl. No. 6 Intake
    Cyl. No. 6 Exhaust

Make corrections as required in the manner outlined above.

54 Rocker arm cover – installation

1   Clean the mating surfaces of the cylinder head and the rocker arm cover.
2   Coat each of the gasket halves with a light coating of non-hardening gasket sealer and locate the gaskets in their proper spots.

3   Set the rocker arm cover in place and install the bolts. Torque the bolts in a 'bow tie' pattern beginning at the middle and working outward. (See Specifications).

55 Engine – preparation for installation

1   Having completed the engine rebuilding, it is now necessary to install the items which were taken off prior to the commencement of major dismantling. These will differ according to the extent of the work done and the original equipment fitted, but will typically be:

   a) *Oil pressure sender:* Coat threads with a non-setting gasket sealant and screw into the cylinder head.
   b) *Water temperature sender:* Coat threads with a non-setting gasket sealant and screw into cylinder block.
   c) *Fan:* Refer to Chapter 3, if necessary.
   d) *Exhaust manifold:* Ensure that the mating surfaces are clean then apply a light even film of graphite grease. Install the manifold and then the bolts in two steps to the specified torque.
   e) *Spark plugs:* Fit new spark plugs of the type stated on the engine emission control decal.
   f) *Intake manifold:* Since the intake manifold is integral with the cylinder head, the carburetor must be kept covered to avoid the ingestion of debris during reinstallation.
   g) *Manifold ancillaries:* Install the manifold ancillaries. These will vary according to the particular vehicle.
   h) *Carburetor:* Install the carburetor, EGR valve and spacer assembly using new gaskets. Do not forget the choke hose; do not fit the air cleaner at this stage.
   i) *Distributor:* Align the index marks and refer to Chapter 5, to ensure that the ignition timing is correct.
   j) *Oil filter:* If not already installed, refer to Section 23.

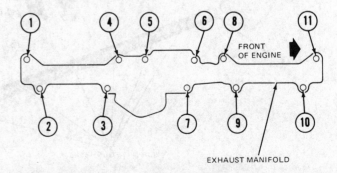

Fig. 2.12 Exhaust manifold tightening sequence (Sec 55)

k)   *Fuel pump:* Refer to Chapter 4, if necessary.
l)   *Alternator:* Refit loosely; do not fit the drivebelt.
m) *Thermactor pump, compressor, PVC system, oil level dipstick, miscellaneous emission control items and associated interconnecting hoses etc.*

56 Engine – installation (without transmission)

1   Raise the engine on the hoist and position it over the car engine compartment so that the rear end is sloping downward.
2   Lower the engine so that the exhaust manifold lines up approximately with the exhaust muffler inlet pipe.
3   *Automatic transmission:* Start the converter pilot into the crankshaft.
4   *Manual transmission:* Start the transmission main drive gear (input shaft) into the clutch hub. If necessary rotate the engine slightly *clockwise* to align the splines.
5   Ensure that the engine is settled on its mounts, then detach the hoist chains.
6   From beneath the car install the flywheel housing or converter upper attaching bolts.
7   *Automatic transmission:* Attach the converter to the flywheel and tighten the nuts to the specified torque. Refer to Chapter 7 for further information, if necessary. Install the converter bolt access plug.
8   Fit the front engine mount nuts.
9   Connect the exhaust pipe to the manifold, using a new gasket (if applicable).
10 Install the starter motor and electrical cables.
11 Remove the plugs from the fuel lines and reconnect them to the fuel pump. If not already done, reconnect the fuel line to the carburetor.
12 Position the power steering pump on its brackets and install the upper bolts.
13 Fit the engine shield.
14 From inside the engine compartment fit the power steering pump pulley.
15 Reconnect the engine ground lead.
16 Fit the alternator adjusting arm bolt and the electrical connector(s).
17 Connect the wire to the electrically assisted choke.
18 Connect the coil wire and vacuum hose to the distributor.
19 Connect the vacuum amplifier.
20 Connect the wire to the water temperature sender in the cylinder block.
21 Connect the idle solenoid wires.
22 Position the accelerator cable on the ball stud and install the ball stud on the clip. Snap the bracket clip into position on the bracket. Where applicable, install the kick-down cable.
23 Install the line to the oil pressure sender.
24 Install the brake vacuum unit hose.
25 Reconnect the engine heater and vacuum hoses.
26 Install the drivebelts to the engine-driven accessories. Refer to Chapter 3 for the correct tension.
27 Install the radiator. Refer to Chapter 3 if necessary.
28 Install the oil cooler lines (where applicable).
29 Install the radiator hoses.
30 Where applicable, install the fan shroud.
31 Refill the cooling system with the correct amount of water/antifreeze (or inhibitor) mixture. Refer to Chapter 3 as necessary.
32 Fill the crankcase with the specified amount and type of oil.
33 Install the air cleaner and the vacuum hoses. Refer to Chapter 4 if necessary.
34 Connect the battery leads.
35 Have a last look round the engine compartment to ensure that no hoses or electrical connections have been left off.

57 Engine – installation (with manual transmission)

1   The procedure for installing the engine and manual transmission is basically as described in the previous Section. However, the following differences should be noted:

a) Support the weight of the transmission with a hydraulic jack prior to installing the rear mountings.
b) Do not forget to reconnect the speedometer cable and transmission electrical connections. Refer to Chapter 7 for further information, if necessary.
c) Check the clutch adjustment after the cable has been reconnected. Refer to Chapter 8 for further information.
d) When reconnecting the driveshaft, ensure that the index marks are correctly aligned. Refer to Chapter 8 for further information if necessary.

58 Engine – initial start-up after overhaul or major repair

1   Make sure that the battery is fully charged and that all lubricants, coolant and fuel are replenished.
2   If the fuel system has been dismantled it will require several revolutions of the engine on the starter motor to pump the gas up to the carburetor.
3   As soon as the engine fires and runs, keep it going at a fast idle only (no faster) and bring it up to normal working temperature. When the thermostat opens the coolant level will fall and must therefore be topped-up again as necessary.
4   As the engine warms up there will be odd smells and some smoke from parts getting hot and burning off deposits. The signs to look for are leaks of water or oil, which will be obvious, if serious. Check also the exhaust pipe and manifold connections as these do not always find their exact gastight position until the warmth and vibration have acted on them and it is almost certain that they will need tightening further. This should be done, of course, with the engine stopped.
5   When normal running temperature has been reached, adjust the engine idle speed, as described in Chapter 4.
6   Stop the engine and wait a few minutes to see if any lubricant or coolant is dripping out when the engine is stationary.
7   After the engine has run for 20 minutes remove the engine rocker cover and recheck the tightness of the cylinder head bolts. Also check the tightness of the oil pan bolts. In both cases use a torque wrench.
8   Install the hood to the previously drawn alignment marks and check that the hood fits correctly when shut.
9   Road test the car to check that the timing is correct and that the engine is giving the necessary smoothness and power. Do not race the engine; if new bearings and/or pistons have been installed it should be treated as a new engine and run in at a reduced speed for the first 1000 miles (2000 km).

Chapter 2 Part B V8 engines

Contents

Specifications

Engine displacement
Displacement .... 4.2L (255 cu in), 5.0L (302 cu in), or 5.8L (351 cu in)

Type .... 90° V8 pushrod-operated OHV

Bore and stroke
4.2L .... 3.68 in x 3.00 in
5.0L .... 4.00 in x 3.00 in
5.8L .... 4.00 in x 3.50 in

Firing order
4.2L and 5.0L 1-5-4-2-6-3-7-8
5.8L 1-3-7-2-6-5-4-8

Oil pressure (hot at 2000 rpm)
4.2L and 5.0L .... 40 to 60 psi
5.8L .... 40 to 65 psi

Compression test .... Lowest cylinder (psi) must be within 75% of highest cylinder pressure

Cylinder head and valve train
Valve guide bore diameter .... 0.3433 in to 0.3443 in

Valve seat width
Intake .... 0.060 in to 0.080 in
Exhaust .... 0.060 in to 0.080 in

Valve face runout limit .... 0.002 in

Valve seat angle .... 45°

Valve arrangement (front to rear)
Right bank .... I-E-I-E-I-E-I-E
Left bank .... E-I-E-I-E-I-E-I

Valve stem-to-guide clearance
Intake .... 0.0010 in to 0.0027 in
Exhaust .... 0.0015 in to 0.0032 in
Service clearance limit .... 0.0055 in

Valve head diameter
1975 and 1976 (all)
    Intake .... 1.773 in to 1.791
    Exhaust .... 1.442 in to 1.460
1977 5.0L
    Intake .... 1.773 in to 1.791 in
    Exhaust .... 1.442 in to 1.460 in
1977 5.8L
    Intake .... 1.773 in to 1.791 in
    Exhaust .... 1.468 in to 1.453 in
1978 thru 1980 4.2L and 5.0L
    Intake .... 1.770 in to 1.794 in
    Exhaust .... 1.439 in to 1.463 in
1978 thru 1980 5.8L
    Intake .... 1.770 in to 1.794 in
    Exhaust .... 1.439 in to 1.463 in

Valve stem diameter
Standard
    Intake .... 0.3416 in to 0.3423 in
    Exhaust .... 0.3411 in to 0.3418 in
0.003 in oversize
    Intake .... 0.3446 in to 0.3453 in
    Exhaust .... 0.3441 in to 0.3448 in
0.015 in oversize
    Intake .... 0.3566 in to 0.3573 in
    Exhaust .... 0.3561 in to 0.3568 in
0.030 in oversize
    Intake .... 0.3716 in to 0.3723 in
    Exhaust .... 0.3711 in to 0.3718 in

Valve springs
Compression pressure (lbs at spec. length)
    1975 thru 1978 5.0L
        Intake .... 76 to 84 at 1.69
                 190 to 210 at 1.31
        Exhaust .... 76 to 84 at 160
                 190 to 210 at 1.20

    1975 thru 1978 5.8L
        Intake .... 71 to 79 at 1.790
                 190 to 210 at 1.340
        Exhaust .... 76 to 84 at 1.60
                 190 to 210 at 1.20

    1979 5.0L
        Intake .... 74 to 82 at 1.78
                 190 to 212 at 1.36
        Exhaust .... 76 to 84 at 1.60
                 190 to 210 at 1.20

1979 5.8L
    Intake .... 74 to 82 at 78
           215 to 237 at 1.39
    Exhaust .... 76 to 84 at 1.60
           190 to 210 at 1.20
1980 4.2L
    Intake .... 74 to 82 at 1.78
           190 to 212 at 1.30
    Exhaust .... 76 to 84 at 1.60
           190 to 210 at 1.20
Free length (approximate)
  1975 thru 1978 5.0L
    Intake .... 1.94 in
    Exhaust .... 1.87 in
  1975 thru 1978 5.8L
    Intake .... 2.06 in
    Exhaust .... 1.87 in
  1979 and 1980 (all)
    Intake .... 2.04 in
    Exhaust .... 1.85 in
    Service limit .... 10% pressure loss at specified length
Out-of-square limit .... 5/64 in (0.078 in)

Rocker arm, pushrods and tappets
Rocker arm lift ratio .... 1.61 : 1
Pushrod runout .... 0.015 in
Valve tappet diameter (standard) .... 0.8749 in to 0.0875 in
Valve tappet clearance-to-bore .... 0.0007 in to 0.0027 in
Collapsed tappet gap
  1975 5.0L
    Desired .... 0.115 in to 0.130 in
    Allowable .... 0.106 in to 0.200 in
  1975 5.8L
    Desired .... 0.131 in to 0.181 in
    Allowable .... 0.106 in to 0.200 in
  1976 5.0L
    Desired .... 0.115 in to 0.165 in
    Allowable .... 0.090 in to 0.190 in
  1976 5.8L
    Desired .... 0.131 in to 0.181 in
    Allowable .... 0.106 in to 0.206 in
  1977 and 1978 all
    Desired .... 0.096 in to 0.168 in
    Allowable .... 0.071 in to 0.193 in
  1979 5.0L
    Desired .... 0.096 in to 0.165 in
    Allowable .... 0.071 in to 0.193 in
  1979 5.8L
    Desirable .... 0.123 in to 0.173 in
    Allowable .... 0.098 in to 0.198 in
  1980 all
    Desirable .... 0.123 in to 0.173 in
    Allowable .... 0.098 in to 0.198 in

Camshaft

Endplay
Endplay .... 0.001 in to 0.007 in
Service limit .... 0.009 in

Journal-to-bearing clearance
Journal-to-bearing clearance .... 0.001 in to 0.003 in
Service limit .... 0.006 in

Journal diameter
No. 1 .... 2.0805 in to 2.0815 in
No. 2 .... 2.0655 in to 2.0665 in
No. 3 .... 2.0505 in to 2.0515 in
No. 4 .... 2.0355 in to 2.0365 in
No. 5 .... 2.0205 in to 2.0215 in
Runout limit .... 0.005 in max.
Out-of-round limit .... 0.0005 in max.

Bearing inside diameter
No. 1 .... 2.0825 in to 2.0835 in
No. 2 .... 2.0675 in to 2.0685 in
No. 3 .... 2.0525 in to 2.0535 in
No. 4 .... 2.0375 in to 2.0385 in
No. 5 .... 2.0225 in to 2.0235 in

Front bearing location .... 0.005 in to 0.020 in distance that the front edge of the bearing is below the front edge of the cylinder block

Cylinder block
Head gasket surface flatness .... 0.003 in for every 6 inches; 0.006 in overall

Cylinder bore diameter
4.2L .... 3.6800 in to 3.6835 in
5.0L .... 4.0004 in to 4.0052 in
5.8L .... 4.0000 in to 4.0048 in

Tappet bore diameter .... 0.8752 in to 0.8767 in

Main bearing bore diameter
4.2L and 5.0L .... 2.4412 in to 2.4420 in
5.8L .... 3.1922 in to 3.1930 in

Distributor shaft bearing bore diameter
4.2L and 5.0L .... 0.4525 in to 0.4541 in
5.8L .... 0.5155 in to 0.5171 in

Crankshaft and flywheel
Main bearing journal diameter
4.2L .... 2.2482 in to 2.2490 in
5.0L .... 2.2482 in to 2.2490 in
5.8L .... 2.9994 in to 3.0002 in
Out-of-round limit .... 0.0006 in
Taper limit .... 0.0006 in
Journal runout limit .... 0.002 in
Wear limit .... 0.005 in

Thrust bearing journal length .... 1.137 in to 1.139 in

Connecting rod journal diameter
4.2L and 5.0L .... 2.1228 in to 2.1236 in
5.8L .... 2.3103 in to 2.3111 in
Out-of-round limit .... 0.0006 in max.
Taper limit .... 0.0006 in max.

Main bearing thrust face runout limit .... 0.001 in

Flywheel face runout .... 0.010 in

Flywheel ring gear lateral runout
Manual transmission .... 0.030 in
Automatic transmission .... 0.060 in

Crankshaft free endplay .... 0.004 in to 0.008 in
Service limit .... 0.012 in

Connecting rod bearings
Clearance to crankshaft
    Desired .... 0.0008 in to 0.0015 in
    Allowable .... 0.0008 in to 0.0025 in
Bearing wall thickness (standard*) .... 0.0572 in to 0.0577 in

*For 0.002 in undersize add 0.001 in to standard thickness
Main bearings-to-crankshaft
1975 5.0L
    Desired .... No. 1 bearing 0.001 in to 0.0005 in; all others 0.0005 in to 0.0015 in
    Allowable .... No. 1 bearing 0.0001 in to 0.0020 in; all others 0.0005 to 0.0024 in

1975 5.8L
    Desired .... 0.0008 in to 0.0015 in
    Allowable .... 0.0008 in to 0.0026 in
1976 5.0L
    Desired .... 0.0008 in to 0.0015 in
    Allowable .... No. 1 bearing 0.0001 in to 0.0020 in; all others 0.0005 in to 0.0024 in

1976 5.8L
    Desired .... 0.0008 in to 0.0015 in
    Allowable .... 0.0008 in to 0.0026 in

1977 and 1978 5.0L
    Desired ....   No. 1 bearing 0.0001 in to 0.0015 in;
                                                 all others 0.0005 in to 0.0015 in
    Allowable ....   No. 1 bearing 0.0001 in to 0.0020 in;
                                                 all others 0.0008 in to 0.0026 in

1977 and 1978 5.8L
    Desired .... 0.0008 in to 0.0015 in
    Allowable .... 0.0008 in to 0.0026 in

1979 5.0L
    Desired ....   No. 1 bearing 0.0001 in to 0.0015 in;
                                                   all others 0.0004 in to 0.0015 in
    Allowable ....   No. 1 bearing 0.0001 in to 0.0017 in;
                                                   all others 0.0004 in to 0.0021 in

1979 5.8L
    Desired .... 0.0008 in to 0.0015 in
    Allowable .... 0.0008 in to 0.0026 in
1980 4.2L
    Desired ....   No. 1 bearing 0.0001 in to 0.0015 in;
                                                   all others 0.0008 in to 0.0015 in
    Allowable ....   No. 1 bearing, 0.0961 in to 0.0966 in;
                                                   all others 0.0957 in to 0.0962 in

Bearing wall thickness (standard*)
4.2L and 5.0L ....   No. 1 bearing 0.0961 in to 0.0966 in;
                                                    all others 0.0957 in to 0.0962 in
5.8L .... 0.0957 in to 0.0960 in

*For 0.002 in undersize add 0.001 in to standard thickness
Connecting rods, pistons and rings
Piston pin inside bore diameter
1975 and 1976 .... 0.9104 in to 0.9112 in
1977 thru 1979 .... 0.9096 in to 0.9112 in
1980 .... 0.9124 in to 0.9127 in

Connecting rod bearing bore diameter
4.2L and 5.0L .... 2.2390 in to 2.2398 in
5.8L .... 2.4265 in to 2.4273 in
Out-of-round limit .... 0.0004 in
Taper .... 0.0004 in
Length (center to center)
    4.2L and 5.0L .... 5.0885 in to 5.0915 in
    5.8L .... 5.9450 in to 5.9575 in
Alignment (bore-to-bore max. difference)
    Twist .... 0.024 in
    Bend .... 0.012 in
Side clearance .... 0.010 in to 0.020 in
Service limit .... 0.023 in

Piston diameter (measured at the pin bore centerline at 90° to the pin)
Coded red
    4.2L .... 3.6784 in to 3.6790 in
    5.0L .... 3.9984 in to 3.9990 in
    5.8L .... 3.9978 in to 3.9984 in
Coded blue
    4.2L .... 3.6798 in to 3.6804 in
    5.0L .... 3.9996 in to 4.0002 in
    5.8L .... 3.9990 in to 3.9996 in
    0.003 in oversize
        4.2L .... 3.6812 in to 3.6818 in
        5.0L .... 4.0008 in to 4.0014 in
        5.8L .... 4.0002 in to 4.0008 in
Coded yellow
    5.0L .... 4.0020 in to 4.0026 in
    5.8L .... 4.0014 in to 4.0020 in

Piston-to-bore clearance
.... 0.0018 in to 0.0026 in

Pin bore diameter
4.2L and 5.0L .... 0.9122 in to 0.9126 in
5.8L .... 0.9124 in to 0.9127 in

Ring groove width
Compression (top) .... 0.077 in to 0.078 in
Compression (bottom) .... 0.077 in to 0.078 in

Side clearance

Compression (top) .... 0.002 in to 0.004 in
Compression (bottom) .... 0.002 in to 0.004 in
Oil .... Snug fit
Service limit .... 0.006 in

Ring gap

Compression (top) .... 0.010 in to 0.020 in
Compression (bottom) .... 0.010 in to 0.020 in
Oil ring (steel rail) .... 0.015 in to 0.055 in

Lubrication system
Oil pump

Relief valve spring tension (lbs at specified length)
    4.2L and 5.0L .... 10.6 to 12.2 at 1.704 in
    5.8L .... 18.2 to 20.2 at 2.49 in
Driveshaft-to-housing bearing clearance .... 0.0015 in to 0.0030 in
Relief valve-to-bore clearance .... 0.0015 in to 0.0030 in
Rotor assembly end clearance (assembled) .... 0.004 in max.
Outer race-to-bearing clearance .... 0.001 in to 0.013 in

Torque specifications

	ft-lb	Nm
Carburetor attaching nut	12 to 15	16 to 20
Camshaft sprocket gear-to-camshaft bolt	40 to 45	54 to 61
Camshaft thrust plate-to-cylinder block bolt	9 to 12	12 to 16
Connecting rod nuts		
1975 thru 1979		
5.0L	19 to 24	26 to 32
5.8L	40 to 45	54 to 61
1980 only		
4.2 and 5.8L	19 to 24	26 to 32
5.0L	40 to 45	54 to 61
Cylinder block front cover bolt	12 to 18	16 to 24
Cylinder head bolt		
Step 1	55 to 65	75 to 88
Step 2	65 to 72	88 to 97
Damper-to-crankshaft bolt	70 to 90	95 to 122
EGR valve-to-carburetor spacer	12 to 18	16 to 24
Exhaust manifold-to-cylinder head	18 to 24	24 to 32
Fan-to-water pump hub	12 to 18	16 to 24
Flywheel-to-crankshaft	75 to 85	102 to 115
Intake manifold-to-cylinder head	20 to 22	28 to 30
Main bearing cap bolts		
1975 thru 1979		
5.0L	60 to 70	81 to 95
5.8L	95 to 105	129 to 142
1980 only		
4.2 and 5.8L	60 to 70	81 to 95
5.0L	95 to 105	129 to 142
Oil inlet tube-to-oil pump bolt	10 to 15	14 to 20
Oil pan drain plug	15 to 25	20 to 34
Oil pan-to-cylinder block	9 to 11	12 to 15
Oil pump-to-cylinder block	22 to 32	30 to 43
Oil inlet tube-to-main bearing cap nut	22 to 32	32 to 43
Pulley-to-damper bolt	35 to 50	47 to 68
Rocker arm stud bolt	18 to 35	24 to 47
Spark plug	10 to 15	14 to 22
Valve rocker cover bolt	3 to 5	4 to 7
Water outlet housing bolt	9 to 12	12 to 16
Water pump-to-front cover	12 to 18	16 to 24

1 General information

All V8-equipped models have engines of the same basic design, varying only in displacement. Engines are of 5.8 liter (351 cu in), 5.0 liter (302 cu in) or 4.2 liter (255 cu in) displacement.

All engines have hydraulically operated valve lifters (tappets). The valves and lifters are actuated by a camshaft located in the engine block and driven from the front of the crankshaft via a chain and sprockets.

A gear on the front of the camshaft drives the distributor which in turn drives the oil pump by an intermediate shaft.

2 Engine removal – general

The following operations can be carried out without removing the engine from the vehicle:

Removal and installation of the cylinder heads
Removal and installation of the engine front cover and timing gear
Removal and installation of the engine mounts
Removal and installation of the camshaft
Removal and installation of the oil pan

Removal and installation of the connecting rod bearings, pistons and connecting rods
Removal and installation of the oil pump

2   The engine should be removed for the following operations:

Removal and installation of the flywheel
Removal and installation of the rear main bearing oil seal
Removal and installation of the crankshaft and crankshaft main bearings

3   Engine removal – without transmission

1   Remove the hood (Chapter 12). Disconnect the battery and alternator ground cables at the cylinder block.
2   Drain the radiator and the crankcase into suitable containers.
3   Remove the air cleaner and ducting and disconnect the upper and lower radiator hoses.

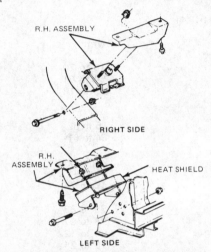

Fig. 2.13 Front engine supports (Secs 3 and 4)

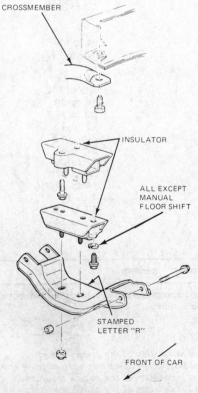

Fig. 2.14 Rear engine supports (Secs 3 and 4)

4   On automatic transmission equipped vehicles, disconnect the transmission oil lines at the radiator.
5   Remove the radiator shroud bolts. Remove the radiator, fan, spacer, drivebelts, pulley and shroud.
6   Loosen the alternator bolts and position the alternator out of the way.
7   Disconnect the oil pressure sending unit wire at the unit. Disconnect the flexible fuel line at the fuel tank line and plug the line from the tank.
8   Disconnect the accelerator cable from the cable.
9   On automatic transmission equipped vehicles, disconnect the throttle valve vacuum line at the intake manifold. Disconnect the manual shift rod and at the shift rod stud, disconnect the retracting spring. Remove the transmission filler tube from the cylinder block.
10   If the vehicle is equipped with air conditioning, the compressor should be unbolted and moved out of the way without disconnecting the hoses. **Note:** *The system is under pressure and if the hoses must be disconnected, the job should be left to a qualified technician.*
11   If equipped with power steering, remove the pump bracket from the cylinder head, remove the drivebelt and position the pump out of the way in a position where the fluid won't drain out.
12   On vacuum assisted brake equipped vehicles, disconnect the brake vacuum line from the intake manifold.
13   Disconnect the heater hoses at the water pump and intake manifold. Remove the coolant sending wire from the sending unit.
14   Remove the upper bolts on the flywheel or converter housing.
15   Remove the wire harness from the left rocker arm cover and position it out of the way. Disconnect the primary wiring connector at the ignition coil and remove the ground strap from the block.
16   Raise the front of vehicle and support it securely.
17   Disconnect the muffler inlet pipe(s) from the exhaust manifold(s).
18   Disconnect the engine support insulators from the brackets on the frame.

Automatic transmission
19   Disconnect the transmission cooler lines from the retainer and remove the converter housing inspection cover. Secure the converter assembly to the housing and remove the remaining converter-to-housing bolts.

Manual transmission
20   Remove the clutch equalizer bar attaching bolts at the frame rail and remove the equalizer from the engine block. Remove the remaining flywheel housing-to-engine bolts.
21   Lower the vehicle and support the transmission.
22   Attach lifting chains to the exhaust manifolds and check to make sure that all cables, controls or emissions hoses are disconnected.
23   Take up the slack in the lifting chains, lift the engine slightly and carefully pull it from the transmission. On automatic transmissions, make sure that the torque converter remains attached to the transmission unit.
24   Lift the engine carefully out of the engine compartment, taking care that the rear cover plate does not contact the radiator brace.
25   With the engine lifted out, lower it to the floor, a firm bench or an engine stand, mounting it securely in an upright position.

4   Engine removal – transmission attached

1   It is not recommended that the engine be removed with the automatic transmission attached, due to the weight involved. Should it be necessary to remove both units, refer to Chapter 7 and remove the transmission first. The engine can then be removed as described in Section 3.
2   To remove the engine with manual transmission attached, follow the procedure described in Section 3, paragraphs 1 through 23, except for those having to do with the automatic transmission.
3   Remove the gearshift lever, referring to Chapter 7.
4   From beneath the car, remove the transmission drain plug and allow the oil to drain for five minutes. Replace the plug.
5   After marking its position, remove the driveshaft (refer to Chapter 8).
6   Support the weight of the transmission with a small jack.
7   Remove the bolts attaching the crossmember to the transmission extension and the body and remove the crossmember.

8   Check that all cables and controls have been detached and are out of the way.

9   With the jack still in position under the transmission, start lifting and moving the engine forward.

10   Because the transmission is attached, the engine will have to be lifted out at an extreme angle. As the weight is toward the rear, it will be fairly easy to achieve this angle.

12   Continue to raise the engine and move it forward at the necessary angle. At this stage the forward edge of the bellhousing is likely to catch against the front crossmember and the tail of the gearbox will need raising until the whole unit is forward and clear of it.

13   As the maximum height of the lifting tackle is reached, it will be necessary to switch the entire engine/transmission unit so that the tail can be lifted clear while the hoist is moved away or the vehicle is lowered from the jack stands and rolled rearward.

14   The whole unit should be lowered to the ground or workbench as soon as possible and the transmission separated from the engine.

5   Engine dismantling – general

Ideally, the engine should be mounted on a proper stand for overhaul but it is anticipated that most owners will have a strong bench on which to place it instead. If a sufficiently large strong bench is not available, then the work can be done at ground level. It is essential, however, that some form, of substantial wooden surface is available. Timber should be at least $\frac{3}{4}$ inch thick, otherwise the weight of the engine will cause projections to punch holes straight through it.

It will save a great deal of time later if the exterior of the engine is thoroughly cleaned down before any dismantling begins. This can be done by using a solvent which can be brushed on and then the dirt sprayed off with a water jet. This will dispose of all the heavy muck and grit once and for all so that later cleaning of individual components will be a relatively clean process.

As the engine is stripped down, clean each part as it comes off. Try to avoid immersing parts with oilways in solvent as pockets of liquid could remain and cause oil dilution in the critical first few revolutions after reassembly. Clean oilways with pipe cleaners. or, preferably, an air jet.

Where possible avoid damaging gaskets on removal, especially if new ones have not been obtained. They can be used as patterns if new ones have to be specially cut.

It is helpful to obtain a few blocks of wood to support the engine while it is in the process of being dismantled. Start dismantling at the top of the engine and then turn the block over and deal with the oil pan and crankshaft etc. afterwards.

Nuts and bolts should be refitted in their locations where possible to avoid confusion later. As an alternative keep each group of nuts and bolts (all the timing gear cover bolts for example) together in a jar or can.

Many items when dismantled must be refitted in the same position, if they are not being replaced. These include valves, rocker arms, valve lifters, pistons, pushrods, bearings and connecting rods. Some of these are marked on assembly to avoid any possibility of mixing them up during overhaul. Others are not, and it is a great help if adequate preparation is made in advance to classify these parts. Suitably labelled cardboard boxes or trays should be used. The time spent in this preparation will be amply repaid later.

6   Engine accessories – removal

1   Before beginning a complete overhaul, or if the engine is being exchanged for a rebuilt unit, the following items should be removed:

Fuel system components:
    Carburetor
    Intake and exhaust manifolds
    Fuel pump
    Fuel lines
Ignition system components:
    Spark plugs
    Distributor
    Coil
Electrical system components (if not removed already):
    Alternator and mounting brackets
    Starter motor

Cooling system components:
    Fan and fan pulley
    Water pump thermostat housing and thermostat
Engine:
    Crankcase ventilation tube
    Oil filter element
    Oil pressure sender unit (if fitted)
    Oil level dipstick
    Oil filler cap
    Engine mounting brackets
Clutch:
    Clutch pressure plate and total assembly
    Clutch friction plate and total assembly
Optional equipment:
    Air conditioning compressor
    Power steering pump
    Thermactor pump

7   Cylinder heads – removal with engine in vehicle

1   Open the hood.

2   For safety reasons disconnect the battery.

3   Remove the air cleaner from the carburetor installation, as described in Chapter 4.

4   Disconnect the accelerator linkage from the carburetor.

5   Refer to Chapter 3 and drain the cooling system.

6   Detach the HT leads from the spark plugs, release the distributor cap securing clips and remove the distributor cap.

7   Loosen the clips and disconnect the hose from the water pump to the water outlet.

8   Detach the vacuum pipe from the distributor body and carburetor installation.

9   Refer to Chapter 4, and remove the carburetor and inlet manifold assembly. This will necessitate removal of the distributor.

10   Remove the two rocker covers by undoing and removing the securing screws and lifting away together with their rspective gaskets.

11   Loosen the alternator adjusting arm bolt and remove the alternator mounting bracket bolt and spacer. Push the alternator down out of the way.

12   Remove the accelerator shaft bracket from the left-hand cylinder head and position it out of the way.

13   Loosen the rocker arm stud nuts just enough to enable the rocker arms to be rotated to one side.

14   Lift out the pushrods and keep them in the correct order of removal by pushing them through a piece of cardboard with the valve numbers marked on it (1 to 6).

15   Detach the exhaust downpipes from the exhaust manifold and move the downpipes to the sides of the engine compartment. Leave the manifolds in place as they will act as a lever to assist removal of the heads.

16   Taking each cylinder head in turn, loosen the eight holding down bolts in the order shown. When all are free of tension remove all the bolts.

17   On occasions the heads may have stuck to the head gasket and cylinder block, in which case if pulling up on the exhaust manifolds does not free them they should be struck smartly with a soft faced hammer in order to break the joints. **Do not** try to pry them off with a blade of any description or damage will be caused to the faces of the head or block, or both.

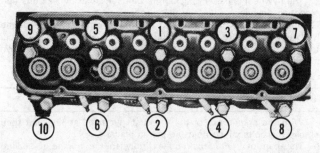

Fig. 2.15 Cylinder head bolt loosening and tightening sequence (Secs 7 and 44)

18 With the help of an assistant, lift off the cylinder heads, remove them from the vehicle and place them on the workbench. Remove the exhaust manifolds.

19 Remove the cylinder head gaskets. New ones will be required for reassembly.

8 Cylinder heads – removal with engine out

Follow the sequence given in Section 7, paragraphs 6 to 19 inclusive, disregarding information on parts mentioned that have been previously removed.

9 Cylinder heads – dismantling of valves and springs

1 Remove the rocker arm retaining nuts and lift off the fulcrum seats and rocker arms.

2 Lay the cylinder head on its side and using a proper valve spring compressor place the 'U' shaped end over the spring retainer and screw on the valve head so as to compress the spring.

3 Sometimes the retainer will stick, in which case the end of the compressor over the springs should be tapped with a hammer to release the retainer from the locks (collets).

4 As the spring is compressed two tapered locks will be exposed and should be taken from the recess in the retainer.

5 When the compressor is released the spring may be removed from the valve. Lift off the retainer, spring and oil seal. Withdraw the valve from the cylinder head.

6 It is essential that the valves, springs, retainer, locks and seals are all kept in order so that they may be refitted in the original positions.

10 Valve lifters – removal

1 Remove the valve lifters and lay them out in the correct order of removal so that they may be refitted in their original bores.

2 Use a magnet to remove the tappets from the bores.

11 Crankshaft damper – removal

1 Remove the retaining bolts and remove the pulley wheel from the front of the damper.

2 Remove the bolt and washer locating the damper to the front of the crankshaft. The damper is keyed to the crankshaft and must be drawn off with a proper socket puller. Attempts to lever it off with long bladed articles such as screwdrivers or tire levers are not suitable in this case because the timing cover behind the damper is a light and relatively fragile casting. Any pressure against it could certainly crack it and possibly break a hole in it.

3 The damper may be removed with the engine in the car but it will be necessary to remove the radiator, and drivebelts.

4 Recover the Woodruff key from the crankshaft nose.

12 Flywheel – removal

1 Remove the clutch assembly, as described in Chapter 8.

2 The flywheel is held in position to the crankshaft by six bolts and a locating dowel.

3 Remove the six bolts, taking care to support the weight of the flywheel as they are slackened off in case it slips off the flange. Remove it carefully, taking care not to damage the mating surfaces on the crankshaft and flywheel.

13 Oil pan – removal

1 With the engine out of the car, first invert the engine and then remove the bolts which hold the pan in place.

2 The pan may be stuck quite firmly to the engine if sealing compound has been used on the gasket. It is in order to lever it off in this case. The gasket should be removed and discarded in any case.

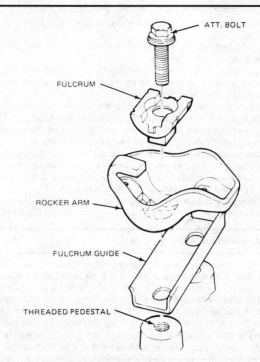

Fig. 2.16 Rocker arm components (Sec 9)

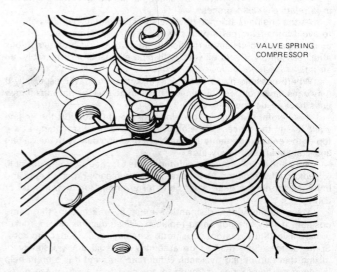

Fig. 2.17 Removing valve locks (Sec 9)

3 The oil pan can be removed with the engine still fitted in the vehicle but it is first necessary to raise the engine within the engine compartment approximately 4 inches to provide the necessary clearance.

4 Open the hood and drain the cooling system as described in Chapter 3.

5 Jack up the front of the vehicle, support it on jack stands and drain the engine oil into a suitable container. If vehicle is equipped with a dual sump oil pan, both drain plugs must be removed to thoroughly drain the crankcase.

6 Refer to Section 3 and disconnect all controls and components that will impede the upward movement of the engine; this will include the radiator shroud and hoses, the two front exhaust pipes, the air cleaner and carburetor linkage, alternator and transmission linkage etc. Disconnect the steering flex coupling and remove the 2 bolts attaching the steering gear to the frame crossmember. Rest the steering gear on the frame away from the oil pan.

7 Remove the converter inspection cover and the front engine

mounting securing nuts. Place a jack and wooden block under the oil pan and slowly raise the engine at least 4 inches. Place wooden blocks between the engine and crossmember to hold it in the raised position. Remove the jack.

8 Remove all the retaining bolts and lower the oil pan as far as possible, unbolt the oil pump assembly from inside the crankcase. Allow it to drop into the oil pan and withdraw the oil pan complete with pump.

9 Remove the oil pan gasket. A new one must be obtained for reassembly.

14 Front cover – removal

1 With the engine out of the car, remove the oil pan, crankshaft pulley wheel and damper. Disconnect the fuel pump outlet line, unbolt the fuel pump and move it to one side with the fuel line still attached.

2 Remove the water pump retaining bolts and lift the water pump from the front cover. It may be necessary to tap it with a soft-faced mallet if a jointing compound has been used.

3 Remove the front cover securing nuts and lift it away. If it is stuck, carry out the instructions in paragraph 2. Remove the front cover gasket.

4 If the engine is still in the vehicle it will be necessary to remove the front oil pan bolts which run through the timing cover. It will also be necessary to remove the fan belt, crankshaft pulley wheel and fuel pump.

15 Timing chain and sprockets – removal

1 Remove the front timing chain cover as described in the previous Section and withdraw the oil slinger from the front of the crankshaft.

2 Remove the camshaft sprocket securing bolt and remove the fuel pump eccentric from the sprocket. Replace the front damper bolt and use a wrench to rotate the engine until the sprocket timing marks are aligned.

3 Using a suitable puller, withdraw the crankshaft sprocket and, if necessary the camshaft sprocket; remove both sprockets and chain as a complete assembly.

4 Recover the Woodruff key from the groove in the crankshaft.

5 To test the chain for wear, refer to Section 34 of this Chapter.

16 Camshaft – removal

1 The camshaft can be removed with the engine in the vehicle. Should camshaft replacement be necessary it will probably be necessary to overhaul other parts of the engine too. If this is the case engine removal should be considered.

2 Refer to Chapter 3 and remove the radiator.

3 Detach the spark plug leads from the spark plugs, release the cap securing clips and place the cap to one side.

4 Detach the distributor vacuum line and then remove the distributor as described in Chapter 5.

5 Remove the alternator as described in Chapter 11.

6 Remove the screws that secure each rocker cover to the cylinder heads. Lift away the rocker covers and gaskets.

7 Refer to Chapter 3 and remove the intake manifold and carburetor installation.

8 Loosen the rocker arm retaining nuts just enough to enable the rocker arms to be rotated to one side.

9 Remove the pushrods and note each rod's original location, and also which way up they are fitted. Keep them in order and the right way up by pushing them through a piece of stiff card with valve numbers marked.

10 Refer to Section 14 and remove the front cover.

11 Refer to Section 15 and remove the camshaft timing sprocket and chain.

12 Remove the 2 screws which secure the camshaft thrust plate to the cylinder block face. Lift away the plate and spacer.

13 Using a magnet, recover the valve lifters from the 'Vee' in the cylinder block. Keep in order as they must be replaced in their original positions.

14 If any valve lifters cannot be removed, retain in their maximum height positions with clips.

15 The camshaft may now be drawn forwards through the cylinder block. Take care that the sharp edges of the cams do not damage the bearings.

17 Oil pump – removal

1 Refer to Section 13 and remove the oil pan.

2 Remove the 2 bolts that secure the pump to the crankcase. Lift away the pump and recover the gasket.

3 The long hexagonal section driveshaft will come out with the pump. This is driven by the distributor shaft.

18 Pistons, connecting rods and bearings – removal

1 Pistons and connecting rods may be removed with the engine in the vehicle, provided the oil pan and cylinder heads are first removed. The bearing shells may be removed with the heads on.

2 Loosen the two nuts holding each bearing cap to the connecting rod. Use a good quality socket wrench for this work. A box wrench may be used for removal only – not replacement which calls for a special torque wrench. Having slackened the nuts 2 or 3 turns tap the caps to dislodge them from the connecting rods. Completely remove the nuts and lift away the end caps.

3 Each bearing cap normally has the cylinder number etched on one end as does the connecting rod. However, this must be verified and if in doubt the cap should be marked with a dab of paint or punch mark to ensure that its relationship with the connecting rod and its numerical position in the cylinder block is not altered.

4 The piston and connecting rod may then be pushed out of the top of each cylinder.

5 The connecting rod bearing shells can be removed from the connecting rod and cap by sliding them round in the direction of the notch at the end of the shell and lifting them out. If they are not being replaced it is vital they are not interchanged – either between pistons or between cap and connecting rod.

19 Piston rings – removal

1 Remove the pistons from the engine.

2 The rings come off over the top of the pistons. Starting with the top one, lift one end of the ring out of the groove and gradually ease it out all the way round. With the second and third rings an old feeler blade is useful for sliding them over the other grooves. However, as rings are only normally removed if they are going to be replaced it should not matter if breakages occur.

20 Piston pin – removal

The piston pins need removing if the pistons are being replaced. New pistons are supplied with new pins for fitting to the existing connecting rods. The piston pin is semi-floating, that is it is a tight shrink fit with the connecting rod and a moving fit in the piston. To press it out requires considerable force and under usual circumstances a proper press and special tools are essential, otherwise piston damage will occur. If damage to the pistons does not matter, then the pins may be pressed out using suitable diameter pieces of rod and tube between the jaws of a vise. However, this is not recommended as the connecting rod might be damaged also. It is recommended that piston pins and pistons are removed from, and refitted to, connecting rods, by Ford dealers with the necessary facilities.

21 Crankshaft rear oil seal – removal and installation

1 It is possible to remove the crankshaft rear oil seal with the engine in or out of the vehicle. Where the engine is being completely removed, refer to Section 22 and remove the crankshaft. Remove the two halves of the seal from the upper rear main bearing and cap.

2 With the engine in the vehicle, drain the engine oil and remove the oil pan and pump as described in Section 13.

3   Undo the two bolts and carefully pry the rear main bearing cap from the crankshaft. Remove the oil seal from the cap and if a locating pin is fitted in the bottom of the groove in the cap, drive it out using a pin punch.

4   Loosen all the main bearing cap bolts to enable the crankshaft to drop down slightly, but not more than $\frac{1}{32}$ in (0.002 mm).

5   Using a piece of brass rod, push one end of the upper half of the oil seal upwards to rotate it around the crankshaft. When the other end of the seal is protruding sufficiently, grip it with a pair of pliers and carefully pull it out while continuing to push on the other end with the piece of wire. Great care must be taken not to scratch the crankshaft oil seal surface.

6   Clean out the oil seal grooves in the cylinder block and cap using a suitable solvent.

7   Soak the new rubber seals in clean engine oil prior to fitting.

8   Fit the upper half of the seal in the cylinder block with the inner lip facing towards the front of the engine. Slide the seal around the crankshaft until $\frac{3}{8}$ in (9 mm) protrudes from the base of the block.

9   Repeat the procedure for the lower half of the seal, allowing an equal amount of seal to protrude beyond the opposite end of the bearing cap.

10 Fit the rear bearing cap and seal ensuring the protruding ends of the seals correctly enter the respective grooves. Apply a bead of sealer to the rear corners of the block and sides of the cap.

11 Tighten all the main bearing cap bolts to the specified torque wrench setting.

12 Fit the oil pan seals and gaskets and refit the oil pump and oil pan as described in Sections 41 and 43 respectively.

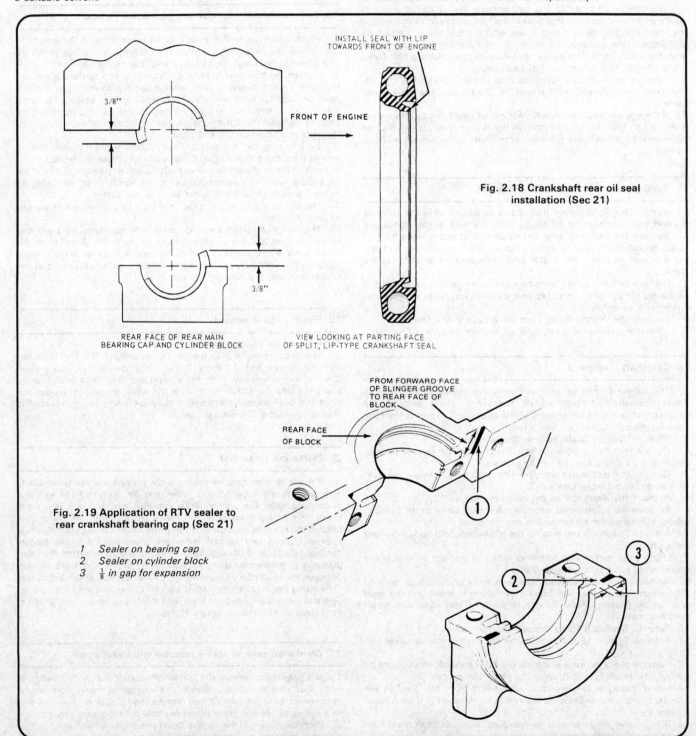

Fig. 2.18 Crankshaft rear oil seal installation (Sec 21)

Fig. 2.19 Application of RTV sealer to rear crankshaft bearing cap (Sec 21)

1   *Sealer on bearing cap*
2   *Sealer on cylinder block*
3   *$\frac{1}{8}$ in gap for expansion*

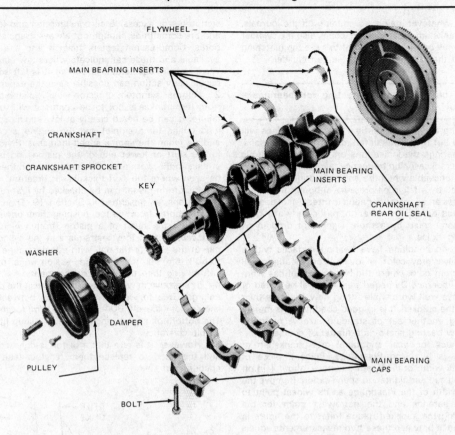

Fig. 2.20 Crankshaft, bearings and components (Sec 22)

22 Main bearings and crankshaft – removal

1 The engine should be taken from the vehicle and the oil pan cylinder heads, timing gears and pistons removed.
2 With a good quality socket wrench undo the ten bolts holding the five main bearing caps.
3 When all the bolts are removed lift out the caps. If they are tight, tap the sides gently with a piece of wood or soft mallet to dislodge them.
4 On some engines the main bearing caps are marked from 1 - 5. However, if they are not, identify the position of each cap with paint marks or light center punch marks to ensure correct reassembly.
5 Lift out the crankshaft from the cylinder block taking care not to damage the journals.
6 Slide out the bearing shells from the cylinder block and bearing caps noting that the center shells also function as thrust bearings.

23 Lubrication and crankcase ventilation systems – description

1 The oil pump is located in the crankcase and is driven from the distributor by a hexagonal driveshaft. An oil pressure relief valve is incorporated in the pump body. Oil under pressure is directed via a full flow filter to the main, connecting rod and camshaft bearings and to the hydraulic valve lifters pushrods and rocker arms.
2 A drilling in the front cylinder block face enables oil to pass through to the timing chain and sprocket.
3 Oil from the valve gear drains down over the camshaft lobes and distributor drive gear before passing back into the oil pan.
4 The cylinder bores are lubricated by a squirt of oil from a drilling in each connecting rod. The piston pins are lubricated continuously by the oil mist thrown up inside the crankcase.
5 The crankcase has a positive ventilation system (PCV). Instead of allowing engine fumes to escape into the atmosphere they are drawn back into the engine via a hose and non-return valve connected between the oil filler cap on the rocker cover and the intake manifold.

24 Oil filter – removal and installation

1 The oil filter is a complete throw-away cartridge screwed into the left-hand side of the engine block. Simply unscrew the old unit, clean the seating on the block and screw the new one in, taking care not to cross the thread. Continue until the sealing ring just touches the block face. Then tighten one half turn. Always run the engine and check for signs of leaks after installation.

25 Engine components – examination for wear

1 When the engine has been stripped down and all parts properly cleaned, decisions have to be made as to what needs replacement and the following Sections tell the examiner what to look for. In any border-line case it is always best to decide in favor of a new part. Even if a part may still be serviceable its life will have been reduced by wear and the degree of trouble needed to replace it in the future must be taken into consideration. However, these things are relative and it depends on whether a quick 'survival' job is being done or whether the car as a whole is being regarded as having many thousands of miles of useful and economical life remaining.

26 Crankshaft – inspection and overhaul

1 Look at the 5 main bearing journals and the 8 crankpins and if there are any scratches or score marks then the shaft will need grinding. Such conditions will nearly always be accompanied by similar deterioration in the matching bearing shells.
2 Each bearing journal should also be round and can be checked with a micrometer or caliper gauge around the periphery at several points. If there is more than 0.006 in (0.0152 mm) of ovality regrinding is necessary.
3 A Ford dealer or engine rebuilder will be able to decide to what extent regrinding is necessary and also supply the special under-size

shell bearings to match whatever may need grinding off the journals.

4   Before taking the crankshaft for regrinding, check also the cylinder bores and pistons as it may be more convenient to have the matching operations performed at the same time by the same rebuilder.

27 Crankshaft (main) bearings and connecting rod bearings – inspection and overhaul

1   With careful servicing and regular oil filter changes bearings will last for a very long time but they can still fail for unforeseen reasons. With connecting rod bearings the indications are a regular rhythmic loud knocking from the crankcase, the frequency depending on engine speed. It is particularly noticeable when the engine is under load. This symptom is accompanied by a fall in oil pressure although this is not normally noticeable unless an oil pressure gauge is fitted. Main bearing failure is usually indicated by serious vibration, particularly at higher engine revolutions, accompanied by a more significant drop in oil pressure and a 'rumbling' noise.

2   Bearing shells in good condition have bearing surfaces with a smooth, even, matte silver/grey color all over. Worn bearings will show patches of a different color where the bearing metal has worn away and exposed the underlay. Damaged bearings will be pitted or scored. It is nearly always well worthwhile fitting new shells as their cost is relatively low. If the crankshaft is in good condition it is merely a question of obtaining another set of standard size. A reground crankshaft will need new bearing shells as a matter of course.

3   A good way to check for wear and taper of a crankshaft or connecting rod journal is by using Plastigage. Place a piece of Plastigage across the full width of the bearing surface, about $\frac{1}{4}$ in off center, install the bearing cap and tighten to specification. Remove the cap and measure the width of the Plastigage as its widest point to obtain the minimum clearance and the narrowest point for the maximum clearance using the supplied gauge (refer to the figure in Chapter 2A). The difference between these two measurements equals the taper. Be sure to remove all traces of the Plastigage from the journal after measurement.

28 Cylinder bores – inspection and overhaul

1   A new cylinder is perfectly round and the walls parallel throughout its length. The action of the pistons tends to wear the walls at right angles to the wrist pin due to side thrust. This wear takes place principally on that section of the cylinder swept by the piston rings.

2   It is possible to get an indication of bore wear by removing the cylinder heads with the engine still in the car. With the piston down in the bore first signs of wear can be seen and felt just below the top of the bore where the top piston ring reaches and there will be a noticeable lip. If there is no lip it is fairly reasonable to expect that bore wear is low and any lack of compression or excessive oil consumption is due to worn or broken piston rings or pistons (see next Section).

3   If it is possible to obtain a bore measuring micrometer, measure the bore in the thrust plane below the lip and again at the bottom of the cylinder in the same plane. If the difference is more than 0.010 inch (0.254 mm) then a rebore is necessary. similarly, a difference of 0.005 inch (0.127 mm) or more across the bore diameter is a sign of ovality calling for a rebore.

4   Any bore which is significantly scratched or scored will need reboring. This symptom usually indicates that the piston or rings are damaged in that cylinder. In the event of only one cylinder being in need of reboring it will still be necessary for all eight to be bored and fitted with new oversize pistons and rings. Your Ford dealer or local machine shop will be able to rebore and obtain the necessary matched pistons. If the crankshaft is undergoing regrinding it is a good idea to let the same firm renovate and reassemble the crankshaft and pistons to the block. A reputable firm normally gives a guarantee for such work. In cases where engines have been rebored already to their maximum, new cylinder liners are available which may be installed. In such cases the same reboring processes have to be followed and the services of a machine shop are required.

29 Pistons and piston rings – inspection and overhaul

1   Worn pistons and rings can usually be diagnosed when the

symptoms of excessive oil consumption and low compression occur and are sometimes, though not always associated with worn cylinder bores. Compression testers that fit into the spark plug holes are available and these can indicate where low compression is occurring. Wear usually accelerates the more it is left so when the symptoms occur, early action can possibly save the expense of a rebore.

2   Another symptom of piston wear is piston slap – a knocking noise from the crankcase not to be confused with connecting rod bearing failure. It can be heard clearly at low engine speed when there is no load (idling for example) and the engine is cold, and is much less audible when the engine speed increases. Piston wear usually occurs in the skirt or lower end of the piston and is indicated by vertical streaks in the worn area which is always on the thrust side. It can also be seen where the skirt thickness is different.

3   Piston ring wear can be checked by first removing the rings from the pistons, as described in Section 19. Then place the rings in the cylinder bores from the top, pushing them down about 1.5 inches (38 mm) with the head of a piston (from which the rings have been removed) so that they rest square in the cylinder. Then measure the gap at the ends of the ring with a feeler gauge. If it exceeds 0.020 in (0.508 mm) for the top compression rings, or 0.055 in for the oil control ring then they need replacement.

4   The groove in which the rings locate in the piston can also become enlarged due to wear. The clearance between the ring and piston should not exceed 0.004 in (0.1016 mm) for the top and second ring. The bottom oil control ring should be a snug fit in the groove with no visible clearance.

5   However, it is rare that a piston is only worn in the ring grooves and the need to replace them for this fault alone is hardly ever encountered.

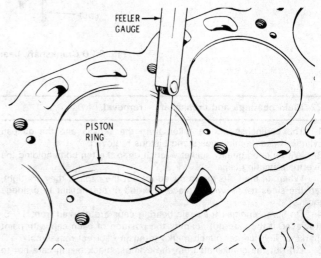

Fig. 2.21 Measure ring end gap at the bottom of ring travel to determine wear (Sec 29)

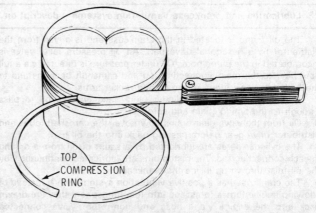

Fig. 2.22 Measuring piston ring side gap (Sec 29)

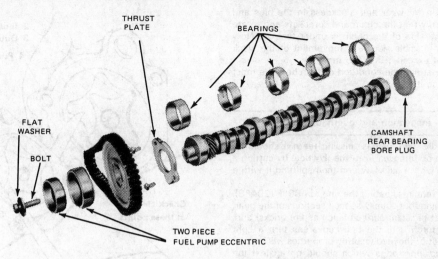

THRUST PLATE

BEARINGS

FLAT WASHER

BOLT

CAMSHAFT REAR BEARING BORE PLUG

TWO PIECE FUEL PUMP ECCENTRIC

Fig. 2.23 Camshaft and components (Sec 31)

30 Connecting rods and piston pins – inspection

1 Piston pins are a shrink fit into the connecting rods. Neither of these components would normally need replacement unless the pistons were being changed, in which case the new pistons would automatically be supplied with new pins.
2 Connecting rods are not subject to wear but in extreme circumstances such as engine seizure, they could be distorted. Such conditions may be visually apparent but where doubt exists they should be changed. The bearing caps should also be examined for indications of filing down which may have been attempted in the mistaken idea that bearing looseness could be remedied in this way. If there are such signs then the connecting rods should be replaced.

31 Camshaft and camshaft bearings – inspection

   The camshaft bearings should be examined for signs of scoring and pitting. If they need replacement they will have to be dealt with professionally as, although it may be relatively easy to remove the old ones, the correct fitting of new ones requires special tools. If they are not fitted evenly and square from the very start they can be distorted, thus causing localized wear in a very short time. See your Ford dealer or local machine shop for this work.
2 The camshaft itself may show signs of wear on the bearing journals, cam lobes or the skew gear. The main decision to take is what degree of wear justifies replacement which is costly. Any signs of scoring or damage to the bearing journals must be rectified and as under-size bearing brushes are not supplied the journals cannot be reground. Replacement of the whole camshaft is the only solution. Similarly, excessive wear on the skew gear which can be seen where the distributor driveshaft teeth mesh, will mean replacement of the whole camshaft.
3 The cam lobes themselves may show signs of ridging or pitting on the high points. If the ridging is light then it may be possible to smooth it out with fine emery cloth. The cam lobes, however, are surface hardened and once this is penetrated wear will be very rapid thereafter. The cams are also offset and tapered to cause the valve lifters to rotate – thus ensuring that wear is even – so do not mistake this condition for wear.

32 Valve lifters – inspection

1 The faces of the valve lifters which bear on the camshaft should show no signs of pitting, scoring or other forms of wear. They should also not be a loose fit in their housing. Wear is only normally encountered at very high mileages or in cases of neglected engine lubrication.
2 Although it is possible to dismantle the valve lifters by removing

the spring clip and tapping out the valve assembly, it is not worthwhile fitting new components to an old valve body and the best policy is to replace all the valve lifters whenever a major engine overhaul is carried out.

33 Valves and valve seats – inspection and overhaul

1 With the valve removed from the cylinder heads examine the heads for signs of cracking, burning away and pitting of the edge where it seats in the port. The seats of the valves in the cylinder head should also be examined for the same signs. Usually it is the valve that deteriorates first but if a bad valve is not rectified the seat will suffer and this is more difficult to repair.
2 Providing the valve heads and seats are not cracked or badly pitted, minor burn marks and blemishes can be removed by using carborundum paste.
3 This may be done by placing a smear of carborundum paste on the edge of the valve and, using a suction type valve holder, lapping the valve in place. This is done with a semi-rotary action, twisting the handle of the valve holder between the hands and lifting it occasionally to redistribute the paste. Use a coarse paste to start with and finish with a fine paste. As soon as a matt grey unbroken line appears on both the valve and the seat the valve is 'lapped-in'. All traces of carbon should also be cleaned from the head and the neck of the valve stem. A wire brush mounted in a power drill is a quick and effective way of doing this.
4 If an exhaust valve requires replacement it should be lapped into the seat in the same way as an old valve.
5 Another form of valve wear can occur on the stem where it runs in the guide in the cylinder head. This can be detected by trying to rock the valve from side to side. If there is any movement at all it is an indication that the valve stem or guide is worn. Check the stem first with a micrometer at points all along and around its length and if they are not within the specified size new valves will probably solve the problem. If the guides are worn, however, they will need reboring for oversize valves or for fitting guide inserts. The valve seats will also need recutting to ensure they are concentric with the stems. This work should be given to your Ford dealer or local machine shop.
6 When all valve lapping is completed it is essential that every trace of paste is removed from the valves and ports in the cylinder head. This should be done by a thorough washing in gasoline or kerosene and blowing out with a jet of air. If particles of carborundum paste should work their way into the engine they would cause havoc with bearings or cylinder walls.

34 Timing chain and sprockets – inspection and overhaul

1 Examine the sprocket teeth for excessive wear and replace if necessary.

2   Check the timing chain for wear and slackness in the pins and
links. As a guide, temporarily refit the chain and sprockets and rotate
the crankshaft so that one side of the chain is under tension. Now
check that the maximum possible sideways movement of the slack
side of the chain does not exceed $\frac{1}{2}$ in (12.5 mm).
3   If any doubt exists regarding the condition of the chain the most
sensible policy is to replace it.

35 Flywheel ring gear – inspection and overhaul

1   If the ring gear is badly worn or has missing teeth it should be
replaced. The old ring can be removed from the flywheel by cutting a
notch between two teeth with a hacksaw and then splitting it with a
cold chisel.
2   To fit a new ring gear requires heating the ring to 400°F (204°C).
This can be done by polishing four equally spaced sections of the gear,
laying it on a suitable heat resistant surface (such as fire bricks) and,
heating it evenly with a torch until the polished areas turn a light
yellow tint. Do not overheat or the hard wearing properties will be lost.
The gear has a chamfered inner edge which should go against the
shoulder when put on the flywheel. When hot enough place the gear
in position quickly, tapping it home if necessary and let it cool naturally
without quenching in any way.

36 Oil pump – inspection

1   The oil pump maintains a pressure of around 40 to 60 psi. An oil
pressure gauge is fitted to give earlier warning of falling oil pressure
due either to overheating, pump failure or bearing wear.
2   At a major engine overhaul it is as well to check the pump and
exchange it for a reconditioned unit if necessary. The efficient
operation of the oil pump depends on the finely machined tolerances
between the moving parts of the rotor and the body and reconditioning
of these is generally not within the competence of the non-specialist
owner.
3   To dismantle the pump, first remove it from the engine, as
described in Section 17.
4   Remove the two bolts holding the end cover to the body and
remove the cover and relief valve parts which will be released.
5   Remove the four bolts securing the rotor end plate.
6   The necessary clearances may now be checked using a machined
straight edge (a good steel rule) and a feeler gauge.
7   On bi-rotor type pumps the critical clearances are between the
lobes of the center rotor and convex faces of the outer rotor, between
the outer rotor and the pump body, and between both rotors and the
end cover plate.
8   The rotor lobe clearances may be checked as shown in the
accompanying figure. The clearances should not exceed 0.006 in
(0.152 mm). The clearance between the outer rotor and pump body
should not exceed 0.013 in (0.330 mm).
9   The endfloat clearance can be measured by placing a straight edge
across the end of the pump and measuring the gap between the rotors
and the straight edge. The gap on either rotor should not exceed 0.005
in (0.127 mm).
10 If any clearances are out of specification, the oil pump must be
replaced with a new one.
11 When reassembling the pump and refitting the end cover, make
sure that the interior is scrupulously clean and that the pressure relief
valve parts are assembled in the correct positions.

37 Cylinder heads and piston crowns – cleaning

1   When cylinder heads are removed either in the course of an
overhaul or for inspection of bores or valve condition when the engine
is in the vehicle, it is normal to remove all carbon deposits from the
piston crowns and heads.
2   This is best done with a cup-shaped wire brush and an electric drill
and is fairly straightforward when the engine is dismantled and the
pistons removed. Sometimes hard spots of carbon are not easily
removed except by a scraper. When cleaning the pistons with a
scraper take care not to damage the surface of the piston in any way.
3   When the engine is in the vehicle certain precautions must be

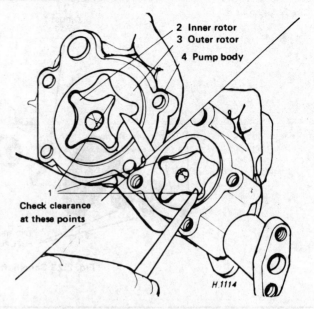

2 Inner rotor
3 Outer rotor
4 Pump body

Check clearance at these points

H.1114

Fig. 2.24 Checking oil pump rotor side clearances (Sec 36)

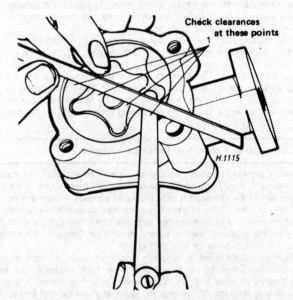

Check clearances at these points

H.1115

Fig. 2.25 Checking oil pump rotor endfloat (Sec 36)

taken when removing the piston crowns, in order to prevent dislodged
pieces of carbon falling into the interior of the engine which could
cause damage to cylinder bores, pistons and rings – or if allowed into
the water passages – damage to the water pump. Turn the engine,
therefore, so that the piston being worked on is at the top of its stroke
and then mask off the adjacent cylinder bore and all surrounding water
jacket orifices with paper and adhesive tape. Press grease into the gap
all round the piston to keep carbon particles out and then scrape all
carbon away by hand carefully. Do not use a power drill and wire brush
when the engine is in the car as it will be virtually impossible to keep
all the carbon dust clear of the engine. When completed carefully clear
out the grease round the rim of the piston with a matchstick or
something similar – bringing any carbon particles with it. Repeat the
process on the other seven piston crowns. It is not recommended that
a ring of carbon is left round the edge of the piston on the theory that
it will reduce oil consumption. This was valid in the earlier days of long
stroke low revving engines but modern engines, fuels and lubricants
cause less carbon deposits anyway and any left behind tends merely
to cause hot spots.

38 Oil pan – inspection

1· Wash out the oil pan with the proper solvent and wipe dry. Inspect the exterior for signs of damage or excessive rust. If evident, a new oil pan must be obtained. To ensure an oil tight joint scrape away all traces of old gasket from the cylinder block mating face.

39 Engine reassembly – general

All components of the engine must be cleaned of oil, sludge and old gasket and the working area should also be cleared and clean. In addition to the normal range of good quality socket wrenches and general tools which are essential, the following must be available before reassembling begins:

Complete set of new gaskets
Supply of clean lint-free cloths
Clean oil can full of new engine oil
Torque wrench
All new spare parts as necessary

40 Engine reassembly – camshaft and crankshaft

1   Insert the camshaft carefully into the block, taking care not to let any of the cam lobes damage the bearing (photo).
2   Replace the camshaft thrust plate and secure it with the two screws. These screws must be tightened firmly.
3   Ensure that the crankcase is thoroughly clean and that all oilways are clear. A thin twist drill is useful for cleaning the oilways, or if possible they may be blown out with compressed air. Treat the crankshaft in the same fashion, and then inject engine oil into the oilways.
4   Select the halves of the five main bearing shells that have the oil slots and grooves and fit them into the crankcase bearing housings Ensure that the notches in the ends of the shells are correctly located in the cut-outs in the housing.
5   Note that the center main bearing shells have flanges, which act as thrust washers. These are available in various thicknesses in order to be able to set the crankshaft endfloat.
6   Push the upper half of the crankshaft oil seal into the recess at the rear of the crankcase. For further information on fitting the rear crankshaft oil seal refer to Section 21.
7   Lubricate the crankshaft journals with engine oil and carefully lower the crankshaft into position.
8   Fit the lower (plain) shells into the main bearing caps.
9   Push the lower half of the crankshaft oil seal into the recess in the rear main bearing cap.
10 Fit the rear and main bearing caps over the crankshaft and temporarily tighten the retaining bolts.
11 Check the crankshaft endfloat using the feeler gauges (photo). If the endfloat is not within 0.004 – 0.008 in (0.101 – 0.202 mm) the crankshaft should be removed and the center thrust bearings replaced with ones of the necessary thickness to achieve this tolerance.
12 When the crankshaft endfloat is correct, fit all the main bearing caps and retaining bolts. Note that the bearing caps should be marked with a number from 1 to 5 and an arrow to ensure it is installed in the correct position.
13 Finally, tighten the main bearing cap bolts to the specified torque wrench setting.

41 Engine reassembly – pistons, connecting rods and oil pump

1   The subsequent paragraphs on assembly assume that all the checks described in Sections 29 and 30 have been carried out. Also the engine has been partially assembled as described in Section 40.
2   The assembly of new pistons to connecting rods should have been carried out as detailed in Section 20. The new pistons should be supplied with rings already fitted.
3   If new rings are being fitted to existing pistons the following procedure should be followed. Having removed the old rings make sure that each ring groove in the piston is completely cleaned of carbon deposits. This is done most easily by using a special groove cleaner tool or by breaking one of the old rings and using the sharp end as a scraper. Be careful not to remove any metal from the groove by mistake.
4   The end-gap of the new piston rings – three for each piston – must be checked in the cylinder bores as described in Section 29.
5   Check Specifications for the minimum end gap for all three rings. If the gap is too small, one end of the ring must be fitted to increase the gap. To do this the ring should be gripped in a vise between two thin pieces of soft metal in such a way that only the end to be filed is gripped and so that it only protrudes above the jaws of the vise a very small distance. This will eliminate the possibility of bending and

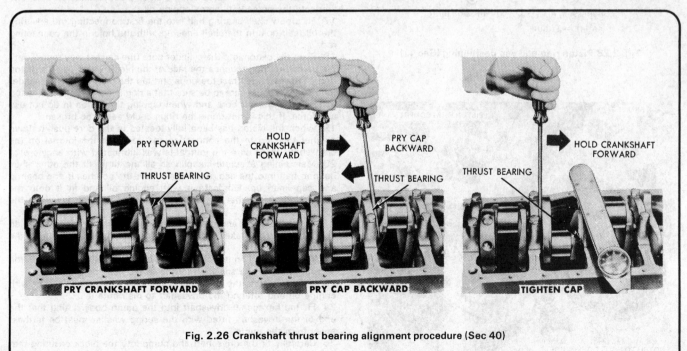

Fig. 2.26 Crankshaft thrust bearing alignment procedure (Sec 40)

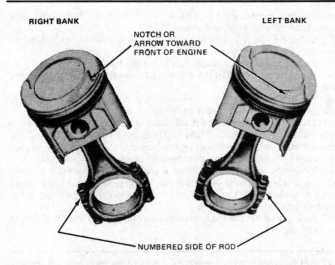

RIGHT BANK   LEFT BANK

NOTCH OR
ARROW TOWARD
FRONT OF ENGINE

NUMBERED SIDE OF ROD

Fig. 2.27 Correct piston and connecting rod positioning (Sec 41)

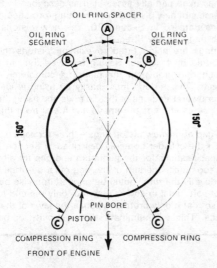

OIL RING SPACER

OIL RING   OIL RING
SEGMENT   SEGMENT

150°   150°

PIN BORE

PISTON

COMPRESSION RING   COMPRESSION RING

FRONT OF ENGINE

Fig. 2.28 Piston ring end gap positioning (Sec 41)

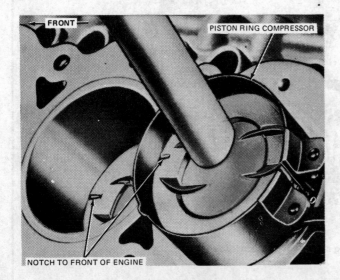

FRONT   PISTON RING COMPRESSOR

NOTCH TO FRONT OF ENGINE

Fig. 2.29 Installing piston (Sec 41)

breaking the ring while filing the end. Use a thin, fine file and proceed in easy stages – checking the gap by refitting the ring in the bore until the necessary minimum gap is obtained. This must be done with every ring, checking each one in the bore to which it will eventually be fitted. To avoid mistakes it is best to complete one set of rings at a time and refit the piston in the cylinder bore before proceeding to the next.

6   To fit the rings onto the pistons calls for patience and care if breakages are to be avoided. The three rings for each piston must all be fitted over the crown, so obviously the first one to go on is the slotted oil control ring. Hold the ring over the top of the piston and spread the ends just enough to get it around the circumference. Then, with the fingers, ease it down, keeping it parallel to the ring grooves by 'walking' the ring ends alternately down the piston. Being wider than the compression rings no difficulty should be encountered in getting it over the first two grooves in the piston.

7   The lower compression ring, which goes on next, must only be fitted one way up. It is marked 'TOP' to indicate its upper face.

8   Start fitting this ring by spreading the ends to get it located over the top of the piston.

9   The lower compression ring has to be guided over the top ring groove and this can be done by using a suitable cut piece of tin which can be placed so as to cover the top groove under the ends of the ring.

10   Alternatively, a feeler blade may be slid around under the ring to guide it into its groove.

11   The top ring may be fitted either way up as it is barrel faced.

12   With the rings fitted, the piston/connecting rod assembly is ready for refitment in the cylinder.

13   Each connecting rod and bearing cap should have been marked on removal but in any case the cylinder number is etched lightly on the end of the cap and connecting rod alongside (photo).

14   The connecting rod and bearing caps are numbered from 1 to 4 in the right bank of the cylinder block and from 5 to 8 in the left bank with the lower number commencing at the front of the block. The numbered side of the rod and cap must face toward the outside of the cylinder block and the notch in the top of the piston must face toward the front of the engine.

IMPORTANT: One side of the bearing cap and connecting rod is chamfered and this must be positioned toward the crankpin thrust face of the crankshaft to allow for the small radius between the journal and web (photo).

15   Before refitting the pistons, position the three rings around each piston so that the gaps are spaced from each other as shown in the accompanying figure.

16   Clean the cylinder bores using a clean piece of lint-free cloth and lubricate the bores with some engine oil.

17   Fit a new shell bearing half into the first connecting rod ensuring the oil feed hole in the shell lines up with the hole in the connecting rod.

18   Push the piston into the cylinder bore (the correct way round) until the oil control ring touches the face of the block. Then, using a piston ring compressor contract the rings and tap the piston into the cylinder (photo). Take great care to be sure that a ring is not trapped on the top edge of the cylinder bore and when tapping the piston in do not use any force. If this is not done the rings could easily be broken.

19   When the piston has been fully located in the bore push it down so that the end of the connecting rod seats on the journal on the crankshaft. Make sure the journal is well lubricated with engine oil.

20   Maintaining absolute cleanliness all the time, fit the other shell bearing half into the cap, once again with the notches in the bearing and cap lined up. Lubricate it with engine oil and fit it onto the connecting rod so that the holes in the cap fit to the dowels in the connecting rod.

21   Refit all pistons and connecting rods in a similar manner and do not make any mistakes locating the correct number piston in the correct bore.

22   When all the connecting rod caps are correctly fitted, tighten the securing nuts to the specified torque wrench setting.

23   Before refitting the oil pump, prime it by filling the inlet port with engine oil and rotating the driveshaft to distribute it.

24   Fit the hexagonal driveshaft into the pump body noting that the end of the driveshaft fitted with the spring washer must be furthest away from the pump.

25   Carefully fit the driveshaft and pump into the block ensuring that the end of the shaft is correctly entered into the distributor aperture.

26   Secure the pump in place with the two retaining bolts and fit the filler and pipe assembly.

Fig. 2.30 Aligning timing gear marks (Sec 42)

Fig. 2.31 Fuel pump eccentric and oil slinger installation (Sec 42)

42 Engine reassembly – timing chain and timing cover

1   Fit the spacer onto the end of the camshaft ensuring the slot is correctly located over the dowel.
2   Rotate the camshaft so that the dowel is facing downward and then rotate the crankshaft so that the keyway in the front end of the crankshaft is facing upward in line with the camshaft dowel.
Note: *If the task is being carried out with the engine in the vehicle and the distributor has not been removed, lift off the distributor cap and check that the rotor is pointing toward the No. 1 cylinder spark plug lead position. If it is not, rotate the camshaft a full 360° until it is.*
3   Lay the camshaft and crankshaft sprockets on the bench so that the single dot on the camshaft sprocket perimeter is directly opposite the mark on the crankshaft sprocket. Maintain them in this position and fit the timing chain around both sprockets.
4   Carefully fit both sprockets and the chain onto the camshaft and crankshaft and tap the onto the dowel and keyway respectively.
5   Now make a careful check to ensure the timing marks are still correctly aligned.
6   Position the fuel pump eccentric on the camshaft dowel and secure it with the washer and bolt. Tighten the bolt to the specified torque wrench setting.
7   Place the oil thrower in position on the end of the crankshaft.
8   Fit a new seal in the timing cover aperture ensuring it is the correct way around. Tap it home using a flat block of wood.
9   Select the front cover gasket and using a suitable sealing compound position it on the engine front plate and install the cover.
10 Place the front cover bolt in position and screw them up loosely. Fit the crankshaft damper onto the keyway of the crankshaft (photo). See that the boss of the damper is lubricated where the oil seal runs.
11 Refitting the crankshaft damper before tightening the cover bolts centralises the seal to the damper. The bolts holding the cover may then be tightened to the specified torque wrench setting.

43 Engine reassembly – rear plate, crankshaft damper, oil pan and flywheel

1   If the engine rear plate has been removed it should now be

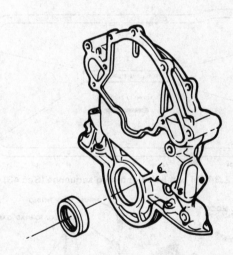

Fig. 2.32 Timing cover seal installation (Sec 42)

refitted. Make sure that both metal faces are quite clean before refitting. No gasket is used.
2   Refit the bolt and washer which locates the crankshaft damper, block the crankshaft with a piece of wood against the side of the crankcase and tighten the bolt to the specified torque wrench setting.
3   Clean all traces of old gasket which may remain from the oil pan joint faces and cover the faces of both the crankcase and pan with sealing compound. The oil pan gasket is in four-sections which dovetail together and these should be carefully positioned and the joints interlocked.
4   The engine is then ready for the oil pan to be reinstalled.
5   Clean the interior of the pan thoroughly, apply sealer to the joint edge and place it in position.
6   Install all the oil pan bolts and tighten them evenly to the specified torque wrech setting.

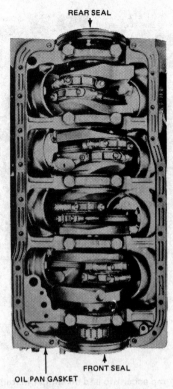

REAR SEAL

FRONT SEAL

OIL PAN GASKET

Fig. 2.33 Oil pan gasket and seals (Sec 43)

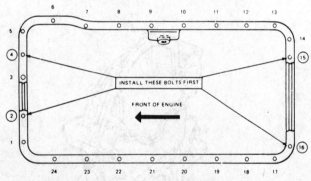

INSTALL THESE BOLTS FIRST

FRONT OF ENGINE

Fig. 2.34 Oil pan bolt tightening sequence (Sec 43)

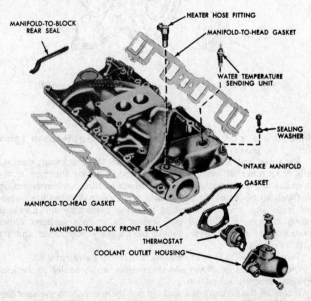

MANIFOLD-TO-BLOCK REAR SEAL

HEATER HOSE FITTING

MANIFOLD-TO-HEAD GASKET

WATER TEMPERATURE SENDING UNIT

SEALING WASHER

INTAKE MANIFOLD

GASKET

MANIFOLD-TO-HEAD GASKET

MANIFOLD-TO-BLOCK FRONT SEAL

THERMOSTAT

COOLANT OUTLET HOUSING

Fig. 2.35 Intake manifold and components (Sec 43)

7   The flywheel may now be re-installed. Make sure that the mating flanges are clean and free from burrs and that the bolt holes line up correctly.

8   Screw in six retaining bolts and tighten them evenly to the specified torque wrench setting.

44 Engine reassembly – valve gear, cylinder heads and intake manifolds

1   When the cylinder heads have been cleaned and the valves lapped in as described in Sections 37 and 33, the cylinder heads may be reassembled. If the valves have been removed as described in Section 9, there will be no confusion as to which valve belongs in which position.

2   Make sure all traces of carbon and paste have been removed, lubricate the valve stem with engine oil and place it in the appropriate guide.

3   It will then protrude through the top of the cylinder head.

4   Fit a new seal cup over the valve stem.

5   Place the valve spring over the valve stem.

6   Fit the circular retainer over the spring with the protruding center boss retainer downwards.

7   Using a proper valve spring compressor tool, compress the spring down the valve stem sufficiently enough to enable the two halves of the locks (collets) to be fitted into the groove in the valve stem. If necessary the locks should be smeared with grease to keep them in position. The spring compressor may then be released. Watch to ensure that the locks stay together in position as the retainer comes past them. If the retainer is a little off center it may force one lock out of its groove in which case the spring must be recompressed and the lock repositioned. When the compressor is finally released, tap the head of the valve with a soft mallet to make sure the valve assembly is securely held in position.

8   Stand the engine the right way up on the bench and refit the valve lifters if they have been removed from the block. If these have been kept in order on removal, as suggested, it will be a simple matter to refit them.

9   Make sure that the cylinder head faces are clean and free from grease or oil and place the new head gaskets in position. To ensure

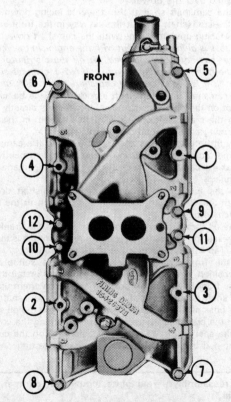

FRONT

Fig. 2.36 Intake manifold bolt tightening sequence for all engines except 1975 5.8L (Sec 44)

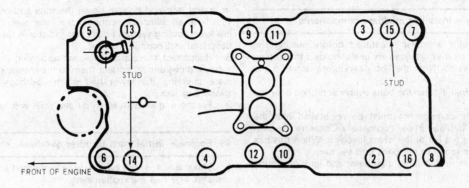

Fig. 2.37 1975 5.8L engine intake manifold bolt tightening sequence (Sec 44)

correct location 'FRONT' is usually marked on the upper side of the gasket.

10 Carefully place the cylinder heads in position on the block.

11 Make sure the cylinder head bolts are clean and lightly oiled and refit them. Nip them all down lightly and then tighten them in the sequence shown in the accompanying figure. The bolts should be tightened down to progressive torque loadings – (see Specifications) and finally to the specified torque wrench setting.

12 Now fit the pushrods into position, making sure that they are refitted the same way up as they came out and according to the original valve position. This will not be difficult if they have been kept in order.

13 Position the rocker arms over the pushrods and valve stems and carefully tighten the remaining nuts just enough to retain the pushrods in their correct position. The valve clearances must be adjusted either now or at a later stage as described in the following Section.

14 To refit the inlet manifold first ensure that the cylinder head faces are clean and then lightly coat them with a suitable jointing compound.

15 Carefully stick the gaskets in place ensuring that the small front and rear pieces are interlocked with the two main gaskets (photo).

16 Lower the intake manifold into place and check that none of the gaskets have been pushed out of position.

17 Insert the intake manifold securing bolts. Note that some of the bolts are longer than others and care must be taken to ensure that they are refitted in the correct hole.

18 Tighten the inlet manifold bolts progressively in the sequence shown in the accompanying figure and then finally tighten them to the specified torque wrench setting.

45 Valve lash – adjustment

1 The engines on all models use hydraulic valve lifters which automatically compensate for valve gear wear once the initial clearance has been correctly set. With the hydraulic lifter collapsed, the valve stem to lifter clearance must be periodically checked to make sure that it is within specification.

2 Repeated valve reconditioning such as valve or seat refacing can decrease the clearances to the point where the lifter cannot compensate and the valve could actually be left open. In this case, a shorter or longer pushrod will be required to bring the valve gear back into proper relationship.

3 To determine whether a shorter or longer pushrod may be required, rotate the engine with the ignition off until No. 1 piston is at TDC. This can be checked by removing the spark plug and placing your finger over the hole and rotating the engine until the pressure is felt. This indicates that the piston is rising on the compression stroke. Continue to rotate the engine until the timing pointer on the front cover is aligned with TDC (position No. 1 in the accompanying figure). At this time, mark positions No. 2 and 3 on the pulley with chalk as shown in the figure.

4 To check the valve clearance, push the rocker arm down so that the valve lifter is fully collapsed and insert a feeler gauge between the rocker arm and the valve stem tip.

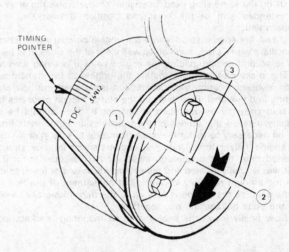

Fig. 2.38 Position of crankshaft pulley for checking and adjusting valve clearance (Sec 45)

Position 1: No. 1 at TDC at end of compression stroke
Position 2: Rotate Crankshaft 180° clockwise from position 1 ($\frac{1}{2}$ turn)
Position 3: Rotate crankshaft 270° clockwise from position 2 ($\frac{3}{4}$ turn)

5 With the No. 1 piston at TDC, check the clearances on the following valves:

4.2L engine		5.8L engine	
No. 1 intake	*No. 1 exhaust*	*No. 1 intake*	*No. 1 exhaust*
No. 7 intake	*No. 5 exhaust*	*No. 4 intake*	*No. 3 exhaust*
No. 8 intake	*No. 4 exhaust*	*No. 8 intake*	*No. 7 exhaust*

6 Rotate the engine to the No. 2 position marked on the pulley and check the following valve clearances:

4.2L engine		5.8L engine	
No. 5 intake	*No. 2 exhaust*	*No. 3 intake*	*No. 2 exhaust*
No. 4 intake	*No. 6 exhaust*	*No. 7 intake*	*No. 6 exhaust*

7 Rotate the engine to position No. 3 and check the clearances on the following valves:

4.2L engine		5.8L engine	
No. 2 intake	*No. 7 exhaust*	*No. 2 intake*	*No. 4 exhaust*
No. 3 intake	*No. 3 exhaust*	*No. 5 intake*	*No. 5 exhaust*
No. 6 intake	*No. 8 exhaust*	*No. 6 intake*	*No. 8 exhaust*

8 A longer pushrod will be required if the clearance is less than in Specifications and a shorter one if the clearance is greater. Pushrods are available at your Ford dealer, be sure to take the old pushrod with you to ensure that the new one is the correct size.

46 Engine reassembly – installing auxiliary components

1 The exhaust manifolds are best reinstalled before putting the engine back into the car as they provide very useful holds if the engine has been manhandled at all. Note that no gaskets are used on the exhaust manifolds.
2 Reinstall each manifold, tighten the bolts evenly and bend over the locking tabs.
3 The auxiliary engine components must be reinstalled and the method of doing this is detailed in the appropriate Chapters. Section 9 of this Chapter gives a full list of the items involved. When this has been done the engine is ready to put back into the car.
4 For details on how to re-install the distributor and ignition timing refer to Chapter 5.

47 Engine – installation

1 The procedure for refitting the engine into the vehicle is basically the reversal of the removal procedure described in Sections 3 and 4.
2 Using the same sling used for engine removal, raise the engine on the extended arm of the hoist and position it over the engine compartment.
3 Lower the engine steadily into the engine compartment, keeping all ancillary wires, pipes and cables well clear of the sides. It is best to have a second person guiding the engine while it is being lowered.
4 The tricky part is finally mating the engine to the transmission, which involves locating the transmission input shaft into the clutch housing and flywheel. Provided that the clutch friction plate has been centered correctly as described in Chapter 8, there should be little difficulty. Grease the splines of the transmission input shaft first. It may be necessary to rock the engine from side to side in order to get the engine fully home. Under no circumstances let any strain be imparted onto the transmission input shaft. This could occur if the shaft was not fully located and the engine was raised or lowered more than the amount required for very slight adjustment of position.
5 As soon as the engine is fully up to the transmission bellhousing refit the bolts holding the two together.
6 Now finally lower the engine onto its mounting brackets at the front and refit and tighten down the nuts and washers.
7 Refit all electrical connections, the fuel lines and carburetor linkages, cooling system hoses and radiator in the reverse order to that described in Sections 3 and 4.
8 Reconnect the clutch cable as described in Chapter 8, refit the exhaust pipes and reconnect them to the manifold extensions, refit the plate covering the lower half of the bellhousing and remove the supporting jack.
9 Fill the engine with fresh oil and refill with coolant.

48 Engine – initial start-up after overhaul or major repair

1 Make sure that the battery is fully charged and that all lubricants, coolants and fuel are replenished.
2 If the fuel system has been dismantled it will require several revolutions of the engine on the starter motor to get the gas up to the carburetor. It will help if the spark plugs are remved and the engine turned over on the starter motor. This will ensure that gas is delivered to the carburetor and also that oil is being centralised around the engine prior to starting.
3 As soon as the engine fires and runs keep it going at a fast idle only (no faster) and bring it up to normal working temperature.
4 As the engine warms up there will be odd smells and some smoke from parts getting hot and burning off oil deposits. The signs to look for are leaks of oil or water which will be obvious if serious. Check also the clamp connections of the exhaust pipes to the manifolds as these do not always 'find' their exact gas tight position until warmth and vibration have acted on them and it is almost certain that they need tightening further. This should be done, of course, with the engine stopped.
5 When the running temperature has been reached adjust the idling speed as described in Chapter 4.
6 Stop the engine and wait a few minutes to see if any lubricant or coolant is dripping out when the engine is stationary.
7 Road test the vehicle to check that the timing is correct and giving the necessary smoothness and power. Do not race the engine – if new bearings and/or pistons and rings have been fitted it should be treated as a new engine and run in at reduced revolutions for 500 miles (800 km).

Chapter 3 Cooling, heating and air conditioning

Contents

Specifications

System type .... Pressurized, assisted by belt-driven water pump and fan

Thermostat type .... Wax pellet

Radiator .... Corrugated fin, light metal construction, crossflow type

Pressure cap operating pressure   psi
Specified 16
Lower limit 13
Upper limit 19

Water pump type .... belt-driven impeller

Cooling system capacities*   US qts
1975 and 1976
    3.3L, all 9.9
    4.1L, air conditioning 10.5
    4.1L, standard 10.7
    5.0L, air conditioning 14.6
    5.0L, standard 14.1
    5.8L, air conditioning 16.7
    5.8L, standard 15.7
1977
    3.3L, all 9.7
    4.1L, air conditioning 10.5
    4.1L, standard 10.8
    5.0L, all 14.6
    5.8L, all 15.7
1978 and 1979
    4.1L, air conditioning 10.6
    4.1l, standard 10.5
    5.0L, air conditioning 14.3
    5.0L, standard 14.2

1980

4.1L, air conditioning	10.8
4.1L, standard	10.6
4.2L, air conditioning	14.7
4.2L, standard	14.6
5.0L, air conditioning	14.3
5.0L, standard	14.2

Approximate figures, consult your owners manual for actual capacity

Coolant type ....   50/50 mix of Ford ESE-M97B18-C coolant or equivalent non-phosphate ethylene glycol anti-freeze

Drivebelt tension

$\frac{1}{4}$ in V-belt

new (A)	50 to 80 lb
used	40 to 60 lb (B)

All other V- and cogged belts

new (A)	120 to 160 lb
used	75 to 120 lb (C)

V-ribbed

new (A)	140 to 170 lb
used	110 to 130 lb (D)

(A)   a new belt has been installed for less than one revolution of the pulley, a used belt for ten minutes of operation, or more
(B)   if less than 40 lb, readust to 40 to 60 lb
(C)   if less than 75 lb, readjust to 90 to 120 lb
(D)   if less than 100 lb, readjust to 90 to 120 lb

Torque specifications

	Ft-lb	Nm
Fan shroud-to-pulley	2 to 4	3 to 5
Fan pulley-to-hub	12 to 18	16 to 24
Automatic transmission oil cooler fittings	9 to 12	12 to 24
Radiator hose clamps	1 to 2	2 to 3
Water pump-to-engine		
3.3L and 4.1L	15 to 20	20 to 27
4.2L and 5.0L	12 to 18	16 to 24

1   Cooling system – general information

The basic components of the cooling system consist of a radiator, which is connected to the engine by top and bottom hoses, a fan and belt-driven water pump. Small bore hoses transfer coolant to the heater and automatic choke control unit.

Vehicles equipped with automatic transmission use radiators with transmission oil coolers incorporated into their tanks.

The cooling system is pressurized so that higher coolant temperatures may be maintained without boiling the coolant. Pressure is controlled by a spring loaded radiator cap. If coolant pressure exceeds the preset limit of the spring, it releases and the pressure is bled from the system.

All models use a coolant recovery system consisting of a plastic reservoir connected to the radiator inlet by a hose. When the coolant in the radiator cools, it contracts and pulls the coolant in the reservoir back into the radiator through a vacuum relief valve in the pressure cap.

Constant coolant temperature is controlled by the thermostat. The

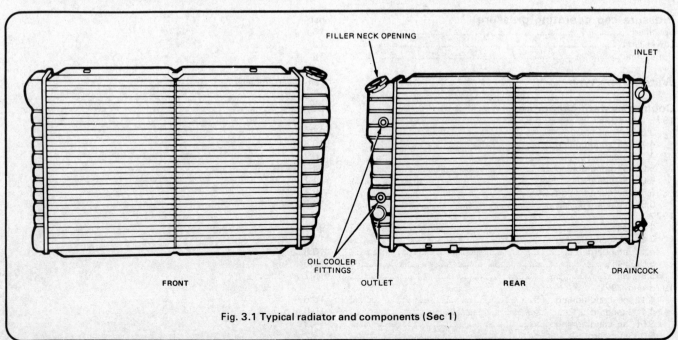

Fig. 3.1 Typical radiator and components (Sec 1)

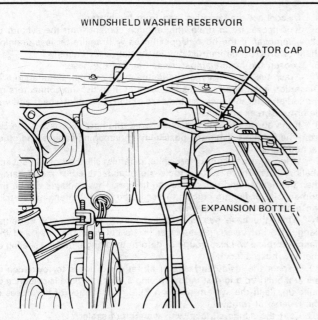

Fig. 3.2 Coolant recovery system (Sec 1)

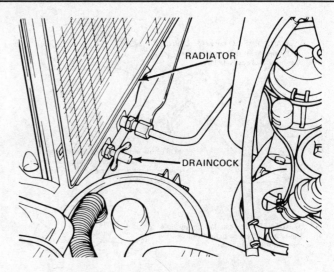

Fig. 3.3 Typical radiator draincock location (Sec 2)

thermostat is closed during initial startup, restricting coolant flow and allowing fast warmup to operating temperature. Once operating temperature is reached, the thermostat opens and allows a free flow of coolant throughout the system.

A belt-driven fan pulls air through the radiator for improved cooling, particularly when the engine is under load. Some models are equipped with a fan with a temperature operated clutch in the hub. The fan free wheels until the air passing through the radiator reaches a certain temperature, activating the bi-metal switch in the hub and engaging the fan.

2 Cooling system – draining, flushing, coolant mixing and filling

1 Do not perform the following tasks if the engine has been run to operating temperature. Hot steam and coolant can scald, and the pressures present in the system can force scalding liquid out causing widespread burning. If you wish to perform these tasks after operating your car, leave it in a shady spot for at least one hour, or until the temperature gauge registers a nearly-cold engine when the ignition is switched on, but the engine is not started.
2 The car must be parked on a level, flat spot. Run the engine only long enough to move the vehicle, then shut if off immediately.
3 Place the heater controls on their hottest setting.
4 Raise the hood of the car and remove the radiator cap. If the engine and radiator are warm enough to give off noticeable heat, do not remove the cap. Once heat cannot be felt or when the engine becomes cool enough to touch comfortably with the palm of your hand, the radiator cap may be removed. Place a towel or heavy rag over the cap and turn the cap to its first detent position and allow any remaining pressure to dissipate, then twist it to the second position and remove.
5 Place a pan beneath the radiator to catch draining coolant. Coolant is poisonous and should not be poured into gutters or dumped into storm drains.
6 Open the drain petcock. On crossflow radiators this is located at the bottom of the right side reservoir tank and faces the rear of the vehicle. Vertical-flow radiators have their drain petcocks located on the right side of the lower reservoir tank.
7 When the system has been drained, close the petcock and tighten it until it is snug. Before disposing of the used coolant, check to see if it is rusty in color. If it is, and the coolant is very cloudy, it is advisable to flush the radiator and engine coolant passages.
8 Flushing may be performed in a number of ways. The easiest method is to flush the system with a brand-name flushing fluid according to the manufacturer's directions. To remove the greatest amounts of scale and deposits, it is further recommended that you

reverse-flush the system prior to filling. At least one manufacturer in the U.S. produces and markets a special fixture for this purpose. These are available through many auto parts stores.
9 If the reverse-flushing fixture is not available, or if you do not wish to undertake the expense, the most common method of flushing the engine block and radiator is with a garden hose adapter which can be installed in the lower spigot of the radiator and the lower hose adapter at the engine. This adapter provides a female garden hose coupling so that a garden hose may be hooked directly to the engine and radiator.
10 Begin reverse flushing by removing the thermostat (Section 12), then installing the hose. Turn the water on to a high pressure, then off several times to loosen the scale and all larger deposits. After this has been done several times, allow a steady stream of water to flow through the engine or radiator to flush out all loosened deposits.
11 If scale build-up is very severe due to the minerals in local water, consider using distilled water in place of tap water when refilling the cooling system.
12 When you are satisfied that the engine block water passages and the radiator are clean, fill the system with a mixture of ethylene glycol-based antifreeze mixed in the proper proportions (see manufacturer's specifications) with water, or with a 50/50 mixture of water and Ford Long Life Coolant, which is available from all authorized dealers. Before filling the system, make sure that the hoses are tightly clamped (Section 3), the drain plug has been tightened, and that the thermostat has been replaced (if it was removed for flushing the engine). The system is filled by pouring coolant into the radiator filler neck opening, which is covered by the radiator cap when the car is in use.
13 When the system has been filled, start the engine and allow it to run until the thermostat opens. Fill the radiator again until the proper levels of coolant are reached.
14 When proper fill levels have been reached, and brief acceleration of the engine does not cause the coolant level to drop, the system is properly filled. Replace the radiator cap and tighten it fully. Continue to run the engine until proper pressure is built up. Inspect all joints and connections for water-tightness.

3 Hoses – removal, inspection, and installation

1 A key ingredient in the proper operation of the cooling system is the routine inspection of hoses and their connectors for condition. Another ingredient to long hose life is the proper removal and installation procedure, as incorrect methods will shorten the useful life of the hose and may also lead to the damaging of other engine components.
2 Routine inspection of hoses involves checking of all connections for watertight fit and all hoses for cracking. Squeeze each hose at several points along its length and closely inspect the surface for cracking, splitting, or breaks. If cracking is severe, replace the hose.
3 To remove the hoses, first park the car on a flat, level surface.

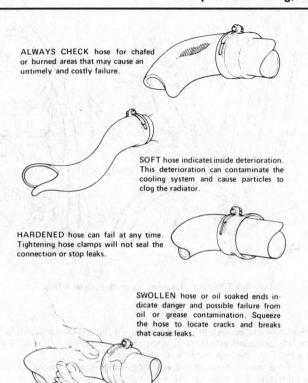

ALWAYS CHECK hose for chafed or burned areas that may cause an untimely and costly failure.

SOFT hose indicates inside deterioration. This deterioration can contaminate the cooling system and cause particles to clog the radiator.

HARDENED hose can fail at any time. Tightening hose clamps will not seal the connection or stop leaks.

SWOLLEN hose or oil soaked ends indicate danger and possible failure from oil or grease contamination. Squeeze the hose to locate cracks and breaks that cause leaks.

Fig. 3.4 Conditions to look for when inspecting hoses (Sec 3)

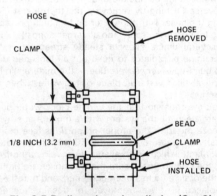

HOSE

HOSE REMOVED

CLAMP

1/8 INCH (3.2 mm)

BEAD

CLAMP

HOSE INSTALLED

Fig. 3.5 Radiator hose installation (Sec 3)

4   Disconnect the negative lead from the battery.

5   It is necessary to drain only enough coolant from the system to allow removal of the hose. Upper hoses will require far less draining than lower. Use the instructions in Section 2 for draining.

6   Loosen the hose clamps at each end of the hose.

7   Grasp the hose firmly, at the flange, twist and pull simultaneously. Discretion is required for this job. Do not 'muscle' the connectors on the radiator, for instance, as they are of soft, thin, alloy sheet and will deform or break very easily.

8   If the above procedure doesn't work, the hose will have to be cut from the flange to avoid the possibility of damaging flanges and other related parts.

9   Using a razor blade or art knife, carefully slit the hose in several shallow cuts. These cutting tools are manufactured of metal harder than the flanges and will gouge the flanges. These gouges will be the primary site of fatigue cracking later in the life of the engine, so take the time to cut the hose, only.

10 When the hose has been cut, carefully peel it away from the flange. Do not insert any tools or levers between the hose and the flange as these will also gouge or deform the flange, making sealing of the new hose difficult.

11 Inspect the inside surfaces of all removed hoses for evidence of mineral build-up and rust in the cooling system. If there is evidence of build-up, flush the system (Section 2).12 Installation of the hoses is the reverse of removal.

13 Coat the flange surface with waterproof sealer.

14 Slide the hose over the flange and position the clamp.

15 Tighten the clamp until the hose is snug on the flange.

16 Fill the cooling system with fresh coolant mixed according to the directions in Section 2.

17 Start the engine and allow it to reach operating temperature. Check all connections for leakage.

4   Radiator – removal and installation

1   Park the car on a flat, level surface.

2   Disconnect the negative cable from the battery.

3   Drain the cooling system (Section 2).

4   Remove the cooling fan and shroud.

5   Remove the upper and lower hoses from the radiator. If the vehicle is equipped with an automatic transmission, disconnect the lines from the transmission oil cooler and plug them. Place a suitable container under the radiator to catch any transmission fluid which may escape during the removal of the radiator.

6   Remove the bolts which hold the radiator to its upper mounts. Remove the upper mounts. Lift the radiator from the vehicle.

7   Installation is the reverse of removal.

4.5 Hold the fitting closest to the radiator with a wrench when removing the transmission cooler lines to avoid damage to the radiator

4.6 Removing the radiator mounting bolts

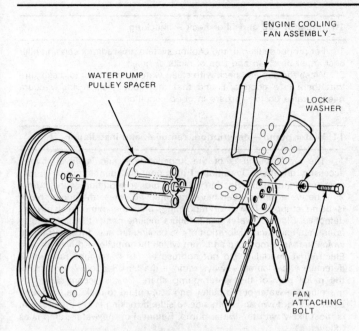

Fig. 3.6 Typical standard fan installation (Secs 1 and 6)

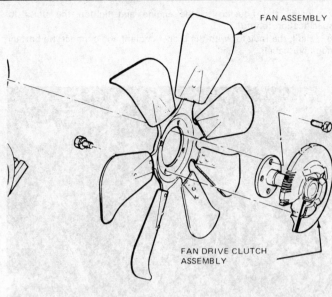

Fig. 3.7 Typical clutch-hub type fan installation (Secs 1 and 6)

8   If a new radiator is to be installed, transfer the draincock from the old radiator. On automatic transmission models, the oil line adapters must also be installed, using an oil resistant sealer.

5   Radiator – pressure testing, repair and service

Other than the procedures outlined in this chapter, we recommend that the radiator be taken to a properly equipped shop for testing, repair or service. These shops have the specialized equipment necessary to perform this work on an efficient basis.

6   Cooling fan – removal and installation

1   Disconnect the negative battery cable.
2   Remove the bolts which hold the fan shroud in place and remove the shroud.
3   Remove the bolts securing the fan to the pulley hub and remove the fan.
4   Installation is the reverse of removal.
5   Tighten the fan bolts and then the fan shroud bolts to specification in a cross pattern.
6   Connect the battery negative cable.

7   Cooling fan – inspection

1   Carefully check each of the fan blades for cracks, bends or other damage. Check also at the hub for loose or broken rivets.
2   If there is any doubt about the condition or safety of the fan, replace it. If it is necessary to drive the car, do not start the engine with the hood open or open the hood while the engine is running.

8   Thermostat – checking

1   Thermostats are designed to go to the full-open position if they fail, generally. If the engine does not reach operating temperature, this is usually a good indication that the thermostat is not working. A good way to determine this is to turn the heater blower on after having

driven 3 or 4 miles from a cold start. If the air from the heater is not hot, the thermostat should be suspected.
2   Another way to check the thermostat is to remove it and hold it up against a lighted background. If light shines through around the thermostat valve, it is not sealing properly.

9   Thermostat – removal and installation

1   Disconnect the battery negative cable.
2   Drain the radiator coolant into a suitable container.
3   The thermostat is located in a housing on the engine at the end of the upper radiator hose. Remove the thermostat housing bolts, lift the housing away from the engine and remove the thermostat.
4   Use a putty knife or gasket scraper to clean the engine and thermostat housing of old gasket material.
5   Coat the gasket with water-resistant sealer and place the gasket in position.
6   Refer to the accompanying figure and insert the new thermostat into the housing with the bridge facing the housing. Turn the thermostat clockwise so that it is locked into the faults cast into the housing.

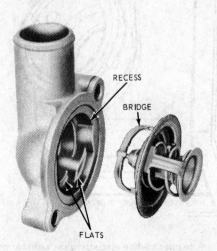

Fig. 3.8 Thermostat installation (Sec 9)

7   Install the housing to the engine and tighten the bolts to specification (photo).
8   Refill the radiator with the proper coolant and connect the battery negative cable.

9.7 The thermostat housing ready for installation with the gasket retained in place with grease or sealer

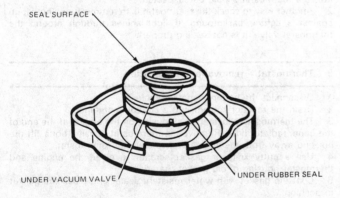

SEAL SURFACE

UNDER VACUUM VALVE

UNDER RUBBER SEAL

RADIATOR CAP

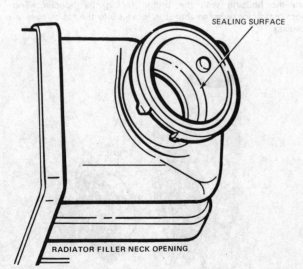

SEALING SURFACE

RADIATOR FILLER NECK OPENING

Fig. 3.9 Areas to check when inspecting the radiator cap and filler neck (Sec 10)

10 Radiator cap and filler neck – checking

1   For proper sealing of the cooling system, the radiator cap and filler neck must be clean and free of nicks or holes.
2   Wash the cap and neck with clean water and inspect to make sure that there is a good seal and that the rubber gasket and vacuum release valve on the cap are in good condition.

11 Water pump – description, removal, and installation

1   The water pump is of the impeller type and is driven by an accessory drivebelt. Operation of the pump is dependent upon proper drivebelt adjustment (Section 13) and proper condition of the pump.
2   The water pump need never be removed unless the engine block is being stripped down for rebuilding, or if the pump itself proves defective. Signs of water pump failure include coolant leakage, noisy operation, and excess vibration of the cooling fan and driveshaft (upon which the fan is mounted and from which the impeller is driven [except Electrodrive models]). Do not confuse an out-of-balance fan with a defective water pump. Always remove the fan (Section 7) and check the radial play of the water pump shaft. This is accomplished by grasping the water pump pulley and attempting to rock the mounting shaft up and down and from side to side. If rocking is felt the problem is most likely with the water pump. Removal of the water pump is as follows:
3   Disconnect the negative lead from the battery.
4   Remove the fan and shroud (Section 6).
5   Drain the cooling system (Section 2).
6   Loosen and remove all drivebelts (Section 13).
7   On some models, one of the water pump mounting bolts is also a bracket for the alternator. Remove the nut which holds the bracket in place and move it out of your work area.
8   Remove the four bolts which hold the fan pulley to the water pump flange and remove the pulley.
9   Remove the hoses which are connected to the water pump.
10   Remove the four bolts which hold the water pump to the engine block.
11   The water pump is located by three locating pins which match up to holes in the engine block. In order to break the seal between the engine and the pump, it is necessary to rap on the water pump flange with a rubber mallet or a hammer and block of wood. Do not insert any tools or other levering devices between the engine block and the water pump in an attempt to pry them apart as damage to the sealing surfaces may result.
12   Clean all sealing surfaces with a gasket removal tool or a putty knife. Do not use a razor blade as this may damage the sealing surfaces.
13   Installation is the reverse of the removal procedure.

11.14 The water pump ready for installation, gasket retained with sealer

14 Coat the water pump gasket with a thin coating or waterproof sealant before installing it on the seal surface of the water pump (photo).
15 Tighten the water pump bolts evenly, wait about five minutes for the sealer to be pushed down, then retighten the bolts.
16 Fill the cooling system with fresh coolant when parts installation and belt adjustment is complete.

12 Water pump – rebuilding

1 Water pumps are not an item which can be rebuilt economically by the home mechanic. We suggest that you purchase a new unit or investigate the purchase of a rebuilt exchange unit from an auto parts store.

13 Drivebelts – description, removal and installation

1 Drivebelts are used to drive all ancillaries including the cooling fan, alternator, Thermactor pump, air conditioning pump and power steering pump. The belts vary in size and design, according to function.
2 Belts are considered stretched after ten minutes of use and must be adjusted. Ford Motor Company and its subsidiaries do not use 'inches of belt deflection' as a means of determining belt adjustment, but refer to 'pounds of adjustment'. This is determined by use of a tensionmeter, available from an authorized Ford dealer. The 'pounds of tension' is based on the design of the belt being tested.
3 Belts are of three types; V-belts, cogged belts and V-ribbed belts. The V-ribbed belt is differentiated by the appearance of its inner surface which appears to be made up of several V-belts placed side by side.
4 Drivebelt adjustment should be performed in the following manner. Locate each of the belts and measure the width. Using the tensionometer, adjust the belt to the tensions given in the Specifications Section at the beginning of the Chapter.
5 If no tensionometer tool is available, belts can be adjusted using a straight-edge and a ruler as shown in the accompanying figure. Belts with a free span of less than twelve inches should have a deflection of between $\frac{1}{4}$ and $\frac{1}{8}$ inch (3 to 6 mm). The deflection of a belt with a span greater than twelve inches should be between $\frac{1}{8}$ and $\frac{3}{8}$ in (3 to 9 mm).
6 Vehicles equipped with ribbed belts must only be checked with the tensionometer because of the higher tension used with this type of belt. The deflection testing method described in Chapter 1 is not valid on these belts.
7 Drivebelts should be inspected periodically for fraying, glazed or burned appearance.
8 To adjust a drivebelt, loosen the bolt(s) on the component the belt is driving and, using a suitable pry bar, hold tension on the belt while the bolt is tightened (photo). Check the belt tension after tightening.

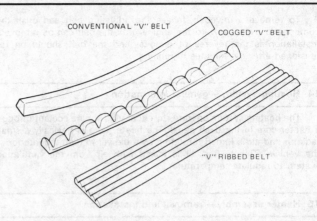

Fig. 3.10 The three types of accessory drivebelts (Sec 13)

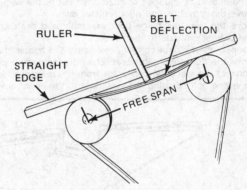

Fig. 3.11 Measuring belt deflection (Sec 13)

SMALL CRACKS on the underside can be enlarged for inspection by flexing the belt. Cracks expose the interior to damage and belts can break without warning.

GREASE rots ordinary rubber belts, making the belt sides slick and causing slippage.
V-belts with Neoprene are resistant to grease.

GLAZED belts with hard surfaces slip causing overheating and low battery voltage, in the case of alternator belts.

ALWAYS CHECK the underside of the belt. Split belts may appear sound from the top, but sides and bottom may be severely split and ready to fail.

13.8 Using a pry bar to maintain tension when adjusting the drivebelt

Fig. 3.12 Condition to look for when inspecting drivebelts (Sec 13)

9   To remove a drivebelt, loosen the adjusting bolt and push the component inward toward the engine until the belt can be removed. Installation is the reverse of removal and the belt should be re-tensioned after ten minutes of running.

14 Heating system – general information

The heating system operates by circulating engine coolant through a heater core in the dash panel. The heater core is basically a small radiator and air is forced through it by a blower to heat the interior of the vehicle. This heated air is mixed with air from the ventilation system to regulate temperature.

15 Heater assembly – removal and installation

1   Drain the cooling system into a suitable container.
2   From inside the engine compartment, disconnect the heater houses at the heater core tubes. The hoses will contain residual coolant and should be plugged or positioned out of the way.
3   Remove the glovebox and right register duct.
4   Remove the floor discharge duct assembly and the clips which secure the defroster nozzle to the heater.
5   Disconnect the air door control cables from the heater and doors.
6   Remove the right vent cable bracket at the instrument panel.
7   Disconnect the electrical connector from the resistor assembly.
8   Remove the bolt securing the vent duct to the upper cowl.

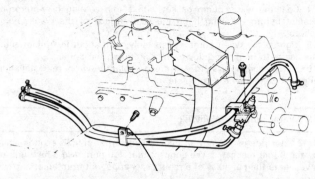

Fig. 3.13 Typical six cylinder engine heater hose routing (Sec 15)

9   Remove the 3 mounting stud nuts securing the heater case to the dash panel and remove the complete heater case and vent duct assembly.
10 Installation is a reversal of removal. After installation adjust the control cable as described in Section 19.

16 Heater core – removal and installation

1   Remove the heater assembly as described in Section 15 and place it on a suitable work surface.

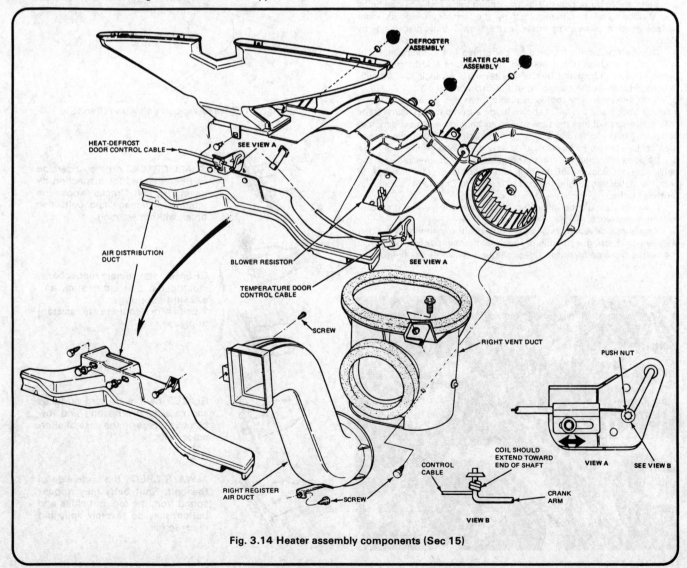

Fig. 3.14 Heater assembly components (Sec 15)

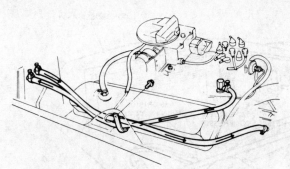

Fig. 3.15 V8 engine heater hose installation (Sec 16)

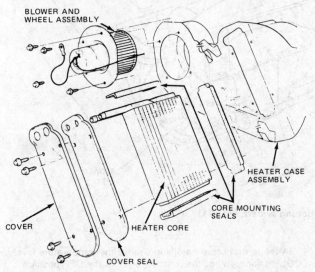

BLOWER AND
WHEEL ASSEMBLY

HEATER CASE
ASSEMBLY

CORE MOUNTING
SEALS

COVER

HEATER CORE

COVER SEAL

**Fig. 3.17 Blower motor, wheel and heater core removal
(Secs 16 and 17)**

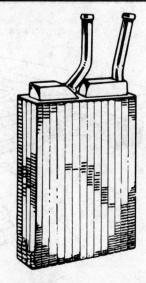

Fig. 3.16 Typical heater core (Sec 16)

2   Remove the heater care cover and pad. Slide the core from the case.
3   Installation is the reverse of removal. If a new core is being installed, transfer the butyl rubber pads from the old core.

17 Heater blower motor and wheel assembly – removal and installation

1   Remove the heater assembly as described in Section 15 and place it on a suitable work surface.
2   Remove the 4 mounting screws and slide the blower motor and wheel assembly from the housing.
3   Installation is the reverse of removal, making sure to attach the ground wire, referring to the accompanying figure.

18 Heater defroster nozzle – removal and installation

1   Remove the upper finish panel from the instrument panel, referring to Chapter 12 if necessary.
2   Remove the radio speaker (if equipped) and instrument panel-to-cowl brace.
3   Remove the screws from the right and left defroster nozzles.
4   Remove the clip which holds the defroster nozzle to the heater core and move the nozzle upward and through the instrument panel opening to remove.
5   Installation is the reversal of removal.

19 Heater control assembly – removal and installation

1   Remove the windshield wiper, light switch and radio control knobs and light switch control bezel.

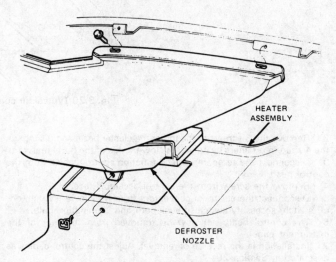

HEATER
ASSEMBLY

DEFROSTER
NOZZLE

Fig. 3.18 Defroster nozzle installation (Sec 18)

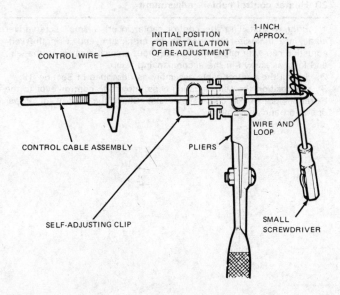

INITIAL POSITION
FOR INSTALLATION
OF RE-ADJUSTMENT

1-INCH
APPROX.

CONTROL WIRE

CONTROL CABLE ASSEMBLY

SELF-ADJUSTING CLIP

WIRE AND
LOOP

PLIERS

SMALL
SCREWDRIVER

Fig. 3.19 Heater control cable adjustment (Sec 19)

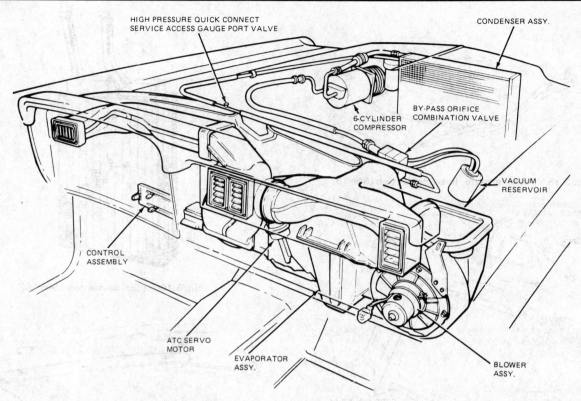

HIGH PRESSURE QUICK CONNECT
SERVICE ACCESS GAUGE PORT VALVE

CONDENSER ASSY.

6-CYLINDER
COMPRESSOR

BY-PASS ORIFICE
COMBINATION VALVE

VACUUM
RESERVOIR

CONTROL
ASSEMBLY

ATC SERVO
MOTOR

EVAPORATOR
ASSY.

BLOWER
ASSY.

Fig. 3.20 Typical air conditioning system (Sec 21)

2   Remove the 3 screws at the top of the cluster bezel and disengage the 4 snap-in retainers by pulling the lower edge of the bezel rearward.
3   Disconnect the temperature and function control cables from the control head.
4   Remove the screw from the control assembly face.
5   Disconnect the electrical connectors from the blower switch, on-off switch, accessory switch (if equipped) and illumination bulb.
6   The control head can now be removed from the rear of the instrument panel.
7   Installation is the reverse of removal. Adjust the control cables as described in Section 20.

20 Heater control cable – adjustment

1   Prior to installing the control cable, insert a small screwdriver blade into the wire and loop at the crank arm end. Grip the self-adjusting clip with pliers and slide it about an inch away from the wire and loop as shown in the accompanying figure.
2   Install the control cable assembly as described in Section 19.
3   To position the self-adjusting clips, move the control lever to the extreme right of the control lever slot. Check the control for proper operation and movement.

4   After control cable installation, move the temperature lever to the COOL position and/or the function lever to the OFF position.
5   With the crank arm held firmly in position, insert the small screwdriver blade into the wire loop as described in paragraph 1, referring to the figure.
6   Move the control levers to the extreme right of the control slot to position the self-adjusting clip.
7   Check for proper movement and operation.

21 Air conditioner – general information

The air conditioner cools the vehicle interior by transferring heat to a refrigerant which is pumped through the condenser mounted in front of the radiator. The refrigerant is then circulated back to the interior of the vehicle through a compressor and back to the condenser.

The volume and circulation of the cooled air is controlled by a four-position blower and a system of outlets and doors in the ventilation system.

Other than keeping the condenser fins free of obstructions, checking the hose condition and drivebelt tension, maintenance or repairs of the air conditioner should be left to your dealer or a qualified repair shop.

Chapter 4 Fuel and exhaust systems

Contents

Specifications

Fuel pump type	Mechanical, operated by the camshaft, diaphragm provides the vacuum
Fuel pump static pressure	
3.3L and 4.1L	5.0 to 7.0 psi
4.2L, 5.0L and 5.8L	6.0 to 8.0 psi
Carburetor	
3.3L and 4.1L	Carter YFA 1-V
4.2L, 5.0L and 5.8L	Motorcraft 2150 2-V, 2700VV 2-V and 7200VV 2-V
Engine speed setting, all	Refer to emission decal
Fuel tank capacity	18.0 US gallons
Fuel filter	Disposable in-line with paper element
Air filter	Replaceable paper element

Torque specifications

	ft-lb	Nm
Fuel pump-to-block		
3.3L and 4.1L	16 to 24	21 to 32
4.2L, 5.0L and 5.8L	19 to 27	26 to 37
Carburetor-to-intake manifold	12 to 15	16 to 19

1 Fuel system – general information

All models use a rear-mounted fuel tank and the fuel is drawn from the carburetor by an engine-driven fuel pump.

2 U.S. Federal regulations – emission controls

1 The fuel system is designed so that the car will comply with all U.S.A Federal regulations covering emission hydrocarbons and carbon monoxide. To achieve this, the ignition system must be accurately set using the proper equipment. Proper ignition timing is a must before attempting any other emission-related adjustments. The information in this Chapter is given to assist the reader to clean and/or replace certain components before taking the vehicle to the local Ford dealer or repair shop for final adjustments. Failure to do this could mean that the car will not comply with the regulations.

3 Thermostatic air cleaner and duct system – general information

The air cleaner contains a replaceable filter element and is retained to the carburetor by a wing nut.

An additional feature of the air cleaner is the control system for the intake air which ensures that fuel atomization within the carburetor takes place using air that is the proper temperature. This is achieved by a duct system which draws in either fresh air or pre-heated air from a heat shroud around the engine exhaust manifold.

When the engine is cold, heated air is directed from the exhaust manifold into the air cleaner, and as the engine warms up cold air is progressively mixed with this warm air to maintain the proper air temperature for proper atomization. At high ambient temperatures the hot air intake is closed off completely.

The mixing of the air is regulated by a vacuum-operated motor in the air cleaner duct, which is controlled by a bi-metal temperature sensor and a cold weather modulator valve.

Some models are equipped with Cold Temperature Actuated Vacuum (CATV) systems which have an ambient temperature sensor mounted within the air cleaner. This switch is operated by air temperature and under certain conditions will override the cold weather modulator system.

4 Thermostatic air cleaner – testing

Vacuum motor and valve assembly

1 Check that the valve is open when the engine is switched off. Start the engine, and check that the valve closes when idling (except where the engine is hot). If this fails to happen, check for disconnected or leaking vacuum lines, and for correct operation of the bi-metal sensor (see below).

2 If the valve closes, open and close the throttle rapidly. The valve should open at temperatures above 55°F (12.7°C) during the throttle operation. If this does not happen, check the valve for binding.

Bi-metal switch

3 The bi-metal switch can be checked by subjecting it to heated air, either from the engine or from an external source (eg. a hair dryer). Do not immerse it in water or damage may occur.

Cold weather modulator valve

4 Without the use of a supply of refrigerant R-12 and a vacuum source, testing is impractical. If the modulator valve is suspected of being faulty it should be tested by your Ford dealer.

5 Air cleaner element – removal and installation

1 Remove the wing nut(s) attaching the air cleaner top plate to the air cleaner housing.

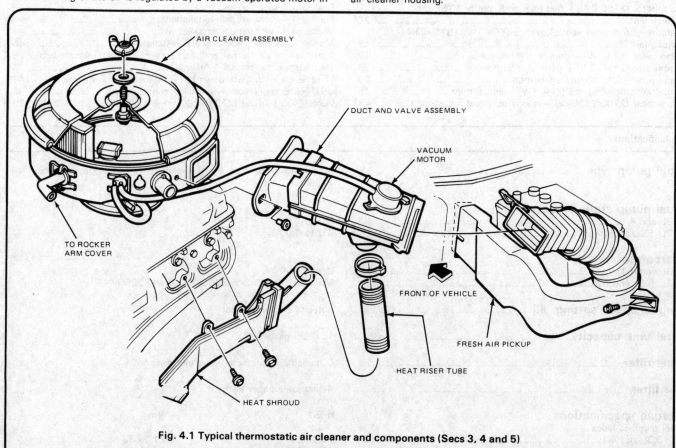

Fig. 4.1 Typical thermostatic air cleaner and components (Secs 3, 4 and 5)

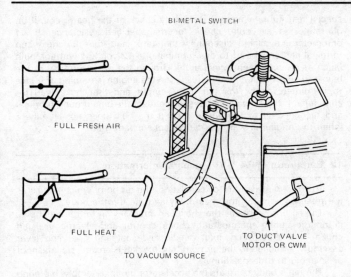

Fig. 4.2 Vacuum-operated duct operation (Secs 3 and 4)

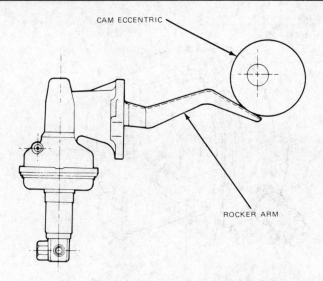

Fig. 4.3 Typical fuel pump (Sec 6)

2 Remove the air cleaner top and take out the air filter element.
3 Installation is the reverse of removal.

6 Fuel pump – general information

The fuel pump is bolted to the left side of the engine front cover. The fuel pump actuator arm is operated by the camshaft or, on V8 models, an eccentric bolted to the end of the camshaft.

The pump is a sealed unit and must be discarded and replaced by a new one if a fault develops.

7 Fuel pump – removal and installation

1 Remove the inlet and outlet pipes at the pipe and plug the ends to stop fuel loss or dirt finding its way into the fuel system (photo).
2 Undo and remove two bolts and spring washers that secure the pump to the cylinder block.
3 Lift away the fuel pump and gasket.
4 Installing the fuel pump is the reverse sequence to removal but there are several additional points that should be noted: (photo).

   a) Tighten the pump securing bolts to the specified torque
   b) Before reconnecting the pipe from the fuel tank to the pump inlet, move the end to a position lower than the fuel tank so that fuel can syphon out. Quickly connect the pipe to the pump inlet
   c) Disconnect the pipe at the carburetor and turn the engine over until gasoline flows from the open end. Quickly connect the pipe to the carburetor union. This last operation will help to prime the pump.

8 Fuel pump – testing (all models)

1 Assuming that the fuel lines and unions are in good condition and that there are no leaks anywhere, check the performance of the fuel pump in the following manner. Disconnect the fuel pipe at the carburetor inlet union, and the high tension lead to the coil and, with a suitable container or large rag in position to catch the ejected fuel, turn the engine over. A good spurt of gasoline should emerge from the end of the pipe every second revolution.

9 Fuel filter – replacement

Fuel filter replacement is covered in Chapter 1.

10 Carburetion – warning

1 Before making any adjustment or alteration to the carburetor or emission control systems (see Section 33), the owner is advised to make himself aware of any Federal, State or Provincial laws which may be contravened by making any such adjustment or alteration.
2 Setting dimensions and specifications are given in this Chapter where relevant to adjustment procedures. Where these differ from those given on the engine tune-up decal, the decal information should be assumed to be correct.
3 Where the use of special test equipment is called for (eg, exhaust gas CO analyzer, etc), and this equipment is not available, any setting or calibration should be regarded as a temporary measure only and should be rechecked by a suitably equipped dealer or carburetion/emission control specialist at the earliest opportunity.
4 Before attempting any carburetor adjustments, first ascertain that the following items are serviceable or correctly set:

   a) All vacuum hoses and connections
   b) Ignition system
   c) Spark plugs
   d) Ignition initial advance

5 If satisfactory adjustment cannot be obtained check the following:

   a) Carburetor fuel level
   b) Crankcase ventilation system
   c) Valve clearance
   d) Engine compression
   e) Idle mixture

11 Electrically assisted choke heater – description and testing

1 Some carburetors have an electrically operated heater to aid in fast choke release and help reduce emissions during warm up.
2 The choke assist system consists of a choke cap, thermostatic spring, bimetal temperature sensing switch and positive temperature coefficient (PTC) heater. The system is grounded to the carburetor and receives current from the center tap of the alternator.
3 At temperatures below 60°F (16°C), the sensing switch remains open and normal thermostatic spring action takes place. Above 60°F the sensing switch allows current from the alternator to activate the heater, warming the thermostatic spring so it opens faster. The thermostatic spring then pulls down the choke.
4 A fast idle cam latch works in conjunction with the choke to hold the cam in the high position until the choke backs off, allowing the latch to rotate to the normal run position.
5 The only test that can be carried out on this assembly, without

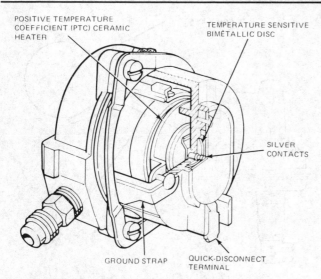

Fig. 4.4 Electrically-assisted choke (Sec 11)

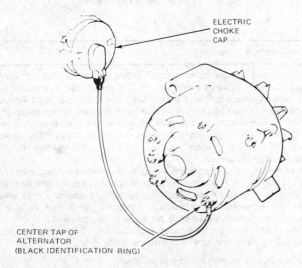

Fig. 4.5 Electrically-assisted choke wiring (Sec 11)

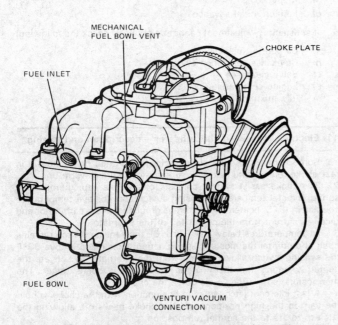

Fig. 4.6 Carter model YFA 1-V carburetor (Sec 12)

special test equipment, is a continuity check of the heater coil. If an ohmmeter is available, check for the specified resistance. If no ohmmeter is available, disconnect the stator lead from the choke cap terminal and connect it to one terminal of a 12 volt low wattage bulb (such as an instrument panel bulb). Ground the other terminal of the bulb and check that it illuminates when the engine is running. If it fails to illuminate, check the alternator output and the choke lead for continuity. If the bulb illuminates, disconnect the bulb ground terminal and reconnect it to the choke lead. If the bulb does not illuminate when the engine is warm, a faulty choke is indicated.

12 Carburetor (YFA 1-V) – general information

The YFA 1-V carburetor consists of the air horn, which serves as the main body cover, the main body and the throttle body.

The air horn contains the choke, an internal vent for the fuel bowl, automatic choke thermostatic choke control and electric assisted choke, fuel inlet fitting, inlet needle and seat and float and lever assembly. Attached to the air horn by a bracket is an anti-stall dashpot or solenoid throttle positioner.

The main body contains the accelerator pump assembly, metering rod, main metering jet, low speed jet, accelerator pump check ball and weight and the main discharge nozzle.

The throttle body contains the throttle plate, throttle shaft and lever and idle mixture screw with plastic limiter cap.

Some models are equipped with solenoid throttle positioners to reduce the engine's tendency to 'run on' because the solenoid allows the throttle plate to close further than normal when the engine is shut off.

The choke on all models is electrically operated.

13 Carburetor fast idle speed (YFA 1-V) – adjustment

1   With the engine at operating temperature, remove the air cleaner, disconnect the EGR vacuum and attach a tachometer.
2   Rotate the fast idle cam so that the fast idle adjusting screw is resting on the cam as shown in the accompanying figure.
3   Turning the fast idle speed adjustment screw clockwise increased the idle speed. Adjust the idle speed to the specification on the emissions decal.
4   Remove the tachometer, connect the EGR vacuum and reinstall the air cleaner.

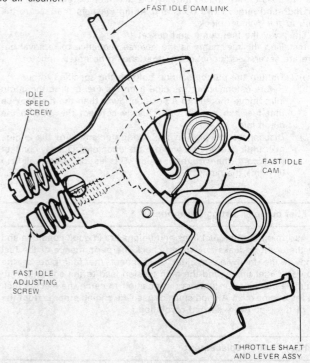

Fig. 4.7 Idle adjustment (YFA 1-V) (Sec 13)

14 Carburetor fast idle cam (YFA 1-V) – setting

1   Position the fast idle screw located on the shoulder of the fast idle cap against the shoulder of the highest step.
2   To adjust the fast idle cam setting, bend the choke plate connecting rod until the specified clearance between the lower edge of the choke plate and the carburetor bore is obtained. The clearance can be checked by inserting a drill bit shank of the specified size between the choke plate and carburetor bore.

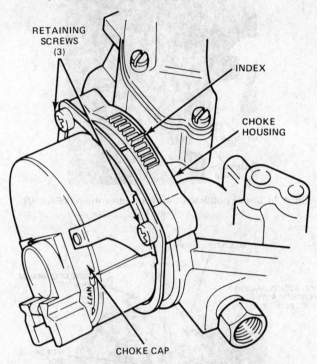

Fig. 4.8 Choke cap adjustment (YFA 1-V) (Sec 15)

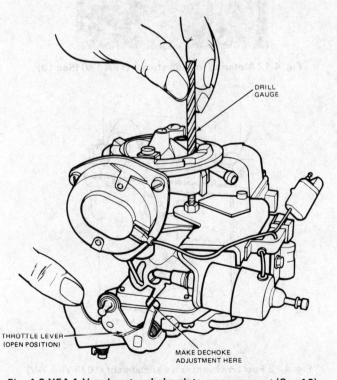

Fig. 4.9 YFA 1-V carburetor choke plate measurement (Sec 16)

15 Carburetor automatic choke (YFA 1-V) – adjustment

1   The automatic choke on most models can be adjusted to control its reaction to engine temprature. This is accomplished by loosening the thermostatic spring housing screws and turning the housing. The engine emissions label contains the information for proper setting.
2   Remove the air cleaner assembly.
3   Loosen the thermostatic spring housing screws and rotate the housing to the marks specified on the emissions decal.
4   Tighten the retaining screws.
5   Install the air cleaner assembly.

16 Carburetor choke plate dechoke (YFA 1-V) – adjustment

1   Remove the air cleaner assembly.
2   Hold the throttle plate fully open and close the choke plate lightly. Insert a proper size drill bit shank (refer to the emissions decal) between the choke plate and air horn wall to check the clearance.
3   Bend the arm of the choke trip lever of the throttle lever if the clearance is not within specifications. Bending the arm upward increases the clearance and bending it downward decreases it.
4   After adjustment, check the clearances and reinstall the air cleaner assembly.

17 Carburetor choke plate pulldown (YFA 1-V) – measurement and adjustment

1975 thru 1977
1   Remove the air cleaner assembly, choke spring housing and heat baffle from the carburetor.
2   Bend a 0.026 in diameter wire at a 90° angle approximately $\frac{1}{8}$ in from the end as shown in the accompanying figure.
3   Insert the bent end of the wire into the choke housing between the choke piston slot and the right slot in the housing. Turn the choke piston lever counterclockwise until the wire gauge fits snugly in the piston slot as shown in the accompanying figure.
4   Hold the gauge in place by keeping light pressure on the choke piston and use the proper size drill to check the clearance between the carburetor bore wall and the choke plate.
5   If adjustment is necessary, bend the choke piston lever as necessary to obtain the proper setting. Use care so that the piston link is not distorted when bending the lever.
6   Reinstall the air cleaner assembly and any components which were removed.

1978 thru 1980
7   With the engine cold, remove the air cleaner assembly.
8   Set the throttle onto the highest step of the fast idle cam.
9   With the choke plate closed, mark the position of the choke cap for use when resetting the cap.

Fig. 4.10 Choke pulldown adjustment tool (YFA 1-V) (Sec 17)

10 Loosen the choke cap retaining screws and rotate the cap 90° to the Rich position. Tighten the screws.

11 Use a vacuum pump to apply vacuum to the choke pulldown motor external vacuum tube, activating the motor.

12 Push down on the choke lever of the pulldown motor and release it to make sure the motor is fully retracted. Push down only on the choke lever and not the linkage or shaft. If the vacuum has not fully retracted the motor, check the motor diaphragm for leakage. Replace the motor if the diaphragm is determined to have a leak.

13 Check the choke plate to make sure that it has not been moved and measure the clearance, adjusting if necessary, following the procedures in steps 2, 3, 4 and 5.

14 After adjustments have been made, reset the choke cap to the position marked in step 9.

15 Replace the air cleaner assembly and any other components which were removed.

18 Carburetor metering rod (YFA 1-V) – adjustment

1 Remove the carburetor air cleaner, air horn and gasket.

2 Back the idle speed adjusting screw out until the throttle plate is closed tightly in the throttle bore.

3 Push down on the end of the pump diaphragm until it bottoms.

4 To adjust the metering rod, hold the diaphragm down and turn the adjustment screw until the metering rod just bottoms in the body casing as shown in the accompanying figure.

5 For final adjustment, turn the metering rod one additional turn clockwise.

6 Install the carburetor air horn with a new gasket and reinstall the air cleaner assembly.

19 Carburetor fuel bowl vent clearance (YFA 1-V, 1975 only) – adjustment

1 Check the curb idle rpm with the throttle positioner activated, as specified on the emissions decal and adjust as necessary.

2 Turn the engine off and leave the ignition key in the On position so that the positioner solenoid is activated.

3 Open the throttle so that the throttle vent lever does not touch the fuel bowl vent rod.

4 Close the throttle and referring to the accompanying figure, measure the travel of the fuel bowl vent rod from the open position to the idle position at point A. The travel should be 0.020 in, plus or minus 0.010 in.

5 If the travel is not correct, adjust by bending the throttle vent lever at the indentation.

20 Carburetor float dry level (YFA 1-V) – adjustment

1 Dry float fuel level is generally the final step after carburetor overhaul and should be done with the carburetor removed.

2 Fabricate or obtain from your Ford dealer the proper float level gauge.

3 Invert the air horn and measure the clearance from the indentation on the top of the float to the bottom of the air horn with the gauge. Hold the air horn at eye level when checking the float level. The float arm should be resting on the needle pin but the needle should not be under load.

4 To adjust, bend the float arm to obtain the proper clearance. Do not bend the tab at the end of the float arm because it would prevent the float from striking the float bowl bottom when empty.

21 Carburetor (YFA 1-V) – removal and installation

1 Remove the air cleaner assembly.

2 Disconnect the throttle cable or rod. At the carburetor, disconnect the EGR vacuum line, venturi vacuum line, distributor vacuum line, fuel line and choke heater tube (if equipped).

3 Disconnect the choke clean air hose external vent hose from the air cleaner.

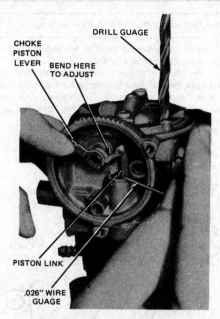

Fig. 4.11 Choke pulldown clearance adjustment (YFA 1-V) (Sec 17)

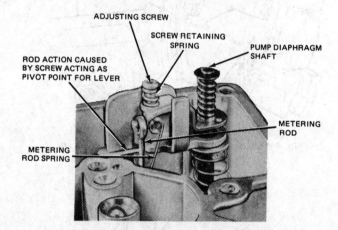

Fig. 4.12 Metering rod adjustment (YFA 1-V) (Sec 18)

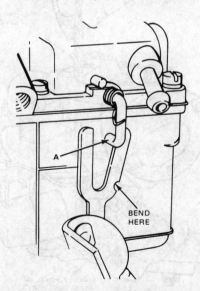

Fig. 4.13 Fuel bowl vent valve adjustment (1975 YFA 1-V) (Sec 19)

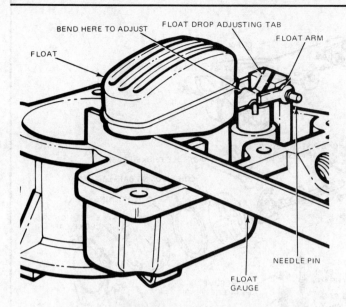

Fig. 4.14 YFA carburetor dry float level adjustment (Secs 20 and 21)

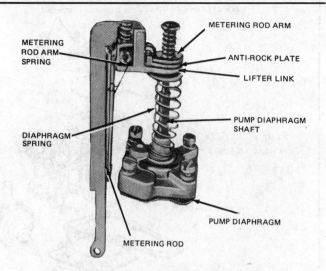

Fig. 4.15 Accelerating pump and lifter link assembly (YFA 1-V) (Sec 22)

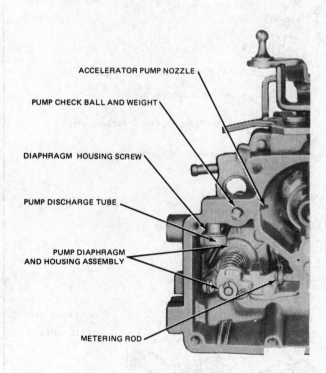

Fig. 4.16 Pump diaphragm and housing components (YFA 1-V) (Sec 22)

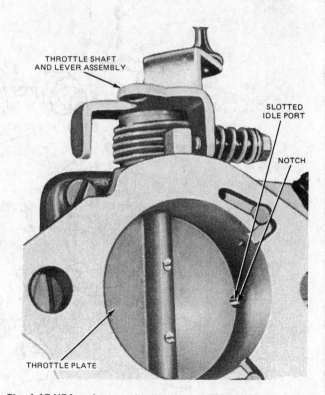

Fig. 4.17 YFA carburetor throttle plate and shaft arm installation (Sec 22)

4   Remove the nuts retaining the carburetor to the intake manifold and remove the carburetor.

5   Place a rag in the carburetor opening in the intake manifold and clean all traces of gasket material from the mounting surface.

6   Installation is the reverse of removal. Install the retaining nuts finger tight and then tighten to specification.

7   Reinstall the air cleaner assembly and other components which were removed.

22 Carburetor (YFA 1-V) – dismantling and reassembly

1   Remove the carburetor as described in Section 21.

2   On models equipped with a choke pulldown motor, remove the retaining screws, disconnect the choke pulldown link and remove the motor assembly, disengaging the link from the choke shaft lever.

3   Remove the choke retaining screws, housing retainers, spring housing assembly, gasket, baffle plate and fast idle link.

4   Remove the screws securing the air horn assembly to the carburetor and remove the air horn, gasket and solenoid bracket assembly.

5   With the air horn assembly upside down, remove the float pin, float and lever assembly. Turn the air horn assembly over and catch the needle pin, spring and needle and remove the needle seat and gasket.

6   Remove the air cleaner bracket. File the staked ends off the

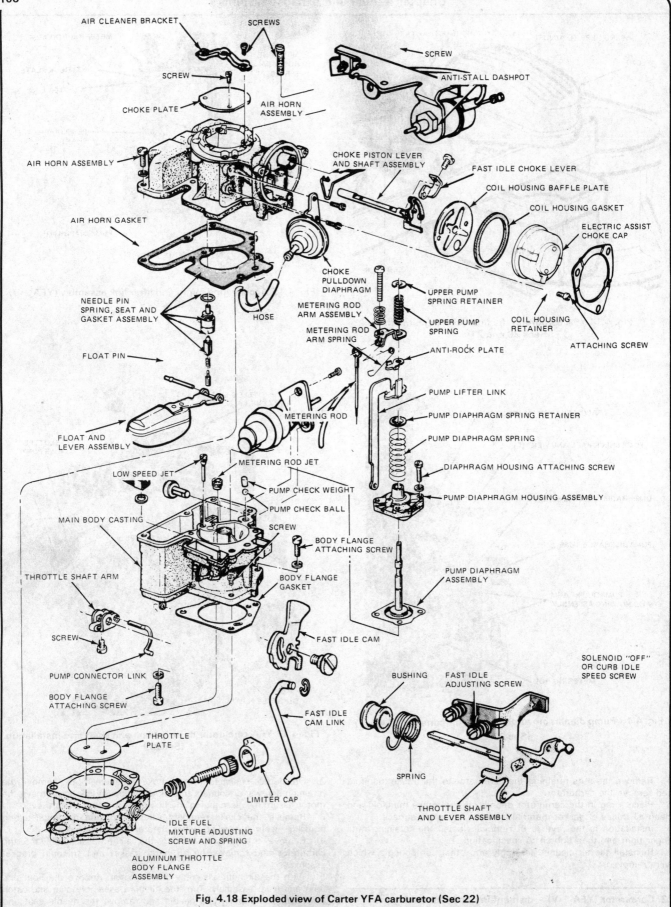

Fig. 4.18 Exploded view of Carter YFA carburetor (Sec 22)

screws retaining the choke plate and remove the screws and plate. Remove the choke link lever and screw.

7   Turn the main body casing upside down and catch the accelerating pump check ball and weight and (if equipped) hot idle compensator.

8   Remove the mechanical bowl vent operating lever assembly from the throttle shaft.

9   Loosen the throttle shaft screw and remove the arm and pump connector link.

10 Remove the fast idle cam and shoulder screw.

11 Remove the accelerating pump diaphragm housing screws and lift the pump diaphragm assembly out as a unit.

12 Disengage the metering rod spring from the rod and remove the rod from the arm assembly. Sketch the location of any washers which may be used in shimming the springs so they can be reinstalled in the same location. Compress the upper pump spring and remove the spring retainer, spring and pump diaphragm assembly from the housing, referring to the accompanying figure.

13 Use the proper size jet tool or screwdriver to remove the main metering rod jet and low speed jet.

14 On models with a temperature-compensated accelerator pump, remove the bleed valve plug from the main body, using a punch. Loosen the bleed valve screw and remove the valve.

15 Remove the retaining screws and separate the throttle body from the main body of the carburetor.

16 File the staked throttle plate retaining screws and remove the screws and plate. Slide the throttle shaft and lever assembly from the carburetor. Make sure to note the location of the ends of the spring on the throttle shaft for proper reinstallation. Also be sure to note the position of the idle limiter cap tab for ease of proper assembly. After removing the cap, count the number of turns to lightly seat the needle and make a note of this for use during reassembly.

17 The carburetor is now completely disassembled and should be cleaned and inspected for wear. After the carburetor components have been cleaned in the proper solvent of dirt, gum and carbon deposits, they should be rinsed in kerosene and dried, preferably with compressed air. Do not use a wire brush to clean the carburetor and clean all passages with compressed air rather than wire or drills as these could enlarge them. Inspect the throttle and choke shafts for grooves, wear or excessive looseness. Check the throttle and choke plates for hicks and smoothness of operation. Inspect the carburetor body and components for cracks. Check the floats for leaks by submerging them in water which has been heated to just below boiling. Leaks will be indicated by the appearance of bubbles. Check the float arm needle contact surface for grooves. If the grooves are light, polish the needle contact surface with crocus cloth or steel wool. Replace the floats if the shafts are badly worn. Inspect the gasket metering surfaces for burrs and nicks, replace any distorted springs or screws or bolts with stripped threads.

18 To reassemble, install the throttle shaft and lever assembly in the throttle body flange. Make sure the bushings and springs are in the positions noted during disassembly. Position the throttle plate on the throttle shaft with the notch aligned with the slotted idle port as shown in the accompanying figure. Install the throttle plate, using new screws. Tighten the screws so they are snug and then move the throttle plate around to check that it doesn't bind in the bore. Make sure that the idle speed screw is backed off when checking the throttle plate fit. Reposition the plate as necessary, tighten the screws and stake or peen them in place. Install the idle speed screw the same number of turns recorded during removal.

19 Install the main body to the throttle body flange and fully tighten the screws evenly.

20 Install the low speed jet and main metering rod jet.

21 Install the pump diaphragm in the pump diaphragm housing. Place the pump diaphragm spring on the diaphragm shaft and housing assembly. Install the spring shim washers, spring retainer, pump lifter link, metering rod arm and spring assembly and upper pump spring on the diaphragm shaft. Depress the spring and install the upper pump and spring retainer.

22 Assemble the metering rod on the metering rod arm and place the looped end of the metering rod arm spring as shown in the accompanying figure. Align the diaphragm pump with the housing, making sure the holes are lined up. Install the housing attachment screws to maintain alignment.

23 Install the assembly into the carburetor main body, engage the pump lifter link with the body and insert the metering rod in the main

metering rod jet. Install the pump housing screws so that they are snug, but not tight. Push down on the diaphragm shaft and then tighten the screws. Adjust the metering rod as described in Section 18.

24 Place the pump bleed valve and washer in position and install the retaining screw. Install a new welch plug, using a $\frac{1}{4}$ in flat drift punch to seat it.

25 Install the fast idle cam and shoulder screw, throttle shaft arm and pump connector link and tighten the lock screw.

26 Install the E-clip, spacer, wave washer, bowl vent actuating lever and tighten the retaining screw. Install the hot idle compensator valve and accelerator pump check ball and weight.

27 Install the choke shaft assembly through the choke housing, the pulldown link lever into the air horn and tighten the retaining screw.

28 Place the choke plate in position on the choke shaft and install the retaining screws snugly, but not tight. Check the choke plate for binding and tighten the screws and peen or stake them in place.

29 Install the needle seat and gasket into the air horn. Turn the air horn over, and install the needle, pin spring, needle pin, float and lever assembly and float pin. Adjust the float level as described in Section 20.

30 Align the bowl vent flapper valve with the vent rod, making sure that the spring is properly installed on the vent rod shaft. Install the spring retainer.

31 Place a new air horn gasket in position and install the air horn, making sure that the mechanical fuel bowl vent engages the forked actuating lever. Install the solenoid bracket.

32 Install the choke coil housing with the identification marks facing out, the gasket and baffle plate. The thermostatic spring must engage the choke lever tang and not be stopped by the baffle plate retaining tab (if equipped). Set the choke housing to the index specified on the emissions decal and tighten the screws.

33 Install the air cleaner bracket and fast idle link.

34 Engage the choke pulldown link with the choke fast lever and the pulldown diaphragm rod. Place the diaphragm bracket on the air horn and install the attaching screws. Connect the pulldown vacuum hose to the diaphragm housing.

35 Adjust the carburetor to the operating specifications on the emissions decal.

23 Carburetor (2150-2V) – general information

The Motorcraft 2150-2V carburetor is used on various V8 engines.

The 2150-2V carburetor is composed of two main assemblies; the main body and the air horn. The air horn assembly serves as the main body cover and contains the choke plate and fuel bowl vent valve. Also

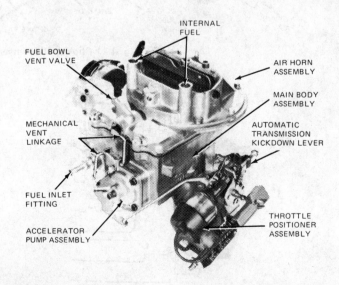

Fig. 4.19 Typical Motorcraft 2150 2-V carburetor (Sec 23)

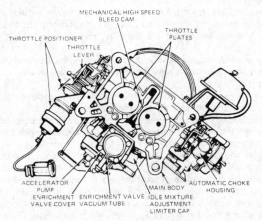

Fig. 4.20 Bottom view of the 2150 2-V carburetor (Sec 23)

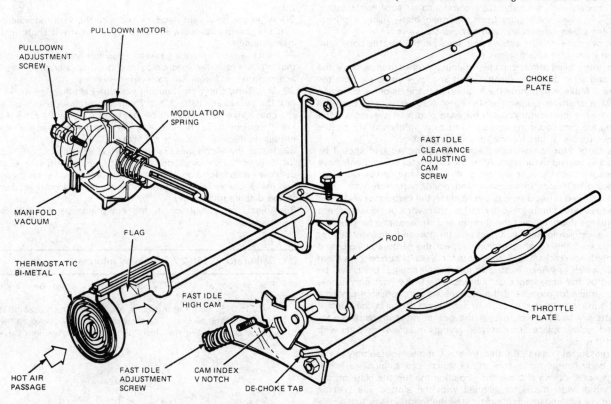

Fig. 4.21 Choke pulldown assemblies (2150 2-V) (Sec 24)

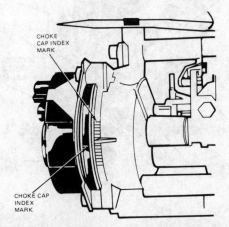

Fig. 4.22 2150 carburetor choke housing (Sec 24)

in this assembly is the pullover enrichment system which provides additional fuel flow when there is high air flow through the air horn.

Fuel is drawn from the fuel bowl into the air flow through bleeds in the metered orifice.

In the main body are the throttle plate, accelerator pump assembly, fuel bowl and mechanical high-speed bleed cam.

Some models are equipped with high altitude compensators which consists of a choke in the bypass air intake for improved high altitude cold starts.

On most vehicles the choke is electronically operated.

24 Choke plate vacuum pulldown (2150-2V) – adjustment

1   Run the engine until it is up to operating temperature (about 5 minutes) and then shut it off.
2   Remove the carburetor air cleaner to provide access to the carburetor.
3   Rotate the choke housing to the rich setting which will lightly close the choke plate. Rotate the housing an additional 90°.

4   Push the choke pulldown diaphragm to the closed position.
5   Use a $\frac{1}{2}$ in drill bit shank to measure the clearance between the air horn wall and lower edge of the choke plate.
6   To decrease the choke pulldown, turn the adjusting screw clockwise and to increase it, turn the screw counterclockwise.
7   The fast idle cam must be adjusted after choke vacuum pull-down has been adjusted.

25 Fast idle cam (2150-2V) – adjustment

1   With the choke housing rotated to the rich position as described in Section 24, push the throttle open to set the fast idle cam.
2   Close the choke as described in step 4 of Section 24.
3   Open the throttle while watching the fast idle cam and idle speed screw. The cam should drop to the kickdown step and idle speed screw should be opposite the 'V' notch on the cam.
4   To align the fast idle speed screw with the 'V' notch, turn the hex headed screw in the plastic fast idle cam lever.

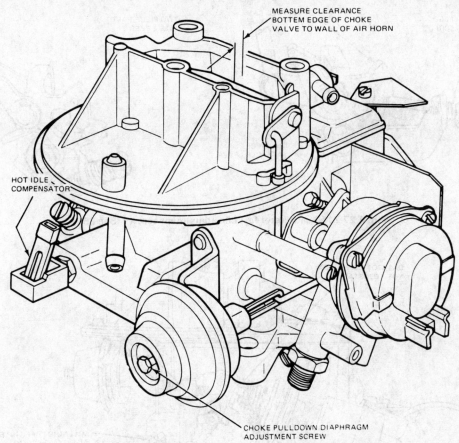

Fig. 4.23 Measuring 2150 carburetor choke plate clearance (Sec 24)

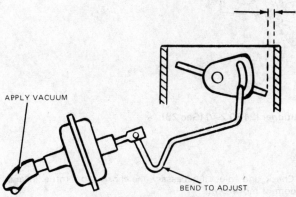

Fig. 4.24 Choke pulldown adjustment (2150 2-V) (Sec 24)

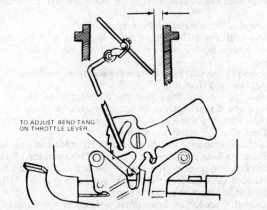

Fig. 4.26 Adjusting the fast idle speed lever tang (2150 2-V) (Sec 25)

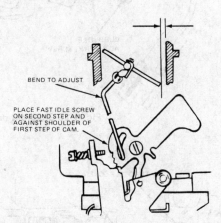

Fig. 4.25 Fast idle cam adjustment (2150 2-V) (Sec 25)

5 To de-choke after adjusting the choke vacuum pulldown fast idle cam, hold the throttle wide open.

6 Measure the clearance between the choke plate lower edge and the air horn wall as described in step 5, Section 24. To adjust the clearance, bend the metal tang on the fast idle speed lever.

7 After all adjustments are made, reset the choke thermostat housing to the specifications on the emissions decal.

26 Carburetor (2150-2V) – fast idle, curb idle and TSP off adjustment

1 Start the engine and run it up to operating temperature. Shut the engine off and remove the air cleaner. The air cleaner assembly must be in position when engine speeds are measured.

2 Apply the parking brake and block the rear wheels.

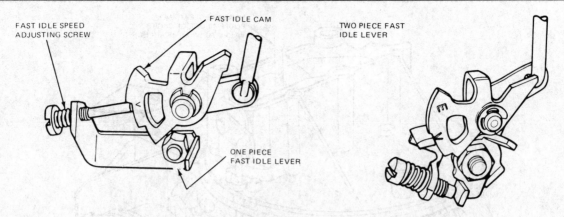

Fig. 4.27 2150 carburetor fast idle adjustment screws (Sec 26)

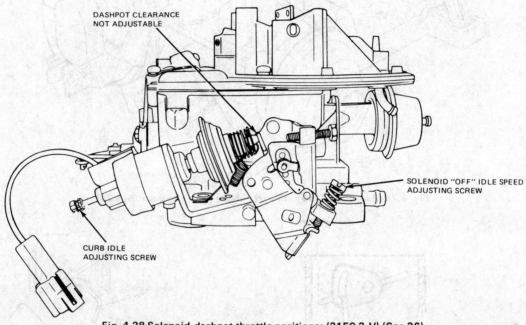

Fig. 4.28 Solenoid-dashpot throttle positioner (2150 2-V) (Sec 26)

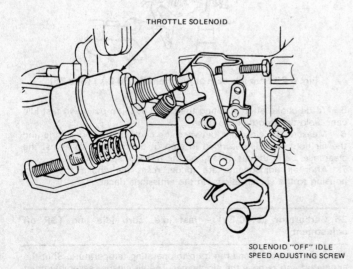

Fig. 4.29 2150 carburetor throttle solenoid throttle positioner (Sec 26)

3   Check, and adjust if necessary, the choke and throttle linkages for freedom of movement.

4   Where applicable, turn the air conditioner to OFF.

5   Disconnect the evaporative purge line from the carburetor and plug it.

6   Connect a tachometer to the engine.

7   Disconnect the EGR vacuum hose and plug it. If the vehicle is equipped with a ported vacuum switch (PVS), do not disconnect the EGR line.

8   Disconnect the distributor vacuum hose from the advance side of the distributor and plug it.

9   Follow the vacuum hose from the thermactor dump valve to the carburetor and disconnect the dump valve vacuum hose nearest the carburetor. Plug the original vacuum source and connect the dump valve directly to the manifold vacuum.

10 With the transmission in Park (automatic) or Neutral (manual) and the choke plate fully open, run the engine at 2500 rpm for 15 seconds. Place the fast idle lever on the step of the fast idle cam specified on the emissions decal. Allow the engine speed to stabilize (10 to 15 seconds) and measure the fast idle rpm.

11 Repeat this procedure three times and adjust the fast idle rpm if not as specified.

12 Before adjusting the curb idle, it is necessary to determine which

of the various throttle positioners and engine speed control devices the carburetor is equipped with. Refer to Chapter 6 for a description of these devices.

13 Make all adjustments after determining the curb idle speeds by following the procedure described in steps 1 through 11.

14 On vehicles without air conditioning or other solenoid devices, the curb idle is adjusted by turning the throttle screw.

15 If the carburetor is equipped with a dashpot to control the throttle closing, the dashpot plunger must be collapsed with the engine off. Check the clearance between the plunger and the throttle lever pad and adjust, if necessary, to the specifications on the emissions label. Each time the curb idle is adjusted, the dashpot clearance must also be adjusted.

16 On anti-diesel TSP-equipped vehicles, the curb idle is adjusted by collapsing the TSP plunger by forcing the throttle lever pad against the plunger. The curb idle is then adjusted by turning the throttle stop adjusting screw.

17 If equipped with air conditioning, dashpot and TSP, turn the air conditioning off and determine the curb idle rpm. Adjust to the specified air conditioning curb idle by turning the throttle stop screw. Turn the engine off, collapse the TSP plunger and check the clearance between the plunger and throttle lever pad. To adjust, turn the long screw which is part of the assembly mounting bracket.

18 Reconnect all vacuum lines and Thermactor hoses to their proper locations and re-install the air cleaner.

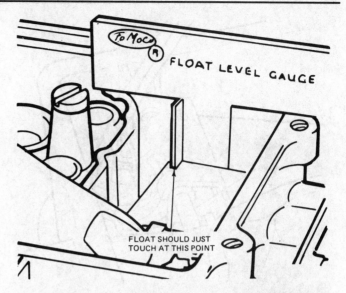

Fig. 4.30 Measuring 2150 carburetor dry float level with Ford gauge (Sec 77)

27 Carburetor (2150-2V) – dry float setting

1 The dry float setting can only be checked at the appropriate stage of carburetor disassembly.

2 Remove the carburetor air horn, raise the float and seat the fuel inlet needle.

3 Remove the gasket and depress the float tab to assure seating of the fuel inlet needle while being careful not to damage the needles Viton tip.

4 Measure from a point near the center, $\frac{1}{8}$ in (3.2 mm) from the free end of the float to the top surface of the carburetor body. This measurement must be $\frac{7}{16}$ in. Bend the tab on the float to adjust the level. Alternatively, the float level can be checked using a cardboard gauge available at your Ford dealer.

28 Carburetor – idle mixture adjustment

1 On 1979 and later models idle mixture adjustment can only be carried out by using special test equipment. Refer to your local dealer or repair shop for proper adjustment.

2 1975 thru 1978 YFA 1-V and 2150 2-V carburetors' idle mixture can be adjusted to some extent. The idle mixture screws on these carburetors have limiter stops to limit adjustment within a narrow range.

3 Idle mixture adjustment on these models can be accomplished at the same time that fast and curb idle is set.

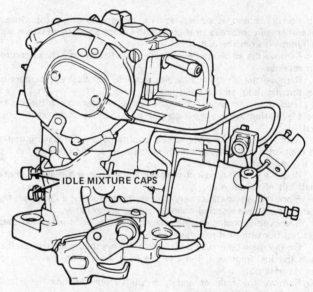

Fig. 4.31 YFA carburetor idle mixture screw (Sec 28)

29 Carburetor (2150, 2700VV and 7200VV) – removal and installation

1 Remove the air cleaner as described in Section 5.

2 Disconnect the fuel feed line from the carburetor.

3 Disconnect the electrical leads and vacuum lines from the carburetor.

4 Disconnect the throttle cable/kick-down cable from the carburetor.

5 Using suitable cranked wrenches, remove the carburetor mounting nuts and lift the carburetor, gasket and spacer (if equipped) from the manifold.

6 Installation is basically a reverse of the removal procedure, but ensure that a new flange gasket is used.

30 Carburetor (2150-2V) – dismantling and reassembly

1 Before dismantling, wash the exterior of the carburetor in the proper solvent and wipe off using a lint-free rag. Select a clean area of

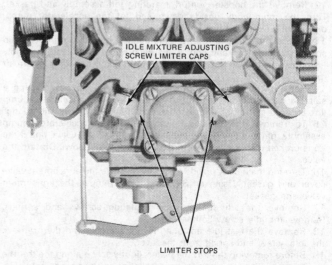

Fig. 4.32 2150 carburetor idle mixture screws (Sec 28)

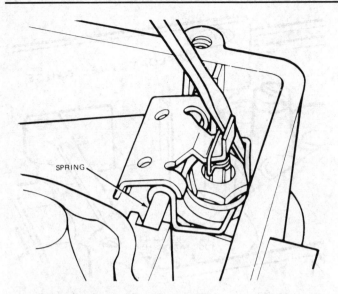

Fig. 4.33 Removing the 2150 float shaft retainer (Sec 30)

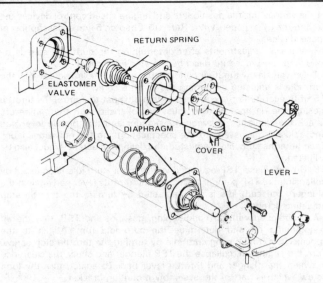

Fig. 4.34 2150 carburetor accelerator pump assembly (Sec 30)

the workbench and lay several layers of newspaper on the top. Obtain several small containers to segregate the many small parts which will be removed from the carburetor.

2   Remove the air cleaner anchor screw and automatic choke control rod retainer.

3   Remove the air horn attaching screws, lockwashers, carburetor identification tag, air horn and gasket.

4   Loosen the screw securing the choke control rod to the choke shaft lever. Remove the choke control rod and slide out the plastic dust seal.

5   Remove the choke plate screws after removing the staking marks on their ends and remove the choke plate by sliding it out of the top of the air horn.

6   Remove the bypass air choke plate and screws and slide the choke shaft out of the air horn.

7   From the automatic choke, remove the fast idle cam retainer, the thermostatic choke spring housing, clamp and retainer.

8   Remove the choke housing assembly, gasket and the fast idle cam and rod from the fast idle cam lever.

9   On the main body, use a screwdriver to pry the float shaft retainer from the fuel inlet seat. Remove the float, float shaft and fuel inlet needle assembly.

10   Remove the retainer and float shaft from the float lever and remove the fuel filler bowl.

11   Remove the fuel inlet needle, seat filter screen and main jets.

12   Remove the booster venturi, metering rod assembly and gasket. Turn the main body upside down and let the accelerator pump, discharge weight and ball fall into your hand.

13   Disassemble the lift rod from the booster by removing the lift rod spring retaining clip and spring and separating the lift rod assembly from the booster. Do not remove the metering rod hanger from the lift rod.

14   Remove the roll pin from the accelerator pump cover, using a suitable punch. Retain the roll pin and remove the accelerator pump link and rod assembly, pump cover, diaphragm assembly and spring.

15   To remove the Elastomer valve from the accelerator pump assembly, grasp it firmly and pull it out. Examine the valve, and if the tip is broken off, be sure to remove it from the fuel bowl. Discard the valve.

16   Turn the main body upside down and remove the enrichment valve cover and gasket. Using an 8-point socket, remove the enrichment valve and gasket.

17   Remove the idle fuel mixture adjusting screws and springs. Remove the idle screw limiter caps.

18   Remove the fast idle adjusting lever assembly and then remove the idle screw and spring from the lever.

19   Before removing the throttle plates, lightly scribe along the throttle shaft and mark each plate for re-installation in the proper bore (Fig. 4.36). File off the staked portion of the throttle plate screws before

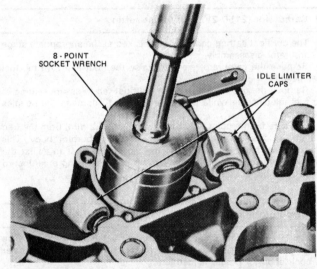

Fig. 4.35 2150 carburetor enrichment valve removal (Sec 30)

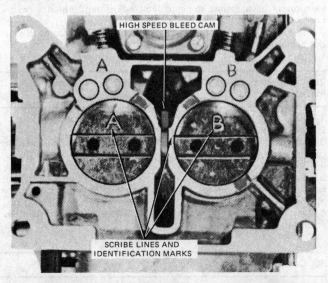

Fig. 4.36 Marking the throttle plates prior to removal (2150 2-V) (Sec 30)

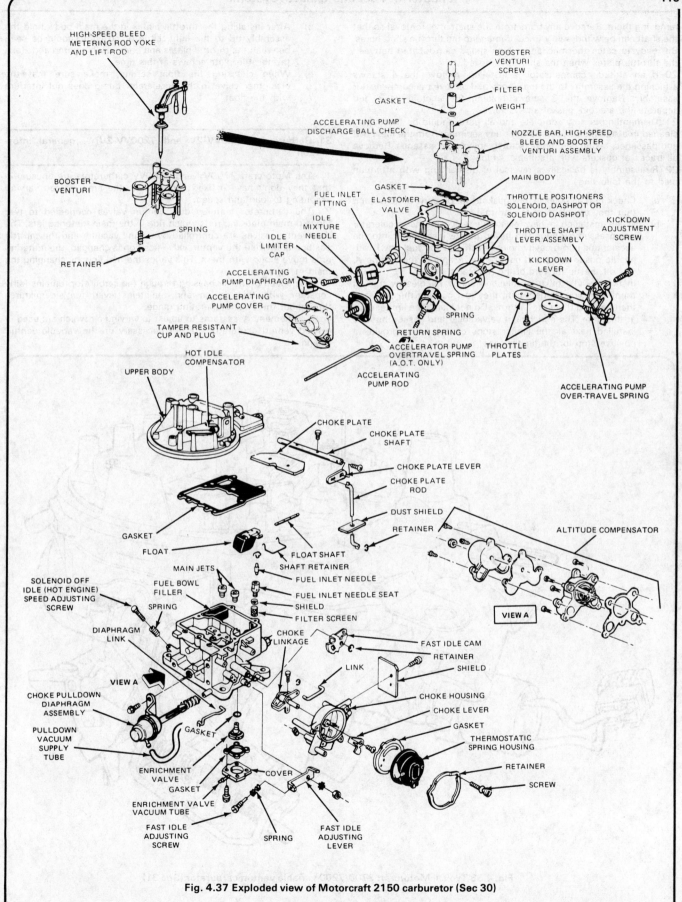

Fig. 4.37 Exploded view of Motorcraft 2150 carburetor (Sec 30)

removing them. Remove any burrs from the shaft after removal so that the shaft can be withdrawn without damage to the throttle shaft bores. Be ready to catch the mechanical high-speed cam located between the throttle plates when the shaft is removed.

20 If an altitude compensator is installed, remove the 4 screws attaching the assembly to the main body and remove the compensator assembly. Remove the 3 screws holding the aneroid valve and separate the aneroid, gasket and valve.

21 Dismantling is now complete and all parts should be thoroughly cleaned in a suitable solvent. Remove any sediment from the fuel bowl and passages, taking care not to scratch any of the passages. Remove all traces of gaskets with a suitable scraper.

22 Reassembly is basically a reversal of dismantling with attention paid to the following:

a) Check that all holes in new gaskets are properly punched and that they are clean of foreign material

b) When installing a new elastomer valve in the accelerator pump assembly, lubricate its tip before inserting it into the accelerator pump cavity hole. Reach into the fuel bowl with needle nosed pliers and pull the valve tip into the fuel bowl. Cut off the tip forward of the retainer shoulder

c) Install the idle mixture adjusting screw needles by turning them with your fingers until they just contact the seat and then backing them off 1½ turns. Do not install the limiter caps at this time. The enrichment valve cover and gasket must be installed next as the limiter stops on the cover provide a positive stop for the limiter caps

d) After installing the throttle plates in the main body, hold the assembly up to the light. Little or no light should be seen between the throttle plates and bores. Fully tighten and stake the throttle plate screws at this time

e) When checking the float setting, make sure that the elastomer valve in the accelerator pump does not interfere with the float

31 Carburetor (2700VV-2V and 7200VV-2V) – general information

1 The Motorcraft 2700VV and 7200VV carburetors are unusual in that they don't have a fixed venturi area, the area instead varying according to load and speed.

2 The carburetor features dual venturi valves connected to two tapered main metering rods which ride in the main metering jets. The dual venturi valves are controlled by engine vacuum and the throttle position and when the venturi valve position is changed, the metering rods move along with them. This varies the fuel flow by changing the main metering jets.

3 The speed of the air passing through the carburetor remains fairly constant with this design and maintains even fuel/air mixtures throughout the engine operating range.

4 Supplementary systems to adjust to varying air which are used in a fixed venturi carburetor are not necessary on the variable venturi design.

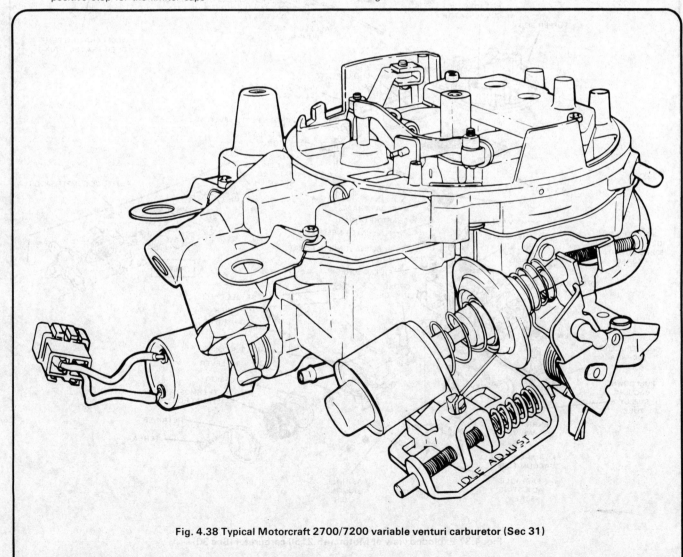

Fig. 4.38 Typical Motorcraft 2700/7200 variable venturi carburetor (Sec 31)

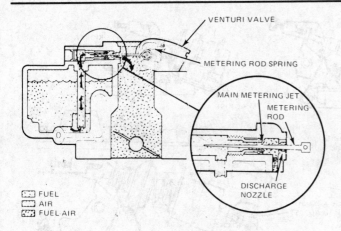

FUEL
AIR
FUEL-AIR

Fig. 4.39 Variable venturi main metering system (Sec 31)

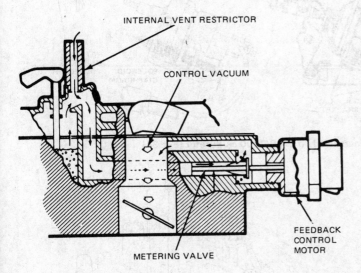

Fig. 4.40 7200VV carburetor backsuction feedback system (Sec 31)

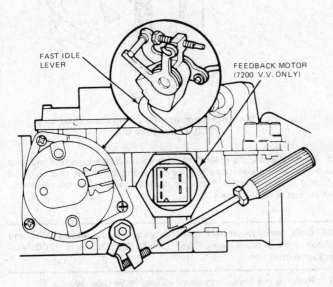

Fig. 4.41 Fast idle speed adjustment (2700/7200) (Sec 33)

5   The Motorcraft 7200VV variable venturi carburetor is basically the same design as the 2700VV, the major difference being the addition of feedback control system designed to work in conjunction with an onboard electronic control system (EEC). The EEC system is described in Chapter 5.

6   The feedback system improves drivability, fuel economy and exhaust emissions by more precisely controlling the fuel/air ratio because of the continuous response to the flow of commands from the EEC system.

7   The 7200VV carburetor has no provision for vacuum adjustment as vacuum control is set at the factory.

32 Carburetor (2700VV and 7200VV) – adjustments, notes and precautions

1   When making any adjustments to the carburetor, make sure that all hoses and lines are connected to the air cleaner assembly even when the assembly is moved to clear the carburetor. The air cleaner assembly, including the filter, should be fitted for any adjustment governing engine speed.

2   Due to the interaction of emission controls and temperature changes, the engine speed may oscillate. If this is encountered, use the average engine speed.

3   Do not allow the vehicle to idle for long periods of time as overheating of the catalytic converter may result in excessive under-body temperatures.

4   Always apply the parking brake and block the wheels before making any underhood carburetor adjustments.

5   Except where otherwise noted, turn all accessories to Off.

6   The fuel evaporative purge valve MUST be disconnected. Disconnect as follows: Trace the purge valve vacuum hose from the purge valve to the first place the vacuum hose can be disconnected from the underhood routing, eg: vacuum tee connection. Disconnect the hose and plug both the hose and the open connection.

33 Fast idle rpm (2700VV and 7200VV) – adjustment and check

1   Connect a tachometer to the engine.

2   Disconnect the EGR hose from the valve and plug the hose.

3   With the choke off and the engine running at normal operating temperature, raise the speed of the engine to 2500 rpm for 15 seconds. Place the fast idle lever on the specified step of the fast idle cam (refer to the emission decal in the engine compartment).

4   Allow the engine speed to stabilize and measure the engine speed (rpm). Depending upon the engine and the state of tune, it may require anywhere from 15 seconds to 2 minutes for the engine speed (number of rpm) to stabilize.

5   Repeat the above step three times to ensure accuracy.

6   Adjust the fast idle screw as necessary.

7   Repeat the rpm check if an adjustment has been made.

8   Turn the engine off then reconnect the EGR hose.

34 Curb idle speed (2700VV and 7200VV) – adjustment and check

1   Connect a tachometer to the engine.

2   Disconnect the EGR hose from the valve and plug the hose.

3   Disconnect the fuel evaporative purge hose as described in step 6, Section 32.

4   Check the engine curb idle as described in steps 1 through 5 of Section 33.

5   The method of adjustment of curb idle is determined by the type of throttle positioning device installed on the carburetor. The adjustment procedures are as follows:

   a)   2700VV carburetors with solenoid positioners must be in Drive when the curb idle rpm is checked. The curb idle is adjusted by turning the adjustment screw in the bracket

   b)   On vehicles with no solenoids or positioners, turn the throttle adjustment screw to obtain the specified curb idle rpm

   c)   On dashpot equipped carburettors, adjust the curb idle with the throttle stop adjustment screw. Turn the engine off, collapse the dashpot plunger and measure the distance

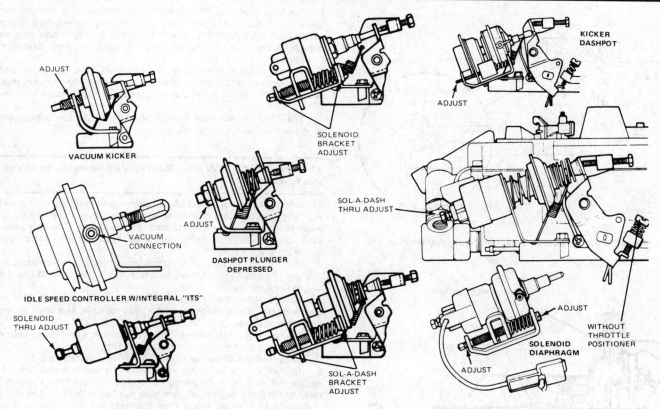

Fig. 4.42 Alternative types of throttle positioners used on 2700/7200 carburetor (Sec 34)

between the throttle lever and the pad and adjust to specifications if necessary. Start the engine and check the curb idle, repeating the procedure until the proper curb idle is obtained

d) On 7200VV carburetors equipped with vacuum-operated throttle modulator (VOTM), turn the throttle stop screw counterclockwise and recheck. If the curb idle rpm is below specifications, shut off the engine and turn the throttle stop screw a full turn clockwise. Start the engine and recheck the curb idle, repeating the procedure until the idle is within specifications

35 Accelerator pump lever lash (2700VV and 7200VV) – checking and adjustment

1   Each time the curb idle is adjusted, the accelerator pump lever lash must be checked and if necessary, adjusted.
2   After setting curb idle adjustment as described in Section 34, take up the accelerator pump clearance by pushing down on the nylon nut on the top of the pump.
3   Use a feeler gauge to check the clearance between the accelerator pump stem and lever.
4   Turn the nylon nut on the accelerator pump clockwise until the clearance is between 0.010 and 0.020 in.
5   To set the accelerator lever lash preload, turn the accelerator pump rod counterclockwise one turn.

36 Choke cap (2700VV and 7200VV) – removal and installation

1   The choke cap on 2700VV and 7200VV carburetors is held in place by 3 screws or in the case of California vehicles, 3 rivets.
2   To remove the choke cap, remove the 3 screws and lift the cap and gasket away from the carburetor. On California vehicles, the 2 top rivets are removed by drilling them out. The bottom rivet is located in a blind hole and must be tapped out, using a suitable punch and hammer. The choke cap, gasket and retainer can then be removed from the carburetor.

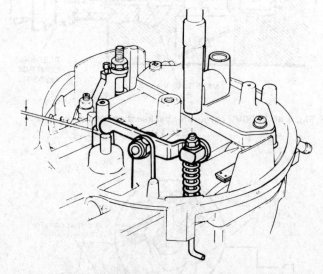

Fig. 4.43 Measuring accelerator pump stem clearance (2700/7200) (Sec 35)

3   Re-installation is a reverse of removal on choke caps retained with screws. California vehicles require the use of a suitable rivet gun and three $\frac{1}{8}$ in by $\frac{1}{2}$ in rivets. It may be necessary to remove the carburetor when installing the rivets.

37 Cold enrichment rod, control vacuum regulator (CVR) and choke control diaphragm, 75°F (24°C) (2700VV and 7200VV) – adjustment

1   Remove the choke cap as described in Section 36.
2   Remove the choke pulldown diaphragm and spring.
3   Install a choke weight on the choke bimetal lever, Ford part

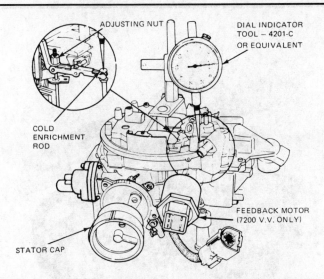

Fig. 4.44 Cold enrichment rod adjustment (2700/7200) (Sec 37)

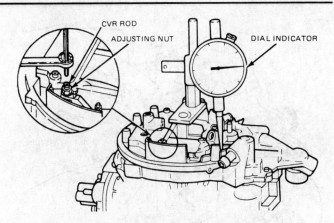

Fig. 4.45 Control vacuum regulator (CVR) adjustment (2700/7200) (Sec 37)

T77L-9848-A or equivalent. Place the fast idle pick-up lever on the first highest step of the fast idle cam.

4   Install a dial indicator (Ford tool 4201-C or equivalent) on the carburetor so that the indicator tip contacts the top surface of the enrichment rod and adjust the dial to zero. Slightly raise the choke weight and then release it, making sure that the zero reading repeats.

5   Remove the choke weight.

6   After installing the stator cap at the index position, the dial indicator should read to specification. If it doesn't, adjust the rod height by turning the adjusting nut clockwise to increase height and counterclockwise to decrease it referring to the figure.

7   To check the setting, repeat steps 3 through 6.

8   To adjust the control vacuum regulator (CVR), remove the stator cap and leave the dial indicator installed but not reset to zero.

9   Set the fast idle on the highest step.

10 Press the CVR rod down until it bottoms in its seat and read the travel on the dial indicator.

11 If adjustment is necessary, place a $\frac{3}{8}$ in box wrench on the CVR adjusting nut to prevent it from turning referring to the accompanying figure.

12 Using a $\frac{3}{32}$ in allen wrench, turn the CVR rod counterclockwise to increase its travel or clockwise to decrease it.

13 With the stator cap removed and dial indicator still installed but not reset to zero, seat the choke diaphragm assembly in the direction of the fast idle cam.

14 If the dial indicator reading is not within specification, turn the choke diaphragm clockwise to decrease or counterclockwise to increase the height.

15 The cold idle enrichment rod height must be checked after each adjustment of the CVR and choke control diaphragm.

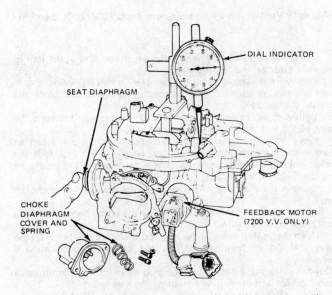

Fig. 4.46 Choke diaphragm adjustment (2700/7200) (Sec 37)

38 Fast idle cam (2700VV and 7200VV) – adjustment

1   Remove the choke cap as described in Section 36.

2   Counting the highest step as the first, install the fast idle lever in the corner of the step specified on the emissions label.

3   Install the stator cap and rotate it clockwise until the lever contacts the adjusting screw.

4   Line up the index mark on the stator cap with the specified mark on the choke casing by turning the fast idle cam adjusting screw. This screw may be hard to turn as it was coated with Loc-Tite at the time of manufacture.

5   Remove the startor cap and re-install the choke cap to the setting specified on the emissions label.

39 Venturi valve limiter (2700VV and 7200VV) – adjustment

1   Remove the carburetor.

2   Remove the venturi valve cover, gasket and roller bearings.

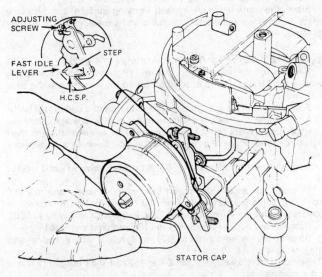

Fig. 4.47 Fast idle cam setting (2700/7200) (Sec 37)

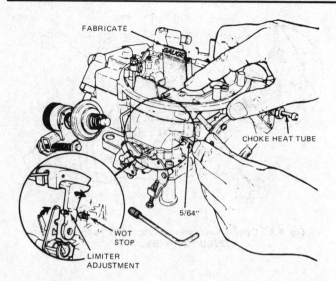

Fig. 4.48 Venturi valve limiter adjustment (2700/7200) (Sec 39)

Fig. 4.49 Removing the cold enrichment and CVR assembly (2700/7200) (Sec 40)

3   Using a suitable punch, remove the expansion plug at the rear of the main body on the throttle side.

4   Remove the venturi valve limiter screw assembly, using a $\frac{5}{32}$ in allen wrench, as shown in the accompanying figure, and block the throttle plates open.

5   Lightly close the venturi valve and check the gap between the valve and the air horn wall. Adjust if necessary.

6   Move the venturi valve to the wide open position and insert an allen wrench into the stop screw hole. To adjust the gap, turn the limiter adjusting screw counterclockwise to decrease the clearance and clockwise to increase it.

7   Remove the allen wrench, lightly close the valve and re-check the gap.

8   Re-install the venturi valve limiter stop screw and turn it clockwise until it contacts the valve.

9   Open the venturi valve all the way and check the gap between the valve and the air horn. Adjust the stop screw to specification if necessary.

10   After installing a new expansion plug, re-install the venturi valve cover, gasket and bearing and re-install the carburetor.

40 Carburetor (2700VV and 7200VV) – disassembly

1   Remove the carburetor as described in Section 29.

2   Place the carburetor on a clean working surface and obtain a variety of small containers for collecting and separating parts as they are removed.

Upper body (refer to the accompanying figure)

3   Remove the fuel inlet fitting (1), filter (2), gasket (3) and spring (4). Remove the E-rings on the accelerator pump rod and remove the rods (5, 6 and 7).

4   Remove the air cleaner stud (not shown) from the carburetor body.

5   Remove the 7 screws holding the upper body in place and remove the upper body. Mark the 2 long screws (8) for re-installation in their original location. Place the upper body upside down in a clean work area.

6   Remove the float hinge pin (10), float assembly (11) and gasket (12).

7   Remove the accelerator pump link retaining screw and nut (17 and 17A), adjusting nut and pump link (20 and 18). Remove the accelerator pump overtravel spring (6A), E-clip (6C) and washer (6B).

8   Remove the accelerator pump rod (6) and dust seal (16).

9   Remove the choke control rod (7) and carefully lift the retainer and slide the dust seal (16) out.

10   Remove the choke hinge pin E-ring (5) and slide the pin (21) out of the casting.

11   Remove the cold enrichment rod adjusting nut (22), lever (23),

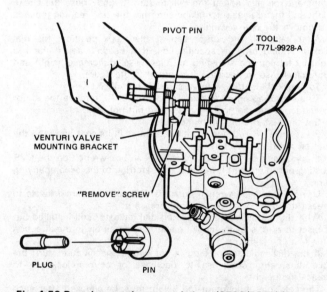

Fig. 4.50 Pressing out the tapered plugs (2700/7200) (Sec 40)

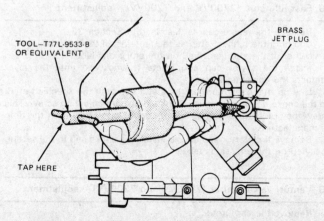

Fig. 4.51 Removing the 2700/7200 carburetor cap plugs (Sec 40)

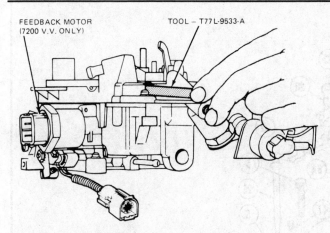

Fig. 4.52 Removing the 2700/7200 main jets (Sec 40)

Fig. 4.53 Positioning the throttle stop shaft pin prior to shaft removal (2700/7200) (Sec 40)

adjusting swivel control vacuum regulator (24), and adjusting nut (25) as an assembly as shown in the accompanying figure. Slide the cold enrichment rod (26) out of the upper body.

12 Remove the 2 screws securing the venturi valve cover (27 and 28). Hold the cover in place as you turn the carburetor over and remove the cover, gasket (29) and bearings (30).

13 Press out the tapered plugs (32) from the venturi valve pivotal pins using Ford tool T77P-9928-A or equivalent.

14 Push the venturi plugs (31) out as you slide the venturi valve (32) to the rear and clear of the casting. Remove the venturi valve pivot pin bushings (34).

15 Remove the metering rod pins (35) from the outboard sides of the venturi valve, the metering rods (36) and the springs (37). Mark the rods 'throttle' and 'choke' for ease of proper reassembly. Make sure to always block the venturi valve wide open whenever working on the jets.

16 Remove the cap plugs (38) recessed into the upper body casting using Ford tool T77L-9533-B or equivalent as shown in the accompanying figure.

17 The main jet setting is crucial to the carburetors overall calibration so *the following sequence must be strictly adhered to:*

   a) Using Ford tool T77L-9533-A, turn each main jet (39 and 40) clockwise, counting the turns as you go. Write down the number of turns to the nearest quarter turn

   b) Unscrew the jet assembly (39) and then remove the O-ring (40). For ease of proper reassembly, identify the jets as to 'throttle' or 'choke' side

   c) Remove the accelerator pump plunger assembly and then remove the pump return spring (41), pump cup (42) and plunger (43)

   d) If necessary for cleaning, remove the $\frac{1}{8}$ in pipe plug (45) from the fuel inlet boss

   e) From the throttle side of the venturi valve, remove the venturi valve limiting screw (44)

Main body (refer to the accompanying figure)

18 Remove the venturi valve diaphragm screws, cover, spring guide and spring (1, 2, 3 and 4). Loosen the cover by tapping lightly. Do not pry. Carefully loosen the venturi valve diaphragm (5) and slide it from the main body.

19 Turn the carburetor upside down, holding your hand under it to catch the accelerator pump check ball (9) and weight (10).

20 Remove the five throttle body retaining screws and remove the throttle body and gasket (11).

21 On the 7200VV only, use a $\frac{5}{8}$ in socket to remove the feedback stepper motor (12), gasket (12A), pintle valve (12B) and spring (12C).

22 On the 2700VV only, remove the choke heat seal screw and shield (14 and 14A).

Throttle body (refer to the accompanying figure)

23 Remove the throttle return control device assembly (1, 2, 3, 4, and 37).

24 Remove the choke thermostatic spring and housing assembly (6, 7, 8 and 9). On California vehicles this housing is retained by rivets, refer to Section 35 for the removal procedure.

25 Remove the choke thermostatic lever (11) and screw (10) and slide the choke shaft and lever assembly (12) out of the casting. Remove the fast idle cam (13) and E-clip (13A) and the adjusting screw (36). Remove the fast idle intermediate lever (14).

26 Remove the choke control diaphragm lever assembly (15, 16 and 17). Remove the choke control diaphragm assembly (18) and rod (19).

27 Should the choke housing bushing (20) have to be removed, it will have to be pressed out, while the casting is being supported, so that it is not damaged. The bushing is staked in place and the staked areas will have to be ground off before pressing.

28 Remove the TSP Off idle speed screw (22), throttle shaft nut (23), nylon bushing (24A), fast idle lever (24), fast idle adjusting lever (25) and screw (26).

29 On the 7200VV only, remove the large E-clip (25A), throttle positioning sensor (25B) and roll pin (25C).

30 If the throttle plates are to be removed, lightly scribe along the shaft and mark the plate 'T' and 'C' to ensure proper reassembly. The throttle plate screws are staked in place so their staked areas must be filed or ground off. Remove the throttle plate screws (27) and discard them and remove the plates (28).

31 When removing the throttle shaft assembly, the limiter lever stop pin (29) will have to be driven down until it is flush with the shaft.

32 Remove the E-clip (33) adjacent to the venturi valve limiter and slide the throttle shaft assembly (30) from the casting and remove the adjusting screw (31).

33 Remove the venturi valve limiter and bushing assembly.

34 Disassembly is now complete and all components should be cleaned in the proper solvent and inspected for wear. All traces of gasket should be removed from the carburetor body and all passages cleaned of dirt or gum deposits.

---

41 Carburetor (2700VV and 7200VV) – reassembly and adjustment

Throttle body (refer to the accompanying figure)

1 After supporting the throttle shaft assembly, carefully drive out the venturi valve limiter stop pin and roll pin (if equipped). Place the venturi valve limiter assembly (32) in the throttle body (35) and insert the throttle shaft (30) and install the E-clips (33).

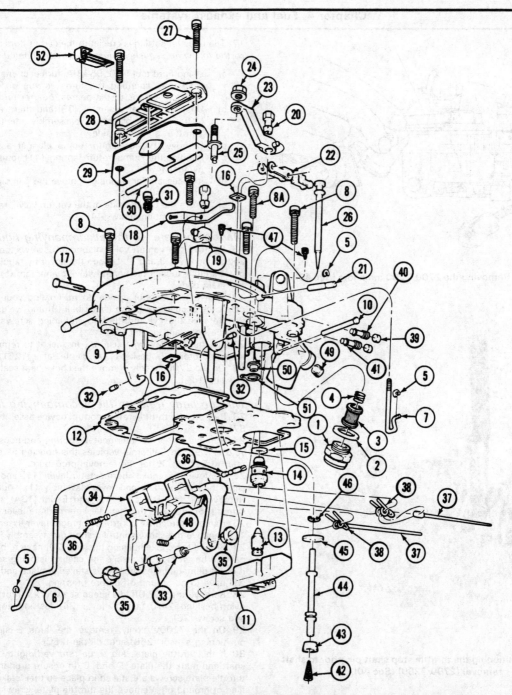

Fig. 4.54 Exploded view of the Motorcraft 2700/7200 carburetor upper body (Secs 40 and 41)

1 Fuel inlet fitting	17 Pin – .12 x 69	29 Gasket	41 O-ring
2 Fuel inlet fitting gasket	18 Accelerator pump link	30 Roller bearing	42 Accelerator pump return spring
3 Fuel filter	19 Accelerator pump swivel	31 Venturi air bypass screw and torque retention spring	43 Accelerator pump cup
4 Fuel filter spring	20 Nut – nylon		44 Accelerator pump plunger
5 ⅛ retaining E-ring	21 Choke hinge pin	32 Venturi valve pivot plug	45 Internal vent valve
6 Accelerator pump rod	22 Cold enrichment rod lever	33 Venturi valve pivot pin	46 ¾ retaining E-ring
7 Choke control rod	23 Cold enrichment rod swivel	34 Venturi valve	47 Idle trim screw
8 Screw (2) 8-32 x .88	24 Control vacuum regulator adjusting nut	35 Venturi valve pivot pin bushing	48 Venturi valve limiter adjusting screw
8A Screw (5) 8-32 x .75		36 Metering rod pivot pin	49 Pipe plug
9 Upper body	25 Control vacuum regulator	37 Metering rod	50 Cold enrichment rod seal
10 Float hinge pin	26 Cold enrichment rod	38 Metering rod spring	51 Seal retainer
11 Float assembly	27 Screw (2) 8-32 x .75	39 Cup plug	52 Hot idle compensator
12 Float bowl gasket	28 Venturi valve cover plate	40 Main metering jet assembly	
13 Fuel inlet valve			
14 Fuel inlet seat			
15 Fuel inlet seat gasket			
16 Dust seal			

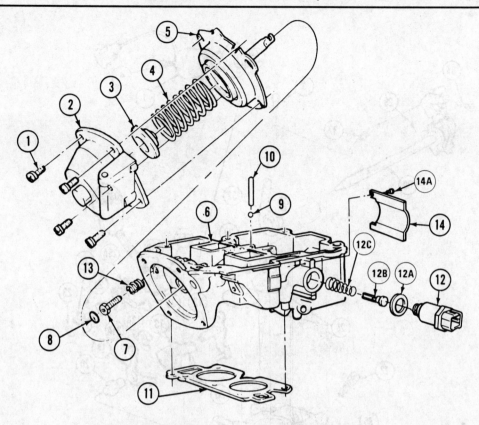

Fig. 4.55 2700/7200 carburetor main body (Secs 40 and 41)

1	Screw (4) 8.32 x .56	6 Main body	10 Accelerator pump check ball weight	12B Pintle valve – 7200 only
2	Venturi valve diaphragm cover	7 Venturi valve limiter stop screw and torque retention spring	11 Throttle body gasket	12C Pintle spring
3	Venturi valve diaphragm spring guide	8 Plug expansion	12 Feedback stepper motor 7200VV only	13 Torque retention spring
4	Venturi valve diaphragm spring	9 Acceleration pump check ball	12A Gasket – 7200VV only	14 Choke heat shield 2700VV only
5	Venturi valve diaphragm assembly			14A Screw 6.32 x .38

2   Install the throttle plates (28), according to the scribed marks made during disassembly. Close the throttle, tap the plates to center them and tighten the screws (27). Stake the ends of the screws so that they won't come loose.

3   Drive the new venturi valve limiter stop pin (29) into the shaft, leaving about $\frac{1}{8}$ in exposed. Install the roll pin (25B) and on the 7200VV, install the throttle positioner sensor (25C) and E-clip (25A).

4   Install the fast idle adjusting lever (24), nylon bushing (24A), fast idle lever (25), throttle shaft retaining nut (26). Install the TSP Off idle speed adjusting screw (22).

5   The choke housing bushing (20) must be pressed into position with the housing supported and the bushing then staked in place.

6   Install the fast idle intermediate diaphragm rod (18) into position and engage the rod (19) and E-clip (19A). After sliding the choke shaft pin and lever assembly (12) into the casting, install the choke thermostatic lever (11) and screw (12). Install the choke control diaphragm spring (17), cover (16) and screws (15).

7   Install the choke thermostat gasket (9), housing (8), and retaining ring 7). On California vehicles, follow the procedure in Section 36. Adjust the cap to the specified setting.

8   Install the throttle return control devices (1, 2, 3, 4 and 5), if equipped.

Main body (refer to the accompanying figure)

9   Place the throttle body gasket (11) on the main body (6) and install the main body to the throttle body.

10   Drop the accelerator pump check ball (9) and weight (10) into the pump discharge channel.

11   The venturi valve limiter stop screw, torque retention spring (7), and plug (8) are not to be installed at this time, but as one of the final steps of upper body assembly.

12   Slide the venturi valve diaphragm (5) into the main body and install the venturi valve spring (4), spring guide (3), cover (2) and screws (1).

13   On the 7200VV only, install the feedback motor (12), gasket (12A), pintle valve (12B) and pintle spring (12C).

14   On the 2700VV only, install the choke heat shield.

Upper body (refer to the accompanying figure)

15   Install the $\frac{1}{8}$ in pipe plug (45) into the fuel inlet boss.

16   Install the venturi valve limiter screw (44) in the venturi valve (33).

17   Install the O-rings (40) on the main metering jets. Lubricate the O-rings with mild soapy solution prior to installation.

18   Install each main metering jet by turning it clockwise with Ford tool T77L-9533-A or equivalent, until seated in the casting. At this point, turn each jet counterclockwise the same number of turns recorded in Steps 18 of Section 40.

19   Install the jet plugs (38), using the Ford jet plug driver tool T77L-9533-C or equivalent. Tap lightly on the end of the tool until it bottom against the face of the casting.

20   Install the metering rods (36), springs (37) and pivot pins (35) on the venturi valve (33). Install the venturi valve and carefully guide the metering rods into the main metering jets. Press downward on the metering rods and if the springs are properly assembled, they will spring back.

21   Install the venturi valve pivot pin bushings (34) and pivot pins (35). Use Ford tool T77P-9928-A or equivalent to press the tapered plugs into the venturi valve pivot pins.

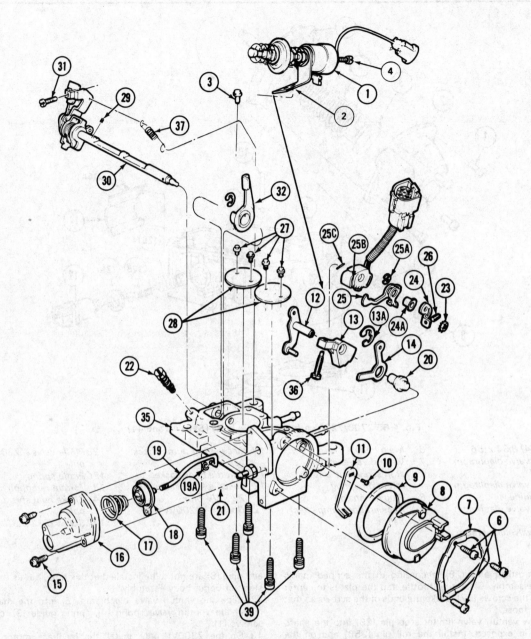

Fig. 4.56 2700/7200 carburetor throttle body (Secs 40 and 41)

1	Throttle return control device
2	Throttle return control device bracket
3	Mounting screw 10.32 x 50
4	Adjusting screw (TSP on)
5	(Not applicable)
6	Screw (3) 8.32 x 50
7	Choke thermostatic housing retainer
8	Choke thermostatic housing
9	Choke thermostatic housing gasket
10	Screw 6.32 x 50
11	Choke thermostatic lever
12	Choke shaft lever and pin assembly
13	Fast idle cam 13A large E-clip
14	Fast idle intermediate lever
15	Screw (2) 8.32 x .75
16	Choke control diaphragm cover
17	Choke control diaphragm spring
18	Choke control diaphragm
19A	Clip
20	Choke housing bushing
21	Choke heat tube (if equipped)
22	Curb idle adjusting screw (TSP off)
23	Retaining nut 10.32
24	Fast idle adjusting lever
24A	Fast idle lever
25A	Large E-clip
25B	Roll pin
25C	Throttle position sensor (7200VV only)
26	Fast idle adjusting screw
27	Throttle plate screws (4)
28	Throttle plates
29	Venturi valve limiter stop pin
30	Throttle shaft assembly
31	Transmission kickdown adjusting screw
32	Venturi valve limiter lever and bushing assembly
33	E-clip
34	(Not applicable)
35	Throttle body
36	Fast idle cam adjusting screw
37	Transmission kickdown lever return spring equipped
38	(Not applicable)
39	Screw (5) 8.32 x .75

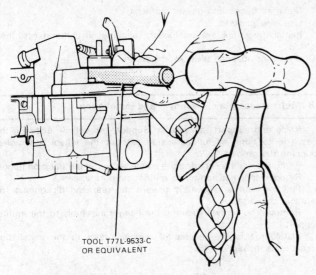

Fig. 4.57 Installing 2700/7200 main jet plugs (Sec 41)

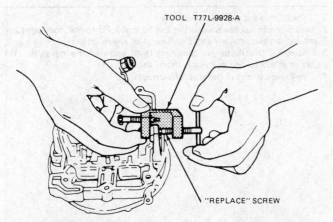

Fig. 4.58 Installing 2700/7200 tapered plugs (Sec 41)

22 Install the venturi valve cover plate (28), roller bearings (30), gasket (29) and attaching screws (27).
23 Install the accelerator pump operating rod (6) and dust seal (16). Attach the E-clip (6C) and washer (6B). Slide the overtravel spring (6A) over the accelerator pump operating rod.
24 Insert the accelerator pump lever and swivel assembly (18) into the pump link. Install the accelerator pump link screw (17), nut (17), nut (17A) and the accelerator pump adjustment nut (20).
25 Install the fuel inlet valve seat gasket (15), the seat (14) and valve (13). Install the float gasket (12), float assembly (11) and hinge pin (10).
26 Assemble the accelerator pump return spring (41), cup (42) and plunger (43). Place the pump piston assembly in the hole in the upper body.
27 Assemble the upper body to the main body. Holding the pump piston with your finger, guide it into the main body pump cavity, making sure the venturi valve limiter diaphragm stem engages the venturi valve. Install screws (8 and 8A).
28 Install the fuel filter spring (4), filter (3), inlet filter gasket (2) and fitting (1).
29 Install the air cleaner stud.
30 Install the choke control rod assembly (16). Tap it gently to straighten the retainer.
31 Slide the cold enrichment rod (26) into the upper body. Assemble the cold enrichment assembly consisting of lever (22), adjusting rod nut (20), swivel (23), control vacuum regulator (25) and adjusting nut (24) and install it.
32 Install the choke control rod (7). See Section 37 for final adjustment procedure.

33 Engage the accelerator pump operating rod (6) to the choke control rod (7) and install the E-ring retainers (5).
34 At this point, install the venturi valve limited stop screw and torque retention spring (7, in the accompanying figure). Follow the adjustment procedure in Section 39, installing the plug after the adjustment is made.
35 Adjust the carburetor to the operating specifications on the emission label.

42 Fuel tank – removal and installation

1   Disconnect the battery terminals.
2   Using a suitable length of pipe siphon out as much gas from the tank as possible. Do not use your mouth to start the flow.
3   Remove the four screws securing the filler pipe to the bodywork aperture and carefully ease the bottom end of the pipe out of the sealing ring in the side of the tank.
4   Jack up the rear of the car and suitably support it for access beneath.
5   Disconnect the fuel feed and vapor pipes at the tank and detach them from the clips along the tank front edge.
6   Disconnect the electrical leads from the sender unit.
7   Undo and remove the two support strap retaining nuts at the rear of the tank while supporting the weight of the tank.
8   Push the straps downwards and lift the tank outward the rear of the car.
9   If it is necessary to remove the sender unit, this can be unscrewed from the tank using the appropriate special tool. Alternatively a suitable C-wrench or drift can probably be used, but great care should be taken that the flange is not damaged and that there is no danger from sparks if a hammer has to be used.
10 Taking care not to damage the sealing washer, pry out the tank-to-filler pipe seal.
11 When installing, ensure that the rubber pads are stuck in position.
12 Install a new filler pipe seal.
13 Refit the sender unit using a new seal, as the original one will almost certainly be damaged.
14 The remainder of the installation procedure is the reverse of removal. A smear of engine oil on the tank filler pipe exterior will aid its fitting.
15 Do not overtighten the tank retaining strap nuts.

43 Fuel tank – cleaning and repair

1   With time it is likely that sediments will collect in the bottom of the fuel tank. Condensation, resulting in rust and other impurities, will usually be found in the fuel tank of any car more than three or four years old.
2   When the tank is removed it should be vigorously flushed out with hot water and detergent and, if facilities are available, steam cleaned.
3   **Note:** *Never weld, solder or bring a naked light close to an empty fuel tank. All repairs should be done by a professional due to the extremely hazardous conditions.*

44 Throttle cable and kick-down rod – removal and installation

1   Pry the throttle cable retainer bushing from the top end of the accelerator pedal and remove the inner cable from the pedal assembly. **Note:** *On later model cars the cable is retained by a Tinnerman type fastener which must be pried off the end of the cable.*
2   Remove the circular retaining clip holding the inner cable to the underside of the dash panel.
3   Remove the two screws retaining the outer cable to the dash panel.
4   Disconnect the control rod from the carburetor linkage.
5   Remove the screw or spring clip retaining the outer cable to the engine bracket.
6   The complete cable assembly can now be removed.
7   To remove the kick-down rod (automatic transmission only), remove the 'C' type spring clips and pins at each end of the rod and remove the rod.
8   Install the throttle cable and kick-down rod using the reverse procedure to removal.

45 Accelerator pedal – removal and installation

1   Remove the inner throttle cable from the pedal assembly as described in the previous Section.
2   Undo the two nuts retaining the pedal to the floor bracket and remove the pedal assembly. **Note**: *If a pedal extension pad is fitted this will have to be uncrimped from the pedal prior to pedal removal.*
3   Install the accelerator pedal using the reverse procedure to removal.

46 Exhaust system – general information

All models use a single exhaust system consisting of an inlet pipe, catalytic converter and muffler. Some models also use a resonator.

The exhaust system is serviced in four pieces: the rear section of the inlet pipe, catalytic converter, muffler inlet pipe and muffler.

Due to the high operating temperatures of the exhaust system, do not work on the exhaust system until at least one hour after the car has been run or driven.

47 Inlet pipe – removal and installation

1   Raise and support the vehicle.
2   Support the muffler assembly with a length of wire.
3   Remove the converter-to-inlet pipe mounting bolts.
4   Remove the front hanger mounting screws from the inlet pipe.
5   Remove the nuts securing the inlet pipe to the exhaust manifold.
6   Installation is the reverse of removal with the following precautions.

7   Clean all flange and gasket surfaces.
8   Use new gaskets.
9   Install the entire system loosely, aligning all components, then tighten.
10 Check for absence of leaks and noise.

48 Muffler assembly – removal and installation

1   Raise and support the vehicle. Support the vehicle allowing the rear axle to hang at full extension without the wheel assemblies touching the ground.
2   Remove the nuts securing the converter to the muffler pipe flange.
3   Remove the rear hanger to muffler support screws.
4   Pull the muffler assembly toward the rear and disconnect the catalytic converter.
5   Remove the screws securing the hanger assembly to the muffler support.
6   Installation is the reverse of removal; refer to the installation precautions in Section 45.

49 Catalytic converter – removal and installation

1   Raise and support the vehicle.
2   Remove the screws securing the heat shields to the converter and carefully remove the shield. Be careful of sharp edges.
3   Remove the fasteners securing both ends of the catalytic converter and lower the converter from the car.
4   Installation is the reverse of removal.

Chapter 5 Engine electrical system

Contents

Specifications

Distributor

Type	Solid state, breakerless
Automatic advance	Vacuum and centrifugal
Direction of rotation	
3.3L and 4.1L	Clockwise
4.2L, 5.0L and 5.8L	Counterclockwise
Static advance	Refer to Emissions Control Decal

Coil .... 8 volt, oil filled

Firing order

3.3L and 4.1L	1-5-3-6-2-4
4.2L and 5.0L	1-5-4-2-6-3-7-8
5.8L	1-3-7-2-6-5-4-8

Spark plugs .... Refer to Emissions Control decal

Alternator (rear terminal)

Stamp color codes	Orange, black and green
Amp rating at 15 volts	
Orange	40 amp
Black	65 amp
Green	60 amp
Watt rating at 15 volts	
Orange	600 watts
Black	975 watts
Green	900 watts
Brush length	
New	$\frac{1}{2}$ in
Wear limit	$\frac{5}{16}$ in

Alternator (side terminal)

Color codes .... Red, black
Amp rating at 15 volts
    Red .... 70 amps
    Black .... 100 amps
Watt rating at 15 volts
    Red .... 1050 watts
    Black .... 1350 watts
Brush length
    New .... $\frac{1}{2}$ in
    Wear limit .... $\frac{5}{16}$ in

Starter

Type .... Positive engagement
Diameter .... 4 in or $4\frac{1}{2}$ in

Torque specifications

	Ft-lb	Nm
Spark plugs	10 to 15	13 to 20
Distributor hold-down clamp		
3.3L and 4.1L	17 to 25	23 to 34
4.2L and 5.0L	18 to 26	24 to 34
Alternator through-bolt	3 to 4	4 to 6
Alternator pulley nut	60 to 100	82 to 135
Alternator brush holder screw	60 to 100	82 to 135
Starter mounting bolt	15 to 20	20 to 27
Starter through-bolt	4 to 6	6 to 8
Starter cable attaching screw	6 to 8	8 to 12

1 Ignition system – general information

All models are equipped with an electronic (breakerless) – type distributor. Mechanically, this system is similar to the contact breaker type with the exception that the distributor cam and contact breaker are replaced by an armature and magnetic pick-up. The coil primary circuit is controlled by an amplifier module.

The system is made up of a primary (low voltage) circuit and a secondary (high voltage) circuit.

When the ignition is switched on, the ignition primary circuit is energized. When the distributor armature teeth approach the magnetic coil assembly, a voltage is induced which signals the amplifier to turn off the coil primary current. A timing circuit in the amplifier module turns the coil current on after the coil field has collapsed.

When on, current flows from the battery through the ignition switch, through the coil primary winding, through the amplifier module and then to ground. When the current is off, the magnetic field in the ignition coil collapses, inducing a high voltage in the coil secondary winding. This is conducted to the distributor where the rotor directs it to the appropriate spark plug. This process is repeated for each power stroke of the engine.

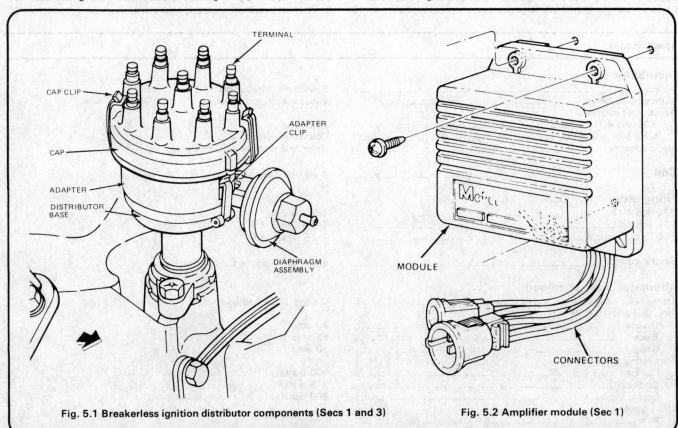

Fig. 5.1 Breakerless ignition distributor components (Secs 1 and 3)   Fig. 5.2 Amplifier module (Sec 1)

Measuring plug gap. A feeler gauge of the correct size (see ignition system specifications) should have a slight 'drag' when slid between the electrodes. Adjust gap if necessary

Adjusting plug gap. The plug gap is adjusted by bending the ground electrode inwards, or outwards, as necessary until the correct clearance is obtained. Note the use of the correct tool

Normal. Gray brown deposits, lightly coated core nose. Gap increasing by around 0.001 in (0.025 mm) per 1000 miles (1600 km). Plugs ideally suited to engine, and engine in good condition

Carbon fouling. Dry, black, sooty deposits. Will cause weak spark and eventually misfire. Fault: over-rich fuel mixture. Check: carburetor mixture settings, float level and jet sizes; choke operation and cleanliness of air filter. Plugs can be re-used after cleaning

Oil fouling. Wet, oily deposits. Will cause weak spark and eventually misfire. Fault: worn bores/piston rings or valve guides; sometimes occurs (temporarily) during running-in period. Plugs can be re-used after thorough cleaning

Overheating. Electrodes have glazed appearance, core nose very white – few deposits. Fault: plug overheating. Check: plug value, ignition timing, fuel octane rating (too low) and fuel mixture (too weak). Discard plugs and cure fault immediately.

Electrode damage. Electrodes burned away; core nose has burned, glazed appearance. Fault: pre-ignition. Check: as for 'Overheating' but may be more severe. Discard plugs and remedy fault before piston or valve damage occurs

Split core nose (may appear initially as a crack). Damage is self-evident, but cracks will only show after cleaning. Fault: pre-ignition or wrong gap-setting technique. Check: ignition timing, cooling system, fuel octane rating (too low) and fuel mixture (too weak). Discard plugs, rectify fault immediately

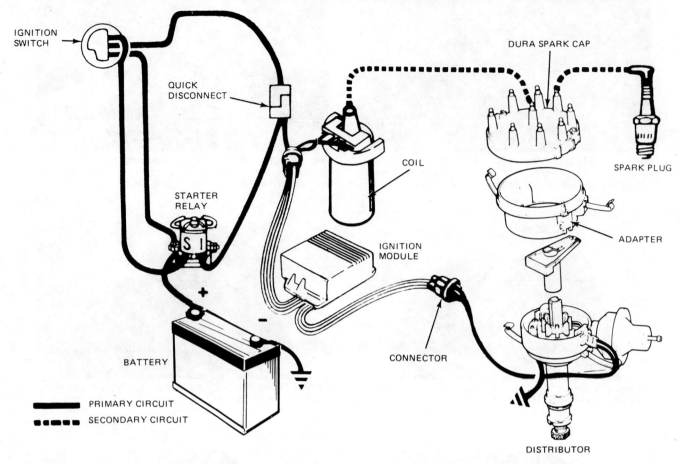

Fig. 5.3 Breakerless ignition system (Secs 1 and 3)

The distributor is equipped with devices to control the actual point of ignition according to the engine speed and load. As the engine speed increases, two centrifugal weights move outwards and alter the position of the armature in relation to the distributor shaft to advance the spark slightly. As engine load increases (as when climbing hills or accelerating), a reduction in intake manifold vacuum causes the base plate assembly to move slightly in the opposite direction under the action of the spring in the vacuum unit, retarding the spark slightly and tending to counteract the centrifugal advance. Under light loading conditions (moderate, steady driving) the comparatively high intake manifold vacuum on the vacuum advance diaphragm causes the baseplate assembly to move in the opposite direction of the distributor shaft rotation, giving a larger amount of spark advance.

Some models are equipped with a fuel diaphragm vacuum assembly which is operated by two different sources of vacuum. The outer (primary) diaphragm is operated by the carburetor venturi vacuum and provides timing advance. The inner (secondary) diaphragm is operated by intake manifold vacuum and retarded ignition timing.

For most practical do-it-yourself purposes, ignition timing is carried out as on conventional systems. A monolithic timing system is incorporated on some models which can only be used with special electronic equipment, a procedure beyond the scope of this manual.

The Electronic Engine Control (EEC) system is installed on some vehicles to provide improved drivability and emissions controls. The EEC system works in conjunction with an onboard computer and a feedback carburetor to control virtually every aspect of engine and ignition operation. Checking or adjusting of the EEC system is possible only with special equipment and procedures described in this chapter pertain only to non-EEC-equipped vehicles.

Faults in the breakerless ignition system which cannot be rectified by the substitution of parts, or by cleaning and tightening connections, should be referred to a properly equipped dealer or repair shop.

2   Ignition system servicing and Federal regulations (all models)

1   In order to conform with the Federal regulations which govern the emission of hydrocarbons and carbon monoxide from car exhaust systems, the engine carburation and ignition systems have been suitably modified.
2   It is critically important that the ignition system is kept in good operational order and to achieve this, accurate analytical equipment is needed to check and reset the distributor function. This will be found at a local repair shop or dealer.
3   Information contained in this chapter is supplied to enable the home mechanic to set the ignition system roughly to enable you to start the engine. Thereafter the car must be taken to the local dealer or repair shop for final tuning.

3   Distributor – removal and installation

V8 engine

1   Remove the air cleaner and disconnect the distributor vacuum lines and wiring connector.
2   Remove the distributor cap and position it out of the way with the wires attached, Use tape or wire to hold the cap and wires to one side.
3   Scribe or paint a mark on the distributor body and engine block to use as a guide when reinstalling the distributor.
4   Remove the hold-down bolt at the base of the distributor from the engine. **Note:** *Be extremely careful to keep the engine from being rotated while the distributor is out, or the engine will have to be re-timed as described in Chapter 1.*
5   If the engine has not been rotated, installation is the reverse of removal, using the alignment marks made in step 3.

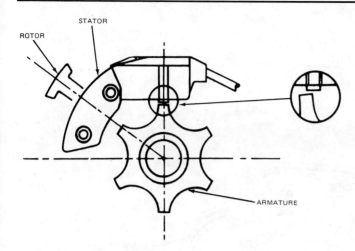

Fig. 5.4 Correct stator position for static timing of six-cylinder engine. Tooth must be perfectly aligned with timing marks. Each $\frac{1}{2}$-tooth error is equal to $7\frac{3}{4}°$ timing error (as in circle) (Sec 3)

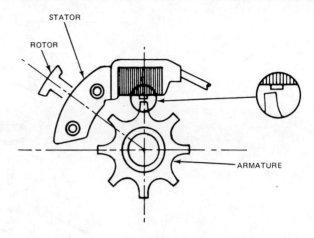

Fig. 5.5 V8 engine correct stator position for static timing. Each $\frac{1}{2}$-tooth error is equal to $7\frac{3}{4}°$ timing error (as in circle) (Sec 3)

Six-cylinder engine

6   Remove one Thermactor pump bolt and swing the pump out of the way.
7   Rotate the engine by hand until the proper timing marks on the crankshaft damper and timing pointer are aligned (see Chapter 1).
8   Remove the distributor cap and check that the rotor and armature are aligned with the magnetic pickup index mark and the marks on the side of the distributor body as described in Chapter 1.
9   Disconnect the vacuum hose and wiring connector from the distributor.
10 Remove the distributor hold-down bolt and lift the distributor from the engine. The oil pump driveshaft may come out with the distributor.
11 If the engine has not been rotated, installation is the reverse of removal, making sure that the marks on the distributor rotor are aligned with the marks on the distributor and armature. If the oil pump driveshaft has been removed, coat one end with heavy grease and

insert it into the hex end hole of the distributor. Make sure that the shaft seats securely in the oil pump.
12 On all engines, install any components which were removed and check the ignition timing as described in Chapter 1.

4   Distributor stator assembly – removal and installation

1   Remove the distributor cap, adapter and rotor from the top of the distributor.
2   Disconnect the electrical harness plug.
3   Using a small gear puller or two screwdrivers, pry the armature from the sleeve and plate assembly.
4   Remove the roll pin, using caution not to damage the pick-up coil wires.

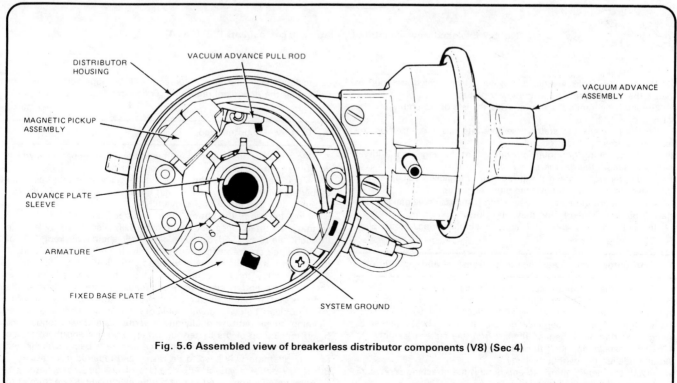

Fig. 5.6 Assembled view of breakerless distributor components (V8) (Sec 4)

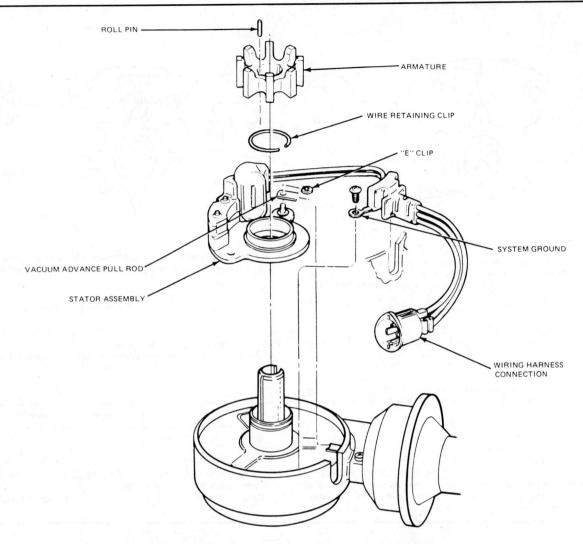

ROLL PIN

ARMATURE

WIRE RETAINING CLIP

"E" CLIP

SYSTEM GROUND

VACUUM ADVANCE PULL ROD

STATOR ASSEMBLY

WIRING HARNESS CONNECTION

Fig. 5.7 Exploded view of distributor stator and components (V8) (Sec 4)

5   Remove the E-clip washer and wave washer which are used to secure the stator assembly to the lower plate.
6   Remove the ground screw and lift the stator assembly off the plate.
7   To install, place the stator assembly into position, inserting the post into diaphragm pull rod hole.
8   Slide the wiring grommet into the slot at the edge of the lower plate and secure the ground screw.
9   Install the washers and E-clip to secure the pickup coil assembly. The wave washer should have the outer edges up.
10 Install the armature on the sleeve and plate assembly making sure the roll pin is engaged in the matching slots.
11 Install the rotor, adapter and cap. Connect the wiring harness plug.

5   Distributor vacuum advance unit – removal and installation

1   Remove the distributor cap, rotor and adapter.
2   Disconnect the vacuum line(s).
3   Remove the attaching screws at the diaphragm unit and lift away the diaphragm unit and identification tag. The unit is best removed by tilting downward to disengage the link from the stator assembly.
4   Upon installation, hook the diaphragm link in position and place the unit against the distributor body.
5   Install the identification tag and tighten the attaching screws.
6   Connect the vacuum hose(s),
7   Install the adapter, rotor and cap.

8   Included with the new diaphragm will be approved method for calibrating the new diaphragm unit. Follow the instructions given.

6   Battery – maintenance

1   Most models are equipped with maintenance-free batteries which do not require the addition of water or electrolyte.
2   Maintenance-type batteries should be checked every week and topped-up with distilled water so that the level is $\frac{1}{4}$ inch above the top of the plates. Be careful not to overfill.
3   Keep the top of the battery clean and free from dirt and moisture so that the battery does not become partially discharged by leakage through dampness and dirt. The terminals should be kept free of corrosion and covered with petroleum jelly. If a felt ring is used under the battery terminals, it should be oiled periodically.
4   Once every three months, remove the battery and inspect the securing bolts, battery clamp plate and leads for corrosion (white fluffy deposits on the metal which are brittle to the touch). If any corrosion is found, clean it off with an ammonia or soda and water solution. After cleaning, smear petroleum jelly on the terminals and lead connectors.
5   If topping-up of the battery becomes excessive and there are no cracks in the case causing leakage, the battery is being overcharged and the alternator will have to be tested and repaired if necessary.
6   If any doubt exists about the state of charge of the battery, a hydrometer should be used to test a little electrolyte drawn from each cell.

7 The specific gravity of the electrolyte at the temperature of 80°F (26.7°C) will be approximately 1.270 for a fully charged battery. For every 10°F (5.5°C) that the electrolyte temperature is above that stated, add 0.04 to the specific gravity or subtract 0.04 if the temperature is below that stated.

8 A specific gravity reading of 1.240 with an electrolyte temperature of 80°F (26.7°C) indicates a half-charged battery.

7 Battery – charging

1 In winter time when heavy demand is placed upon the battery, such as when starting from cold, and much electrical equipment is continually in use, it is a good idea occasionally to have the battery fully charged from an external source at the rate of 3.5 to 4 amps.

2 Continue to charge the battery at this rate until no further rise in specific gravity is noted over a four hour period.

3 Alternatively, a trickle charger charging at the rate of 1.5 amps can be safely used overnight.

4 Specially rapid 'boost' charges which are claimed to restore the power of the battery in 1 or 2 hours are to be avoided as they can cause serious damage to the battery plates through overheating.

5 While charging the battery, note that the temperature of the electrolyte should never exceed 100°F (37.8°C).

8 Battery – removal and installation

1 The battery is located at the front of the engine compartment. It is held in place by a hold-down rod running across the top of the battery.

2 As hydrogen gas is produced by the battery, keep open flames or lighted cigarettes away from the battery at all times.

3 Avoid spilling any of the electrolyte battery fluid on the vehicle or yourself. Always keep the battery in the upright position. Any spilled electrolyte should be immediately flushed with large quantities of water. Wear eye protection when working with a battery to prevent serious eye damage from splashed fluid.

4 Always disconnect the negative (–) battery cable first, followed by the position (+) cable.

5 After the cables are disconnected from the battery, remove the hold-down mechanism, be it a rod or bottom clamp.

6 Carefully lift the battery from its tray and out of the engine compartment.

7 Installation is a reversal of removal, however make sure that the hold-down clamp or rod is securely tightened. Do not over-tighten, however, as this may damage the battery case. The battery posts and cable ends should be cleaned prior to connection.

9 Booster battery (jump) starting

1 Certain precautions are necessary prior to using the booster battery or 'jump' starting procedure.

   a) Before connecting the booster battery, make sure that the ignition switch is in the OFF position.
   b) The eyes should be shielded, safety goggles are a good idea.
   c) Make sure that the booster battery source is 12 volt and not 24 volt, which could damage the starter.
   d) The two vehicles must not touch each other.

2 Connect the end of one jumper cable to the positive (+) terminals of each battery.

3 Connect one end of the other jumper cable to the negative (–) terminal of the good battery. The other end of this cable should be connected to a good ground on the vehicle to be started, such as the engine bolt head.

4 Start the engine using the jumper battery and with the engine running at idle speed, disconnect the jumper cables.

10 Alternator – general information

The main advantage of the alternator lies in its ability to provide a high charge at low revolutions. Driving slowly in heavy traffic with a generator invariably means no charge is reaching the battery. In similar conditions even with the wiper, heater, lights and perhaps radio switched on the alternator will ensure a charge reaches the battery.

The alternator is of rotating field, ventilated design. It comprises 3-phase output winding; a twelve pole rotor carrying the field windings – each end of the rotor shaft runs in ball race bearings which are incorporating the mounting lugs; a rectifier pack for converting AC output of the machine to DC for battery charging, and an output control regulator.

The rotor is belt driven from the engine through a pulley keyed to the rotor shaft. A pressed steel fan adjacent to the pulley draws cooling air through the unit. This fan forms an integral part of the alternator specification. It has been designed to provide adequate air flow with minimum noise, and to withstand the high stresses associated with maximum speed. Rotation is clockwise viewed on the drive end. Maximum continuous rotor speed is 12 500 rpm.

Rectification of the alternator output is achieved by six silicone diodes housed in a rectifier pack and connected as a 3-phase full wave bridge. The rectifier pack is attached to the outer face of the slip ring end bracket and contains also three 'field' diodes. At normal operating speeds, rectified current from the stator output windings flows through these diodes to provide the self excitation of the rotor field, via brushes bearing on face type slip rings.

The slip rings are carried on a small diameter molded form attached to the rotor shaft outboard of the slip ring end bearing. The inner ring is centered on the rotor shaft axle, while the outer ring has a mean diameter of $\frac{3}{4}$ inch approximately. By keeping the mean diameter of the slip rings to a minimum, relative speeds between brushes and rings, and hence wear, are also minimal. The slip rings are connected to the rotor field windings by wires carried in grooves in the rotor shaft.

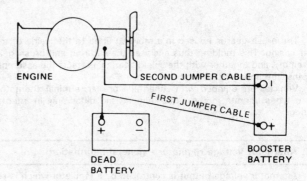

Fig. 5.8 Booster battery cable installation (Sec 9)

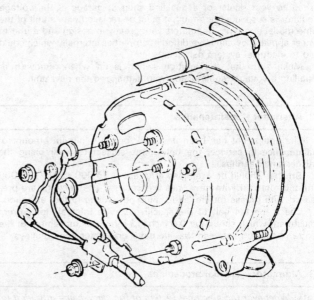

Fig. 5.9 Rear terminal alternator (Secs 10, 12, 13 and 16)

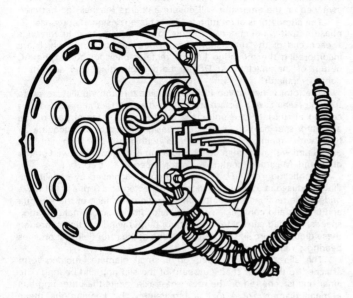

Fig. 5.10 Side terminal alternator (Secs 10, 12, 13 and 17)

The brush gear is housed in a molding fitted to the inside of the rear casing. This molding thus encloses the slip ring and brush gear assembly, and together with the shield bearing, protects the assembly against the entry of dust and moisture.

Vehicles are eqipped with either side or rear terminal alternator. Both types operate in the same manner and differ only in internal wiring.

11 Alternator voltage regulator – general information

Alternator voltage output is controlled by a regulator which is set at the factory. Early models use a contact point type regulator while later models are of the transistorized type.

Special equipment is necessary to check for faults and this should be left to your dealer or a qualified shop or garage. If the voltage regulator is suspected of a fault, it must be replaced with a unit of the same model and type. Regulators vary greatly in design and a unit of similar appearance can have different properties internally which could lead to electrical system damage.

Make sure that the ignition switch is off when removing or installing a voltage regulator to avoid damage to the new unit.

12 Alternator – maintenance

1 The equipment has been designed for the minimum amount of maintenance in service, the only items subject to wear being the brushes and bearings.
2 Brushes should be examined after about 75 000 miles (120 000 km) and replaced with new ones if necessary. The bearings are pre-packed with grease for life, and should not require further attention.
3 Check the fan belt at the specified service intervals for correct adjustment which should be 0.5 inch (13 mm) total movement at the centre of the run between the alternator and water pump pulleys.

13 Alternator – special procedures

Note: *Whenever the electrical system of the car is being attended to, and external means of starting the engine is used, there are certain*

precautions that must be taken, otherwise serious and expensive damage to the alternator can result.

1 Always make sure that the negative terminal of the battery is grounded. If the terminal connections are accidentally reversed or if the battery has been reverse charged the alternator diodes will be damaged.
2 The output terminal on the alternator marked 'BAT' or 'B+' must never be grounded but should always be connected directly to the positive terminal of the battery.
3 Whenever the alternator is to be removed or when disconnecting the terminals of the alternator circuit, always disconnect the battery ground terminal first.
4 The alternator must never be operated without the battery to alternator cable connected.
5 If the battery is to be charged by external means always disconnect both the battery cables before the external charger is connected.
6 Should it be necessary to use a booster charger or booster battery to start the engine always double check that the negative cable is connected to negative terminal and the positive cable to positive terminal.

14 Alternator – removal and installation

1 Disconnect the battery negative cable.
2 Loosen the alternator adjusting bolt.
3 Loosen the alternator pivot bolt.
4 Disconnect the electrical connections.
5 Support the alternator while removing the drivebelt adjusting the pivot bolts.
6 Lift the alternator away from the vehicle.
7 Installation is the reverse of removal. Tighten the bolts to specifications.
8 Adjust the drivebelts to specification.

15 Alternator – fault diagnosis and repair

1 Due to the special training and equipment necessary to test or service the alternator it is recommended that if a fault is suspected the vehicle should be taken to a dealer or a shop with the proper equipment. Because of this the home mechanic should limit maintenance to checking connections and the inspection and replacement of the brushes.
2 The ammeter (ALT) gauge or alternator warning lamp on the instrument panel indicates the charge or discharge (D) current passing into or out of the battery. With the electrical equipment switched on and the engine idling the gauge needle may show a discharge condition. At fast idle or at normal driving speeds the needle should stay on the 'charge' side of the gauge, with the charged state of the battery determining just how far over.
3 If the gauge does not show a charge or (if equipped) the alternator lamp is on, there is a fault in the system. Before inspecting the brushes or replacing the alternator, the battery condition, belt tension and electrical cable connections should be checked.

16 Alternator brushes (rear terminal type) – removal, inspection and installation

1 Remove the alternator as described in Section 13.
2 Scribe a line across the length of the alternator housing to ensure correct reassembly.
3 Remove the housing through-bolts and the nuts and insulators from the rear housing. Make a careful note of all insulator locations.
4 Withdraw the rear housing section from the stator, rotor and front housing assembly.
5 Remove the brushes and springs from the brush holder assembly which is located inside the rear housing.
6 Check the length of the brushes against the wear dimensions given in Specifications at the beginning of the Chapter and replace with new ones if necessary.

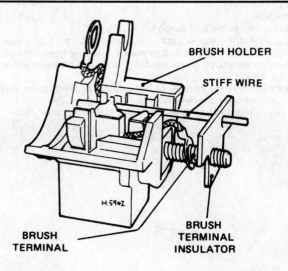

Fig. 5.11 Method of retracting brushes prior to installing on rear terminal alternator (Sec 16)

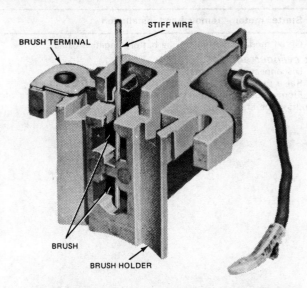

Fig. 5.12 Method of retracting brushes prior to installing brush holder on side terminal alternator (Sec 17)

7   Install the springs and brushes into the holder assembly and retain them in place by inserting a piece of stiff wire through the rear housing and brush terminal insulator. Make sure that enough wire protrudes through the rear of the housing so that it may be withdrawn at a later stage.
8   Install the rear housing rotor and front housing assembly to the stator, making sure that the scribed marks are aligned.
9   Install the housing through-bolts and rear end insulators and nuts but do not tighten at this time.
10   Carefully extract the piece of wire from the rear housing and check that the brushes are seated on the slip ring. Tighten the through-bolts and rear housing nuts.
11   Install the alternator as described in Section 14.

17 Alternator brushes (side terminal type) – removal, inspection and installation

1   Remove the alternator as described in Section 13 and scribe a mark on both end housings and the stator for ease of reassembly.
2   Remove the through-bolts and separate the front housing and rotor from the rear housing and stator. Be careful that you do not separate the rear housing and stator.
3   Use a soldering iron to unsolder and disengage the brush holder from the rear housing. Remove the brushes and springs from the brush holders.
4   Remove the two brush holder attaching screws and lift the brush holder from the rear housing.
5   Remove any sealing compound from the brush holder and rear housing.
6   Inspect the brushes for damage and check their dimensions against Specifications. If they are out of specification, replace them with new ones.
7   To reassemble, install the springs and brushes in the brush holders, inserting a piece of stiff wire to hold them in place.
8   Place the brush holder in position to the rear housing, using the wire to retract the brushes through the hole in the rear housing.
9   Install the brush holder attaching screws and push the holder toward the shaft opening as you tighten the screws.
10   **Caution:** *The rectifier can be overheated and damaged if the soldering is not done quickly.* Press the brush holder lead onto the rectifier lead and solder in place.
11   Place the rotor and front housing in position in the stator and rear housing. After aligning the scribe marks, install the through-bolts.
12   Turn the fan and pulley to check for binding in the alternator.

13   Withdraw the wire which is retracting the brushes and seal the hole with waterproof cement.

18 Starter motor system – general description

The starter motor system consists of a motor with an integral positive engagement drive, the battery, a remote control starter switch, a neutral start switch on some models, the starter relay and the necessary wiring.

When the ignition switch is turned to the start position the starter relay is energized through the starter control circuit. The relay then connects the battery to the starter motor.

Cars equipped with an *automatic transmission and floor shift* have a neutral start switch in the starter control circuit which prevents operation of the starter if the selector lever is not in the 'N' or 'P' positions. Vehicles with *column shift automatic transmission* have an ignition switch mechanism which performs the same function.

With the starter in its rest position one of the field coils is connected directly to ground through a set of contacts. When the starter is first connected to the battery, a large current flows through the grounded field coil and operates a movable pole shoe. The poleshoe is attached to the starter drive plunger lever and so the drive is engaged with the ring gear on the flywheel.

When the movable pole shoe is fully seated, it opens the field coil grounding contacts and the starter is in a normal operational condition.

A special holding coil is used to maintain the movable pole shoe in the fully seated position while the starter is turning the engine.

19 Starter motor – testing on engine

1   If the stater motor fails to operate, then check the condition of the battery by turning on the headlights. If they glow brightly for several seconds and then gradually dim, the battery is in a discharged condition.
2   If the headlights continue to glow brightly and it is obvious that the battery is in good condition, check the tightness of the battery leads and all cables relative to the starting system. If possible, check the wiring with a voltmeter or test light for breaks or short circuits.
3   Check that there is current at the relay when the ignition switch is operated. If there is, then the relay should be suspect.
4   If there is no current at the relay, then suspect the ignition switch. On models with automatic transmission check the neutral start switch.
5   Should the above checks prove negative then the starter motor brushes probably need replacement or at the worst there is an internal fault in the motor.

20 Starter motor – removal and installation

1   On all models, disconnect the battery negative cable.

Six cylinder engine

2   Disconnect the starter cable from the starter motor.

3   Raise the vehicle and support it securely on jack stands.

4   From underneath the vehicle, remove the attaching bolts and withdraw the starter.

V8 engine

5   Raise the vehicle and support it securely.

6   Disconnect the starter cable. On some 4.2L and 5.0L models it will be necessary to unbolt and remove the engine mount insulators.

7   Remove the starter motor attaching bolts and lift the motor away from the vehicle.

8   Installation is the reverse of removal on all models; be sure to tighten starter bolts to specifications.

9   Lower the vehicle and reconnect the battery negative cable.

Chapter 6 Emission control systems

Contents

Specifications

Torque specifications

	ft-lb	Nm
EGR valve-to-carburetor spacer or intake manifold	12 to 18	16 to 24
Thermactor pump pulley-to-hub	11 to 15	15 to 20
Thermactor pump bracket-to-cylinder block		
1975 and 1976		
3.3L and 4.1L	22 to 32	16 to 24
5.0L and 5.8L	15 to 20	20 to 27
1977 and 1978		
3.3L	12 to 18	16 to 24
4.1L, 5.0L and 5.8L	22 to 32	30 to 42
1979 and 1980		
3.3L, 5.0L and 5.8L	12 to 18	16 to 24
4.1L	22 to 32	30 to 42
1980		
4.2L	30 to 45	41 to 61
Thermactor pump pivot bolt		
1975 and 1976		
3.3L and 4.1L	30 to 45	41 to 61
5.0L and 5.8L	22 to 32	30 to 42
1977 thru 1980		
3.3L, 4.2L, 5.0L and 5.8L	22 to 32	30 to 42
4.1L	30 to 45	41 to 61
Thermactor pump adjusting arm-to-pump		
1975 and 1976		
3.3L and 4.1L	27 to 37	37 to 50
5.0L and 5.8L	22 to 32	30 to 42
1977 thru 1979		
3.3L and 4.1L	12 to 18	16 to 24
5.0L to 5.8L	22 to 32	30 to 42
1980		
3.3L and 4.1L	24 to 34	33 to 46
4.2L and 5.0L	22 to 32	30 to 43
Thermactor adjusting arm-to-pump		
1975 and 1976		
All	22 to 32	30 to 42
1977		
All	12 to 18	16 to 24
1978 thru 1980		
3.3L and 4.1L	20 to 28	20 to 38
4.2L, 5.0L and 5.8L	12 to 18	16 to 24

1 General information

In order to meet US Federal anti-pollution laws, vehicles are equipped with a variety of emission control systems, depending on the models and the states in which they are sold.

Since the emissions control so many of the engine's functions, drivability and fuel consumption as well as conformance to the law can be affected should any faults develop. Therefore, it is very important that the emissions systems be kept operating at peak efficiency.

This Chapter will describe all of the systems which may be installed in order to cover all models.

The emissions label located under the hood contains information important to properly maintaining the emissions control systems as well as for keeping the vehicle correctly tuned.

Before beginning any work on the emissions control systems, read Section 2, Chapter 4 to avoid going contrary to any of the emissions control regulations.

Fig. 6.1 Typical emissions label (Sec 1)

FORD MOTOR COMPANY	SHIFT SCHED	Z	MAINT SCHED	F

VEHICLE EMISSION CONTROL INFORMATION

ENGINE FAMILY 2.3(T)'F'(1X92)EGR/AIR/CATALYST
ENGINE DISPLACEMENT 2.3L(140CID)TRANS MAN
SPARK PLUG AWSF-32   GAP .032-.036

EVAPORATIVE FAMILY IS **B**   **CATALYST**

VALVE LASH	HYD— NOT ADJ	TRANSMISSION GEAR		
		NEUTRAL	DRIVE	IDLE SPEED
IGNITION TIMING	2°BTDC			REDUCTION
TIMING RPM	650			(LESS THAN
CHOKE SETTING	2 RICH			100 MILES)
FAST IDLE · 100 RPM	HIGH CAM KICKDOWN	1800		250
CURB IDLE · 50 RPM	A/C ON	1300		
	A/C OFF	900		50
CURB IDLE RPM · 50 RPM	NON A/C	900		50

✳ DE-ENERGIZE THE ELECTRO-MAGNETIC A/C CLUTCH

MAKE ALL ADJUSTMENTS WITH ENGINE AT NORMAL OPERATING TEMPERATURE A/C AND HEADLIGHTS OFF DISCONNECT SENSOR CONNECTOR AT IGNITION MODULE BEFORE SETTING TIMING OR CURB IDLE (IF SO EQUIPPED) CONSULT SERVICE PUBLICATIONS FOR ADDITIONAL INSTRUCTIONS ON THE FOLLOWING PROCEDURES

IGNITION TIMING – A/C OFF – ADJUST WITH HOSES DISCONNECTED AND PLUGGED AT THE DISTRIBUTOR

CURB IDLE –A/C ON–   A/C THROTTLE SOLENOID POSITIONER ENERGIZED ✳

CURB IDLE –A/C OFF–   A/C THROTTLE SOLENOID POSITIONER DE-ENERGIZED

CURB IDLE–A/C ON OR OFF–ADJUST WITH AIR CLEANER IN POSITION REFER TO SERVICE PUBLICATIONS FOR VACUUM HOSE CONNECTIONS DURING IDLE SET

IDLE MIXTURE–A/C OFF–PRESET AT THE FACTORY DO NOT REMOVE THE LIMITER CAP(S) EXCEPT IN ACCORDANCE WITH SERVICE PUBLICATIONS

THIS VEHICLE CONFORMS TO U.S.E.P.A. REGULATIONS APPLICABLE TO 1979 MODEL YEAR NEW MOTOR VEHICLES   D9ZE-9C485-SB   **AJD**

2 Positive Crankcase Ventilation (PCV) system – description and maintenance

1 The PCV system consists of the PCV valve, oil filler cap and associated hoses.

2 The system operates by drawing vapors that escape past the piston rings back into the intake manifold, allowing fresh air to flow through the oil filler cap into the crankcase.

3 Maintenance of the PCV consists of periodically removing the hoses, valve and filler cap, cleaning them and checking for obstructions.

4 If a fault is suspected in the PCV valve, it is removed by grasping it at the elbow and pulling it from the engine. Replacement involves assembling the new valve to the elbow and installing it. For ease of installation the elbow should be soaked in hot water prior to assembling.

5 PCV valve replacement is further covered in Chapter 1.

3 Evaporative Emission Control (EEC) – description and maintenance

1 The EEC system is designed to limit the emission of fuel vapors to the atmosphere. It consists of the fuel tank, pressure and vacuum sensitive fuel filler cap, a restrictor bleed orifice, charcoal canister and associated connecting hoses.

2 When the fuel tank is filled, vapors are discharged to the atmosphere through the filler tube and the space between the inner fuel filler tube and the outer neck. With this system, when fuel covers the filler control tube, vapors can no longer escape because a vapor lock is created by the orifice.

3 When thermal expansion occurs in the fuel tank, vapor is forced through the orifice and is drawn into the carburetor as soon as the engine is started.

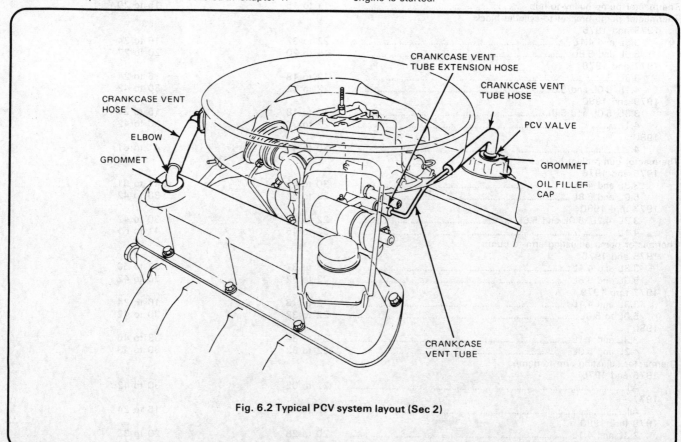

Fig. 6.2 Typical PCV system layout (Sec 2)

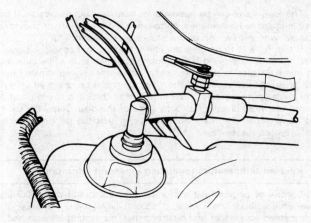

Fig. 6.3 PCV valve installation (V8) (Sec 3)

4   Some models incorporate a fuel bowl vent valve to direct vapors which collect in the carburetor back into the charcoal canister when the engine is off.

5   Maintenance consists of inspecting the system for leaks and checking the purge valve of the canister for proper operation.

4 Exhaust Gas Recirculation (EGR) system – description and maintenance

1   This system is designed to re-introduce small amounts of exhaust gas into the combustion cycle to reduce the generation of oxides of nitrogen (NOx). The amount of gas re-introduced is governed by engine temperature and vacuum.

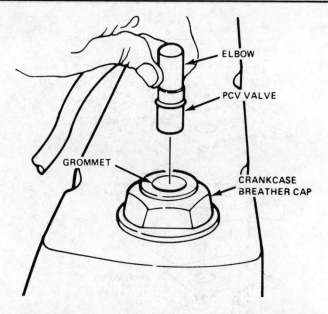

Fig. 6.4 Six-cylinder engine PCV valve installation (Sec 3)

2   The EGR valve is a vacuum-operated unit installed between the carburetor and intake manifold and when it is open it allows exhaust gases to enter the manifold.

3   Three basic types of EGR valves are used, depending on emission requirements. These are the poppet, tapered stem and integral transducer backpressure types.

4   Some models also use a Wide-Open Throttle (WOT) valve which closes the EGR valve when the engine is at or near wide-open throttle.

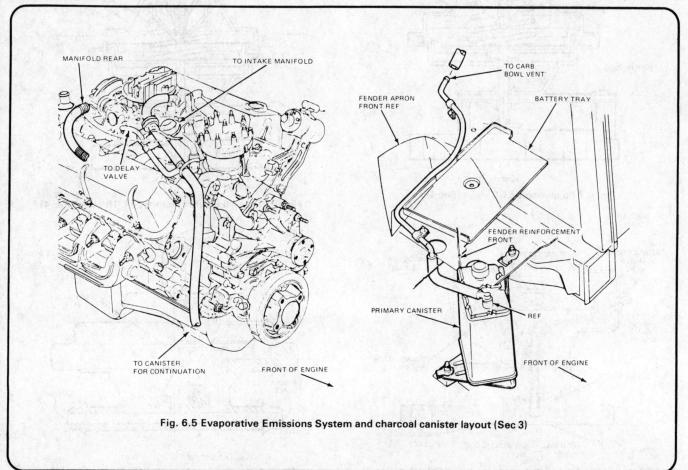

Fig. 6.5 Evaporative Emissions System and charcoal canister layout (Sec 3)

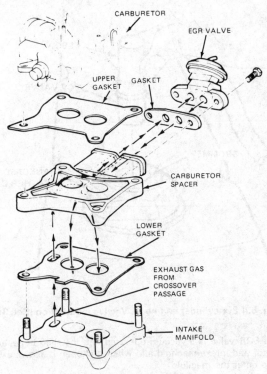

Fig. 6.6 Typical EGR valve installation (Sec 4)

5   The EGR valve can be removed for cleaning and inspection. If the valve is found to be damaged, corroded or extremely dirty it should be replaced with a new unit of the proper specification.

6   If the valve is to be cleaned, check that the orifice in the body is clear of obstructions and be careful not to enlarge it while cleaning. The internal deposits can be removed with a small power-driven rotary wire brush. Deposits around the valve stem can be removed using a steel blade approximately 0.029 in (0.7 mm) thick in a sawing motion around the stem shoulder at both sides of the disc. Clean the cavity and passages in the main body, ensuring that the poppet wobbles axially before reassembly.

5   Inlet air temperature regulation – general information

Control of engine inlet air temperature for better drivability and fewer emissions during warmup is accomplished through the use of a thermostatic air cleaner and duct system. This system is described in Chapter 4.

Some models also incorporate a Cold Weather Modulator (CWM) in the air cleaner assembly. At temperatures below 55° (13°C) the CWM prevents the air cleaner duct door from opening to allow the entry of non-heated intake air. At temperatures below 55°, the CWM does not operate. Under acceleration in cold conditions the CWM will hold the duct door open.

The CWM vacuum motor and valve should be checked periodically for freedom of operation.

6   Thermactor exhaust control system – description and maintenance

The Thermactor system reduces the hydrocarbon (HC) and carbon monoxide (CO) content of the exhaust gasses by continuing the

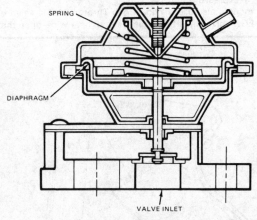

Fig. 6.7 Poppet-type EGR valve (Sec 4)

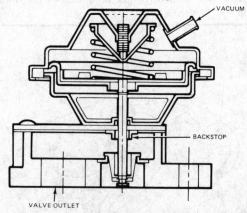

Fig. 6.8 Internal tapered stem-type EGR valve (Sec 4)

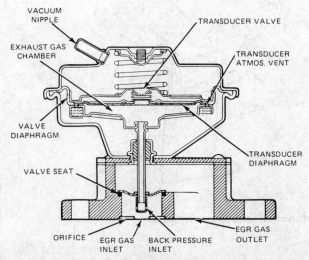

Fig. 6.9 Integral backpressure transducer-type EGR valve (Sec 4)

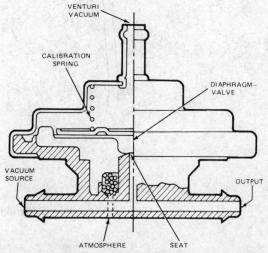

Fig. 6.10 Wide Open Throttle (WOT) valve (Sec 4)

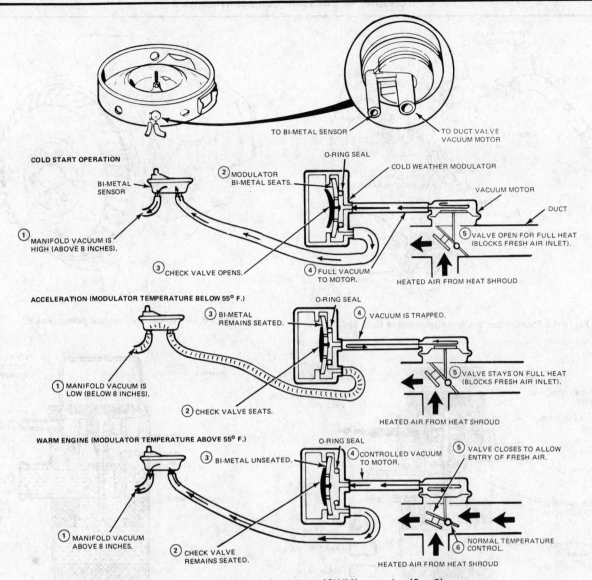

TO BI-METAL SENSOR

TO DUCT VALVE
VACUUM MOTOR

COLD START OPERATION

BI-METAL
SENSOR

② MODULATOR
BI-METAL SEATS.

O-RING SEAL

COLD WEATHER MODULATOR

VACUUM MOTOR

DUCT

① MANIFOLD VACUUM IS
HIGH (ABOVE 8 INCHES).

③ CHECK VALVE OPENS.

④ FULL VACUUM
TO MOTOR.

⑤ VALVE OPEN FOR FULL HEAT
(BLOCKS FRESH AIR INLET).

HEATED AIR FROM HEAT SHROUD

ACCELERATION (MODULATOR TEMPERATURE BELOW 55° F.)

③ BI-METAL
REMAINS SEATED.

O-RING SEAL

④ VACUUM IS TRAPPED.

① MANIFOLD VACUUM IS
LOW (BELOW 8 INCHES).

② CHECK VALVE SEATS.

⑤ VALVE STAYS ON FULL HEAT
(BLOCKS FRESH AIR INLET).

HEATED AIR FROM HEAT SHROUD

WARM ENGINE (MODULATOR TEMPERATURE ABOVE 55° F.)

③ BI-METAL UNSEATED.

O-RING SEAL

④ CONTROLLED VACUUM
TO MOTOR.

⑤ VALVE CLOSES TO ALLOW
ENTRY OF FRESH AIR.

① MANIFOLD VACUUM
ABOVE 8 INCHES.

② CHECK VALVE
REMAINS SEATED.

⑥ NORMAL TEMPERATURE
CONTROL.

HEATED AIR FROM HEAT SHROUD

Fig. 6.11 Cold Weather Modulator (CWM) operation (Sec 6)

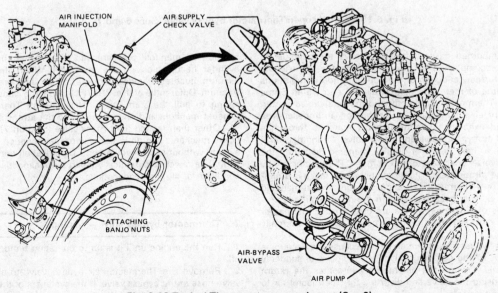

AIR INJECTION
MANIFOLD

AIR SUPPLY
CHECK VALVE

ATTACHING
BANJO NUTS

AIR-BYPASS
VALVE

AIR PUMP

Fig. 6.12 Typical Thermactor system layout (Sec 6)

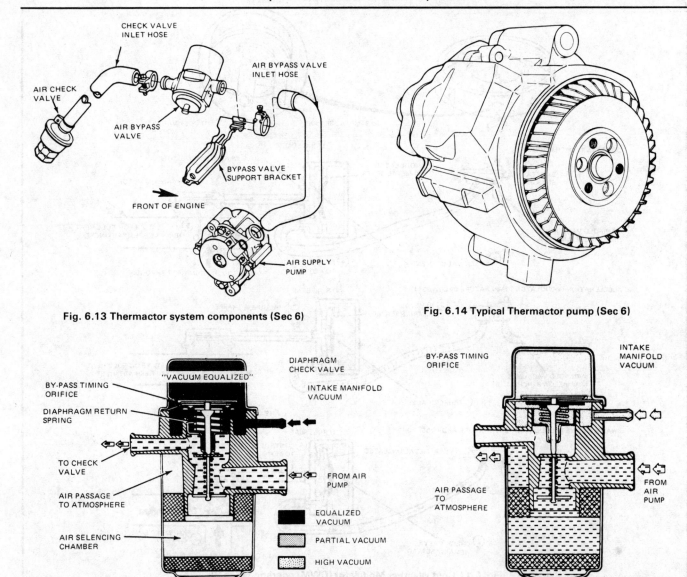

Fig. 6.13 Thermactor system components (Sec 6)

Fig. 6.14 Typical Thermactor pump (Sec 6)

Fig. 6.15 Normally open Thermactor bypass valve (Secs 6 and 7)

oxidation of the unburned gasses after they leave the combustion chamber. This is accomplished by mixing air with the hot exhaust gases, promoting further reduction of the concentration of pollutants and converting some of them into carbon dioxide and water. Some models also inject Thermactor air directly into the catalytic converter.

The Thermactor air pump draws in air through an impeller-type centrifugal fan and exhausts it to the exhaust manifold through a vacuum-controlled air bypass valve and check valve. During deceleration, when there a high level of intake manifold vacuum, the diaphragm check valve operates to shut off the Thermactor air by exhausting it to the atmosphere. The air supply check valve is a one-way type which allows Thermactor air to pass to the exhaust manifold but will not allow exhaust gasses to flow in the reverse direction.

Several models of air bypass valves are used on the Thermactor system, but all are of two main types: normally open or normally closed.

Normally open bypass valves remain open because the vacuum is equal on both sides of the diaphragm. Under conditions of suddenly high intake manifold vacuum the diaphragm overcomes the return spring pressure, closing the valve and diverting the Thermactor air to the atmosphere momentarily.

A normally closed bypass valve is held in the upward or closed

position by manifold pressure and the Thermactor air flows to the cylinder heads, blocking the vent port. When the intake manifold vacuum fluctuates under acceleration or deceleration, the integral Vacuum Differential Valve (VDV) cuts off the vacuum, allowing the spring to pull the stem down. This cuts off Thermactor air to the exhaust manifold and diverts the air to the atmosphere.

Other than testing the bypass valve (Section 7), there is little the home mechanic can do in the way of maintenance of the Thermactor system without special equipment. The drivebelt tension and condition should be checked periodically along with inspecting the security and condition of all hose connections.

7 Thermactor bypass valve – testing

1   Run the engine until it is up to operating temperature and shut it off.

2   Remove the Thermactor air bypass valve-to-air manifold check valve hose at the bypass valve. If the system is of the tee type, remove both hoses which connect the bypass valve to the check valve.

3   With the parking brake on and the transmission in Neutral or Park,

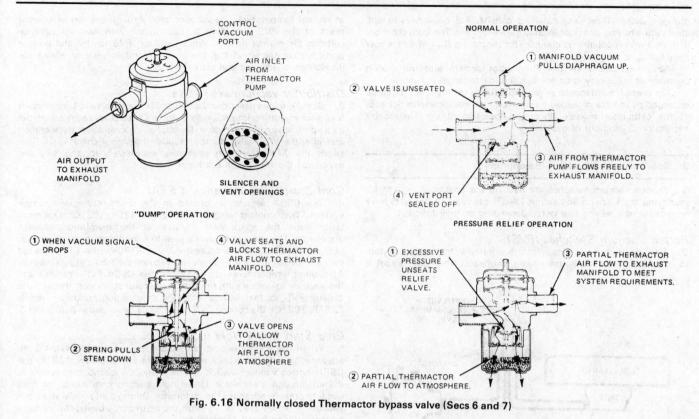

Fig. 6.16 Normally closed Thermactor bypass valve (Secs 6 and 7)

start the engine. Run the engine at a fast idle (approximately 1500 rpm) and place your hand over the air bypass hose connection(s). You should be able to feel as well as hear a definite blast of air. Allow the engine to return to normal idle.

4   Remove the vacuum hose from the bypass valve and plug the hose. Run the engine at a fast idle again with your hand over the bypass hose connection. There should be virtually no air flow felt or heard. Instead, the air should be discharged through the valve silencer cover exhaust ports.

5   If there is a noticable air flow, the bypass valve is defective and it should be replaced with a new one.

6   Shut off the engine and reinstall any components which may have been removed.

8   Catalytic converter – general information

The catalytic converter is incorporated upstream of the exhaust muffler. The converter consists of a ceramic honeycomb-like core housed in a stainless steel pipe. The core is coated with a platinum and paladium catalyst which converts unburned carbon monoxide and hydrocarbons into carbon dioxide and water by a chemical reaction. Converters of this type are called Conventional Oxidation Catalysts (COC) or 'two-way' catalysts because they control two of the three exhaust emissions.

Some later models use a 'three-way' catalyst (TWC) which controls hydrocarbons (HC), carbon monoxide (CO) and oxides of

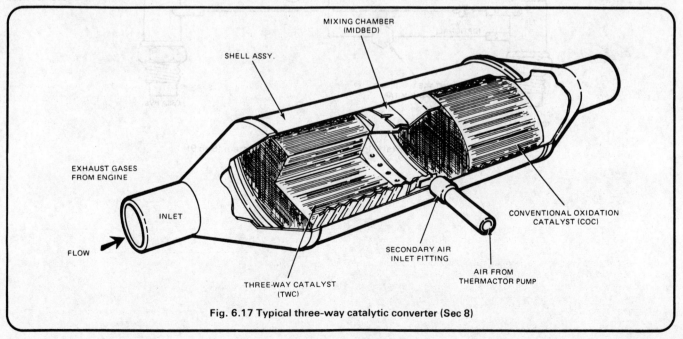

Fig. 6.17 Typical three-way catalytic converter (Sec 8)

nitrogen (NOx). Three-way catalysts consist of 2 converters in one shell with a mixing chamber located between them. The front chamber is coated with rhodium and platinum for controlling NOx while the rear chamber is of the two-way type.

Air is injected from the Thermactor system into the mixing chamber of three-way catalysts to aid in oxidation of pollutants.

No special maintenance of the converter is required, but it can be damaged by the use of leaded fuels, engine misfire, excessive richness of the carburetor mixture, incorrect operation of the Thermactor system or running out of gasoline.

9   Spark control switches – description

1   Various vacuum switches are used in the emissions system for modifying spark timing and engine idle. These vacuum switches have anywhere from two to four ports, depending on their function.

Ported Vacuum Switches (PVS)
2   A typical ported vacuum switch is situated in the cooling system to increase idle rpm when the engine overheats. When the coolant is

at normal temperature, the vacuum goes through the top and center ports of the PVS, providing the distributor with vacuum advance suitable for normal driving. When hot, the PVS center and bottom ports are connected so that the engine manifold vacuum allows the distributor to advance and increase idle.

Distributor vacuum vent valve
3   Some engines use a distributor vacuum vent valve to both prevent fuel from migrating into the distributor advance diaphragm and to act as a spark advance delay valve. During light acceleration, deceleration and idle, the vent valve dumps vacuum through a check valve. This keeps the distributor from advancing excessively for the load and evacuates the fuel in the spark port line.

Cold Start Spark Advance (CSSA)
4   The CSSA system is located in the distributor spark control system. When coolant temperature is below 128°F (53°C), it momentarily traps the spark port vacuum at the distributor advance diaphragm. The vacuum follows a path through the carburetor vacuum tap, the Distributor Retard Control Valve (DRCV), the CSSA ported vacuum switch and then the cooling vacuum switch to the distributor. At coolant temperatures above 128°F, the CSSA PVS operates and the vacuum follows a path from the carburetor spark port through the cooling PVS to the distributor. In an overheating condition (above 225°F, 103°C), the cooling PVS operates as described in paragraph 2.

Cold Start Spark Hold (CSSH)
5   When the engine is cold, the CSSH momentarily provides spark advance for improved cold engine acceleration. Below 128°F, the CSSH ported vacuum switch is closed and the distributor vacuum is routed through a restrictor. Under cold starting conditions, the high vacuum present advances the distributor. During cold acceleration, the vacuum is slowly bled off through the restrictor, slowing the vacuum advance during initial acceleration.

Spark Delay Valve (SDV)
6   SDV's are designed to slow the air flow in one direction while a check valve allows free flow in the opposite direction. This allows closer control of vacuum operated emission devices.

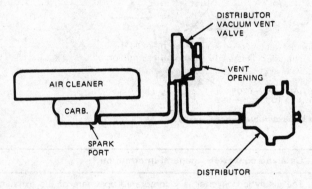

Fig. 6.18 Typical distributor vent valve installation (Sec 9)

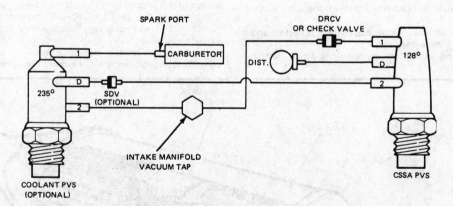

Fig. 6.19 Typical Cold Start Spark Advance (CSSA) system (Sec 9)

Chapter 7 Part A Manual transmission

Contents

Specifications

Transmission type .... 3-speed or 4-speed overdrive, synchromesh in all forward gears

Application
1975 and 1976 .... 3-speed
1977 .... 3-speed and 4-speed
1978 thru 1980 .... 4-speed

Oil capacities
3-speed .... 3.5 US qts
4-speed .... 4.5 US qts

Oil type ESP-M2C83-C

Torque specifications

	Ft-lb	Nm
3-speed		
Shift control-to-transmission	8 to 12	11 to 16
Shift rod lock nuts	10 to 20	14 to 27
Filler plug	10 to 20	14 to 27
4-speed		
Shift control mounting bolts	20 to 30	27 to 41
Shift control rod-to-shifter	10 to 20	14 to 27
Shift control lever attaching nuts	10 to 20	14 to 27
Filler plug	20 to 25	28 to 33
Back-up lamp switch	8 to 12	11 to 16

1 Transmission (3-speed) – general information

The tranmsisison is equipped with three forward gears and one reverse. The forward gears are synchromesh.

All forward gears on the mainshaft and input shaft are in constant mesh with their corresponding gears on the countershaft gear cluster and are helically cut for quiet running. The reverse gear has straight cut gear teeth and drives the first gear through an interposed sliding idler gear.

The gears are engaged by means of two sliding forks and are selected by either a steering column or floor-mounted shift linkage.

2 Floor-mounted shift lever assembly (3-speed) – removal and installation

1 Remove the four screws attaching the lower shift boot to the floor pan and remove the two bolts holding the shift lever to the control assembly.

2 Remove the lock nuts connecting the shift rods to the control assembly, unbolt the assembly from the transmission extension and lower it from the vehicle. The backup light switch can be allowed to hang free.

3 Remove the boot from the control assembly, remove the selector

lever shaft nut and remove the shaft from the assembly. Lift the selector arm and levers out of the support bracket, taking care not to lose the detent spring located between the first-reverse selector lever as shown in the accompanying figure.

4   Prior to assembly, lubricate all of the shift assembly mating surfaces with lithium grease.

5   Place the detent spring in position between the first-reverse selector lever and arm. The wide base of the spring must rest against the selector lever. Next, place the second-third selector arm against the shift selector arm and insert the assembly into the support bracket.

6   Insert the selector shaft through the support bracket and install the retaining nut.

7   Slide the shift control assembly into the shift boot and then attach the entire assembly to the transmission extension housing. Make sure that the spacer is located inside the assembly. Install the backup light.

8   Install the shift control assembly-to-gear shift lever attaching bolts.

9   Adjust the shift linkage as described in Section 3 and check the linkage for smooth operation, adjusting as necessary.

3   Floor-mounted shift linkage (3-speed) – adjustment

1   With the shift rods attached to the transmission levers, rotate the transmission to make sure that it is in neutral.

2   Insert a suitable alignment pin through the hole in the shift boot into the alignment hole in the shift control assembly.

3   Install the slotted ends of the shift rods over the flats of the shift control assembly.

4   Install the slotted ends of the shift rods over the flats of the shift control assembly and install the attaching nuts.

5   Remove the alignment pin and check the shift control for proper operation.

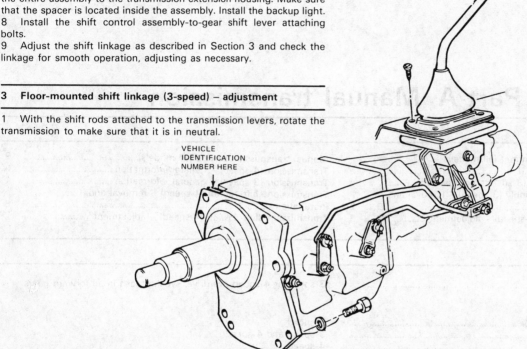

VEHICLE
IDENTIFICATION
NUMBER HERE

Fig. 7.1 Typical 3-speed transmission and linkage layout (Secs 1, 2 and 3)

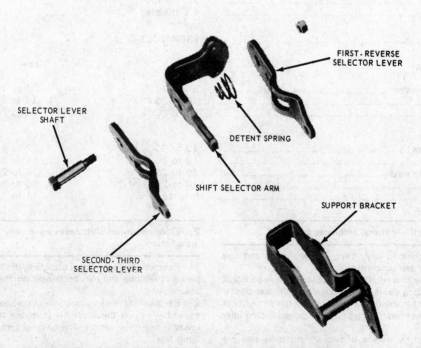

SELECTOR LEVER
SHAFT

SECOND-THIRD
SELECTOR LEVER

FIRST-REVERSE
SELECTOR LEVER

DETENT SPRING

SHIFT SELECTOR ARM

SUPPORT BRACKET

Fig. 7.2 3-speed floor shift selector components (Sec 2)

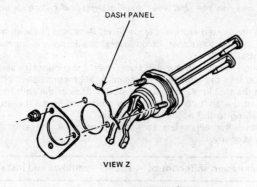

VIEW Z

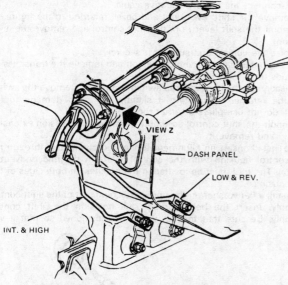

Fig. 7.3 Column shift linkage layout (3-speed) (Sec 4)

4 Column-mounted shift linkage (3-speed) – adjustment

1   Place the gearshift lever in the neutral position and loosen the shift rod adjustment nuts.
2   Making sure that the transmission is in neutral, insert a suitable pin or piece of rod into the shift rods as shown in the accompanying figure.
3   Tighten the shift rod alignment nuts.
4   Remove the alignment pin and check the shift lever for proper operation.

5 Column-mounted shift linkage grommet (all models) – removal and installation

1   All column-mounted shift levers (manual and automatic) use an oil impregnated plastic grommet at the connections between the rods and levers. Any time a rod is disconnected from a grommet connector, the old grommet must be replaced with a new one.
2   To remove a grommet, place the lower jaw of the special Ford tool (or equivalent) between the rod and lever as shown in the accompanying figure.

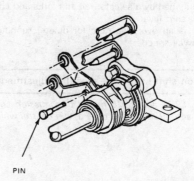

Fig. 7.4 Column shift adjustment (Sec 4)

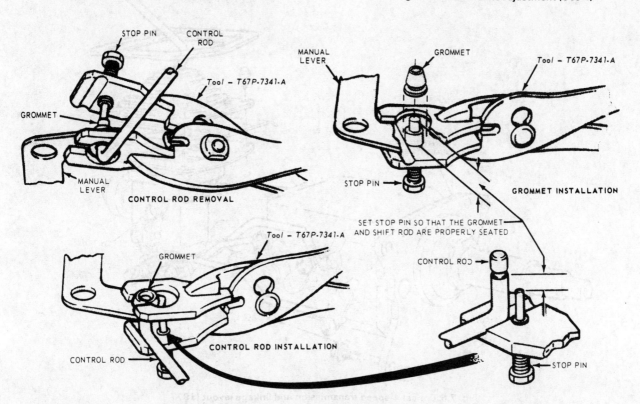

Fig. 7.5 Shift linkage grommet removal and installation (Sec 5)

3   Place the stop pin against the end of the rod and force the rod from the grommet. The grommet can now be removed by cutting off the large shoulder.
4   To install, set the stop pin so that the grommet and shift rod will have the proper clearance.
5   Coat the new grommet with lubricant and position it on the stop pin. Force the grommet into the shift lever hole, rotating the grommet several times to make sure that it is seated properly.
6   Adjust the stop pin to the proper length so that the shift rod can be installed as shown. Improper adjustment could cause damage to the grommet retaining lip.
7   After adjusting the stop pin height, place the shift rod in the tool and force the rod into the grommet so the rod seats in the inner retaining lip of the grommet.

6   Transmission (4-speed) – general information

All forward gears of the the 4-speed transmission are engaged through synchro hubs and rings to obtain smooth, silent gear changes and are helically cut.

The reverse gear has straight-cut spur teeth and drives the toothed 1st/2nd gear synchro-hub on the mainshaft through an interposed sliding idler arm.

Gears are engaged by a selector rail and forks and control is from a floor-mounted shift lever.

Fourth gear is an overdrive ratio for quieter running and better mileage at highway speeds.

7   Transmission shift linkage (4-speed) – adjustment

Note: *Only the 1977 and 1978 model transmission linkage can be adjusted. 1979 and 1980 models have a shift control which cannot be serviced and only the shift lever, backup lamp and switch retainer can be removed.*

1   With the slotted ends of the shift rods detached but with the shift rods attached to the transmission levers, check that the transmission is in Neutral.
2   Through the hole in the shift boot, insert the proper size alignment tool or rod into the shift control assembly alignment hole.
1   With the tool in place, slide the slotted ends of the shift rods over the flats of the shift control assembly studs and install the attaching nuts, referring to the accompanying figure.
4   Remove the alignment tool and check that the shift linkage operates properly.

8   Transmission shift control (4-speed) – removal and installation

1   Disconnect the battery negative cable.
2   Remove the shift lever boot and bezel, referring to the figure.
3   Unbolt the shift lever from the shift control and remove the lever and boot.
4   Raise the vehicle and support it securely.
5   From underneath the vehicle, unbolt and remove the transmission shift rods from the shift control levers.
6   Disconnect the backup lamp switch connector. Remove the switch from the retainer by rotating it slightly. To avoid damage to the switch, do not use pliers or other tools for removal.
7   Unbolt the shift control assembly from the transmission extension housing and remove it.
8   To install, insert an alignment tool or rod completely through the shift control housing with the control levers in the mid or Neutral position. The tool must be located in the notches on both sides of the shift housing.
9   Install a flat washer on the upper attaching bolt of the shift control assembly. Insert the bolts through the holes in the shift control assembly. Be sure that the flat washer is positioned so that it will

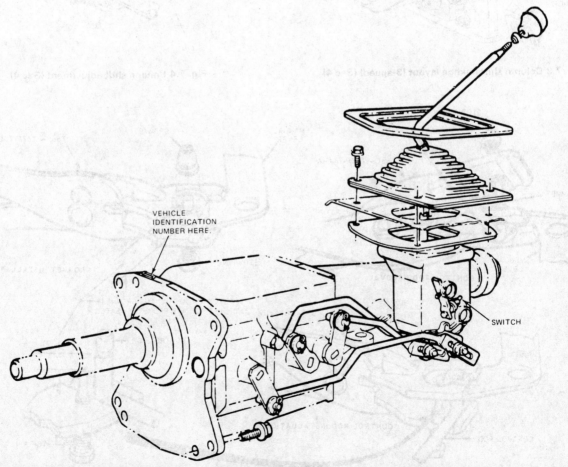

VEHICLE
IDENTIFICATION
NUMBER HERE.

SWITCH

Fig. 7.6 Typical 4-speed transmission and linkage layout (1977 and 1978) (Secs 6, 7 and 8)

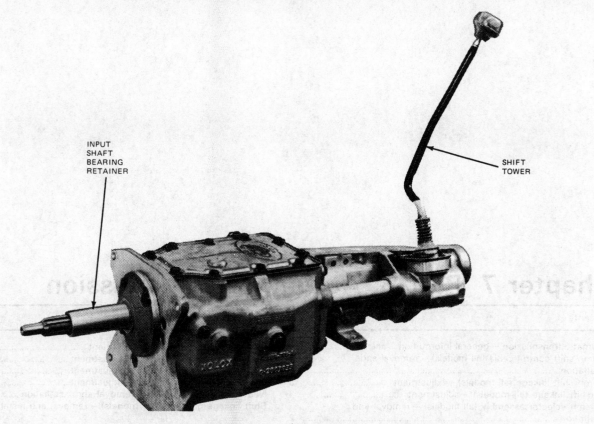

Fig. 7.7 Late models (1979 and 1980) 4-speed transmission (Sec 6)

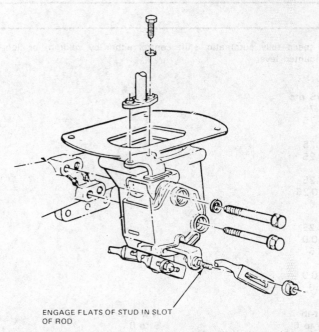

Fig. 7.8 1977 and 1978 transmission shifter installation (Sec 7)

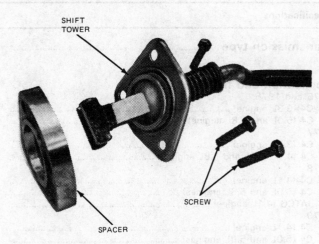

Fig. 7.9 1979 and 1980 shift components (Sec 7)

contact the shift assembly and that the larger diameter bolt is at the top.

10 With the alignment tool still inserted, tighten the attaching bolts to specifications.

11 Shift the transmission into Reverse gear by rotating the center shift lever clockwise.

12 Place the two forward speed shift control rods in position on their corresponding shift levers and install the nuts and washers.

13 Shift the transmission into Neutral by rotating the center lever counterclockwise.

14 Install the reverse shift control rod on the reverse lever and tighten the nuts to specification. Remove the alignment tool.

15 Lubricate all of the shifting components connections.

16 Re-connect the backup light switch to the connector.

17 Lower the vehicle and from inside, install the shift lever to the shift control, tightening the bolts to specification.

18 Install the shift boot and bezel.

19 Check the shift assembly for proper operation. Shifting into reverse will automatically locate the backup light switch.

20 Reconnect the battery negative cable.

9   Manual transmission service (all models)

Because of the special tools and techniques required in the overhauling or dismantling of a transmission, it is recommended that this be left to a dealer or a properly equipped shop.

Chapter 7 Part B Automatic transmission

Contents

Specifications

Transmission type ....

3-speed fully automatic, shift control either by column- or floor-mounted lever

Application and fluid capacities

1975 and 1976	US qts
C4 (3.3L engine)	7.75
C4 (5.0L and 5.8L engine)	8.75
1977	
C4 (3.3L engine)	7.25
C4 (4.1L, 5.0L and 5.8L engines)	8.25
1978	
C4 (4.1L engine)	8.25
C4 (5.0L and 5.8L engines)	10.25
JATCO (4.1L engine)	8.6
1979	
C4 (4.1L engine)	8.25
C4 (5.0L and 5.8L engines)	10.0
JATCO (4.1L engine)	8.6
1980	
C4 (4.1L, 4.2L and 5.0L engines)	10.0
JATCO (4.1 engine)	8.6

Torque specifications

	Ft-lb	Nm
JATCO oil screen-to-lower valve body	4 to 6	5 to 8
JATCO oil pan-to-case	4 to 5	5.42 to 6.77
JATCO intermediate band adjustment screw	9 to 10	6.6 to 13.5
JATCO intermediate band adjustment screw locknut	22 to 29	30 to 39
C4 oil pan-to-case	12 to 16	17 to 21
Shift control cable bolt	10 to 14	13 to 19
C4 cooler line-to-transmission case	12 to 18	17 to 24
C4 low-reverse band adjustment screw	10	13.55
C4 intermediate band adjustment screw	10	13.55
C4 band adjustment locknut	40	54.23
Floorshift selector lever-to-housing nut	20 to 25	28 to 33
Floorshift lever housing bolt	4 to 6	6 to 8
Floorshift manual shift lever retaining nut	10 to 15	14 to 20

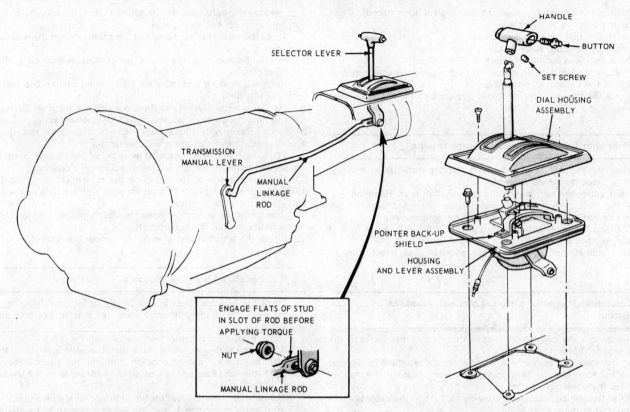

Fig. 7.10 Typical automatic transmission floor shift linkage layout (Secs 2, 3 and 4)

1   Automatic transmission – general information

The automatic transmission takes the place of the conventional clutch and transmission and is composed of the following two main assemblies:

A three element torque converter coupling which is capable of infinitely variable torque multiplication and serves as the link between the engine and transmission.
A hydraulically-operated epicyclic gearbox providing three forward and one reverse ratio.

Due to the complexity of the automatic transmission unit, it is recommended that any major fault diagnosis or repair be left to the dealer or a transmission shop. This Chapter will cover information useful to the owner in routine maintenance and adjustment.

Models are equipped with either a Ford C4 or JATCO transmission depending on engine and year of manufacture. Both transmissions are basically similar and any differences will be described under separate Section headings.

All models feature a transmission oil cooler with the cooler element in the radiator.

Ford specifies a different grade of transmission fluid than other manufacturers and this must be used whenever refilling or adding fluid to the transmission. Transmission fluid which is correct for the vehicle is specified on the certification label on the left front door post.

2   Floor shift selector lever assembly (all models) – removal and installation

1   From under the vehicle, remove the shift rod and nut from the selector lever as shown in the accompanying figure.
2   From inside the vehicle, remove the selector handle set screw.
3   Remove the dial housing and pointer backup shield and disconnect the dial indicator light.
4   Unbolt the selector lever housing and lever assembly and remove them from the vehicle. Remove the nut securing the selector lever to the housing and remove the lever.

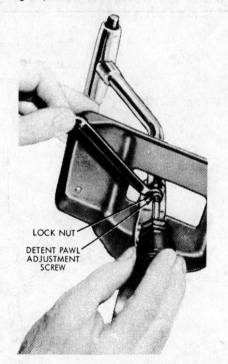

Fig. 7.11 Detent pawl adjustment (Sec 2)

5   To install, secure the selector lever to the housing with the nut and tighten to specification.
6   Before installing the shift detent pawl, check that the highest point on the pawl clears the detent plate. To adjust, hold the adjusting screw stationary and turn the locknut as shown in the accompanying figure.
7   Remove the selector lever handle.
8   Connect the dial indicator light and install the pointer backup shield onto the housing and lever assembly.

9   Referring to the figure, install the housing and lever assembly and tighten the bolts to specification.
10 Install the dial housing and screws.
11 Install the selector lever handle and set screw.
12 Place the selector lever against the Drive stop.
13 From under the vehicle, install the shift rod on the selector lever and adjust the linkage as necessary.
14 Check the transmission for proper operation in each selector lever position.

3   Floor shift linkage (all models) – adjustment

1   Have an assistant position the shift selector in the D position and hold it in place during adjustment.
2   From under the car, loosen the manual shift lever retaining nut. Move the shift lever to the D position on the transmission itself (second detent position from the rear of the transmission).
3   With both the selector lever and the manual lever in the D position, tighten the attaching nut to specification.
4   After adjustment, check the operation of the selector in all positions.

4   Column shift control cable (all models) – removal and installation

1   Disconnect the clip which secures the shift control cable to the brake support bracket.
2   At the steering column lever, remove the cable retaining clip and slide the cable and bushing from the lever. Remove the rubber grommet from the dash panel.
3   Raise the vehicle, support it securely and unbolt the cable bracket assembly from the transmission.
4   Referring to the accompanying figure, remove the nut at point A,

then remove the transmission manual lever stud. Remove the cable by pulling it through the dash panel.
5   To install, insert the round end of the cable through the dash panel opening.
6   Install the cable to the brake pedal support bracket with the retaining clip.
7   Place the bushing and cable on the steering column and secure it with the retaining clip.
8   Put the selector lever in the Drive position and hang an 8 lb weight on it to hold the selector against the Drive position stop.
9   From underneath the vehicle, install the cable and bracket assembly on the transmission with two bolts.
10 Place the transmission manual lever in the Drive position, which is the second detent from the full counterclockwise position.
11 Position the end of the cable on the transmission manual lever stud and carefully align the flats on the stud with the flats on the cable and install the attaching nut.
12 Check that the selector lever has not been moved from the D stop, then tighten the nut to specification.
13 Check the transmission selector for proper operation.

5   Column shift linkage (all models) – adjustment

1   Place the selector lever in the Drive position and hang an 8 lb weight on it to ensure that the lever remains in position during adjustment.
2   Loosen the adjusting nut on the shift rod.
3   At the transmission, make sure that the shift lever is in the D position (the second detent position from the full counterclockwise position). Align the flats on the slotted rod with those on the mounting stud.
4   Tighten the adjusting nut on the shift rod to specification.
5   After adjustment, check that the selector operates properly in all positions.

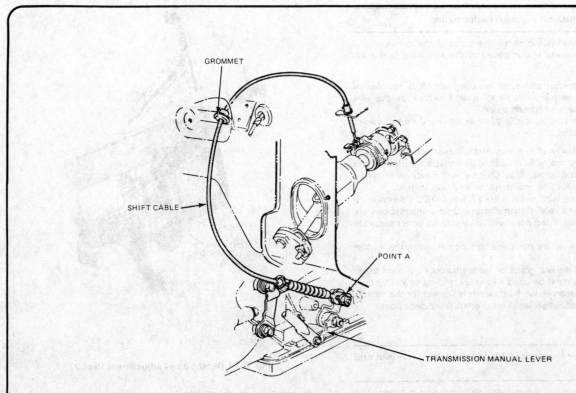

Fig. 7.12 Column shift control cable layout (Secs 4 and 5)

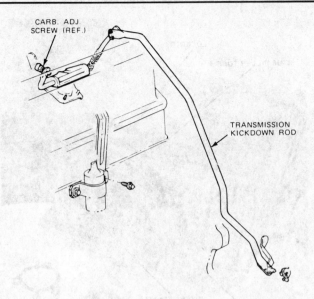

Fig. 7.13 Typical kick-down rod layout (Sec 6)

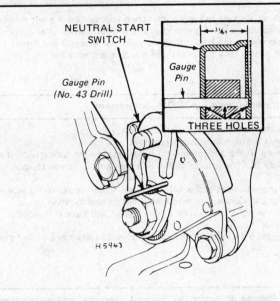

Fig. 7.14 C4 transmission neutral start switch adjustment (Sec 7)

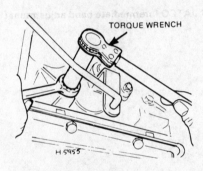

Fig. 7.15 Adjusting the intermediate transmission band (C4)
(Sec 8)

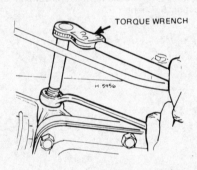

Fig. 7.16 Adjusting the low/reverse band (C4) (Sec 9)

6 Kick-down rod (all models) – adjustment

1   Disconnect the downshift rod return spring and hold the throttle shaft lever in the wide open position.
2   Hold the kick-down rod against the through detent stop.
3   Loosen the lock nut and adjust the downshift screw so as to provide a clearance between the screw top and the throttle shaft lever tab of 0.01 to 0.08 in (0.25 to 2.03 mm).
4   Reconnect the downshift rod return spring.

7 Neutral start switch (C4) – removal and installation

1   Chock the front wheels, jack up the car and support it on firmly based jack stands.
2   From under the car, disconnect the downshift linkage rod from the transmission downshift lever.
3   Apply a little penetrating oil to the downshift lever shaft and nut and allow to soak for a few minutes.
4   Remove the transmission downshift outer lever retaining nut and lift away the lever.
5   Remove the neutral start switch securing bolts.
6   Disconnect the multi-wire connector from the neutral switch and lift away the switch.
7   To reinstall, place the switch on the transmission and secure it finger-tight with the securing bolts.

8   Move the selector lever to the Neutral position. Rotate the switch and fit a No. 43 drill bit into the gauge pin hole. The bit must be inserted a full 0.48 in (12.30 mm) into the 3 holes of the switch (refer to accompanying Figure). Tighten the switch securing bolts fully and remove the drill.
9   Installation is the reverse of the removal procedure. Check that the engine starts only when the selector is in the N and P positions.

8 Intermediate band (C4) – adjustment

1   The intermediate band should be adjusted if there is noticeable slipping or sluggish shifting.
2   Remove the adjustment screw lock nut located on the left side of the transmission case. Tighten the adjusting screw to specification using a torque wrench, as shown in the accompanying figure.
3   Back off the adjustment screw $1\frac{3}{4}$ turns.
4   Install a new lock nut and tighten it to specifications.

9 Low and reverse band (C4) – adjustment

1   Symptoms of an improperly adjusted low and reverse band are that the transmission won't operate in Reverse and there will be little or no engine braking in Low gear.

2　To adjust, remove the adjusting screw lock nut on the left side of the transmission case. Tighten the screw with a torque wrench to specification and then back off the adjustment screw 3 full turns.

3　Install a new lock nut and tighten it to specifications.

10　Intermediate band (JATCO) – adjustment

1　Raise the vehicle and support it securely.

2　Remove the transmission servo cover.

3　Referring to the accompanying figure, loosen the lock nut on the intermediate band adjusting screw and tighten the screw to specification.

4　Back the adjusting screw off two turns. With the adjusting screw held stationary, tighten the screw lock nut to specification.

5　Install the servo cover with a new gasket and tighten the bolts to specification.

6　Lower the vehicle and check the fluid level as described in Chapter 1.

11　Shift linkage grommet (all models) – removal and installation

All column-mounted shift assemblies use an oil impregnated plastic grommet at the connections between rods and levers. The grommet must be replaced with a new one any time a rod is disconnected from it. The procedure for removal and installation can be found in Section 5, Chapter 7A.

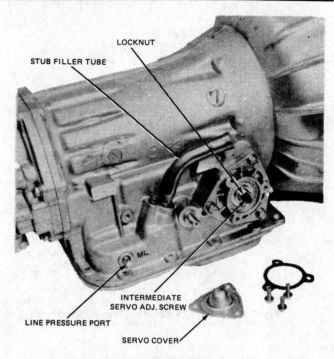

LOCKNUT

STUB FILLER TUBE

INTERMEDIATE SERVO ADJ. SCREW

LINE PRESSURE PORT

SERVO COVER

Fig. 7.17 JATCO intermediate band adjustment (Sec 10)

Chapter 8 Driveline

Contents

Specifications

Clutch
Pedal free play .... 0.136 in

Driveshaft
Runout limit .... 0.035 in

U-joint flange runout limit
All except circular flange-type .... 0.010 in
Circular flange-type .... 0.005 in

Differential/rear axles
Lubricant
Type ESW-M2C-105-A
Capacity
    Integral carrier .... 4.0 US qts
    Removable carrier
        8-in ring gear .... 4.0 US qts
        9-in ring gear .... 5.0 US qts

Pinion bearing preload

	in-lbs	Nm
New bearings	17 to 27	1.92 to 3.05
Used bearings	8 to 14	0.90 to 1.58

Pinion gear-to-side gear backlash .... 0.008 to 0.012 in

Side gear thrust washer thicknesses .... 0.030 to 0.032 in

Pinion gear thrust washer thicknesses .... 0.030 to 0.032 in

Side bearing preload
Integral carrier
    New bearings .... 0.008 to 0.012 in
    Used bearings .... 0.006 to 0.010 in
Removable carrier
    New bearings .... 0.008 to 0.012 in

Ring gear-to-drive pinion backlash .... 0.008 to 0.012 in

Maximum between teeth backlash variation .... 0.003 in

Ring gear runout limit .... 0.003 in

Torque specifications   ft-lb   Nm
Integral carrier axle
Differential bearing cap bolt .... 70 to 85   95 to 115
Differential bearing adjustment nut lock bolts .... 12 to 25   17 to 34
Ring gear attaching bolts .... 70 to 85   95 to 115
Rear cover bolts .... 25 to 35   34 to 46
Filler plug .... 25 to 40   28 to 54
Axleshaft retainer nut .... 20 to 40   28 to 54

Removable carrier axle
Differential bearing cap bolt .... 70 to 85   95 to 115
Carrier-to-housing stud nut .... 25 to 40   34 to 54
Pinion retainer-to-carrier bolts .... 30 to 45   40 to 60
Ring gear attaching bolt .... 70 to 85   95 to 115
Filler plug .... 25 to 50   34 to 67
Rear axleshaft bearing retainer nuts .... 20 to 40   28 to 54

Clutch
Clutch housing-to-engine bolt
    4.1L and 5.0L engine .... 38 to 61   52 to 82
    3.3L engine .... 38 to 55   52 to 73
Pressure plate-to-flywheel .... 12 to 20   17 to 27

Driveshaft
Universal joint-to-flange bolt
    All except circular flange-type .... 8 to 15   9 to 20
    Circular flange-type .... 70 to 90   95 to 120

---

1   Clutch – general information

The clutch is of the single dry disc type, consisting of the clutch disc, pressure plate and clutch release bearing, which is acutated by a pedal and mechanically-operated linkage.

When the clutch pedal is in the up (released) position, the clutch disc is clamped between the friction surface of the engine flywheel and the face of the clutch pressure plate diaphragm, thus transmitting the drive of the engine through the disc which is splined to the transmission. Friction lining material is riveted to the clutch disc and the splined hub is spring-cushioned so as to absorb transmission shocks.

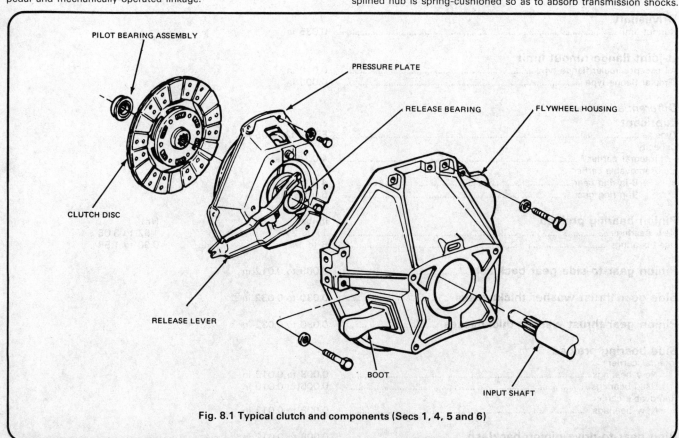

Fig. 8.1 Typical clutch and components (Secs 1, 4, 5 and 6)

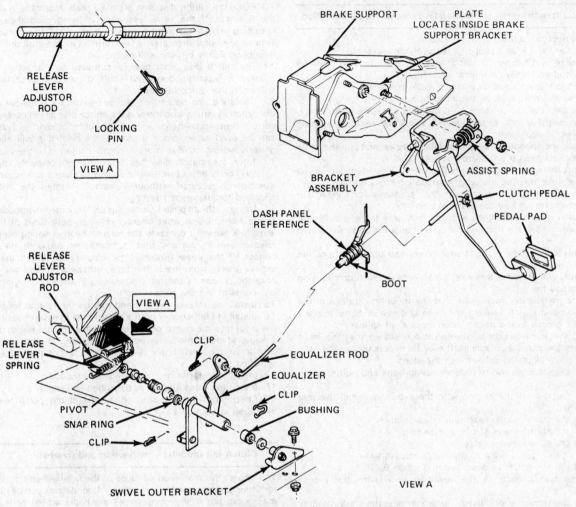

Fig. 8.2 Clutch pedal layout (Secs 2 and 7)

When the clutch is depressed, the clutch release lever moves the release bearing against the clutch diaphragm, which in turns moves the pressure plate away from the clutch disc, disengaging the clutch and disconnecting the drive to the transmission.

Clutch pedal free play should be adjusted after the installation of a new clutch or when the clutch does not engage properly.

2 Clutch pedal free play measurement and adjustment

1   Incorrect clutch pedal adjustment can cause clutch, and possibly transmission damage. The clutch pedal free play should be adjusted whenever the clutch doesn't engage properly.
2   Raise the vehicle and support it securely.
3   Referring to the accompanying figure, disconnect the clutch retainer spring from the release lever.
4   Remove the locking pin from the release lever rod and loosen the adjustment nut.
5   Move the clutch release lever rearward until the release bearing contacts the clutch pressure plate release fingers.
6   Slide the adjuster rod rearward until it seats in the pocket of the release lever.
7   Insert a 0.136 in ($\frac{9}{64}$ in; 3.45 mm) feeler gauge between adjusting nut and the swivel sleeve (referring to the figure) to measure the free play. Tighten the adjusting nut against the feeler gauge.
8   Turn the rod slightly to align the flat with the pinhole and insert the locking pin.
9   Remove the feeler gauge and install the clutch retainer spring.
10 Cycle the clutch pedal at least five times and recheck the free play, readjusting as necessary.
11 Lower the vehicle.

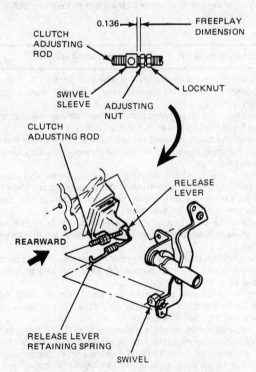

Fig. 8.3 Clutch pedal free play adjustment (Sec 2)

3 Manual transmission (all models) – removal and installation

1   Disconnect the battery negative cable.
2   Raise the vehicle and support it securely on jackstands.
3   Referring to Chapter 7, disconnect the shift linkage, and on floorshift models, remove the lever assembly.
4   Drain the transmission oil into a suitable container.
5   Remove the driveshaft as described in Section 9.
6   Disconnect the clutch cable from the clutch release lever.
7   Disconnect the back-up lamp switch wires and seat belt sensing switch wires (if equipped).
8   Remove the speedometer cable retaining screw and pull the cable out of the transmission extension housing.
9   Support the rear of the engine with a block of wood placed on top of a jack and remove the rear engine mounting crossmember.
10 Remove the bolts retaining the transmission extension crossmember and remove the crossmember.
11 Gradually lower the engine with the jack until there is sufficient clearance to remove the bolts retaining the transmission to the clutch housing.
12 Support the weight of the transmission and unbolt it from the clutch housing.
13 Carefully withdraw the transmission away from the clutch housing and lower it to the ground.
14 Prior to installation, make sure that the mounting surface of the transmission and clutch housing are clean and free of burrs. Apply a dab of light grease to the transmission input shaft splines.
15 Install the transmission by moving it forward so that the input shaft enters the clutch hub splines. It may be necessary to rotate the transmission to align the splines with the shaft.
16 Install the transmission-to-clutch housing bolts and tighten them to specification.
17 Raise the rear of the engine with the jack and install the rear crossmember.
18 Install the transmission extension crossmember.
19 Install the shift linkage and lever assembly.
20 Install the speedometer cable.
21 Connect the clutch cable to the clutch release lever.
22 Install the driveshaft as described in Section 9.
23 Fill the transmission to the specified level with the proper lubricant.
24 Check the transmission linkage for proper operation, adjusting as described in Chapter 7 if necessary.
25 Lower the vehicle and connect the battery negative cable.

4 Clutch (all models) – removal and installation

1   Remove the transmission as described in Section 3.
2   Disconnect the clutch release lever retaining spring from the release lever.
3   Disconnect the starter motor cable, then remove the starter motor attaching bolts and lift away the starter motor.
4   Remove the bolts securing the engine rear plate to the front lower part of the flywheel housing. Remove the flywheel housing lower cover (if so equipped).
5   Remove the flywheel housing securing bolts and move the housing back just far enough to clear the pressure plate, then move it to the right to free the pivot from the clutch equalizer bar. Take care not to disturb the linkage and assist spring.
6   Unscrew the six pressure plate cover securing bolts one turn at a time, to prevent distortion of the cover assembly, when releasing the spring tension.
7   If the same pressure plate and cover assembly is to be reinstalled, mark the cover and flywheel so that the assembly can be installed in its original position.
8   Remove the clutch cover assembly and the clutch disc from the flywheel. Make a note of which way round the clutch disc is installed. The hub faces the rear of the vehicle.
9   It is important that no oil or grease gets on the clutch disc friction linings, or the pressure plate and flywheel faces. It is advisable to handle the parts with clean hands and to wipe down the pressure plate and flywheel faces with a clean dry rag before installing the clutch cover assembly.

10 Place the clutch disc and pressure plate assembly in position on the flywheel. If the same assembly is being reinstalled, align the matching marks made at removal, and install the securing bolts. Tighten the bolts alternately a few turns at a time until the clutch disc is gripped lightly but can still be moved.
11 The clutch disc must now be centered so that when the transmission is installed, the input shaft splines will pass through the splines in the clutch disc hub.
12 Centering can be carried out by inserting a screwdriver through the clutch assembly and moving the clutch disc as necessary to obtain correct centering. Alternatively, if an old input shaft is available, this can be used as an arbor to center the disc; this will eliminate all guesswork and achieve more accurate centering of the clutch disc.
13 After the clutch disc has been located correctly, tighten the securing bolts in an even and diagonal sequence to ensure the cover assembly is secured without distortion. Tighten the bolts to the specified torque wrench setting.
14 Using a lithium based grease, lightly lubricate the outside diameter of the transmission front bearing retainer, both sides of the release lever fork where it contacts the release bearing spring clips, and the release bearing surface that contacts the pressure plate release fingers. Fill the grease groove in the release bearing hub, then clean all excess grease from inside the bore, otherwise grease will be forced onto the splines by the transmission input shaft bearing retainer and will contaminate the clutch disc.
15 Install the release bearing and hub on the release lever.
16 Install the felt washer on the pivot in the flywheel housing and slip the pivot into the clutch equalizer shaft, taking care not to disturb the linkage; at the same time locate the housing on the dowels in the cylinder block. Install the securing bolts and tighten them to the specified torque.
17 Install the starter motor and connect the cable.
18 Install the transmission as described in Section 3.
19 Check and, if necessary, adjust the clutch pedal free play as described in Section 2.

5 Clutch (all models) – inspection and overhaul

1   Inspect the machined surfaces of the flywheel and pressure plate for scoring, ridges and burned marks. Minor defects can be removed by machining, but if any components are badly scored or burned they should be replaced with new ones.
2   Check the wear on the clutch fingers. If there is considerable difference in wear between the fingers, the excessively worn finger is binding which means that the pressure plate assembly must be replaced with a new one. Check the pressure plate for warpage using a steel rule.
3   Lubricate the pressure plate opening with lithium-based grease. Depress the pressure plate fingers fully, apply the grease and then move the fingers up and down until the grease is worked in.
4   Examine the clutch disc for worn or loose lining, distortion, loose nuts at the hub and for broken springs. If any of these defects are found, replace the disc with a new or rebuilt unit.
5   Wipe all oil and dirt off the release bearing but do not clean it in solvent, as it is pre-lubricated. Inspect the bearing retainer for loose spring clips and rivets. Hold the bearing inner race and rotate the outer race and if it is noisy or rough, replace the bearing with a new one. Because of the nominal cost involved it is a good practice to install a new release bearing everytime the clutch is replaced.

6 Pilot bearing (all models) – removal and installation

1   A needle roller bearing of the type shown in the accompanying figure is used as a clutch pilot bearing on all models.
2   Remove the transmission (Section 39, clutch, pressure plate and disc (Section 4).
3   Pull the bearing from the crankshaft using a slide hammer or Ford tool T50T-100A with a puller attachment T58L-101-A.
4   To install a new bearing, coat the opening on the crankshaft with lithium grease. Apply only a small amount of grease as the excess could find its way to the clutch, causing slippage.
5   With the bearing in position, tap it into the crankshaft. A 1-inch, 12-point socket and extension can be used to carefully tap the bearing

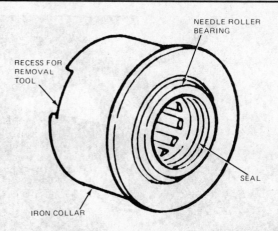

Fig. 8.4 Typical pilot bearing (Sec 6)

squarely into place. Care must be taken when installing the bearing because it is easily damaged, leading to early failure.
6   Reinstall the clutch, pressure plate and transmission.

7   Clutch pedal – removal and installation

1   Disconnect the battery negative cable.
2   Disconnect the pedal pushrod from the pedal.
3   Remove the nuts attaching the clutch pedal and bracket assembly to the brake pedal support bracket and clutch pedal backing plate
4   Remove the clutch pedal, bracket assembly and spring from the pedal backing plate.

5   Place the clutch pedal assembly in a vise. Move the pedal through its full travel so that the spring can be removed.
6   Remove the retaining ring and slide the pedal and bushings out of the bracket hub.
7   Prior to installation, coat the bushings with light oil.
8   Install the bushings into the bracket hub and slide the clutch pedal through the bushings. Install the retaining ring.
9   With the assembly still in the vise, install the clutch pedal assist spring.
10 Install the clutch pedal and spring assembly over the clutch pedal backing plate studs on the brake pedal support bracket. Install the nuts to the studs.
11 Install the pedal pushrod to the clutch pedal and secure it with the retaining clip.
12 Reconnect the battery negative cable.
13 Adjust the clutch pedal free travel as described in Section 2.

8   Driveshaft (all models) – general information

The driveshaft is a one-piece, tubular unit with a cardan-type universal joint installed at each end. The forward end of the front universal joint is splined and fits onto the output shaft of the transmission. The rear universal joint connects to the differential through matching flanges which are bolted together. The universal joints are replaceable components.

9   Driveshaft (all models) – removal and installation

1   Park the vehicle on a level surface.
2   Place the transmission in Park (automatic) or first gear (manual) and set the parking brake.
3   Raise the vehicle and support it firmly on jackstands.
4   Mark the opposing flanges on the rear universal joint and the axle

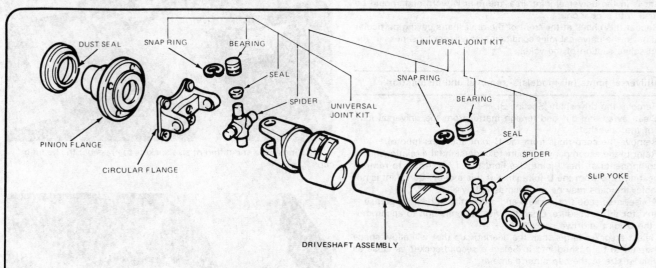

Fig. 8.5 Driveshaft and universal joint components (Secs 8 and 9)

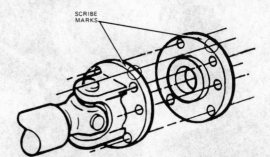

Fig. 8.6 Circular flange-type universal joint marked for installation (Sec 9)

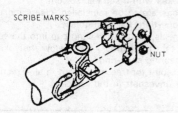

Fig. 8.7 U-bolt-type universal joint marked for easier installation (Sec 9)

pinion prior to removal so that the balance of the unit will not be disturbed on reinstallation.

5   On the rear universal joint, remove the bolts securing the driveshafts to the axle pinion. Support the driveshaft so that it doesn't fall.

6   Remove the driveshaft by lowering the rear carefully and pulling it rearward, sliding the front yoke from the transmission.

7   Plug the rear of the transmission and place a tray underneath to catch any fluid leakage.

8   Prior to installation, check that the front yoke is free of dirt and grit and that the splines are not cracked, rounded or burred.

9   Inspect the transmission tail extension for cracks and make sure that the seal is in good condition.

10 Lubricate the driveshaft slip yoke splines with lithium grease, remove the plug from the transmission and insert the slip yoke into the transmission.

11 Making sure that the marks are lined up, install the bolts through the flanges of the rear universal joint and pinion and tighten them to specification.

12 Lower the vehicle and check the transmission fluid level before driving.

10 Universal joints (all models) – inspection

1   Wear in the universal joints is characterized by vibration in the driveline, 'clunking' noises when starting from a standstill and metallic squeaking and grating sounds. Another symptom of universal joint or driveline bearing problems is a harmonic rumbling at highway cruising speeds.

2   To make a simple check of universal joint condition, park the vehicle on a level surface with the transmission in gear or Park. Block the wheels and engage the parking brake.

3   From underneath the car, hold the axle pinion flange with one hand while moving the driveshaft with the other. If there is noticeable looseness in the universal joint area, the joint is worn and should be replaced with a new one.

4   Repeat this check at the front of the driveshafts paying particular attention to the universal joint condition and wear or looseness in the sliding spline section of the yoke.

11 Universal joints (all models) – removal and installation

1   Remove the driveshaft (Section 9).

2   Clean away any dirt and foreign matter from the universal joint area of the driveshaft.

3   Remove the snap-rings from the U-joint end caps (photo).

4   Refer to the accompanying figure to understand the relationship of the components of the U-joint. Use Ford tool T74P-4635 to remove the bearing caps from the U-joint yoke. If this tool or equivalent is not available, the caps may be removed as follows:

5   A vise, a selection of sockets and a quantity of bearing grease is required for this procedure. Open the vise wide enough to accommodate the U-joint and two sockets.

6   Select a socket larger than the bearing cup that will allow space for the cup to be pushed into it. Select a second socket as close as possible in size to the cup outer diameter.

7   Apply pressure to the vise, forcing the bearing cup from the yoke into the larger of the two sockets (photo).

8   Remove the bearing cup from the yoke (photo).

9   Clean the yokes with a suitable solvent.

10 If the bearings are to be reinstalled, clean and re-grease them, filling the cups one-third full with grease.

11 Using new seals, start the bearing cup into the yoke and press it into position so that the cup is $\frac{1}{4}$ inch below the yoke surface.

12 Install the bearing snap-rings.

13 Check the U-joint for free movement in all directions.

14 Replace the driveshaft to the vehicle.

12 Rear axle – general information

Models are equipped with either of two types of axles: integral carrier or removable carrier.

The differential carrier of the integral-type carrier axle is part of the

11.3 The universal joint snap-rings can be removed with small pliers

11.7 Using a vise and different size sockets to press out the bearing cups

11.8 Extracting the bearing cup with locking pliers

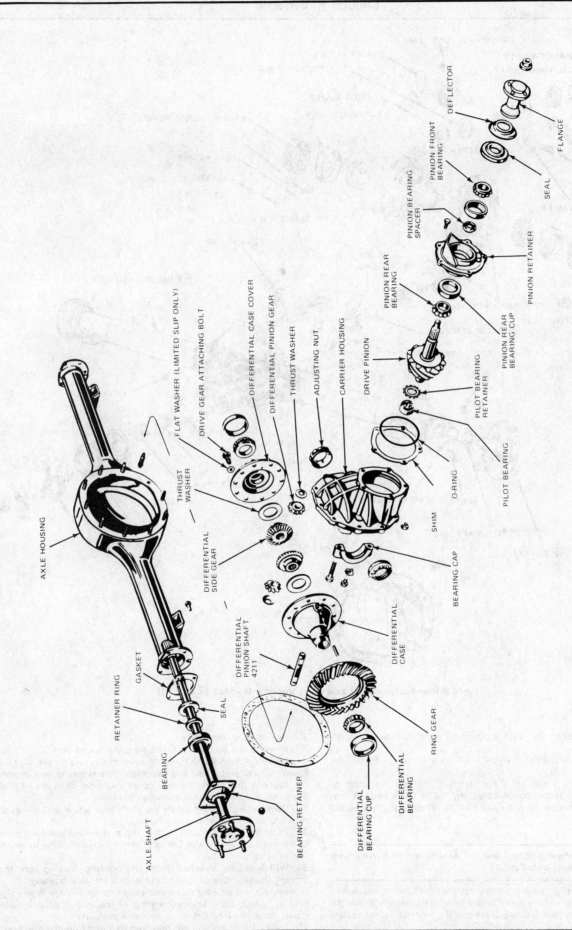

AXLE HOUSING

FLAT WASHER (LIMITED SLIP ONLY)

DRIVE GEAR ATTACHING BOLT

DIFFERENTIAL CASE COVER

DIFFERENTIAL PINION GEAR

THRUST WASHER

ADJUSTING NUT

CARRIER HOUSING

DRIVE PINION

PINION REAR BEARING

PINION BEARING SPACER

PINION FRONT BEARING

DEFLECTOR

FLANGE

SEAL

PINION RETAINER

PINION REAR BEARING CUP

THRUST WASHER

DIFFERENTIAL SIDE GEAR

DIFFERENTIAL PINION SHAFT 4211

PILOT BEARING RETAINER

PILOT BEARING

O-RING

SHIM

BEARING CAP

DIFFERENTIAL CASE

RING GEAR

DIFFERENTIAL BEARING

DIFFERENTIAL BEARING CUP

BEARING RETAINER

AXLE SHAFT

BEARING

SEAL

GASKET

RETAINER RING

Fig. 8.8 Integral carrier axle and components (Secs 12 and 13)

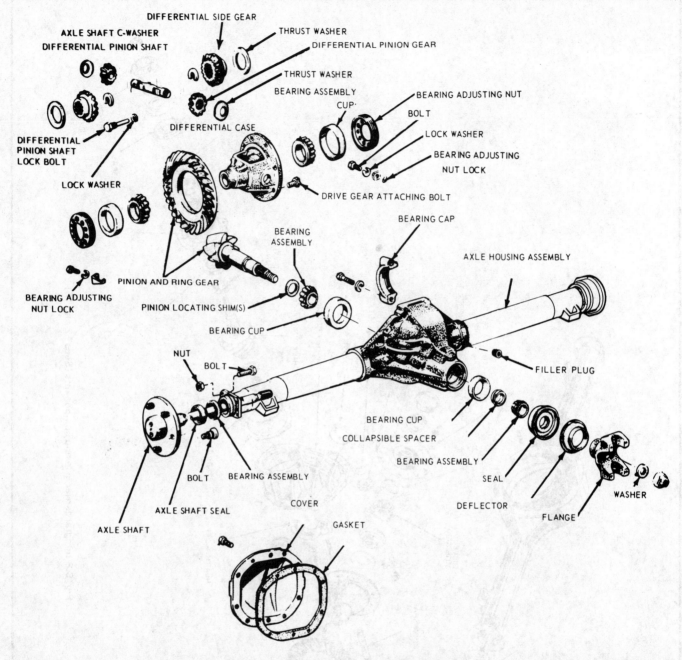

Fig. 8.9 Removable carrier axle and components (Secs 12 and 14)

housing and access to the gears is provided by removal of a stamped, bolt-on cover.

Removable-type carriers can be unbolted and removed from the axle housing as a unit.

Due to the complexity of the differential unit and the need for special tools, it is recommended that any major work beyond that covered in this Chapter be entrusted to a dealer or a qualified repair shop.

13 Axleshaft, wheel bearing and oil seal (integral carrier-type axle) – removal and installation

1   Park the vehicle on level ground, block the front wheels, loosen the lug nuts on the side to be worked on and jack up the vehicle. Place the vehicle securely on jack stands and remove the wheel(s) on the side(s) requiring work.

2   Release the handbrake.
3   Remove the brake drum, retaining the speed nuts.
4   Carefully clean the differential cover of dirt and grease. Use a wire brush, solvent and clean, lint-free rags. Cleanliness is very important.
5   Remove the differential rear cover and allow all of the oil to drain from the differential into a suitable container.
6   Remove the differential pinion shaft lock screw and pinion shaft, referring to the accompanying figure.
7   Push the flanged (outer) end of the axle inward toward the center of the car and remove the C-locks from the groove in the inner end of the axleshaft.
8   Withdraw the axleshaft from the housing, making sure that it doesn't damage the oil seal in the end of the axle housing.
9   Inspect the axle for nicks and rough spots. If there is any sign of blueing, which indicates overheating of the axle, consult a qualified repair shop. Replace any worn or damaged parts.
10   The bearing and seal are removed as a unit from the axle housing,

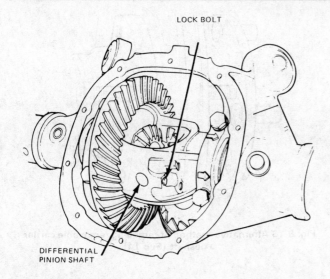

Fig. 8.10 Differential pinion shaft and lock bolt (integral carrier)
(Sec 13)

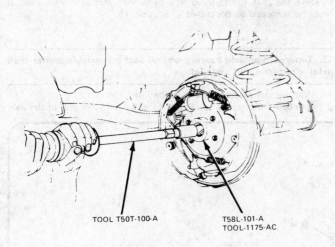
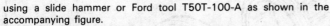

Fig. 8.12 Removal or installation of rear axle seal and bearing
(integral carrier) (Sec 13)

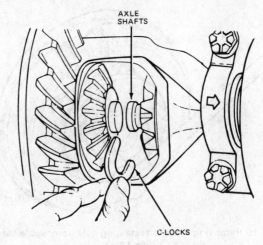

Fig. 8.11 Removing or installing axleshaft C-locks (integral carrier
(Sec 13)

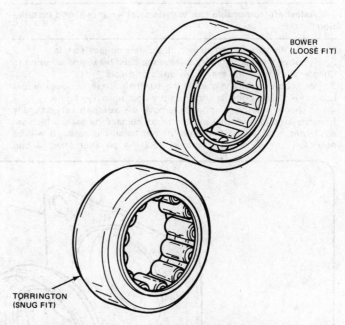

Fig. 8.13 The two types of integral carrier axle bearings (Sec 13)

using a slide hammer or Ford tool T50T-100-A as shown in the
accompanying figure.
11 The new bearing should be lubricated with rear axle oil and
installed squarely in the axle housing bore.
12 Install the new seal, taking care that it is not cocked in the bore.
Tap the seal and bearing into place until seated squarely in the bore.
If the seal or bearing are not installed square, early failure or leakage
could occur.
13 Slide the axleshaft carefully into the axle housing so that the
bearing and seal assembly are not disturbed or damaged. Align the
axleshaft splines with the side gear in the differential and push firmly
until the end of the axle can be seen in the differential case.
14 Slide the C-locks onto the button end of the axleshaft splines.
Push the shaft outward until the shaft splines engage and the C-locks
become seated in the counterbore of the differential side gear.
15 Insert the differential pinion shaft through the case and pinion
gears, lining up the hole in the shaft with the lock screw hole. Install
the differential pinion shaft lock bolt and tighten to specifications.
16 Install the rear cover as described in Section 17.
17 Install the brake drum, wheel and wheel cover.
18 Lower the vehicle to the ground and if oil loss is suspected, check
the rear axle oil level.

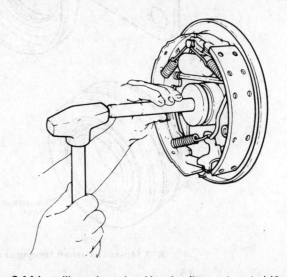

Fig. 8.14 Installing axle seal and bearing (integral carrier) (Sec 13)

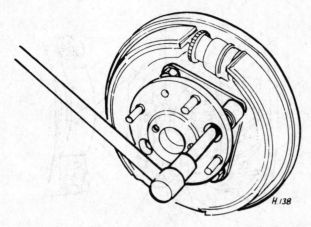

Fig. 8.15 Removing axleshaft retaining nuts (removable carrier) (Sec 14)

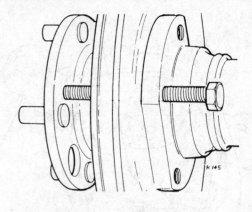

Fig. 8.16 Alternative method of removing removable carrier axleshaft (Sec 14)

14 Axleshaft (removable carrier-type axle) – removal and installation

1   Raise the vehicle and support it securely on jack stands.
2   Remove the rear wheel(s), release the hand brake and referring to Chapter 9, remove the rear brake drum or caliper.
3   Working through the holes in the axleshaft flange, remove the four bearing retaining bolts as shown in the accompanying figure.
4   It should now be possible to remove the axleshaft very carefully from the axle housing, making sure to not contact the seals, which are easily damaged. If the axleshaft will not come out easily, it will be necessary to use a slide hammer tool. As an alternative, a bolt

threaded through the axle flange can be used to push the axleshaft out as shown in the figure.
5   Installation is the reverse of removal, again being very careful not to strike the seal. If a tapered type of bearing and seal is installed, it must be removed as described in Section 15.

15 Tapered-type axle bearing and oil seal (removable carrier-type axle) – removal and installation

1   Remove the axleshaft as described in Section 12.
2   Remove the bearing cup located inside the outer end of the axle

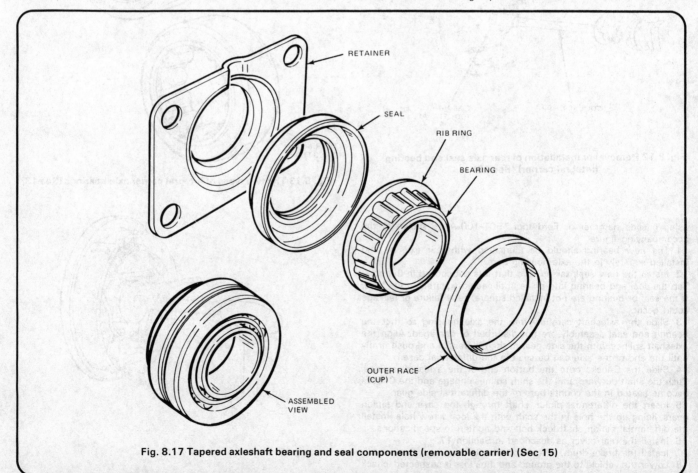

Fig. 8.17 Tapered axleshaft bearing and seal components (removable carrier) (Sec 15)

RETAINER

SEAL

RIB RING

BEARING

OUTER RACE (CUP)

ASSEMBLED VIEW

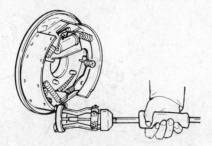

Fig. 8.18 Removing tapered bearing cup from the axle housing (Sec 15)

housing with a slide hammer tool as shown in the accompanying figure.

3   Place the axle assembly securely in a vise which has been suitably padded to prevent damage to the axleshaft.

4   Drill a $\frac{1}{4}$-in hole partially into the retainer and use a chisel to split and remove it as shown in the accompanying figures.

5   The axle assembly should now be taken to a dealer or properly-equipped shop to have the bearing and seal removed and replaced with new ones.

6   Prior to installing the axleshaft with new bearing and seal installed, lubricate the outer edges of the cup and seal.

16 Ball-bearing-type axle bearing and seal (removable carrier-type axle) – removal and installation

1   Remove the axleshaft as described in Section 12.

2   Use a hammer and sharp chisel to make several deep nicks in the bearing retainer ring. This will release the grip on the axleshaft and allow the retainer to be slid off the shaft. If the retainer still fits tightly, it will have to be split with a drill and chisel as described in paragraph 2 of Section 13.

3   Place the axleshaft upside down in a vise so that the bearing retainer is on top of the jaws and the axleshaft flange is under them. Using a soft-headed hammer, drive the axleshaft through the bearing. If this proves difficult, it will be necessary to use a press. Make a note of the direction in which the bearing faces.

4   Place the retainer plate and new bearing (facing in the proper direction) on the axleshaft.

5   Place the axleshaft vertically between the jaws of the vise with the flange at the top and the inner track resting on top of the jaws. Drive the axleshaft through the bearing until it is fully seated against the shaft shoulder, using a soft-headed hammer.

6   Follow the same procedure to install the new bearing retainer. The retainer and bearing should always be installed in separate steps.

7   Pack the bearing with a small amount of multi-purpose grease.

8   Install the axleshaft as described in Section 14.

17 Pinion oil seal (all models) – removal and installation

1   Raise the vehicle and support it securely on jack stands.

2   Remove the rear wheels and brake drums.

3   Mark the driveshaft and axle pinion flange for ease of realignment during reassembly as described in Section 8.

4   Install a torque wrench to the pinion nut and record the torque through several revolutions.

5   Mark the relationship between the pinion and flange as shown in the figure.

6   Hold the flange to keep it from turning and remove the pinion nut and remove the differential flange.

7   Pry out the old seal with a slide hammer and reversed jaws or Ford tool T65L-4851-A.

8   Clean the oil seal mounting surface.

9   Tap the new seal into place, taking care to insert it squarely.

10   Inspect the splines on the pinion shaft for burrs and nicks. Remove any rough areas with a crocus cloth. Wipe the splines clean.

11   Install the differential flange, aligning it with the marks made during removal.

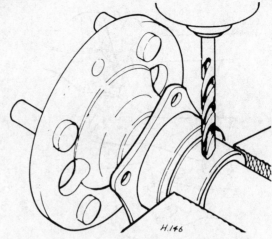

Fig. 8.19 Drilling the tapered bearing retainer (removable carrier) (Sec 15)

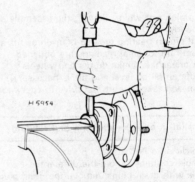

Fig. 8.20 Removing the bearing retainer with a chisel (removable carrier) (Sec 15)

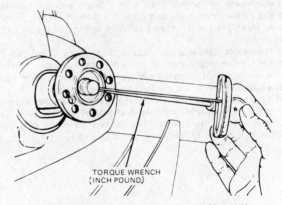

Fig. 8.21 Measuring pinion preload (Sec 17)

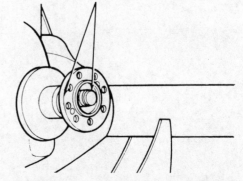

Fig. 8.22 Marking the pinion and flange (Sec 17)

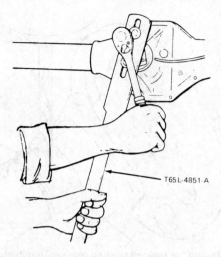

Fig. 8.23 Removing the pinion nut and flange (Sec 17)

12 Tighten the pinion nut while allowing the assembly some movement to seat properly.
13 Take frequent pinion bearing preload measurements as described in paragraph 4 until the original readings are obtained.
14 Reinstall the driveshaft, brake drums and wheels.
15 Check the differential oil level and fill as necessary.
16 Lower the car and take a short test drive to check for leaks.

18 Rear axle oil (all models) – draining and refilling

1 Park the vehicle on a flat surface.
2 Place a suitable container under the differential.
3 On all models with drain plugs, remove the drain plug and allow the oil to drain for 15 minutes.
4 On integral carrier-type axles without drain plugs, clean the area around the cover thoroughly with a wire brush and lint-free rags. Loosen the carrier cover bolts and allow the oil to drain out. Remove the cover, clean the carrier mating surfaces and install a new gasket and the cover.
5 On removable carrier axles without drain plugs, clean the area around the carrier attachment bolts and remove the driveshaft as described in Section 9. Unbolt the carrier and remove it, allowing the oil to drain out. Reinstall the carrier using a new gasket.
6 Refill the axle through the filler hole located on the upper front side of the housing. Removable carrier axles should be fitted to within $\frac{3}{8}$ in of the lower edge of the hole and integral-type to within $\frac{1}{2}$ in.
7 Torque tighten the fill plug and check for leaks.

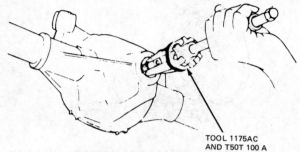

TOOL 1175AC
AND T50T 100 A
Fig. 8.24 Removing the pinion seal (Sec 17)

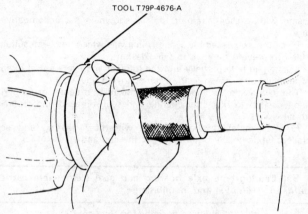

TOOL T79P-4676-A

Fig. 8.25 Installing the pinion seal (Sec 17)

19 Differential cover (integral carrier-type axle) – removal and installation

1 The cover on integral carrier-type axles can be removed to inspect the differential for the cause of noise or vibration, missing or cracked teeth and metal flakes in the oil.
2 Drain the oil as described in Section 9.
3 Remove the bolts securing the differential cover to the axle housing.
4 After inspection, clean the cover and housing mating surfaces. Remove all traces of gasket material with a suitable scraper.
5 Install a new gasket, retaining it in place with gasket sealant.
6 Install the cover and tighten the bolts in a criss-cross pattern to specifications.
7 Refill the axle with oil to the proper level and take a short test drive to check for leaks.

Chapter 9 Braking system

Contents

Specifications

General

Brake fluid type .... Dot type 3

Pedal free height
Power .... 6.6 to 7.5 in
Non-power .... 7.8 to 9.1 in
4-wheel disc .... 6.7 to 7.5 in

Pedal travel
Power .... $2\frac{3}{4}$ in
Non-power .... $2\frac{1}{2}$ in
4-wheel disc .... $2\frac{1}{4}$ in

Master cylinder bore diameter
Disc/drum .... 0.938 in
4-wheel disc .... 1.125 in

Drum brakes
Drum diameter .... 10.0 in

Wear limit .... Specified on drum

Out-of-round limit .... 0.007 in

Brake lining wear limit .... 1/32 in above rivet heads

Adjusting cable length .... $9\frac{3}{4}$ in

Wheel cylinders
Bore diameter .... 0.9375 in
Service limit .... 0.003 in

Disc brakes

Pad lining service limit .... $\frac{1}{8}$ in from shoe surface

Lining-to-disc clearance .... 0.010 in max.

Disc thickness
Front
    Standard .... 0.870 om
    Service .... 0.810 in
Rear
    Standard .... 0.945 in
    Service .... 0.895 in
Allowable variation (all) .... 0.0005 in

Runout limit
Front .... 0.003 in
Rear .... 0.004 in

Caliper bore diameter
Front .... 2.6 in
Rear .... 2.1 in

Torque specifications

	Ft-lb	Nm
Drum brake wheel cylinder-to-backing plate	10 to 20	14 to 28
Drum brake backing plate-to-axle housing	20 to 40	28 to 54
Drum brake wheel cylinder bleeder screw	7.5 to 15	10 to 20
Disc brake caliper bleeder screw	6 to 15	8 to 20
Brake pedal pivot shaft nut	15 to 25	21 to 33
Brake booster-to-dash panel	15 to 25	21 to 33
Master cylinder-to-dash panel	13 to 25	18 to 33
Master cylinder-to-booster	13 to 25	18 to 33
Pressure differential valve bracket	7 to 11	10 to 14
Front brake anchor plate-to-spindle bolt		
Upper	90 to 120	123 to 162
Lower	55 to 75	75 to 105
Rear disc brake anchor plate-to-axle	90 to 120	123 to 162
Rear caliper end retainer	75 to 95	105 to 130
Caliper key retaining screws	12 to 16	22 to 24
Rear disc parking brake retainer screw	16 to 22	22 to 29
Brake hose-to-caliper	10 to 15	14 to 20
Parking brake control mounting screws	12 to 24	16 to 32

1 General information

The standard braking system consists of disc brakes on the front wheels and self-adjusting drum brakes on the rear with a vacuum brake booster available as an option. Rear wheel disc brakes were also available as an option on some models.

The rear drum brake system is of the single anchor, internal expanding and self-adjusting assembly type. A dual piston single hydraulic cylinder is used to expand the shoes against the drum.

The drum brake automatic adjuster operates when the brakes are applied and the vehicle is backed up, or when the secondary shoe is able to move towards the drum beyond a certain limit.

The disc brake assembly is composed of a ventilated disc and caliper. The caliper is of the single-piston, sliding-caliper type and the rear differs from the front only in that it incorporates a parking brake mechanism.

An independent foot-operated parking brake system actuates the rear brakes through a system of cables.

2 Bleeding the hydraulic system

1 Removal of all the air from the hydraulic fluid in the braking system is essential to the correct working of the braking system. Before undertaking this task, examine the fluid reservoir cap to ensure that the hole is clear, also check the level of fluid in the reservoir and top-up if necessary.

2 Check all brake line unions and connections for possible leakage, and at the same time check the condition of the rubber hoses which may be cracked or worn.

3 If the condition of a caliper or wheel cylinder is in doubt, check for signs of fluid leakage.

4 If there is any possibility that incorrect fluid has been used in the system, drain all the fluid out and flush through with methylated spirits. Replace all piston seals and cups as they will be affected and could possibly fail under pressure.

5 Gather together a clean jar, a 12 inch (304 mm) length of rubber tubing which fits tightly over the bleed valves and a container of the correct grade of brake fluid.

6 The primary (front) and secondary (rear) hydraulic brake systems are individual systems and are therefore bled separately. Always bleed the longest line first.

7 To bleed the secondary system (rear) clean the area around the bleed valves and start at the rear right-hand wheel cylinder by first removing the rubber cap over the end of the bleed valve.

8 Place the end of the tube in the clean jar which should contain sufficient fluid to keep the end of the tube submerged during the operation.

9 Open the bleed valve approximately $\frac{3}{4}$ turn with a wrench and depress the brake pedal slowly through its full travel.

10 Close the bleed valve and allow the pedal to return to the released position.

11 Continue this sequence until no more air bubbles issue from the bleed tube. Give the brake pedal two more strikes to ensure that the line is completely free of air, and then re-tighten the bleed valve, ensuring that the bleed tube remains submerged until the valve is closed.

12 At regular intervals during the bleeding sequence, make sure that the reservoir is kept topped-up, otherwise air will enter again at this point. Do not re-use fluid bled from the system.

13 Repeat the whole procedure on the rear left-hand brake line.

14 To bleed the primary system (front), start with the front right-hand side and finish with the front left-hand side cylinder. The procedure is identical to that previously described.

Note: *Some models have a bleed valve incorporated in the master cylinder. Where this is the case, the master cylinder should be bled before the brake lines. The bleeding procedure is identical to that already described. Do not use the secondary piston stop screw which* *is located on the bottom of some master cylinders for bleeding. This could damage the secondary piston on the stop screw.*

15 Top-up the master cylinder to within 0.25 inch of the top of the reservoirs, check that the diaphragm type gasket is correctly located in the cover and then refit the cover.

3 Pressure differential valve – centralization

1 After any repair or bleed operations it is possible that the dual brake warning light will come on due to the pressure differential valve remaining in an off-center position.
2 To centralize the valve, first turn the igntition switch to the ON or ACC position.
3 Depress the brake pedal several times and the piston will center itself again causing the warning light to go out.
4 Turn the ignition off.

4 Flexible hoses – inspection, removal and installation

1 Inspect the condition of the flexible hydraulic hoses leading to each of the front disc brake calipers and the one at the front of the rear axle. If they are swollen, damaged or chafed, they must be replaced.
2 Wipe the top of the brake master cylinder reservoir and unscrew the cap. Place a piece of polythene sheet over the top of the reservoir and refit the cap. This is to stop hydraulic fluid siphoning out during subsequent operations.
3 To remove a flexible hose wipe the union and any supports free from dust and undo the union nuts from the metal pipe ends.
4 Undo and remove the lock nuts and washers securing each flexible hose end to the support and lift away the flexible hose.
5 Refitting is the reverse sequence to removal. It will be necessary to bleed the brake hydraulic system as described in Section 2. If one hose has been removed it is only necessary to bleed either the front or rear brake hydraulic system.

5 Front disc brake caliper and pad – removal and installation

1 Raise the vehicle and support it securely on jackstands.
2 Remove the front wheels.
3 Remove the retaining screw from the caliper retaining key as shown in the accompanying figure.
4 Use a hammer and a punch or rod to carefully tap the caliper retaining key and spring inward or outward away from the anchor plate. It is very important that the key is not damaged.
5 Press the caliper inward and outward against the action of the springs and lift the caliper assembly away from the anchor plate as shown in the accompanying figure.

Fig. 9.2 Removing the caliper retaining screw (Sec 5)

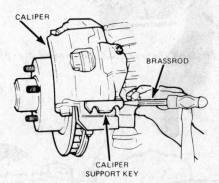
Fig. 9.3 Removing the caliper support (Sec 5)

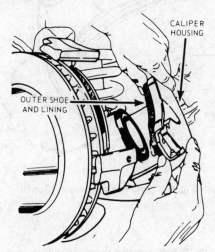
Fig. 9.4 Removing the caliper (Sec 5)

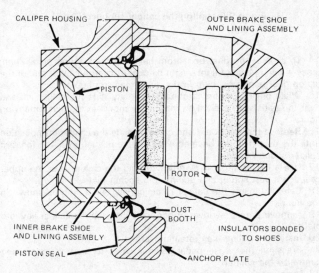
Fig. 9.1 Sectional view of the front brake caliper (Sec 5)

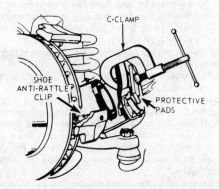
Fig. 9.5 Compressing the piston into the caliper. Use protective pads between shoe surfaces and C-clamp (Sec 5)

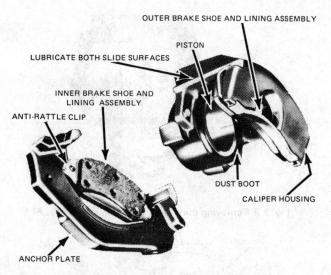

Fig. 9.6 Caliper and pad components (Sec 5)

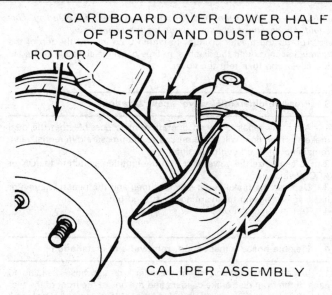

Fig. 9.7 Using thin cardboard to protect the dust boot during installation (Sec 5)

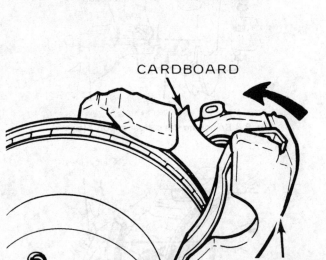

Fig. 9.8 Installing the caliper (Sec 5)

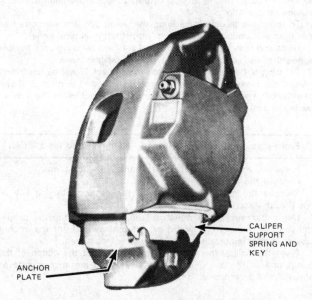

Fig. 9.9 Installing the caliper support (Sec 5)

6 Suspect the caliper from the upper suspension arm with a wire, being careful not to twist or stretch the brake hose.

7 Remove the inner brake pad from the anchor plate, noting the position of the anti-rattle clip. Tap lightly on the outer pad to facilitate removal. If the pads are to be reused, mark them so they will be reinstalled in the original position.

8 Clean the caliper, anchor plate and disc and inspect them for wear, damage, corrosion and leakage.

9 If the pad lining is worn to within $\frac{1}{8}$ in (3.175 mm) of the backing plate, replace all front pads with new ones.

10 If new pads are to be installed, a C-clamp and a block of wood measuring $1\frac{3}{4}$ by $\frac{3}{4}$ in, approximately $\frac{3}{4}$ in long, will be necessary to push the caliper piston into its bore, as shown in the figure.

11 Remove the C-clamp and install the inner and outer brake pads.

12 Prior to installing the caliper, lightly lubricate the 'V' grooves where the caliper slides onto the anchor plate as shown in the accompanying figure.

13 Remove the supporting wire and position the caliper to the anchor plate so that the lower beveled edge of the caliper is on top of the rear caliper support spring.

14 To protect the dust boot from being pinched during installation, place a clean piece of lightweight cardboard over the lower half of the piston dust boot as shown in the accompanying figure.

15 While pulling on the cardboard, carefully slide the caliper on and over the pads with a pivoting motion as shown in the accompanying figure.

16 Remove the cardboard and carefully slide the caliper into position until the caliper upper beveled edge can be pushed over the forward caliper support spring.

17 Use a bar or large screwdriver to hold the caliper over the upper caliper support spring and against the anchor plate.

18 Carefully insert the caliepr retaining key and spring as shown in the figure.

19 Remove the screwdriver or bar and lightly tap the caliper key into place.

20 Install the caliper key retaining screw.

21 Press on the brake pedal several times to seat the pads and centralize the caliper.

22 Install the wheels, lower the vehicle and take it for a short test drive.

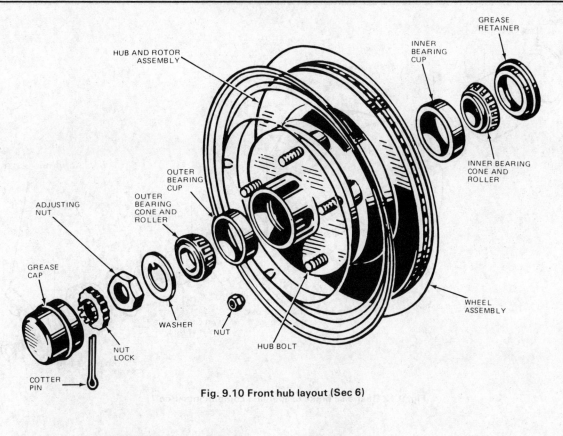

Fig. 9.10 Front hub layout (Sec 6)

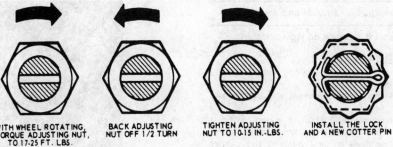

WITH WHEEL ROTATING, TORQUE ADJUSTING NUT, TO 17-25 FT. LBS.

BACK ADJUSTING NUT OFF 1/2 TURN

TIGHTEN ADJUSTING NUT TO 10-15 IN.-LBS.

INSTALL THE LOCK AND A NEW COTTER PIN

Fig. 9.11 Front spindle nut adjustment diagram (Sec 6)

6 Front disc brake disc and hub – removal and installation

1   Refer to Section 5, and remove the caliper and anchor plate assembly. To save extra work and time, if the caliper and anchor plate are not requiring attention, it is not necessary to disconnect the flexible brake hose from the caliper. Suspend the assembly with string or wire from the upper suspension arm.

2   Carefully remove the grease cap from the wheel spindle.

3   Withdraw the cotter pin and nut lock from the wheel bearing adjusting nut.

4   Undo and remove the wheel bearing adjusting nut from the spindle.

5   Grip the hub and disc assembly and pull it outwards far enough to loosen the washer and outer wheel bearing.

6   Push the hub and disc back onto the spindle and remove the washer and outer wheel bearing from the spindle.

7   Grip the hub and disc assembly and pull it from the wheel spindle.

8   Carefully pry out the grease seal and lift away the inner tapered bearing from the back of the hub assembly.

9   Clean out the hub and wash the bearings with solvent making sure that no grease or oil is allowed to get onto the brake disc. Clean any

grease from the rotor with denatured alcohol or an approved brake cleaner.

10 Thoroughly clean the disc and inspect for signs of deep scoring or excessive corrosion. If these are evident the disc may be reground but the minimum thickness of the disc must not be less than the figure given in the Specifications. It is desirable however, to fit a new disc if at all possible. A new disc should be cleaned to remove its protective coating, using carburetor cleaner.

11 To reassemble, first work a suitable grease well into the bearings; fully pack the bearing cages and rollers.

12 To reassemble the hub fit the inner bearing and then gently tap the grease seal back into the hub. A new seal should always be fitted. The lip must face inward to the hub.

13 Replace the hub and disc assembly onto the spindle keeping the assembly centered on the spindle to prevent damage to the inner grease seal or the spindle threads.

14 Place the outer wheel bearing and flat washer on the spindle.

15 Screw the wheel bearing adjusting nut onto the spindle according to the accompanying Figure.

16 Detach the caliper from the upper suspension arm and guide the assembly towards the disc. Be careful not to stretch or twist the brake flexible hose.

17 Install the caliper as described in Section 5.

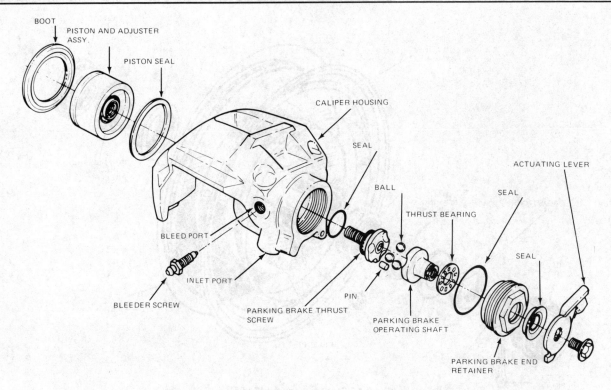

Fig. 9.12 Rear disc brake caliper and components (Sec 7)

7   Rear disc brake caliper and pad – removal and installation

1   Raise the vehicle and support it securely on jackstands.
2   Remove the rear wheels.
3   Disconnect the parking brake cable at the lever.
4   If the caliper is to be removed from the vehicle, disconnect the brake hose and plug it.
5   Referring to the accompanying figure, remove the caliper key retaining screw.
6   Remove the caliper retaining key and support spring, using a hammer and drift to carefully drive the key out as shown in the figure.
7   The caliper can now be removed by first pushing the caliper downward against the anchor plate and then rotating the upper end out of the anchor plate.
8   If the caliper cannot be removed easily, it will be necessary to loosen the caliper and retainer $\frac{1}{2}$ turn which will allow the piston to be forced back into its bore. Before loosening the retainer, remove the parking brake lever and scribe a line across the end retainer and caliper housing to make sure the retainer is not loosened more than $\frac{1}{2}$ turn. If the retainer is moved more than $\frac{1}{2}$ turn, the thrust screw and retainer seal may be broken, allowing fluid leakage.
9   The piston can now be forced back into its bore and the caliper moved as shown in the figure. After removal, hang the caliper out of the way with a piece of wire, taking care not to twist or stretch the brake hose.
10   Remove the inner pad from the anchor plate and tap lightly on the outer pad to ease removal. If the pads are to be reinstalled, mark them so that they can be installed in their original locations. If the anti-rattle clip comes loose, reposition it, as shown in the accompanying figure.
11   Clean and inspect the caliper, anchor plate and disc for corrosion, wear and fluid leakage. If the disc or pads are worn beyond specifications, they must be replaced with new ones. If the pads on one wheel require replacement, the pads on the other wheel must also be replaced to maintain equal braking action.
12   If the end retainer has been loosened $\frac{1}{2}$ turn, the caliper should be installed without the pads. Tighten the end retainer to specification and install the parking brake lever to its keyed spline. Install the parking brake lever downward and rearward.
13   Remove the caliper.
14   Reinstall the brake pads, or if installing new pads it will be

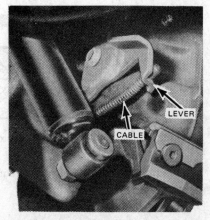

Fig. 9.13 Typical rear disc brake lever and cable installation (Sec 7)

necessary to screw the piston back into the caliper bore using Ford tool T75P-2588-B or equivalent in order to provide sufficient clearance. Remove the brake disc as described in Section 8. Install the caliper, without pads, using the key only. Referring to the accompanying figure, hold the shaft and turn the tool handle counterclockwise until the tool seats firmly against the piston. Loosen the handle $\frac{1}{4}$ turn. Hold the handle and turn the tool shaft clockwise until the piston is fully bottomed in its bore. The piston will continue to turn even when bottomed, so check to make sure there is no further inward movement. Remove the caliper and reinstall the disc.
15   With the anti-rattle clip in place in the lower inner pad support, position the inner pad on the anchor plate.
16   Install the outer pad so that its lower flange ends are against the caliper leg abutments and the upper flanges are over the caliper leg shoulders.
17   Lightly lubricate the areas wherer the caliper and anchor plate will slide on one another. Be careful to use a lubricant which will not melt and get on the braking surfaces.
18   Place the caliper housing lower 'V'-groove on the anchor plate lower abutment surface.

Fig. 9.14 Removing rear caliper retaining screw (Sec 7)

Fig. 9.15 Driving out the rear caliper retaining key (Sec 7)

Fig. 9.16 Removing the rear brake caliper (Sec 7)

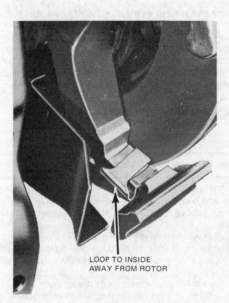

LOOP TO INSIDE AWAY FROM ROTOR

Fig. 9.17 Anti-rattle clip installation (Sec 7)

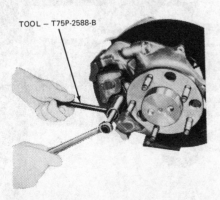

TOOL — T75P-2588-B

Fig. 9.18 Adjusting caliper piston depth (Sec 7)

1/16 INCH OR LESS

Fig. 9.19 Checking lining clearance (Sec 7)

19 Being careful not to damage the piston dust boot, rotate the caliper into position over the disc.

20 Seat the inner pad against the brake disc by pulling the caliper outward. The clearance between the outer pad lining and the disc must be $\frac{1}{16}$ in or less, as shown in the accompanying figure.

21 If the gap is greater than $\frac{1}{16}$ in, remove the caliper and adjust the piston outward following the procedure in Paragraph 16.

22 Hold the caliper in place against the anchor plate and install the caliper support spring and key so that the key's semi-circular slot is over the retaining screw threaded hole in the anchor plate.

23 Install the key retaining screw and tighten to specification.

24 If the brake hose has been disconnected, remove the plug and reinstall it. It will be necessary to bleed the brakes as described in Section 2.

25 Re-connect and adjust the parking brake cable.

26 Install the wheels, lower the vehicle and take it for a short test drive to check for proper braking action.

8   Rear brake disc – removal and installation

1   Remove the brake caliper as described in Section 7. If it is not necessary to repair the caliper, hang it out of the way, anchor plate attached with a piece of wire. Be careful not to damage the brake hose.

2   Remove the two disc-to-axleshaft retaining nuts and withdraw the disc.

3   Inspect the disc for excessive scoring and check its thickness to make sure that it is within wear specifications.

4   If a new disc is to be installed, remove the protective coating with a degreaser, such as carburetor cleaner. The discs have curved fins for cooling and must be installed in the proper direction as shown in the accompanying figure.

5   Install the discs and retaining nuts.

6   Reinstall the brake calipers as described in Section 7.

9   Front disc brake caliper – inspection and overhaul

1   Remove the caliper as described in Section 5. Disconnect the hydraulic line and plug the hose to prevent leakage.

2   Remove the rubber dust boot by striking the caliper sharply on a block of wood.

3   Fit a rag or shop cloth next to the piston bore and again strike the caliper sharply on the block to dislodge the piston, with the cloth catching it. Several attempts may be necessary before the piston comes out.

4   Remove the rubber piston seal from the cylinder bore.

5   Thoroughly wash all parts in the proper solvent or clean hydraulic fluid. Replace all of the rubber seals with new ones during reassembly, making sure they are lubricated with brake fluid.

6   Inspect the piston and bore for signs of wear, score marks or other damage. A new caliper will be necessary if any of these are evident.

7   To resassemble, place the new caliper seal into its groove in the cylinder bore, making sure that it does not become twisted.

8   Install a new dust boot, ensuring that the flange seats correctly in the outer groove of the caliper bore.

9   Carefully insert the piston into the bore. When it is about $\frac{3}{4}$ of the way in, spread the dust boot over the piston. Seat the dust boot in the piston groove and push the piston fully into the bore.

10   Reassembly is now complete and the unit is ready for installation.

11   After installation, bleed the brakes as described in Section 2.

10   Rear disc brake caliper – disassembly, inspection and overhaul

1   Remove the brake caliper as described in Section 7.

2   Remove the caliper end retainer and lift out the operating shaft, thrust bearing and balls.

3   Use a magnet or tweezers to remove the thrust screw anti-rotation pin as shown in the accompanying figure. If the pins are difficult to remove, it will be necessary to use Ford tool T75P-2588-B or equivalent to push the piston back into the housing. Adjust the piston so that it protrudes about one inch. Push the piston back into the

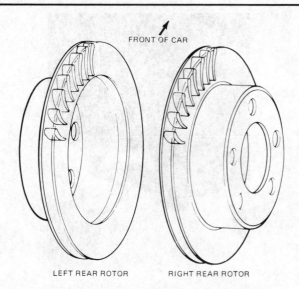

Fig. 9.20 Rear disc rotor identification (Sec 8)

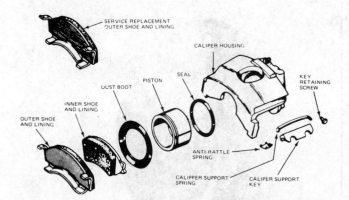

Fig. 9.21 Front caliper and components (Sec 9)

Fig. 9.22 Sectional view of rear caliper housing (Sec 10)

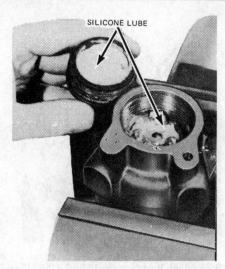

Fig. 9.23 Rear caliper with the end retainer removed (Sec 10)

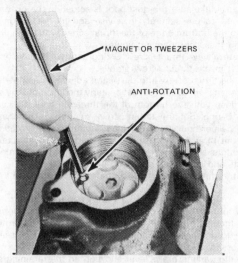

Fig. 9.24 Removing the anti-rotation screw (Sec 10)

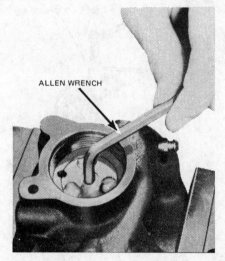

Fig. 9.25 Removing the thrust screw (Sec 10)

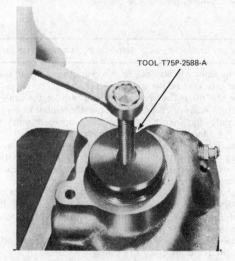

Fig. 9.26 Pushing the piston out with Ford tool (Sec 10)

caliper housing and rotate the tool shaft counterclockwise until the thrust screw is clear of the anti-rotation pin.

4   Remove the thrust screw by turning it counterclockwise with a $\frac{1}{4}$-inch Allen wrench, or on earlier models, a $\frac{1}{4}$-inch square socket drive.

5   Use Ford tool T75P-2588-A or equivalent to push the piston out.

6   Remove the piston seal, boot, thrust screw O-ring seal and end-ring lip seal.

7   Clean all of the metal parts with isopropyl alcohol and dry with compressed air if possible.

8   Inspect the caliper for pitting, scoring or worn parts. If any of these conditions exist to a major degree, or the chrome plating on the bore is worn, the components must be replaced with new parts.

9   Check the adjuster operation by assembling the thrust screw into the assembly and pulling the two apart about $\frac{1}{4}$ in as shown in the figure. The brass drivering must remain stationary during this operation, causing the nut to rotate. The piston/adjuster assembly must be replaced with a new one if this does not occur.

10 Inspect the parking brake lever for damage and replace if necessary.

11 Lubricate the new caliper piston seal with clean brake fluid and seat it fully into the cylinder bore, being careful not to twist it.

12 Install the new dust boot by seating it squarely in the caliper bore outer groove.

13 Lubricate the piston/adjuster assembly with clean brake fluid and install it in the cylinder bore, spreading the dust boot over the seal as

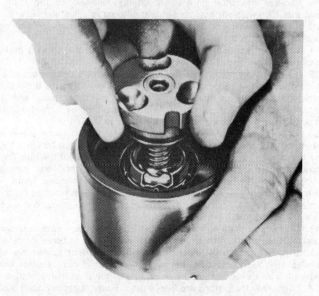

Fig. 9.27 Checking the parking brake adjuster operation (Sec 10)

it is installed. Make sure the dust boot is seated in the piston groove.

14 Place the caliper securely in a vise and fill the piston adjuster assembly to the bottom edge of the thrust screw with clean brake fluid as shown in the accompanying figure.

15 Lubricate a new thrust screw O-ring seal with clean brake fluid and install it in the thrust screw groove.

16 Install the thrust screw into the piston adjuster assembly with a $\frac{1}{4}$-in Allen wrench ($\frac{1}{4}$-in square socket on early models) until the screw tip surface is flush with the bottom of the threaded bore. Be careful not to cut the O-ring. Set the thrust screw so that the notches on the screw and caliper housing are aligned. Install the anti-rotation pin.

17 Place the three balls in their sockets in the thrust screw, apply liberal amounts of silicone grease on the parking brake mechanism components and install the operating shaft on the balls.

18 Cover the thrust bearing with a coat of silicone grease and install it.

19 Install a new O-ring and lip seal onto the end retainer.

20 Lightly lubricate the O-ring seal and lip seal with silicone grease and install the end retainer in the caliper. Hold the shaft firmly during installation to prevent the balls from being dislodged. Reseat the lip seal if necessary. Tighten the end retainer to specification.

21 Install the parking brake lever and tighten the retaining screw to specification.

22 With the caliper in a vise, use tool T75P-2588-B or equivalent to bottom the piston as shown in the figure.

23 Install the caliper, referring to Section 7.

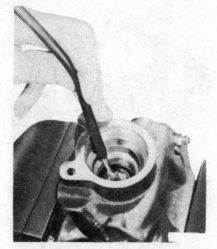

Fig. 9.28 Filling the caliper with brake fluid (Sec 10)

Fig. 9.29 Bottoming the piston (Sec 10)

11 Rear drum brake shoes – inspection, removal and installaton

1 Chock the front wheels, jack up the rear of the car and support on firmly based axle stands. Remove the roadwheel.

2 Remove the three Tinnerman nuts and remove the brake drum.

3 If the drum will not come off, remove the rubber cover from the brake backplate and insert a narrow screwdriver through the slot. Disengage the adjusting lever from the adjusting screw.

4 While holding the adjusting lever away from the screw, back off the adjusting screw with either a second screwdriver or shaped piece of metal as shown in the accompanying figure. Take care not to burr, chip or damage the notches in the adjusting screw.

5 The brake linings should be replaced if they are worn to within 0.03 in of the rivets or will be before the next routine check. If bonded linings are fitted they must be replaced when the lining material has worn down to 0.06 in at its thinnest part.

6 To remove the brake shoes detach and remove the secondary shoe to anchor spring and lift away the spring.

7 Detach the primary shoe to anchor spring and lift away the spring.

8 Unhook the adjusting cable eye from the anchor pin.

9 Remove the shoe hold-down springs followed by the shoes, adjusting screw, pivot nut, socket and automatic adjustment parts.

10 Remove the parking brake link and spring. Disconnect the parking brake cable from the parking brake lever.

11 After the secondary shoe has been removed, the parking brake lever should be detached from the shoe.

12 It is recommended that only one brake assembly be overhauled at a time unless the parts are kept well apart. This is because the brake shoe adjusting screw assemblies are not interchangeable and, if interchanged, would in fact operate in reverse, thereby increasing the drum to lining clearance every time the car is backed up.

13 To prevent any mix-up the socket end of the adjusting screw is stamped with an 'R' or 'L'. The adjusting pivot nuts can be identified by the number of grooves machined around the body of the nut. Two grooves on the nut indicate a right-hand thread and one groove indicates a left-hand thread as shown in the accompanying figure.

14 If the shoes are to be left off for a while, place a warning on the steering wheel as accidental depression of the brake pedal will eject the pistons from the wheel cylinder.

15 Thoroughly clean all traces of dust from the shoes, backplate and brake drums using a stiff brush. Excessive amounts of brake dust can cause judder or squeal and it is therefore important to remove all traces. It is recommended that compressed air is *not* used for this operation as this increases the possibility of the dust being inhaled.

16 Check that the pistons are free in the cylinder, that the rubber dust covers are undamaged and in position, and that there are no hydraulic fluid leaks.

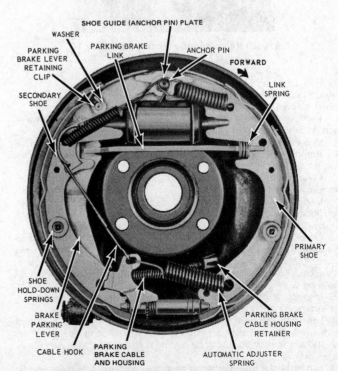

Fig. 9.30 Drum brake components (Sec 11)

17 Prior to reassembly smear a trace of brake grease on the shoe support pads, brake shoe pivots and on the ratchet wheel face and threads.

18 To reassemble install the parking brake lever to the secondary shoe and secure with the spring washer and retaining clip.

19 Place the brake shoes on the backplate and retain with the hold-down springs.

20 Fit new parking brake link and spring. Slacken off the parking brake adjustment and connect the cable to the parking brake lever.

21 Fit the shoe guide (anchor pin) plate on the anchor pin (when fitted).

22 Place the cable eye over the anchor pin with the crimped side towards the backplate.

23 Replace the primary shoe to anchor spring.

24 Fit the cable guide into the secondary shoe web with the flanged hole fitted into the hole in the secondary shoe. Thread the cable around the cable guide groove. It is very important that the cable is positioned in this groove and not between the guide and the shoe web.

25 Fit the secondary shoe to anchor spring.

26 Check that the cable eye is not twisted or binding on the anchor pin when fitted. All parts must be flat on the anchor pin.

27 Apply some brake grease to the threads and socket end of the adjusting screw. Turn the adjusting screw into the adjusting pivot nut fully and then back off by $\frac{1}{2}$ turn.

28 Place the adjusting socket on the screw and fit this assembly between the shoe ends with the adjusting screw toothed wheel nearest to the secondary shoe.

29 Hook the cable hook into the hole in the adjusting lever. The adjusting levers are stamped with an 'R' or 'L' to show their correct fitment to the left or right brake assembly.

30 Position the hooked end of the adjuster spring completely into the large hole in the primary shoe web. The last coil of the spring must be at the edge of the hole.

31 Connect the loop end of the spring to the adjuster lever holes.

32 Pull the adjuster lever, cable and automatic adjuster spring down and towards the rear to engage the pivot hook in the large hole in the secondary shoe web.

33 After reassembly check the action of the adjuster by pulling the section of the cable between the cable guide and the anchor pin towards the secondary shoe web far enough to lift the lever past a tooth on the adjusting screw wheel.

34 The lever should snap into position behind the next tooth and releasing the cable should cuase the adjuster spring to return the lever to its original position. This return motion of the lever will turn the adjusting screw one tooth.

35 If pulling the cable does not produce the desired action, or if the lever action is sluggish instead of positive and sharp, check the position of the lever on the adjusting screw toothed wheel. With the brake unit in a vertical position (the anchor pin at the top), the lever should contact the adjusting wheel 0.1875 in $\pm$ 0.0313 in above the center-line of the screw.

36 Should the contact point be below this center-line the lever will not lock on the teeth in the adjusting screw wheel, and the screw will not be turned as the lever is actuated by the cable.

37 Incorrect action should be checked as follows:

a) Inspect the cable and fittings. They should completely fill or extend slightly beyond the crimped section of the fittings. If this is not so, the cable assembly should be replaced.

b) Check the cable length. The cable should measure $9\frac{3}{4}$ in from the end of the cable anchor to the end of the cable hook.

c) Inspect the cable guide for damage. The cable groove should be parallel to the shoe web, and the body of the guide should lie flat against the web. Replace the guide if it is damaged.

d) Inspect the pivot hook on the lever. The hook surfaces should be square to the body of the lever for correct pivoting action. Replace the lever if the hook shows signs of damage

e) Check that the adjustment screw socket is correctly seated in the notch in the shoe web.

38 Install the brake drum and wheel, lower the car to the ground and take it for a short test run to check the operation of the parking brake and footbrake.

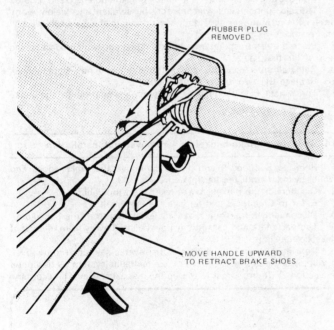

Fig. 9.31 Retracting the brake shoes (Sec 11)

RUBBER PLUG REMOVED

MOVE HANDLE UPWARD TO RETRACT BRAKE SHOES

12 Rear drum brake wheel cylinder – removal and installation

1   Referring to Section 11, remove the brake shoes as described in paragraphs 1 thru 11.

2   On the back side of the brake backing plate, loosen the brake line fitting at the wheel cylinder. Do not try to pull the brake tube from the wheel cylinder as this could bend it, making installation difficult.

3   Remove the 2 bolts securing the wheel cylinder to the brake backing plate and lift the cylinder away from the vehicle.

4   Plug the brake line to stop hydraulic fluid leakage.

5   Installation is the reverse of removal. After reinstallation it will be necessary to bleed the hydraulic system as described in Section 2.

13 Rear drum brake wheel cylinder – inspection and overhaul

1   Remove the wheel cylinder as described in the previous Section.

2   To dismantle the wheel cylinder, first remove the rubber boot from each end of the cylinder and push out the two pistons, cup seals and return spring (see the accompanying figure).

3   Inspect the pistons for signs of scoring or scuff marks; if these are present the pistons should be replaced.

4   Examine the inside of the cylinder bore for score marks or corrosion. If these conditions are present the cylinder can be taken to a machine shop for boring (maximum oversize 0.003 in). However the best policy is to replace it.

5   If the cylinder is sound, thoroughly clean it out with fresh hydraulic fluid.

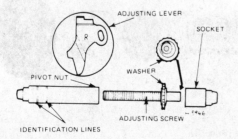

ADJUSTING LEVER

SOCKET

PIVOT NUT

WASHER

ADJUSTING SCREW

IDENTIFICATION LINES

Fig. 9.32 Brake adjuster components and identification marks (Sec 11)

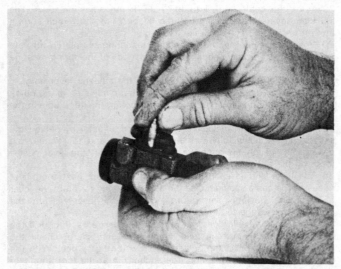

13.6 Checking the bleed screw for obstructions

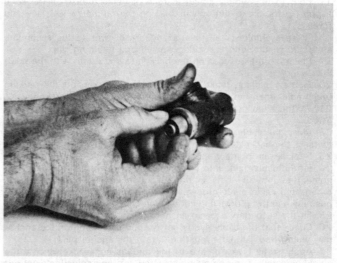

13.9 Inserting the seal and piston into the bore

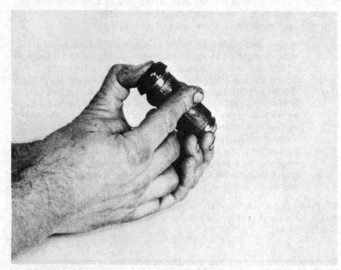

13.10 Installing the wheel cylinder boots after lubricating them with fresh brake fluid

6   Remove the bleed screw and check that the hole is clean (photo).
7   The old rubber cups will probably be swollen and visibly worn. Smear the new rubber cups and insert one into the bore followed by one piston.
8   Place the return spring in to bore and push up until it contacts the rear of the first seal.
9   Reinstall the second seal and piston into the cylinder bore (photo).
10   Replace the two rubber boots (photo).
11   The wheel cylinder is now ready for installation to the brake backplate.

14 Rear drum brake backplate – removal and installation

1   Refer to Sections 9 and 10, and remove the brake shoes and wheel cylinder from the backplate.
2   Disconnect the parking brake lever from the cable.
3   Refer to Chapter 8 and remove the axle shaft.
4   Disconnect the parking brake cable retainer from the backplate.
5   The backplate and gasket may now be lifted away from the end of the axle housing.
6   Refitting the brake backplate is the reverse sequence to removal. It will be necessary to bleed the brake hydraulic system as described in Section 2. Do not forget to top-up the rear axle oil level if necessary.

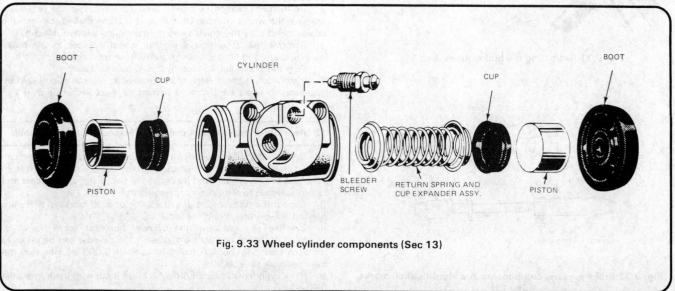

Fig. 9.33 Wheel cylinder components (Sec 13)

15 Rear drum brake shoes – adjustment

Automatic adjusters are fitted to the rear drum brakes and these operate when the car is backed-up and stopped. Should car use be such that it is not backed-up very often and the pedal movement has increased then it will be neceesary to adjust the brakes as follows:

1 Drive the car rearwards and apply the brake pedal firmly. Now drive it forwards, and again, apply the brake pedal firmly.

2 Repeat the cycle until a desirable pedal movement is obtained. Should this not happen, however, it will be necessary to remove the drum and hub assemblies and inspect the adjuster mechanism as described in Section 11, paragraphs 33 to 37 inclusive.

16 Brake master cylinder – removal and installation

1 Unscrew the brake pipes from the primary and secondary outlet parts of the master cylinder. Plug the ends of the pipes to prevent contamination. Take suitable precautions to catch the hydraulic fluid as the unions are detached from the master cylinder body.

2 Undo and remove the two screws securing the master cylinder to the dashpanel (or servo unit).

3 Pull the master cylinder forward and lift it upward from the car. Do not allow brake fluid to contact any paintwork as it acts as a solvent (photo).

4 Refit the master cylinder using the reserve procedure to removal. It will be necesasary to bleed the hydraulic system as described in Section 2.

17 Brake master cylinder – dismantling, inspection and reassembly

If a replacement master cylinder is to be fitted, it will be necessary to lubricate the seals before fitting to the car as they have a protective coating when originally assembled. Remove the blanking plugs from the hydraulic pipe union seatings. Inject some clean hydraulic fluid into the master cylinder and operate the pushrod several times so that the fluid spreads over all the internal working surfaces.

If the master cylinder is to be dismantled after removal proceed as follows:

1 Clean the exterior of the master cylinder and wipe dry with a lint free rag.

2 Remove the filler cover and gasket from the top of the reservoir and pour out any remaining hydraulic fluid.

3 Undo and remove the secondary piston stop bolt from the bottom of the master cylinder body.

4 Undo and remove the bleed screw.

5 Depress the primary piston and remove the snap-ring from the groove at the rear of the master cylinder bore (photo).

6 Remove the pushrod and the primary piston assembly (photo).

7 **Do not** remove the screw that retains the primary return spring retainer, return spring, primary cup and protector on the primary piston. This is factory set and must not be disturbed.

8 Remove the secondary piston assembly (photo).

9 **Do not** remove the outlet pipe seats, outlet check valves and outlet check valve springs from the master cylinder body.

10 Examine the bore of the cylinder carefully for any signs of scores or ridges. If this is found to be smooth all over new seal can be fitted. If, however, there is any doubt of the condition of the bore than a new master cylinder must be fitted. Minor scratches or scoring in the bore can be removed using a honing tool (photo).

11 If the seals are swollen, or very loose on the pistons, suspect oil contamination in the system. Oil will swell these rubber seals and if one is found to be swollen it is reasonable to assume that all seals in the braking system will need attention.

12 Thoroughly clean all parts in clean hydraulic fluid or methylated spirits. Ensure that all ports are clear.

13 All components should be assembled wet after dipping in fresh brake fluid.

14 Carefully insert the complete secondary piston and return spring assembly into the master cylinder bore, easing the seals into the bore,

16.3 Lifting the master cylinder from the engine compartment. Note the newspaper to catch any spilled brake fluid.

17.5 Removing the snap ring from the cylinder piston

17.6 Removing the primary piston

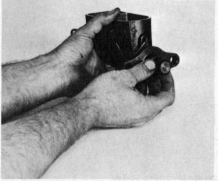
17.8 Removing the secondary piston

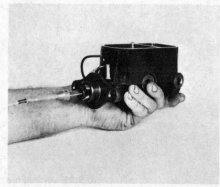
17.10 Using a hone and drill motor to remove minor scratches from the bore

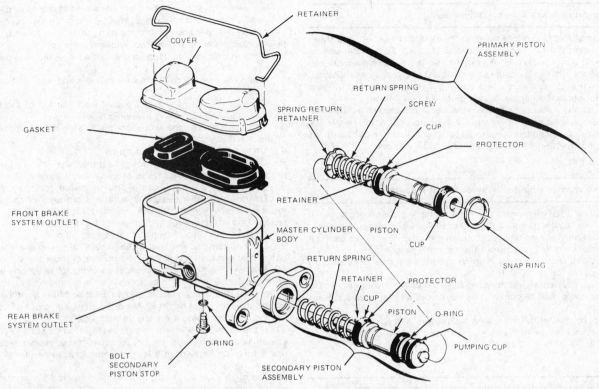

Fig. 9.34 Exploded view of master cylinder (Sec 17)

taking care that they do not roll over. Push the assembly fully home.

15 Insert the primary piston assembly into the master cylinder bore.

16 Depress the primary piston and fit the snap-ring into the cylinder bore groove.

17 Refit the pushrod, boot and retainer onto the pushrod and fit the assembly into the end of the primary piston. Check that the retainer is correctly seated and holding the pushrod securely.

18 Place the inner end of the pushrod boot in the master cylinder body retaining groove.

19 Fit the secondary piston stop bolt and O-ring into the bottom of the master cylinder body.

20 Reinstall the diaphragm into the filler cover making sure it is correctly seated and replace the cover. Secure in position with the spring retainer.

18 Brake pedal – removal and installation

1   Disconnect the negative battery cable.

2   Disconnect the stop light switch wire from the switch.

3   Remove the clutch cable clevis from the pedal on manual transmission equipped vehicles.

4   Loosen the brake booster nuts approximately $\frac{1}{4}$ inch and remove the pushrod retainer and washer.

5   Slide the stop light switch out along the brake pedal to clear the pin. Lower the stop light switch to remove.

6   Remove the black stop light switch bushing from the push rod.

7   Note the location of the pivot location and washers before removing the pedal.

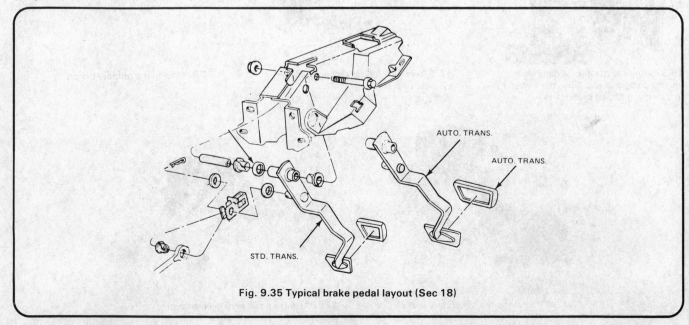

Fig. 9.35 Typical brake pedal layout (Sec 18)

8 Installation is the reverse of removal. However, during installation, coat any pivot points with a small drop of 10W30 motor oil to prolong bearing life and ease of operation.
9 Check the proper operation before driving.

19 Pressure differential valve assembly – removal and installation

1 Disconnect the brake warning light connector from the warning light switch.
2 Disconnect the front inlet and rear outlet pipe unions from the valve assembly. Plug the ends of the pipes to prevent loss of hydraulic fluid or dirt ingress.
3 Undo and remove the two nuts and bolts securing the valve bracket to the underside of the fender apron.
4 Lift away the valve assembly and bracket taking care not to allow any brake fluid to contact paintwork as it acts as a solvent.
5 The valve assembly cannot be overhauled or repaired, so if its performance is suspect a new unit will have to be obtained and installed.
6 Reinstalling the pressure differential valve assembly and bracket is the reverse sequence to removal. It will be necessary to bleed the brake hydraulic system as described in Section 2.

20 Brake pedal travel – checking

1 With the parking brake fully released, measure the brake pedal free height by first inserting a needle through the carpet and sound deadening material until it contacts the metal floorboard.

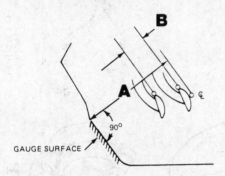

GAUGE SURFACE

Fig. 9.36 Brake pedal travel measurement (Sec 20)

2 Measure the distance from the top center of the brake pedal pad to the floor. This should be within the limits given in the Specifications.
3 If the measurement obtained ('A' in the accompanying figure) is not within specified limits, check the brake pedal linkage for missing, worn or damaged bushings or loose bolts. Replace defective parts as necessary.
4 If the measurement is still incorrect, the master cylinder should be checked.
5 To check the brake pedal travel, measure and record the distance from the pedal free height to a point in the center of the six o'clock position of the steering wheel rim.
6 Depress the brake and take a second measurement. The differences between the brake pedal free height and the depressed pedal measurement ('B' in the figure) should be within the pedal travel figure in Specifications.
7 If the pedal travel is more than specified, back the car up and apply the brakes several times to adjust the brakes as described in Section 15.
8 If this does not bring the pedal to the proper height, check the brake pads or shoes for excessive wear.

21 Parking brake control assembly – removal and installation

1 Release the parking brake.
2 Back off the parking brake adjusting nut to relieve the tension from the rear cables.
3 Disconnect the control assembly release cable or vacuum release motor (if equipped).
4 Disconnect the parking brake warning light connector.
5 Remove the 3 screws which attach the control assembly to the cowl inner panel.
6 Remove the hairpin clip retaining the parking brake cable to the assembly housing and disconnect the cable.
7 Remove the assembly from the vehicle.
8 Installation is the reverse of removal. Tighten the securing screws to specification.

22 Parking brake (all models) – adjustment

Note: *If the parking brake cables have been installed, apply approximately 100 pounds of pedal effort several times to the parking brake foot pedal prior to adjustment.*
1 Fully release the parking brake.
2 Place the transmission in the Neutral position.

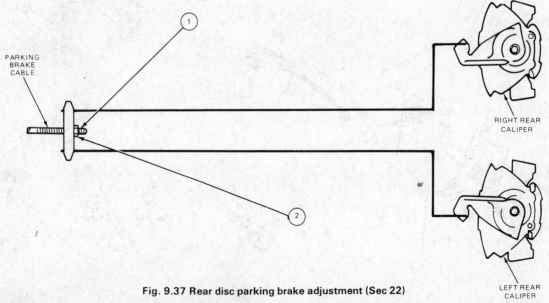

PARKING
BRAKE
CABLE

RIGHT REAR
CALIPER

LEFT REAR
CALIPER

Fig. 9.37 Rear disc parking brake adjustment (Sec 22)

1 *Backing off the adjustment nut loosens the cables*

2 *Tightening the adjustment nut tightens the cable, applying the adjuster*

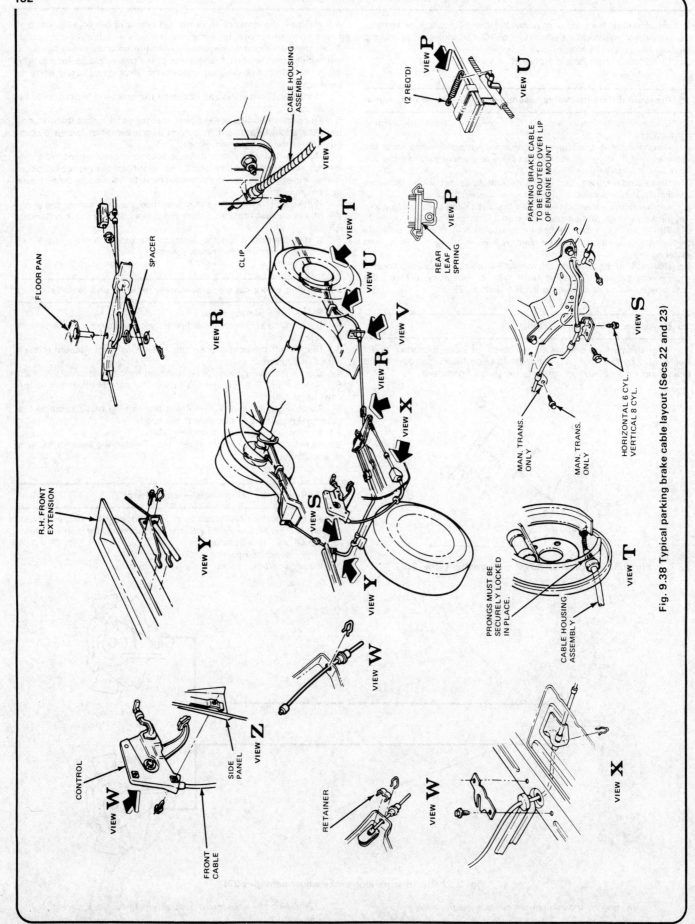

Fig. 9.38 Typical parking brake cable layout (Secs 22 and 23)

FLOOR PAN

SPACER

CABLE HOUSING ASSEMBLY

CLIP

VIEW V

VIEW R

VIEW U

VIEW T

REAR LEAF SPRING

VIEW P

VIEW P

(2 REQ'D)

VIEW U

PARKING BRAKE CABLE TO BE ROUTED OVER LIP OF ENGINE MOUNT

VIEW R

VIEW V

VIEW X

VIEW S

VIEW Y

MAN. TRANS. ONLY

MAN. TRANS. ONLY

HORIZONTAL 6 CYL. VERTICAL 8 CYL.

VIEW S

R.H. FRONT EXTENSION

VIEW Y

VIEW W

PRONGS MUST BE SECURELY LOCKED IN PLACE.

CABLE HOUSING ASSEMBLY

VIEW T

CONTROL

VIEW W

FRONT CABLE

SIDE PANEL

VIEW Z

RETAINER

VIEW W

VIEW X

3   Raise the vehicle and support it securely on jack stands.
4   Tighten the adjusting nut on the cable equalizer until the rear wheels just begin to drag on the shoes (drum brakes) or the calipers just start to move (disc brakes).
5   Loosen the nut on drum brake systems just enough so that the shoes no longer drag. On disc brake systems, loosen the nut so that the levers on the calipers just return to the stop position. The stop position is determined by inserting a $\frac{1}{4}$-in pin into the socket of the caliper housings. If the lever can be moved rearward, it is too tight and must be readjusted.
6   Lower the vehicle and check the parking brake operation.

23 Parking brake cables (all models) – removal and installation

Note: *After replacing any cables, adjust the parking brake system as described in Section 22.*

Front cable
1   Loosen the adjuster assembly nut.
2   Disconnect the cable from the equalizer lever assembly and remove the clip retaining the cable to the body.
3   From inside the vehicle, disconnect the cable from the control assembly.
4   Remove the cable from inside the vehicle.
5   To install, insert the cable through the floor pan holes and attach it to the control assembly from inside the vehicle.
6   From underneath the vehicle, fasten the cable to the body bracket and attach it to the equalizer lever assembly.

Intermediate cable
7   From under the vehicle, remove the cable adjusting nut.
8   Disconnect the intermediate cable ends at the left rear and at the transverse cable.
9   Remove the cable and equalizer lever assembly, keeping track of the order in which the cotter pin, washer and spring were removed for ease of reassembly.
10 Install the equalizer assembly onto the pin, holding it in place while installing the spring, washer and cotter pin.
11 Connect the cable ends to the left rear and the transverse cable.
12 Install the cable adjusting nut.

Transverse cable
13 Remove the cable adjusting nut.
14 Disconnect the cable ends at the right rear of the transverse cable and the intermediate cable.
15 Remove any retaining clips or brackets and remove the cable.
16 With the cable held in position, install the retaining clips or brackets holding the cable to the body.
17 Reconnect the cable ends.
18 Reinstall the adjusting nut.

24 Vacuum servo unit – description

A vacuum servo unit is installed into the brake hydraulic circuit in series with a master cylinder, to provide assistance to the driver when the brake pedal is depressed. This reduces the effort required by the driver to operate the brakes under all braking conditions.

The unit operates a vacuum obtained from the induction manifold and comprises basically a booster diaphragm and check valve. The servo unit and hydraulic master cylinder are connected together so that the servo unit piston rod acts as the master cylinder pushrod. The driver's braking effort is transmitted through another pushrod to the servo unit piston and its built-in control system. The servo unit piston does not fit tightly into the cylinder, but has a strong diaphragm to keep its edges in constant contact with the cylinder wall, so ensuring an air tight seal between the two parts. The forward chamber is held under the vacuum conditions created in the inlet manifold of the engine, and during periods when the brake pedal is not in use, the controls open a passage to the rear chamber, so placing it under vacuum conditions as well. When the brake pedal is depressed, the vacuum passage to the rear chamber is cut off and the chamber opened to atmospheric pressure. The consequent rush of air pushes the servo piston forward in the vacuum chamber and operates the main pushrod to the master cylinder.

The controls are designed so that assistance is given under all conditions and, when the brakes are not required, vacuum in the rear chamber is established when the brake pedal is released. All air from the atmosphere entering the rear chamber is passed through a small air filter.

Under normal operating conditions the vacuum servo unit will give trouble-free service for a very long time. If, however, it is suspected that the unit is faulty, ie, increase in foot pressure is required to apply the brakes, it must be exchanged for a new unit. No attempt should be made to repair the old unit as it is not a serviceable item.

25 Vacuum servo unit – removal and installation

1   Remove the stoplight switch and actuating rod from the brake pedal as described in Section 18.
2   Working under the hood, remove the air cleaner from the carburetor and the vacuum hose from the servo unit.
3   Remove the master cylinder as described in Section 16.
4   From inside the vehicle, remove the nuts securing the servo unit to the dash panel.
5   From inside the engine compartment, move the servo unit forward until the actuating rod is clear of the dash panel, rotate it and lift it upward until it is clear of the engine compartment.
6   Installation is the reverse of removal. After installation, bleed the brakes as described in Section 2.

Chapter 10 Chassis electrical system

Contents

Specifications

Bulbs	Number
Air conditioning and heater control	161
Alternator warning lamp	194
Clock illumination	194
Instrument cluster illumination	194
Defogger indicator	2162
Dome lamp	561
Dome and map light switches	211-2
Dual brake warning	194
Engine compartment lamp	89
Headlamp on indicator lamp	194
Heated backlite warning indicator lamp	2162
High beam indicator lamp	194
Backup lamp	1156
Cornering lamp	1295
Side marker lamp	97NA
Headlamp	6014
Rear running lamp	1157
Turn signal lamp	1157
Parking lamp	1157
Stop lamp	1157
Turn indicator lamp	194
License plate	168
Low fuel indicator lamp	194
Luggage compartment	89
Oil pressure/temperature warning lamp	194
Column shift PRNDL lamp	194
Floor shift PRNDL lamp	1893
Seat belt warning indicator	194
Radio illumination	1893

1 General information

The electrical system is of the 12 volt negative ground type.

Power for the lighting system and all electrical accessories is supplied by a lead/acid-type battery which is charged by an alternator. Circuits are protected from overload by a system of fuses and fuse links.

This Chapter covers repair and service procedures for various lighting and electrical components not associated with the engine. Information on the battery, alternator, voltage regulator and starter motor can be found in Chapter 5.

Note: *Whenever the electrical system is worked on, the negative battery cable should be disconnected to prevent electrical shorts and/or fires.*

2 Fuses

1 The electrical circuits of the car are protected by a combination of fuses, circuit breakers and fusible links.
2 The fuse panel or fuse box is located in most models underneath the dashboard, on the left side of the vehicle. It is easily accessible for fuse inspection or replacement without completely removing the box from its mountings.

3 Each of the fuses is designed to protect a specific circuit, and the various circuits are identified on the fuse panel itself.
4 If an electrical component has failed, your first check should be the fuse. A fuse which has 'blown' can be readily identified by inspecting the element inside the glass tube. If this metal element is broken, the fuse is inoperable and must be replaced with a new one.
5 When removing and installing fuses it is important that metal objects are not used to pry the fuse in or out of the holder. Plastic fuse pullers are available for this purpose.
6 It is also important that the correct fuse be installed. The different electrical circuits need varying amounts of protection, indicated by the amperage rating on the fuse.
7 At no time should the fuse be bypassed by using metal or foil. Serious damage to the electrical system could result.
8 If the replacement fuse immediately fails do not replace again until the cause of the problem is isolated and corrected. In most cases this will be a short circuit in the wiring system caused by a broken or deteriorated wire.

3 Fuse links

1 In addition to fuses, the wiring system incorporates fuse links for overload protection. These links are used in circuits which are not ordinarily fused.

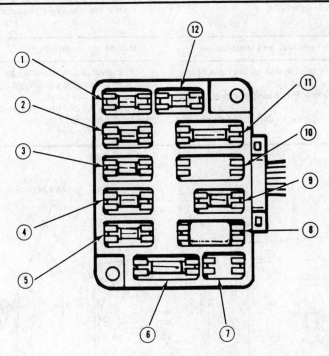

Fig. 10.1 Typical fuse panel (Sec 2)

1 Heater (15 amp fuse)
   Air conditioning (30 amp fuse)
2 Turn signal, back-up lamps (15 amp fuse)
3 Courtesy, stop lamps (15 amp fuse)
4 Horns, cigar lighter (20 amp fuse)
5 Hazard flasher (15 amp fuse)
6 Instrument panel warning lamps (14 amp fuse)

7 Blank
8 Windshield wiper (6 amp circuit breaker)
9 Windshield washer, accessories (15 amp fuse)
10 Blank
11 Radio or tape player
12 Instrument panel, cluster and shift quadrant lights
   (4 amp fuse)

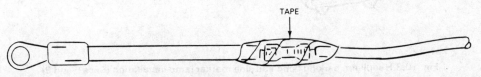

Fig. 10.2 Typical fuse link repair (Sec 3)

2   Fuse links are several wire gauges smaller than the circuit they are incorporated into. The fuse links are green or black and have a molded color identification tag. The tag color identifications are as follows:

  Green – 14 gauge
  Orange – 16 gauge
  Yellow – 17 gauge
  Red – 18 gauge
  Blue – 20 gauge

3   Fuse links cannot be repaired. A new fuse link of the same gauge, length and insulation must be used to replace a blown link. This process is as follows:
4   Disconnect the battery ground cable.
5   Disconnect the fuse link or fuse link eyelet terminal from the battery terminal of the starter relay.
6   Determine which circuit is damaged and the cause of the overload.
7   Cut the damaged fuse link from the circuit and discard it. Strip the insulation from the circuit wire back from the cut approximately $\frac{1}{2}$ inch.
8   Determine the proper replacement fuse link and crimp it into place in the wiring circuit. It may be necessary to cut one or both eyelets off the fuse link when reinstalling.
9   Use a resin core solder at each end of the new link to obtain a good solder joint.
10   Use plenty of electrical tape around the soldered joint. No exposed wiring should show.
11   Connect a fuse link at the starter solenoid. Connect the battery ground cable. Test the circuit for proper operation.

4   Turn signal and hazard flasher – removal and installation

1   The turn signal and hazard flashers are located to the right of the steering column, below the instrument panel.
2   Either flasher is removed by twisting it 90° counterclockwise and withdrawing it.
3   To install, insert the flasher and rotate it 90° in a clockwise direction.

5   Horn – fault testing

1   If horn proves inoperable, the first check should be the fuse. A blown fuse can be readily identified at the fuse panel in the left side of the instrument panel.
2   If the fuse is in good condition, disconnect the electrical lead at the horn. Run jumper wires from the battery positive and negative terminals to the horn terminals.
3   If the horn does not work and there is no evidence of spark at the battery terminal, turn the adjusting screw $\frac{1}{4}$ to $\frac{3}{8}$ of a turn counter-clockwise, making sure to secure the adjustment screw by clinching the housing extrusion with pliers.
4   If the horn does not sound after adjustment, replace it with a new unit.

6   Headlight sealed beam unit – removal and installation

1   Remove the headlamp screws, door and retaining ring. Make sure that the *retaining* screws and not the *adjustment* screws are removed.
2   Pull the headlight forward and support it as you disconnect the wiring plug.
3   Install the plug to the new headlight and position it by locating the glass tabs at the back in the slots in the receptacle.
4   Install the headlight retaining ring, screws and door.
5   Check the headlight alignment.

7   Headlight – alignment

1   It is always advisable to have the headlights aligned on proper optical beam setting equipment but if this is not available the following procedure may be used.
2   Position the car on level ground 10ft (3.048 meters) in front of a dark wall or board. The wall or board must be at right-angles to the center-line of the car.

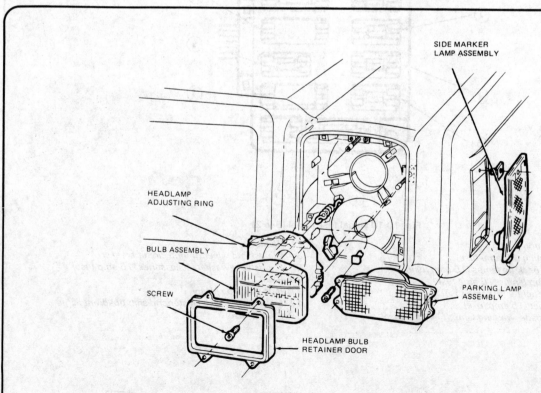

SIDE MARKER
LAMP ASSEMBLY

HEADLAMP
ADJUSTING RING

BULB ASSEMBLY

SCREW

PARKING LAMP
ASSEMBLY

HEADLAMP BULB
RETAINER DOOR

Fig. 10.3 Headlight, parking lamp and side marker lamp installation (Secs 6 and 8)

3   Draw a vertical line on the board or wall in line with the center-line of the car.

4   Bounce the car on its suspension to ensure correct settlement and then measure the height between the ground and the center of the headlights.

5   Draw a horizontal line across the board or wall at this measured height. On this horizontal line mark a cross on either side of the vertical center-line, the distance between the center of the light unit and the center of the car.

6   Remove the headlight rims and switch the headlights onto full beam.

7   By careful adjusting of the horizontal and vertical adjusting screws on each light, align the centers of each beam onto the crosses which were previously marked on the horizontal line.

8   Bounce the car on its suspension again and check that the beams return to the correct position. At the same time check the operation of the dipswitch. Replace the headlight rims.

9   This is a temporary, emergency operation until the headlights can be adjusted using the proper equipment.

8   Bulb replacement – front end

Parking lamp

1   Remove the headlamp door to gain access to the parking lamp assembly.

2   Remove the parking lamp and remove the bulb by twisting it and withdrawing.

3   Install a new bulb and reinstall the parking lamp and headlamp door.

Side marker lamp

4   Remove the side marker lamp retaining screws and lens.

5   Twist the bulb and withdraw it from the housing.

6   Installation is the reverse of removal.

9   Bulb replacement – rear end

1   The various rear lamp bulbs are accessible from inside the trunk. It may be necessary to remove some panels to reach the lamps.

2   Two types of lamp bulb sockets are used, as seen in the accompanying figures. On the plastic socket type, the bulb is removed by twisting it counterclockwise to the stop and removing the socket. On the metal socket type, the socket is pressed down from the keying slot and then rocked from side to side for removal.

10   Dome lamp – bulb replacement

1   Use a screwdriver blade inserted between the lamp housing and lens to compress the retaining tabs. By moving the screwdriver handle toward the side of the car and holding the tabs in the depressed position, the dome can be removed by grasping it and pulling downward.

2   Insert a screwdriver between the glass portion of the bulb and the lamp base and gently pry it out.

3   Place a new bulb in position in the mounting clips and push it gently upward to install it.

4   Position the lens in place on the dome and push upwards gently until it snaps in place.

11   Bulb replacement – instrument panel

1   The instrument panel cluster panel must be removed to gain access to the instrument panel bulbs (Section 15).

2   Some instrument panel bulb replacement requires the removal of the printed circuit (Section 18).

12   Headlight switch – removal and installation

1   Disconnect the battery negative cable.

2   Pull the control knob to the ON position.

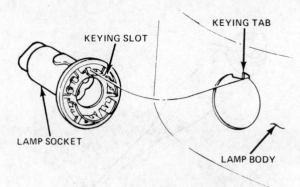

Fig. 10.4 Keying tab-type bulb socket (Sec 9)

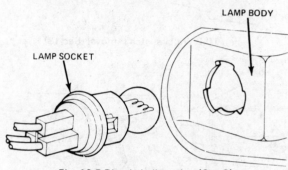

Fig. 10.5 Plastic bulb socket (Sec 9)

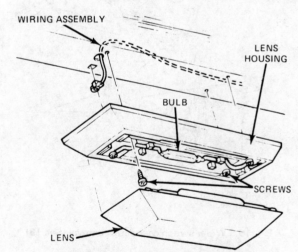

Fig. 10.6 Dome lamp installation (Sec 10)

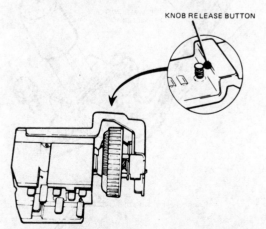

Fig. 10.7 Headlight switch release knob (Sec 12)

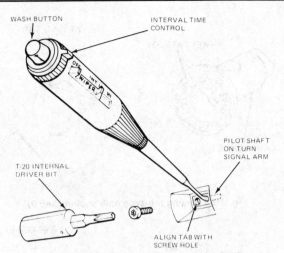

WASH BUTTON

INTERVAL TIME CONTROL

T 20 INTERNAL DRIVER BIT

PILOT SHAFT ON TURN SIGNAL ARM

ALIGN TAB WITH SCREW HOLE

Fig. 10.8 Wiper switch removal (Sec 13)

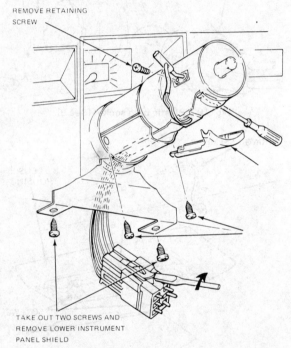

REMOVE RETAINING SCREW

TAKE OUT TWO SCREWS AND REMOVE LOWER INSTRUMENT PANEL SHIELD

Fig. 10.9 Wiper switch connector removal (Sec 13)

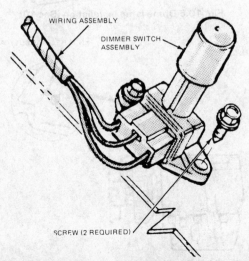

WIRING ASSEMBLY

DIMMER SWITCH ASSEMBLY

SCREW (2 REQUIRED)

Fig. 10.10 Headlight dimmer switch installation (Sec 14)

3   Reach under the instrument panel and press the release button on the switch. With the release button pushed in, pull the control knob out of the switch.

4   Unscrew the bezel nut which retains the switch to the instrument panel.

5   Detach the switch, disconnect the electrical connector and remove the switch.

6   To reinstall, connect the electrical plug to the connector, place the switch in position on the instrument panel and install the bezel nut.

7   Insert the knob and shaft into the switch, rotating it slightly until a click is heard.

8   Connect the battery ground cable and check the switch for proper operation.

13 Windshield wiper switch – removal and installation

1   Removing the screw retaining the windshield wiper to the steering column with an internal driver bit or Allen wrench as shown in the accompanying figure.

2   Use a screwdriver inserted into the locking tabs to release the connector by twisting it as it is pulled apart.

3   Remove the lower instrument panel shield, the two halves of the steering column and the wiring cover.

4   Disconnect the connectors and remove the switch, referring to the figure.

5   Installation is the reverse of removal.

14 Headlight dimmer switch – removal and installation

1   Pull the carpeting back to expose the switch. On some models it may be necessary to loosen the scuff plate and remove the left cowl plate to remove the carpet.

2   Remove the switch mounting screws as shown in the accompanying figure.

3   Disconnect the connector and remove the switch.

4   Installation is the reverse of removal.

15 Instrument cluster – removal and installation

1   Disconnect the battery negative cable.

2   Remove the lower cluster applique cover retaining screws located below the steering column.

3   Remove the steering column shroud.

4   Remove the headlight switch as described in Section 12.

5   Remove the four cluster front cover retaining screws as shown in the accompanying figure. Insert a flat-bladed screwdriver under the edge of the finish panel and carefully dislodge the panel mounting studs.

6   Remove the cluster front cover.

7   If equipped with column shift automatic transmission, remove the PRNDL control cable attaching screw.

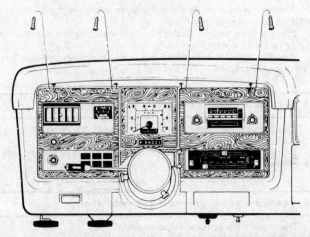

Fig. 10.11 Instrument cluster finish panel installation (Sec 15)

8 Disconnect the speedometer cable as described in Section 17.

9 Remove the cluster screws and withdraw the cluster from the instrument panel.

10 Disconnect the cluster feed plug at the printed circuit and the fuel gauge if equipped with low fuel warning light and remove the cluster from the panel.

11 To install, angle the cluster lens downward, move it up to the opening and connect the connector and (if equipped) low fuel warning lamp.

12 Install the cluster to the instrument panel.

13 Install the automatic transmission cable assembly over the retainer pin on the socket casting and install the screw.

14 With the shift lever in the Drive position, loosen the bracket screw and slide the bracket so that the pointer is aligned with the D and install the screw.

15 Install the speedometer cable.

16 With the cluster front studs aligned with the retainers, push the cover onto the outer edge, working around the cover. Install the retaining screws.

17 Install the headlight switch, column shroud and applique cover.

18 Connect the battery negative cable.

16 Speedometer head – removal and installation

Note: *U.S. Federal law requires that the odometer in any replacement speedometer must register the same mileage as that registered in the removed speedometer.*

1 Disconnect the battery negative cable.

2 Remove the instrument cluster as described in Section 15.

3 If the cluster is equipped with a clock, remove the reset knob and retainer. Remove the 5 screws retaining the mask and lens to the backplate and remove the mask and lens.

4 Disconnect the speedometer cable at the back of the speedometer.

5 After removing the 2 attaching screws, remove the speedometer from the cluster.

6 To reinstall, place the speedometer in the backplate and install the 2 retaining screws.

7 Apply a $\frac{3}{16}$ inch ball of silicone damping grease to the speedometer head drive hole.

8 Place mask and lens in position on the backplate and install the 4 attaching screws.

9 Install the instrument cluster as described in Section 15.

10 Connect the battery negative cable.

17 Speedometer cable – removal and installation

1 Disconnect the speedometer cable from the speedometer head.

2 Push the cable and grommet through the dash panel opening.

3 From underneath the vehicle, disengage the cable retaining clips.

4 Disconnect the cable at the transmission and remove the driven gear.

5 To install, connect the new cable to the driven gear and install to the transmission.

6 Engage the cable to the retaining clip at the marker tapes on the cable housing, route it through the dash panel opening and push the grommet in place.

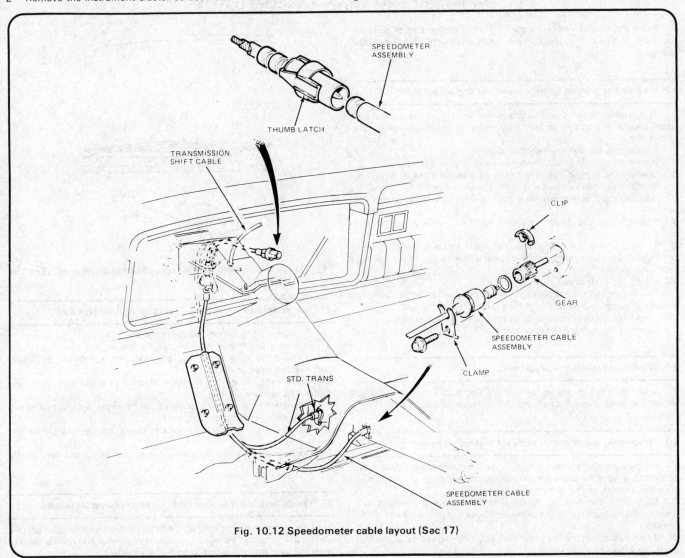

Fig. 10.12 Speedometer cable layout (Sec 17)

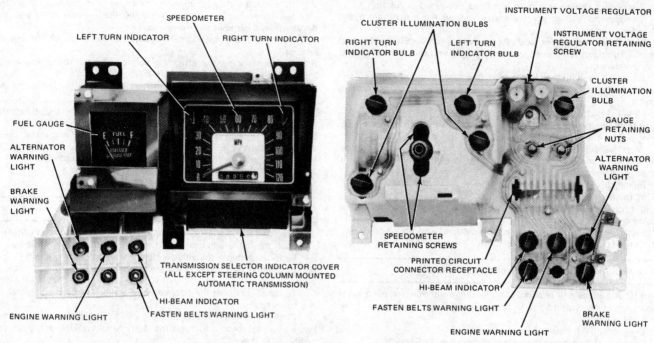

Fig. 10.13 Front and back of printed circuit (Secs 11 and 18)

7   From inside the vehicle, apply a $\frac{3}{16}$ in diameter ball of silicone damping grease in the speedometer head drive hole and install the cable.

18 Instrument printed circuit – removal and installation

1   The printed circuit that comprises the 'wiring' of the instrument panel should be handled as little as possible to avoid damage to the circuit sheet.
2   Disconnect the battery negative cable.
3   Remove the instrument cluster as described in Section 15.
4   Unsnap the printed circuit from the instrument voltage regulator.
5   Remove the illumination and indicator assemblies.
6   Remove the 2 screws retaining the cluster resistor and remove the resistor.
7   Remove the fuel gauge attaching nuts and remove the printed circuit.
8   To install, place the printed circuit over the backplate locating pins.
9   Install the illumination and indicator assemblies and fuel gauge attaching nuts.
10 Install the instrument cluster resistor.
11 Place the instrument voltage regulator in position, install the attaching screw and snap the printed circuit to the regulator.
12 Install the instrument cluster as described in Section 15.
13 Connect the battery negative cable.

19 Windshield washer – adjustment

1   A pin inserted in the windshield washer nozzle can be used to adjust the spray pattern as shown in the accompanying figure.

20 Windshield wiper arm – removal and replacement

1   Before removing a wiper arm, turn the windshield wiper switch on and off to ensure the arms are in their normal parked position parallel with the bottom of the windshield.
2   To remove the arm, swing the arm away from the windshield, depress the spring clips in the wiper arm boss and pull the arm off the spindle.
3   When replacing the arm, position it in the parked position and push the boss onto the spindle.

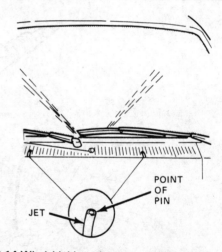

Fig. 10.14 Windshield washer spray pattern adjustment (Sec 19)

21 Windshield wiper motor – removal and installation

1   Disconnect the battery negative cable.
2   Referring to Chapter 12, remove the instrument panel pad.
3   Remove the speaker mounting bracket and speaker (if equipped) and heater/defroster ducts.
4   Disconnect the electrical lead and drive arm clip and unbolt the motor and remove it.
5   If a new motor is to be installed, transfer the drive arm and clip and connect the electrical lead.
6   Install the motor, defroster/heater ducts, speaker assembly and panel pad.
7   Connect the battery negative cable and test the wiper motor operation.

22 Windshield washer assembly – removal and installation

1   Use a small screwdriver to unlock the tabs and disconnect the electrical connector. Remove the retaining screws and lift the washer reservoir and motor assembly from the vehicle.

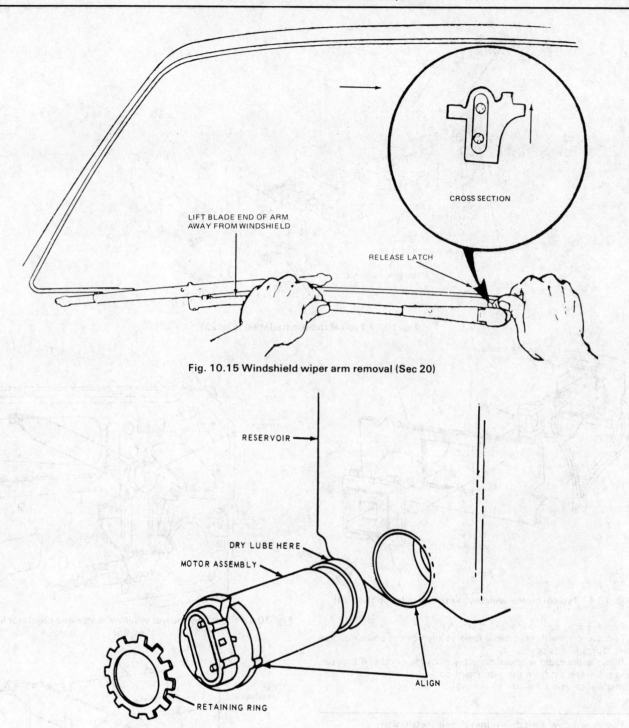

Fig. 10.15 Windshield wiper arm removal (Sec 20)

LIFT BLADE END OF ARM
AWAY FROM WINDSHIELD

CROSS SECTION

RELEASE LATCH

Fig. 10.16 Windshield washer motor installation (Sec 22)

RESERVOIR

DRY LUBE HERE

MOTOR ASSEMBLY

ALIGN

RETAINING RING

2   Drain the reservoir by disconnecting the hose with a small screwdriver.
3   Pry out the retaining ring which holds the motor in the reservoir.
4   Grasp one wall around the electrical terminals with a pair of pliers and pull the motor, seal and impeller assembly out. If the impeller and seal become separated they can be reassembled. Inspect the reservoir for foreign matter before installing the old motor in a new reservoir.
5   Prior to installation, lubricate the outside of the seal with powdered graphite for ease of assembly.
6   Position the small projection on the motor end cap with the slot in the reservoir and assemble so that the seal seats against the bottom of the motor cavity.
7   Use a 1 inch twelve-point socket to hand press the retaining ring against the motor end plate.

8   Fill the reservoir and check for leaks.
9   The cowl mounted nozzle jets can be adjusted for the proper spray pattern by carefully bending them with needle-nosed pliers, taking care not to crimp them.

23 Radio – removal and installation

1   Disconnect the battery negative cable.
2   Disconnect the electrical power leads, speaker and antenna lead-in cable.
3   Remove the control knobs, nuts and retainers.
4   Remove the ash tray and bracket.

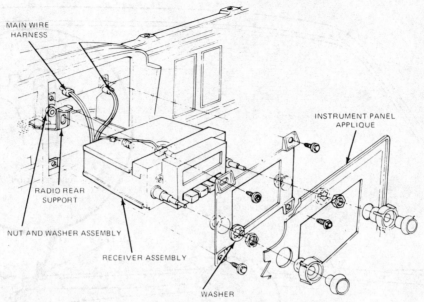

Fig. 10.17 Typical radio installation (Sec 23)

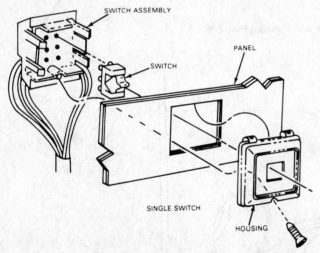

Fig. 10.18 Typical power window switch installation (Sec 24)

5   Remove the radio rear support attaching nut.
6   Remove the instrument panel lower reinforcement and air conditioning ducts (if equipped).
7   Remove the radio receiver assembly from the bezel and the rear support, lowering it from the instrument panel.
8   Installation is the reverse of removal.

24 Power window switch – removal and installation

2-door
1   Disconnect the battery negative cable.
2   Remove the retaining screw from the switch bezel and pivot the lower edge of the bezel out and up to remove as shown in the accompanying figure.
3   The switch is retained by the electrical contact pins. To remove, use a small screwdriver to carefully pry the switch from the connector.
4   To install, press the switch firmly into place on the connector.
5   Reinstall the bezel.

4-door
6   Perform steps 1 and 2 above.
7   Disconnect the multiple connector.
8   Installation is the reverse of removal.
9   Connect the battery negative cable.

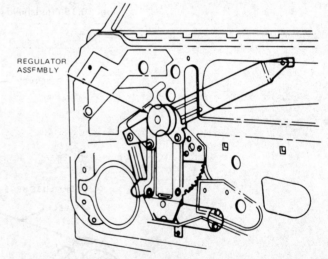

Fig. 10.19 Front door power window motor and regulator layout (Sec 25)

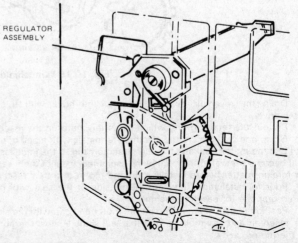

Fig. 10.20 Layout of rear door power window motor and regulator (Sec 25)

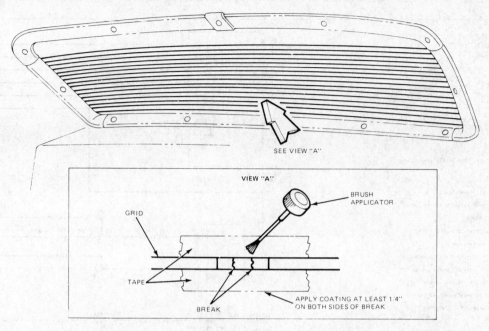

Fig. 10.21 Grid-type defogger repair (Sec 27)

25 Power window motor – removal and installation

Front door

1 Remove the door trim and watershield (Chapter 12).
2 Unplug the motor multiple connector.
3 Working through the access holes, remove the three motor and drive-to-regulator screws.
4 Remove the motor from the door.
5 To install, place the motor in position on the regulator and install the attaching screws snugly.
6 Attach the multiple connector and check the motor operation to make sure the gears are properly engaged.
7 Tighten the motor and drive attaching screws to specifications and check the motor for proper operation.
8 Reinstall the door trim.

Rear door

9 If possible, raise the glass to the full up position. If the glass cannot be raised to full up, it must be supported so that it doesn't fall during motor removal.
10 Disconnect the battery negative cable.
11 Remove the door trim and watershield.
12 Disconnect the motor wiring leads and fasten them out of the way.
13 Use a $\frac{3}{4}$-inch hole saw with a $1\frac{1}{4}$-inch pilot to drill three holes at the dimples located on the inner door panel to gain access to the motor and drive attaching screws.
14 Working through the holes, remove the motor mounting screws and disengage the motor and drive assembly from the regulator. If the glass is in the down position, it will be necessary to use a screwdriver to disengage the drive gear.
15 Install the new motor and drive assembly, reconnect the wiring and reinstall the door trim.
16 Connect the battery negative cable.

26 Stoplight switch removal – removal and installation

1 Disconnect the battery negative cable.
2 Disconnect the wiring harness connector at the switch.
3 On models with power brakes, loosen the brake booster nuts at the pedal support about $\frac{1}{8}$ in to eliminate binding during removal.
4 Remove the hairpin retainer and washer. Slide the switch off the brake pedal pin just enough so that the outer arm clears the pin and remove the switch.

5 Installation is the reverse of removal. Be sure to re-tighten the brake booster nuts on power brake models.
6 Connect the battery negative cable.

27 Grid-type heated rear window defogger – testing and repair

1 The rear window defogger consists of a rear window with a number of horizontal elements that are baked onto the glass.
2 Small breaks in the element system can be successfully repaired without removing the rear window.
3 To test the grids for proper operation, start the engine and turn on the system.
4 Use a strong light inside the vehicle to visually inspect the wire grid from the outside. A broken wire will appear as a brown spot.
5 From inside the car, use a 12-volt DC voltmeter and contact the broad reddish brown strips on the back window. The meter reading should be 10 to 13 volts. A lower voltage reading indicates a loose connection on the ground side of the glass.
6 Make a good ground contact with the meter's negative lead. The voltage should remain the same.
7 Ground the meter's negative lead and touch each grid line at its midpoint with the positive lead. The reading should be approximately 6 volts, indicating the line is good.
8 No reading indicates that the line is broken between the midpoint of the line and the side.
9 A reading of 12 volts means that the circuit is broken between the midpoint and passenger side or the grounding pigtail on the passenger side of the glass is loose.
10 Once the area needing repair is determined, it is recommended that a grid repair kit be obtained from a dealer.
11 Clean the area to be repaired with alcohol to remove dirt, grease or other foreign material.
12 With the area clean and dry, mark the spot to be repaired on the outside of the glass.
13 Shake the bottle of grid repair compound for at least one minute and shake it frequently during use. The compound and the glass must be at room temperature.
14 Mask the area above and below the break with electrical tape so that the gap is the same as the width of the grid.
15 Apply several smooth continuous strokes of the coating, using the brush applicator cap. The repair coating should extend $\frac{1}{4}$ in on both sides of the break.
16 Allow the repair to dry for at least 3 minutes and remove the tape. The repair can be energized within 3 minutes. Optimum hardness occurs after 24 hours.

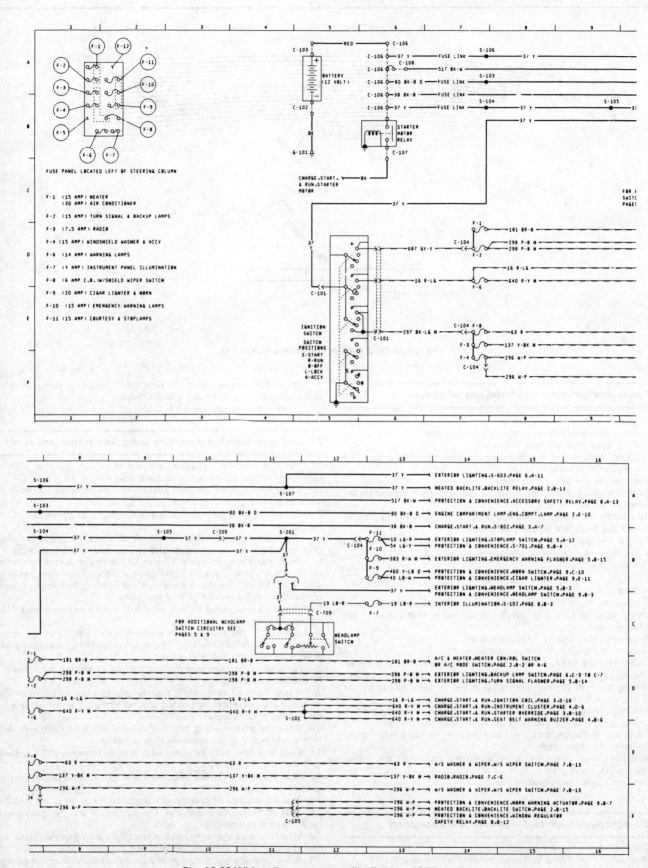

Fig. 10.22 Wiring diagram, power distribution, 1975 models

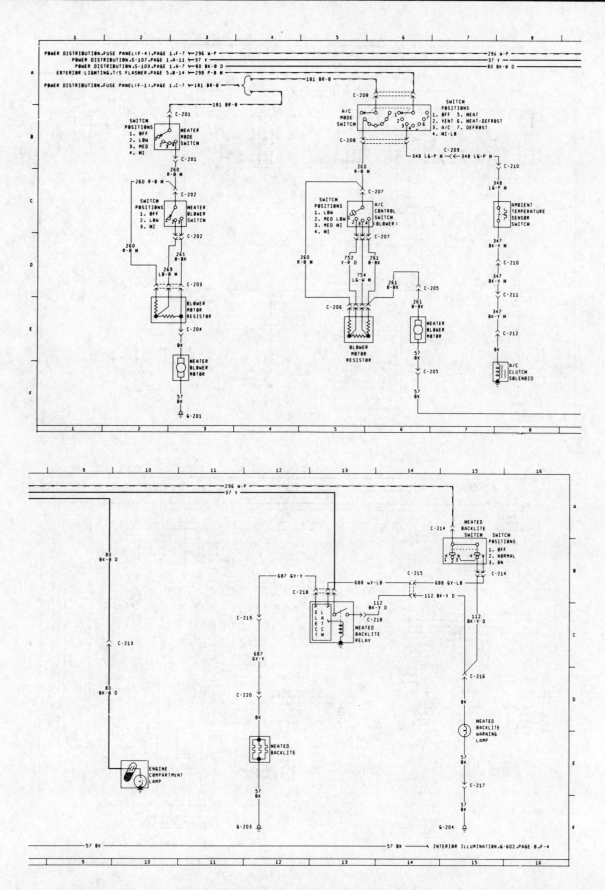

Fig. 10.23 Wiring diagram, air conditioning and/or heater, engine compartment lamp and heated backlite, 1975 models

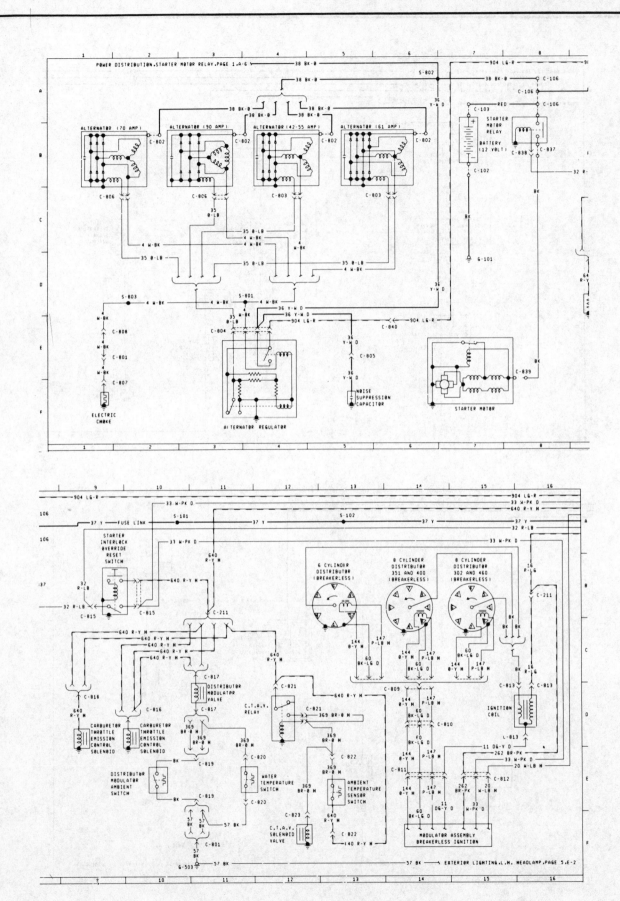

Fig. 10.24 Wiring diagram, charge, start, run, 1975 models

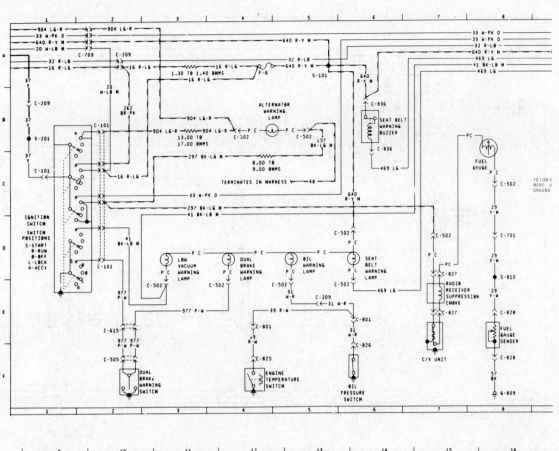

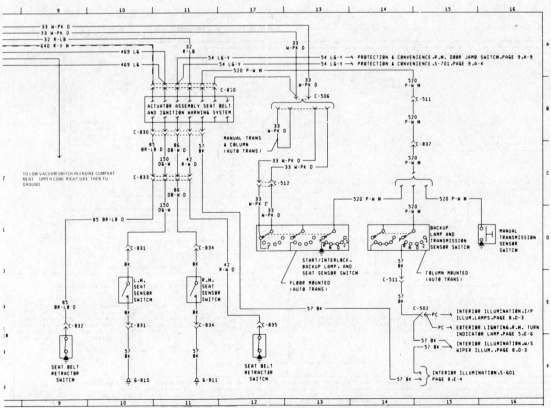

Fig. 10.25 Wiring diagram, charge, start, run 1975 models (cont.)

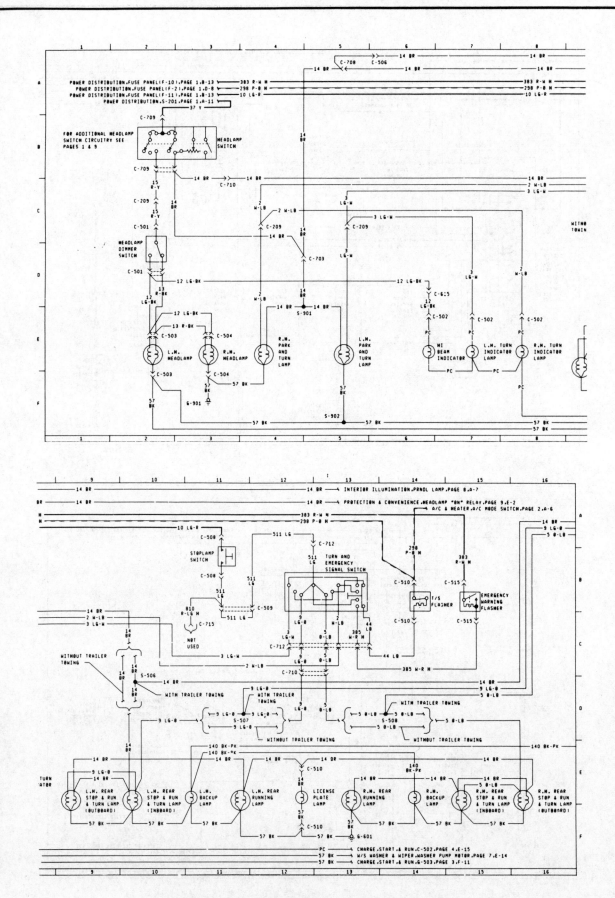

Fig. 10.26 Wiring diagram, exterior lighting, 1975 models

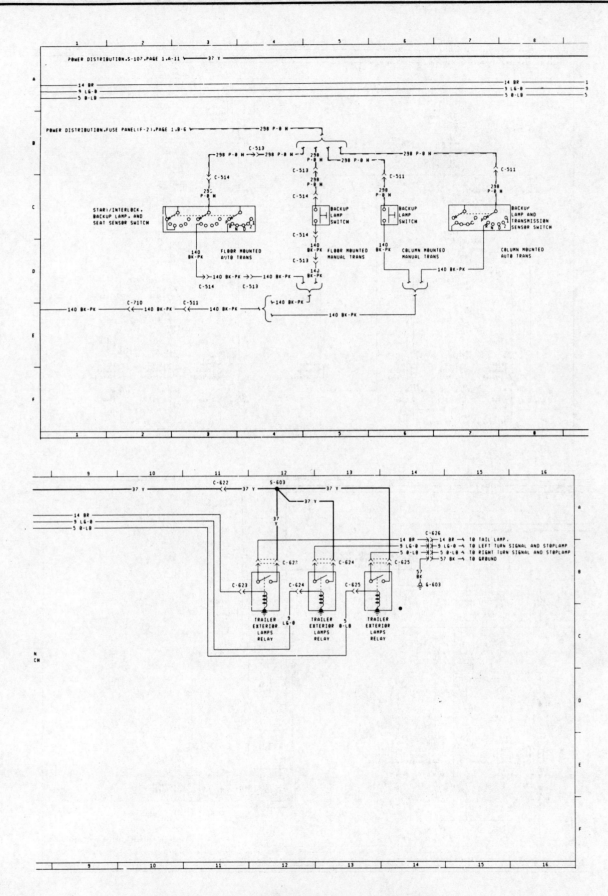

Fig. 10.27 Wiring diagram, exterior lighting, 1975 models (cont.)

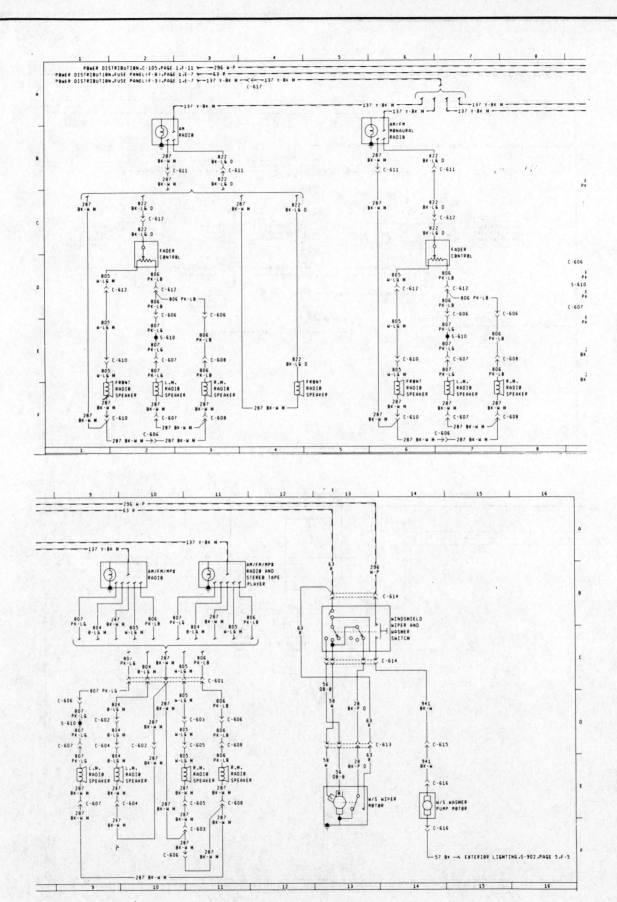

Fig. 10.28 Wiring diagram, windshield wiper, washer, 1975 models

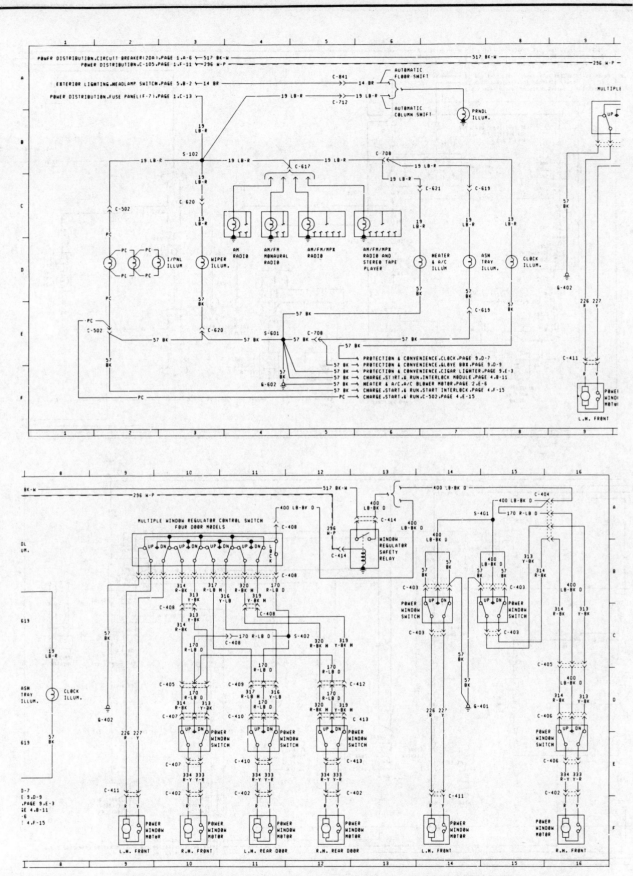

Fig. 10.29 Wiring diagram, illumination lamps and power windows, 1975 models

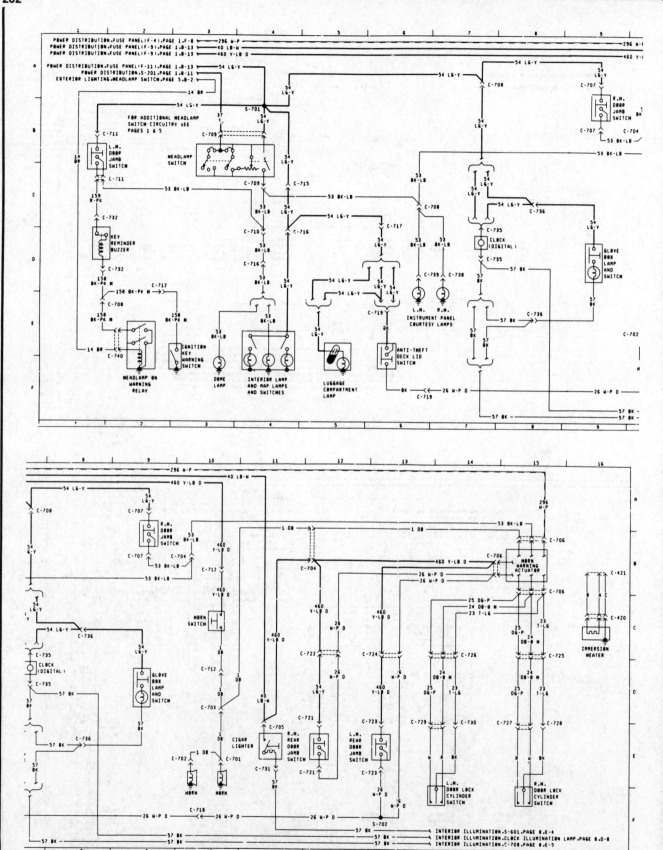

Fig. 10.30 Wiring diagram, protection and convenience, power door locks, 1975 models

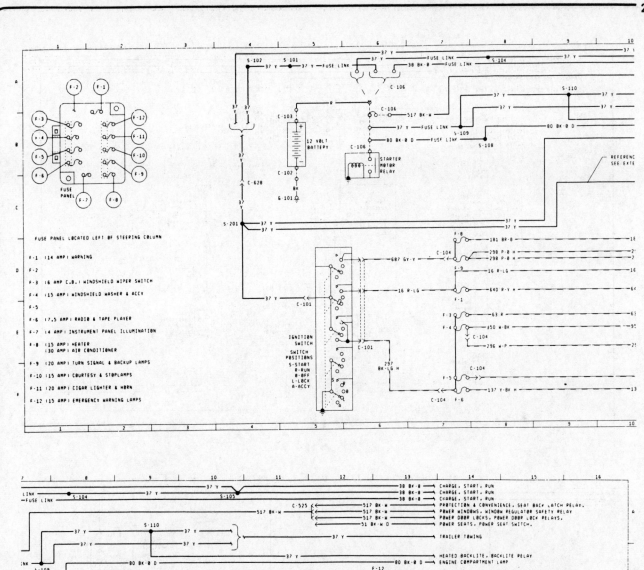

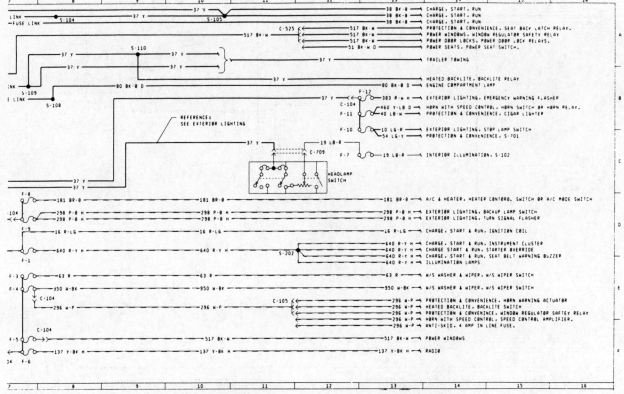

Fig. 10.31 Wiring diagram, power distribution, 1976 models

204

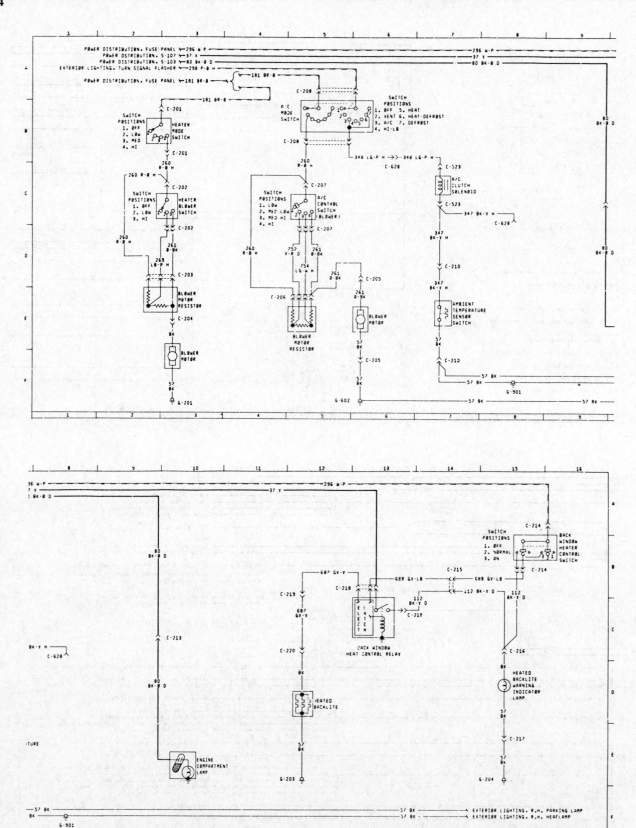

Fig. 10.32 Wiring diagram, air conditioning and/or heater, engine compartment lamp and heated backlite. 1976 models

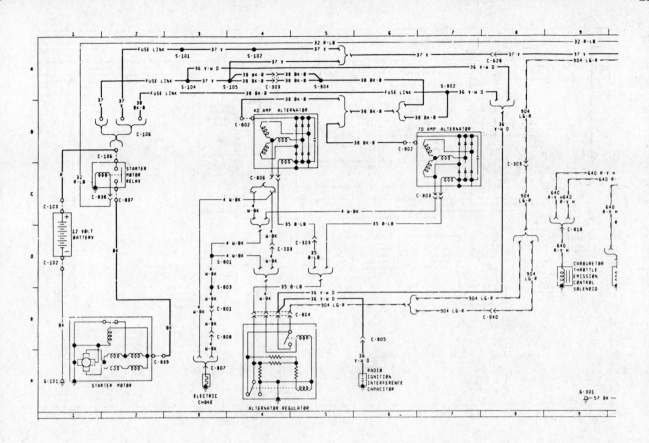

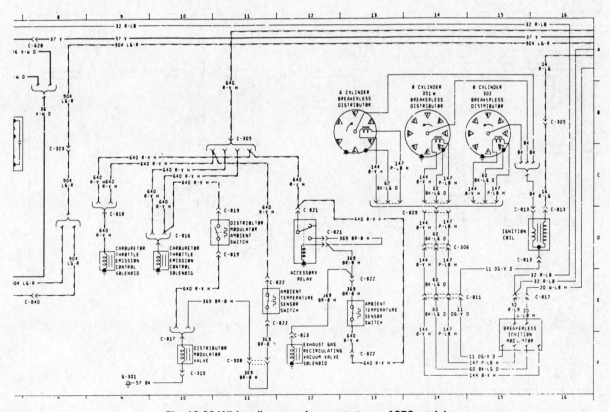

Fig. 10.33 Wiring diagram, charge, start, run, 1976 models

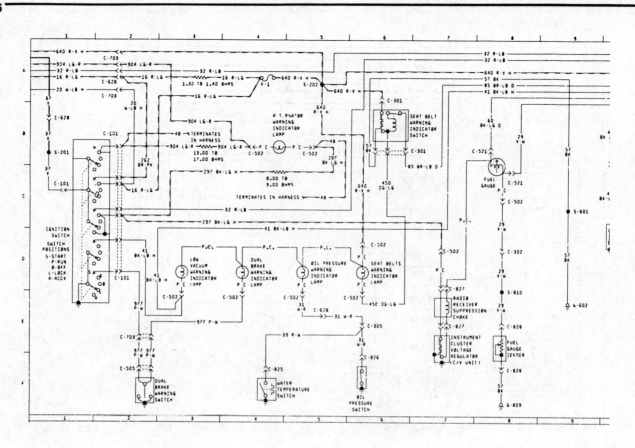

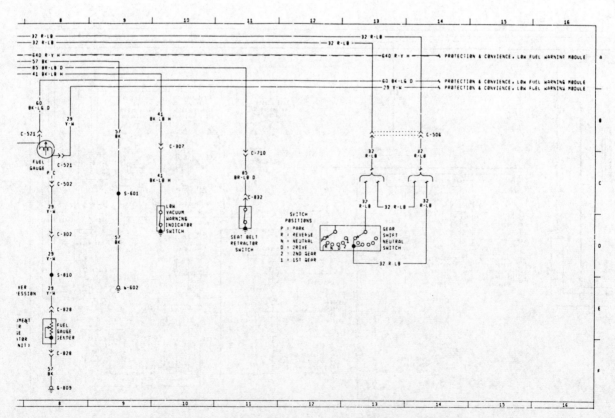

Fig. 10.34 Wiring diagram, charge, start, run, 1976 models (cont.)

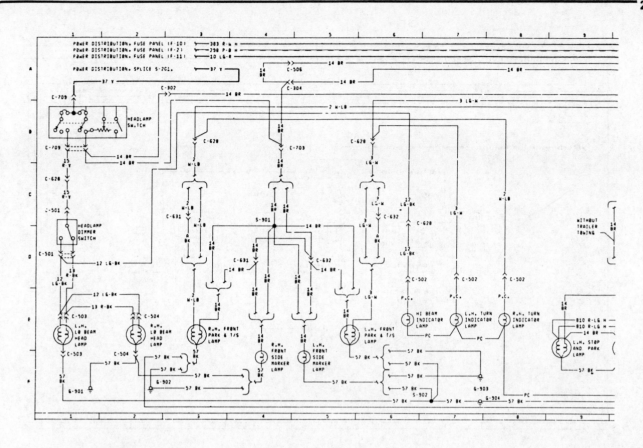

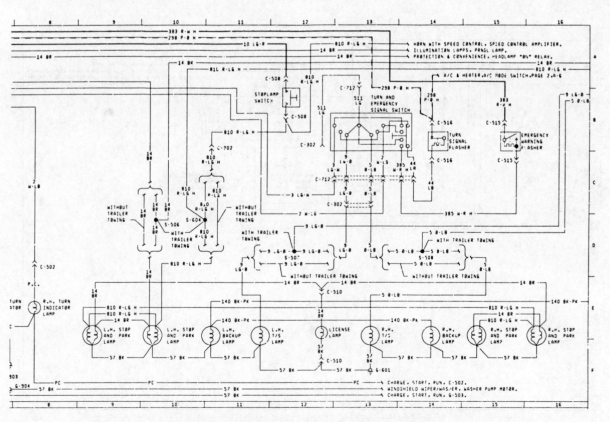

Fig. 10.35 Wiring diagram, exterior lighting, 1976 models

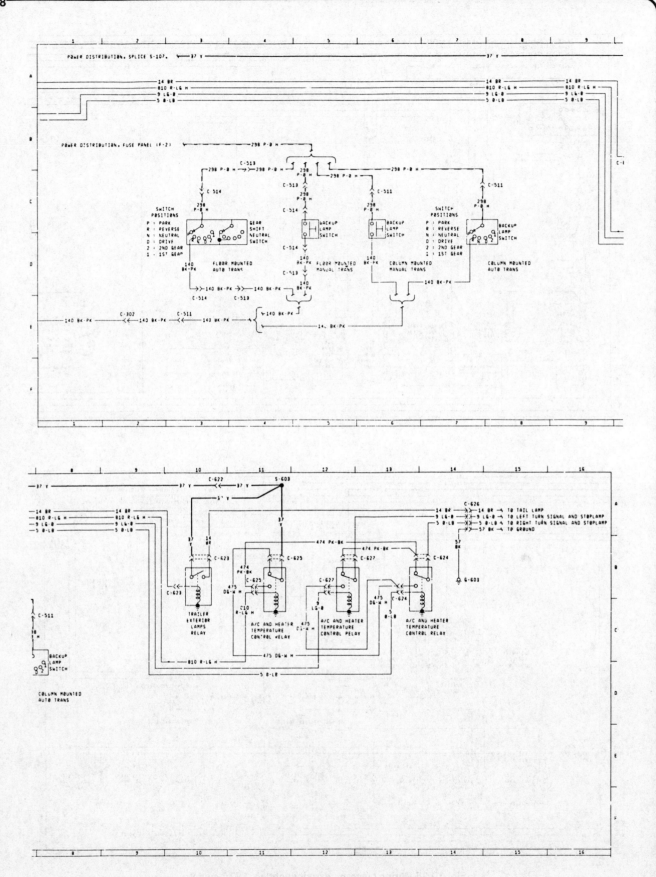

Fig. 10.36 Wiring diagram, exterior lighting, 1976 models (cont.)

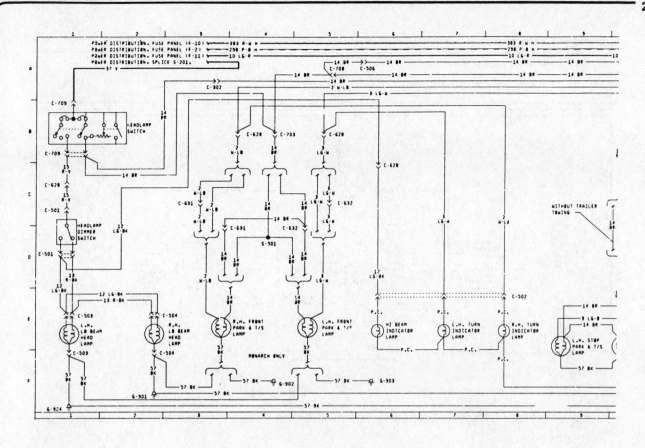

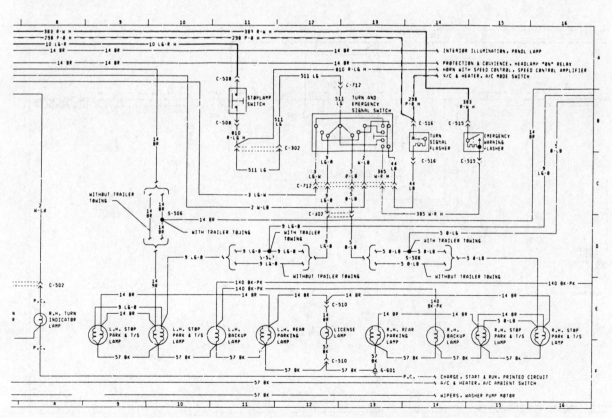

Fig. 10.37 Wiring diagram, exterior lighting, 1976 models (cont.)

210

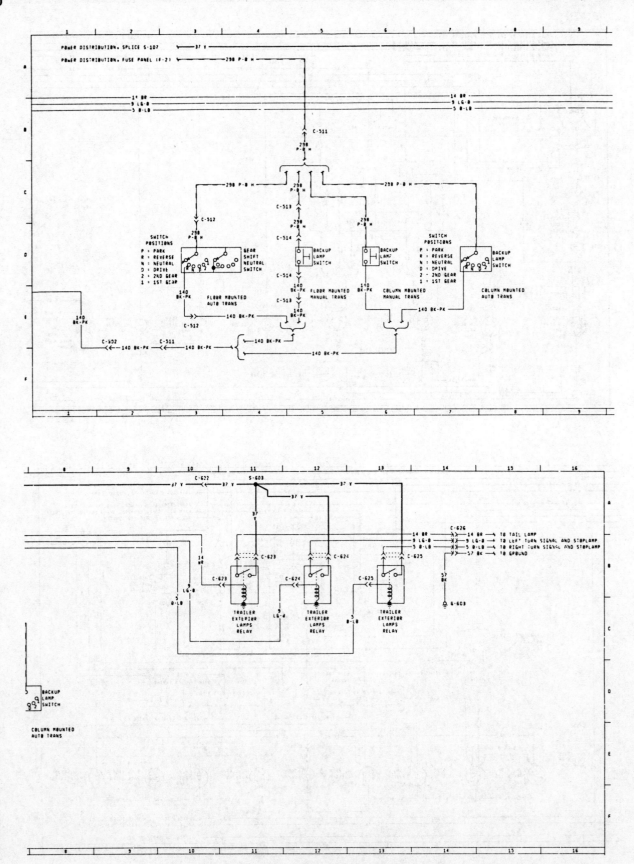

Fig. 10.38 Wiring diagram, exterior lighting, 1976 models (cont.)

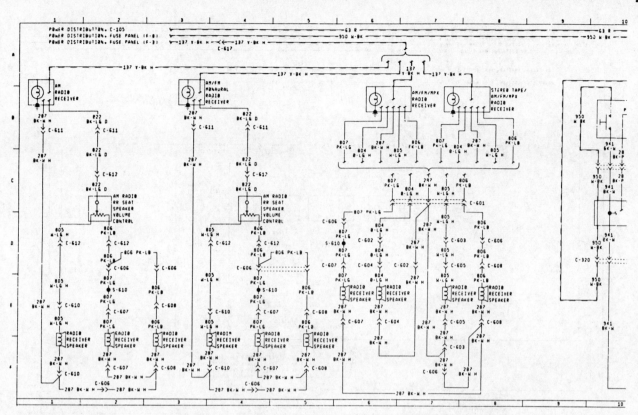

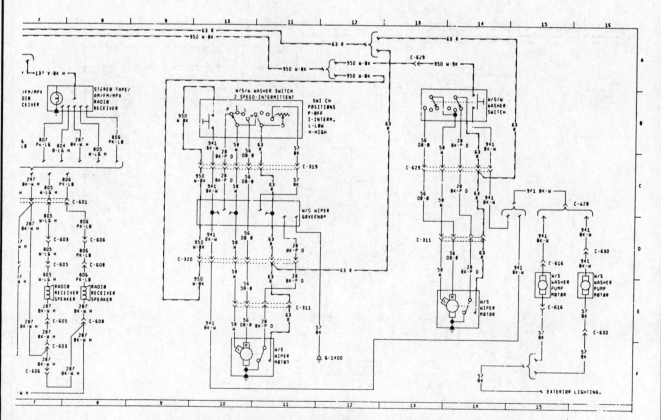

Fig. 10.39 Wiring diagram, radio, windshield wiper/washer, 1976 models

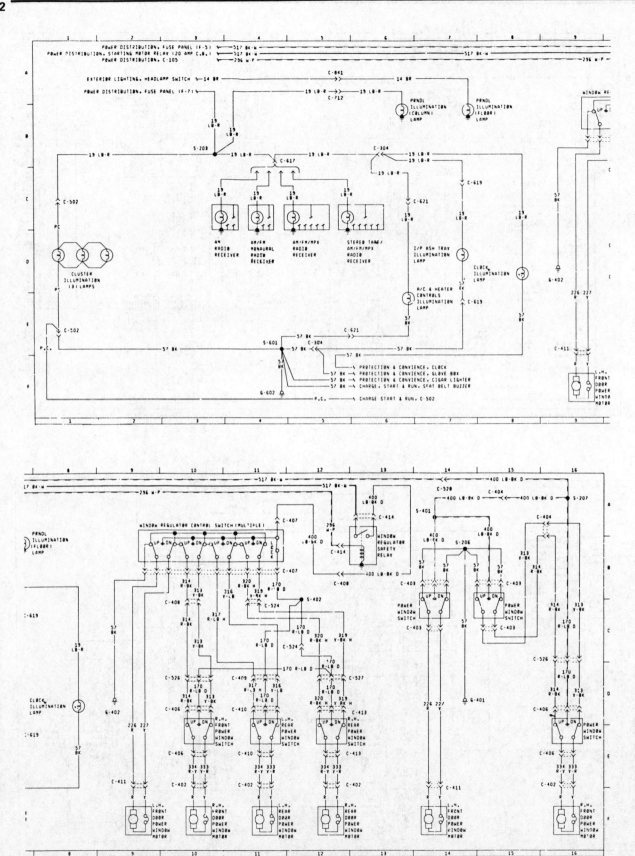

Fig. 10.40 Wiring diagram, illumination lamps, power windows, 1976 models

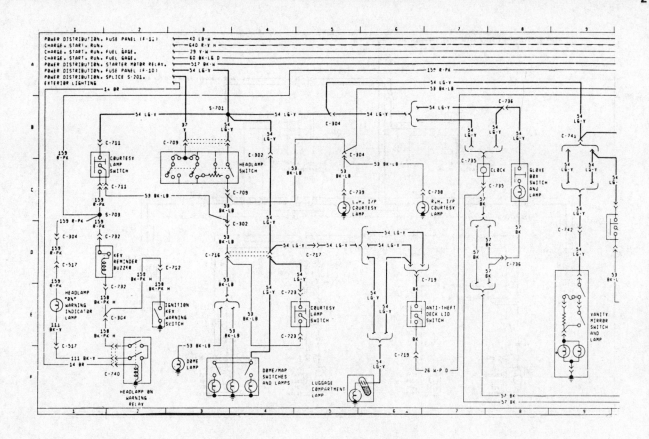

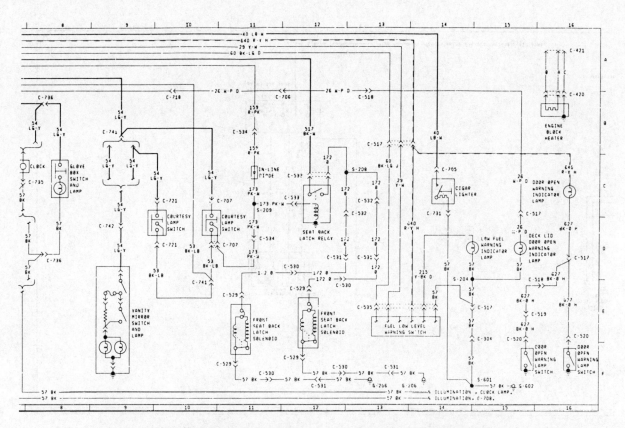

Fig. 10.41 Wiring diagrams, protection and convenience, heater, 1976 models

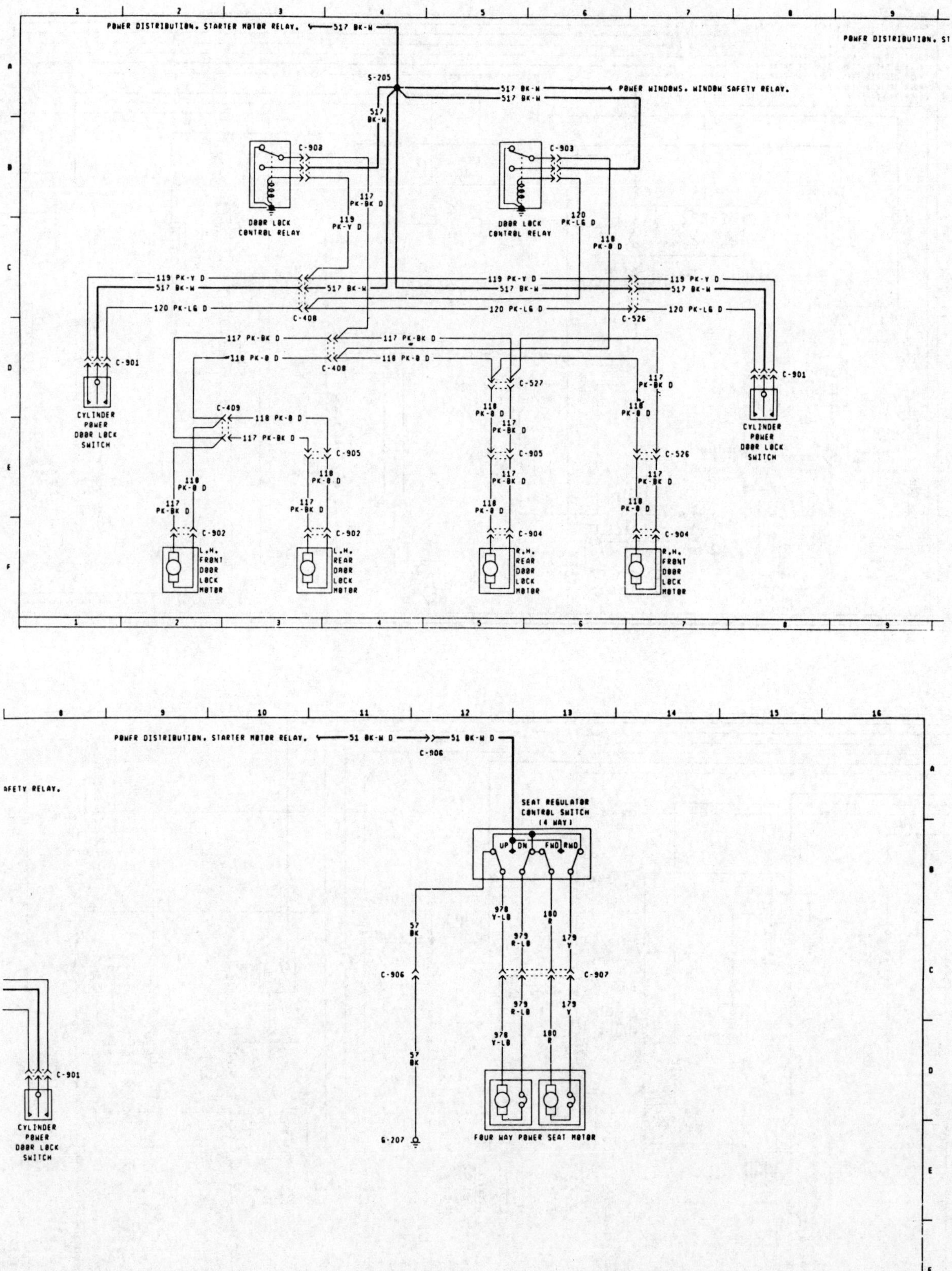

Fig. 10.42 Wiring diagram, power door lock, seats, 1976 models

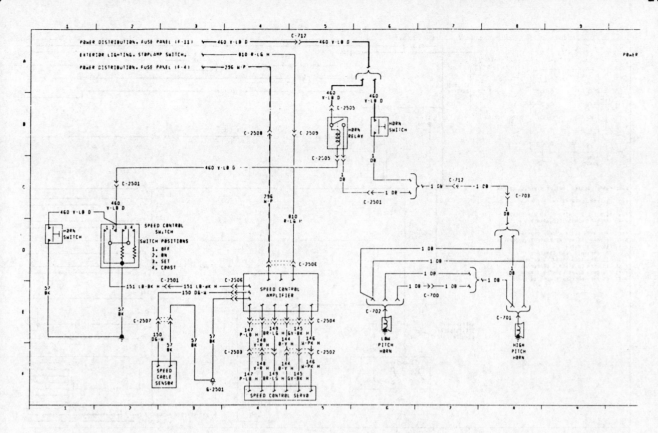

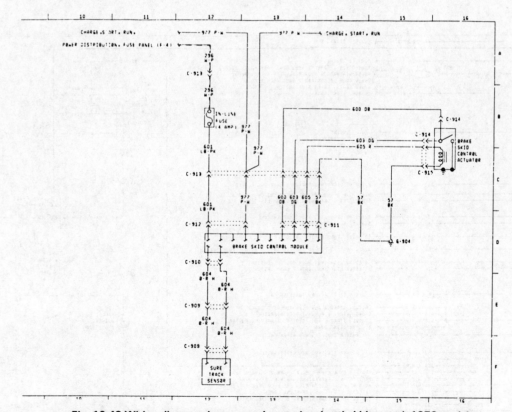

Fig. 10.43 Wiring diagram, horn, speed control and anti-skid control, 1976 models

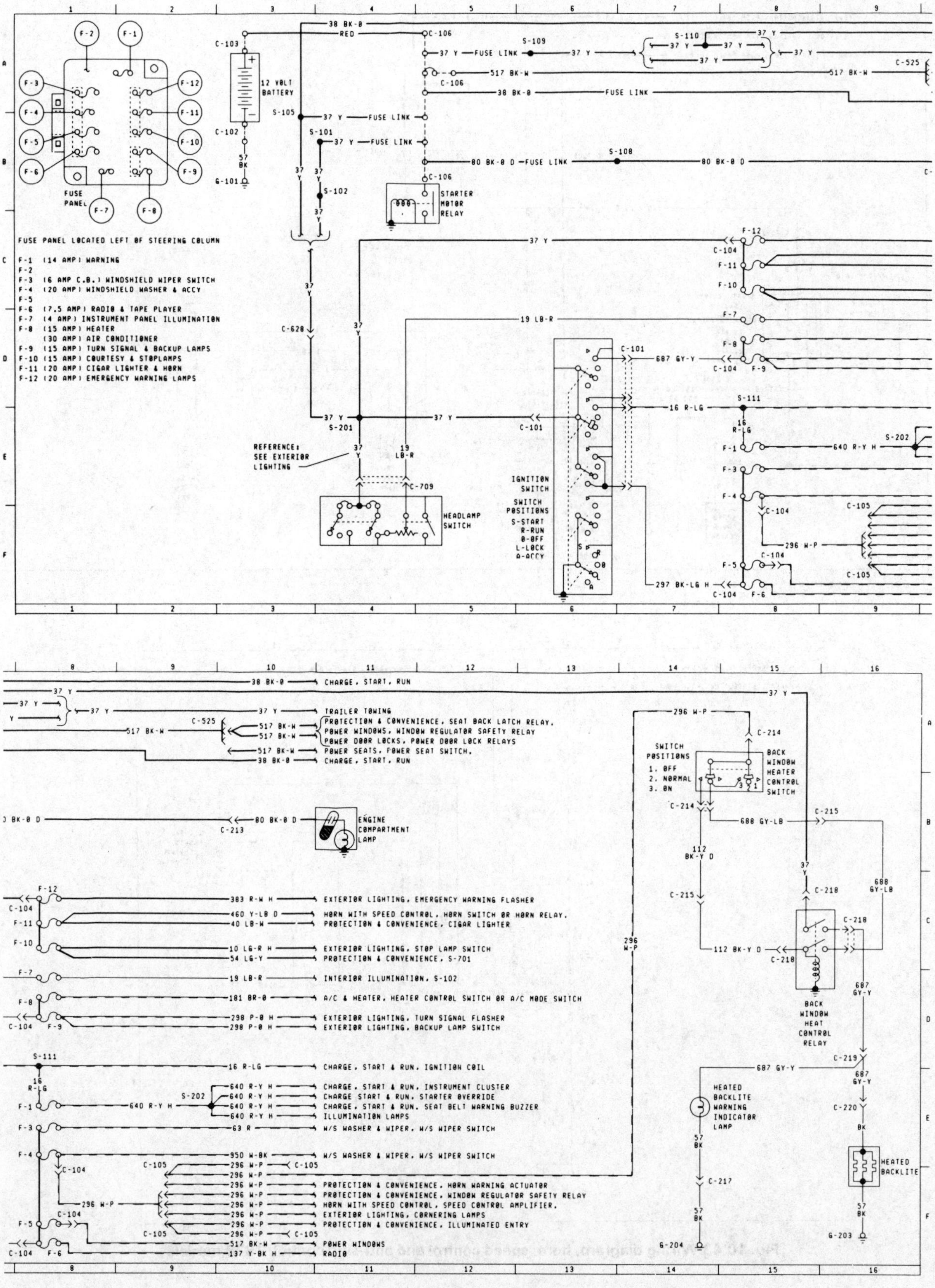

Fig. 10.44 Wiring diagram, power distribution, engine compartment lamp, heated backlite, 1977 models

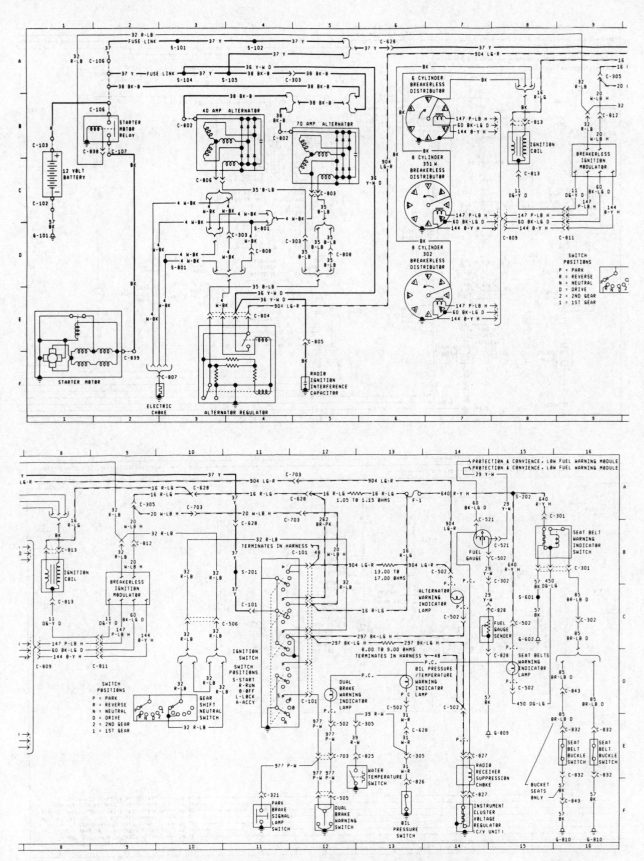

Fig. 10.45 Wiring diagram, charge, start, run, 1977 models

218

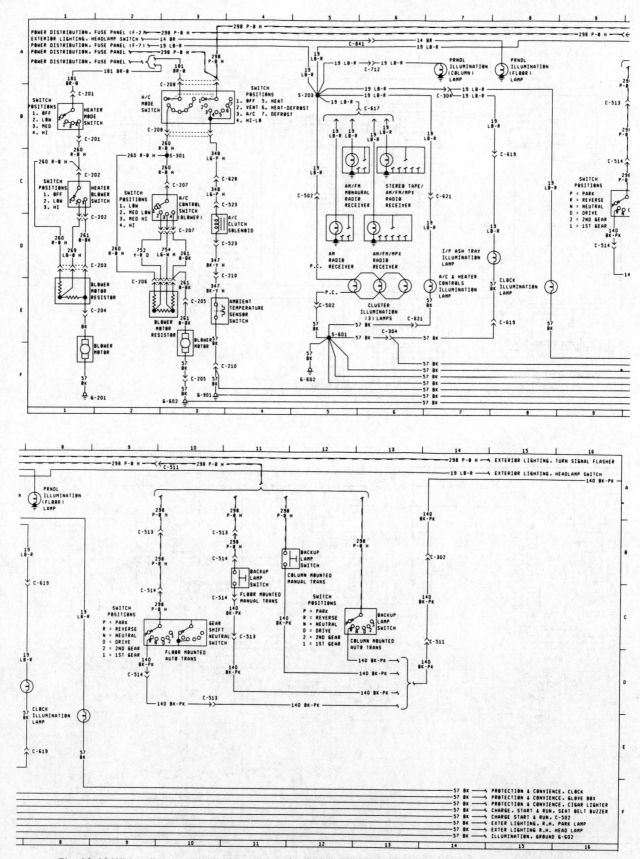

Fig. 10.46 Wiring diagram, air conditioning and/or heater, illumination lamps, exterior lighting, 1977 models

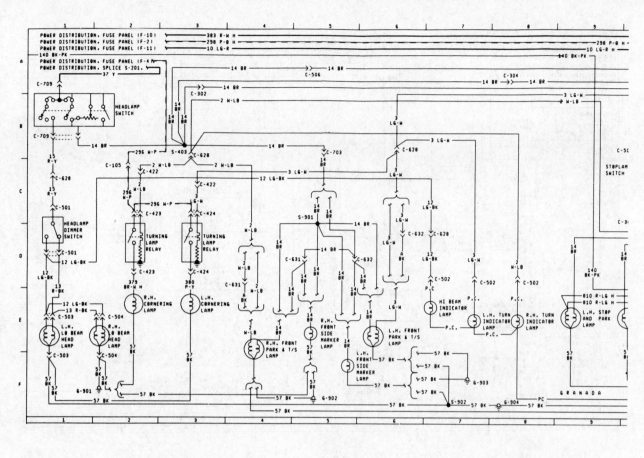

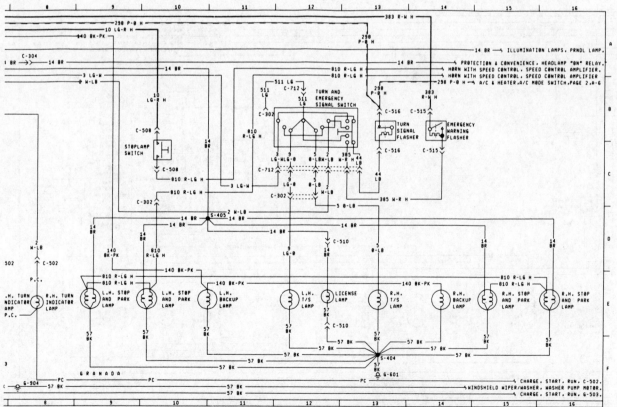

Fig. 10.47 Wiring diagram, exterior lighting, 1977 models

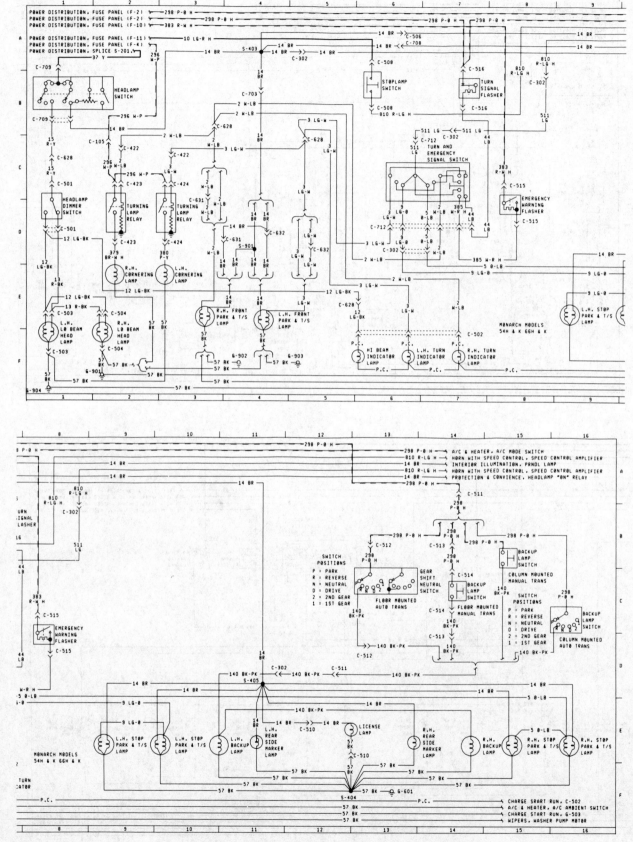

Fig. 10.48 Wiring diagrams, exterior lighting, 1977 models (cont.)

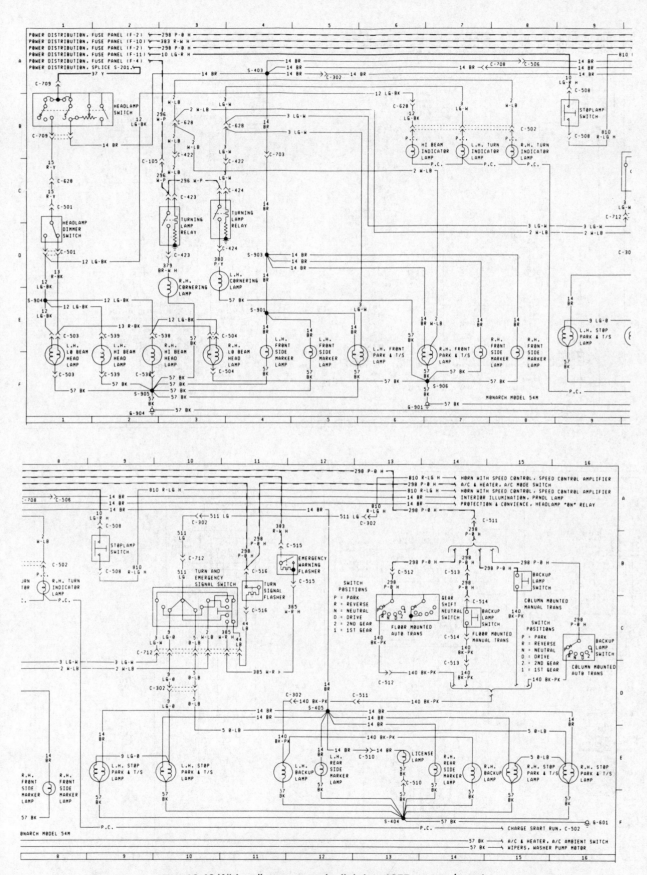

Fig. 10.49 Wiring diagram, exterior lighting, 1977 models (cont.)

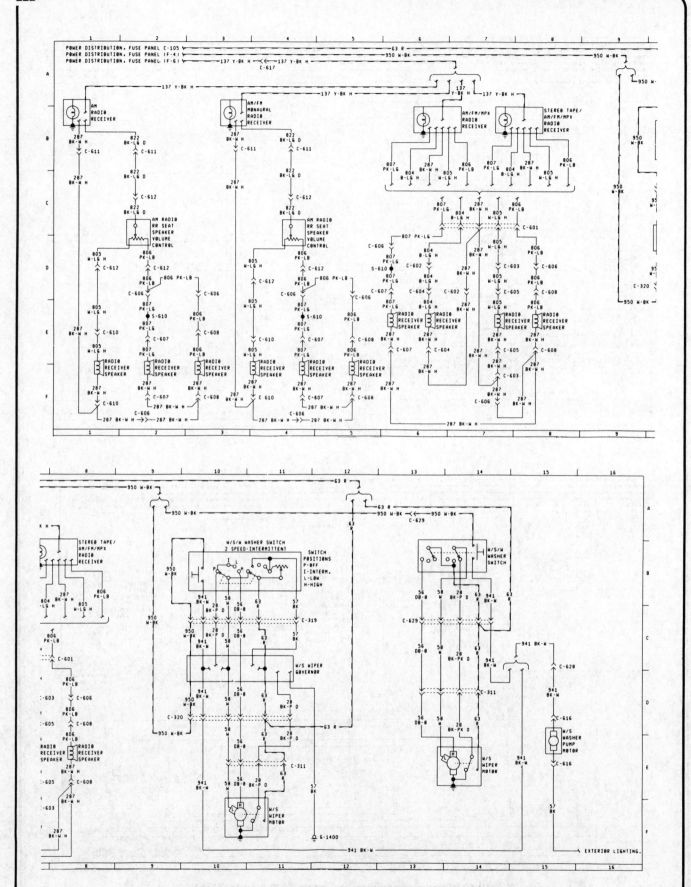

Fig. 10.50 Wiring diagram, radio, windshield wiper/washer, 1977 models

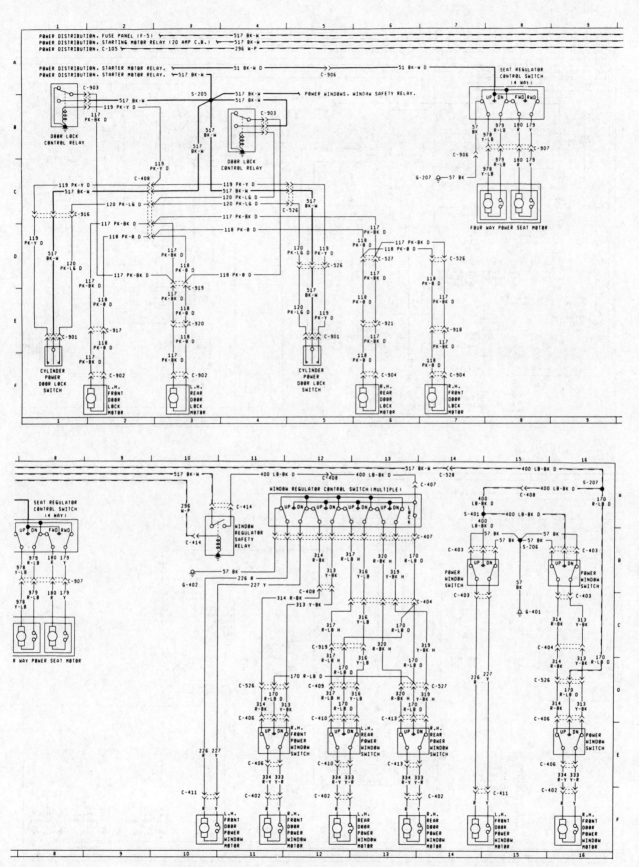

Fig. 10.51 Wiring diagram, power door locks, seats, windows, 1977 models

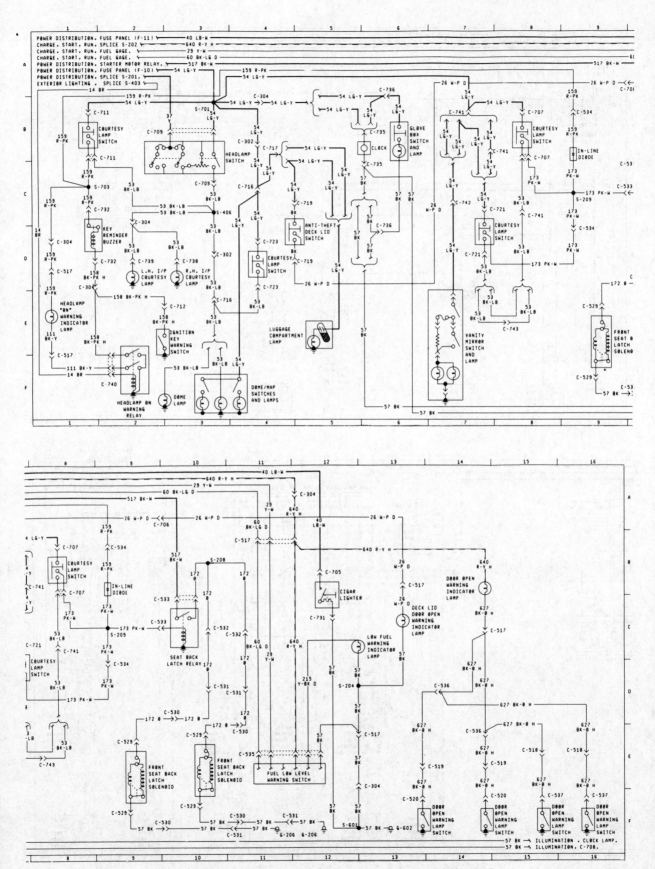

Fig. 10.52 Wiring diagram, protection and convenience, 1977 models

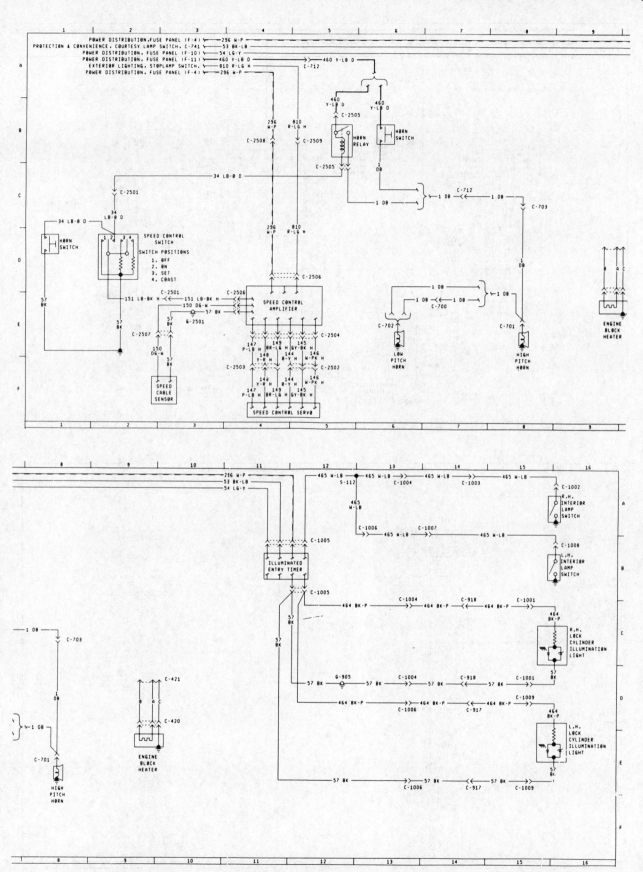

Fig. 10.53 Wiring diagram, horn with speed control, heater, protection and convenience, 1977 models

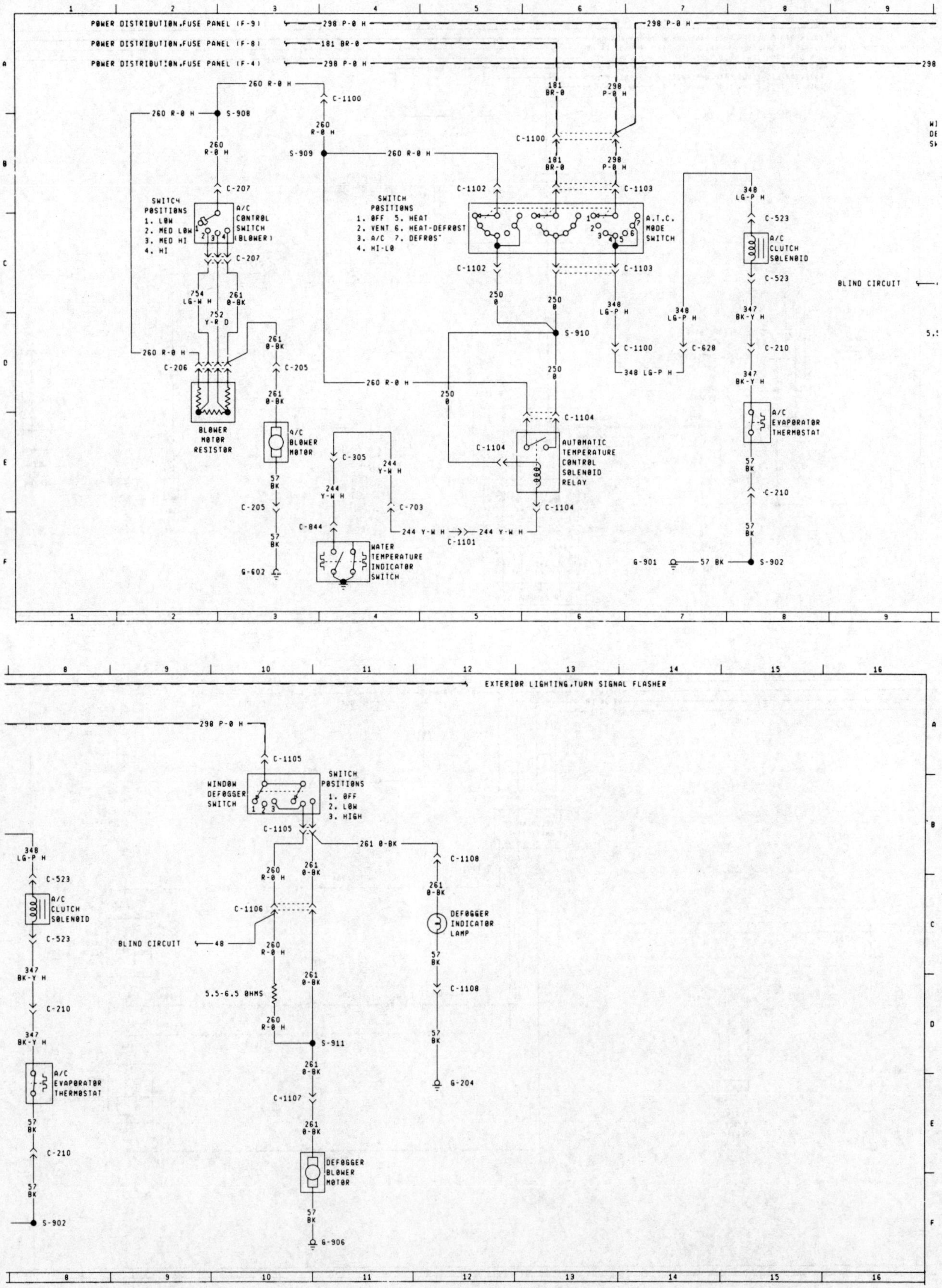

Fig. 10.54 Wiring diagram, automatic temperature control, rear window defogger, 1977 models

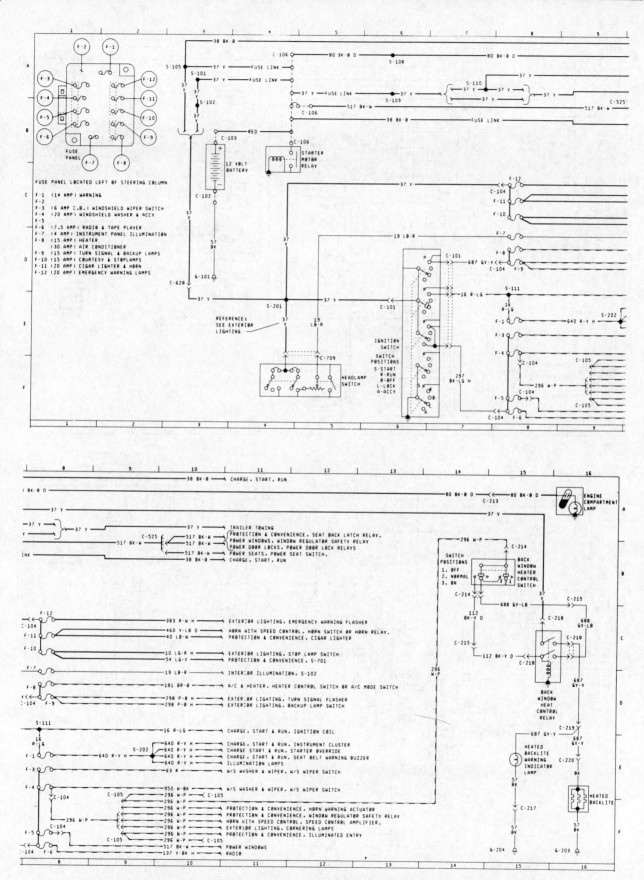

Fig. 10.55 Wiring diagram, power distribution, heated backlite, engine compartment lamp, 1978 models

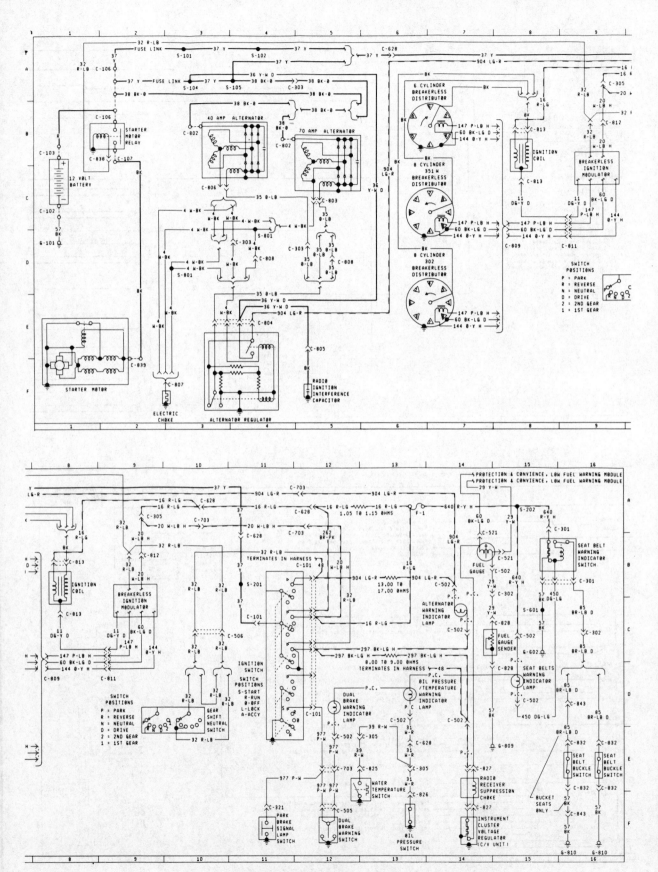

Fig. 10.56 Wiring diagram, charge, start, run, 1978 models

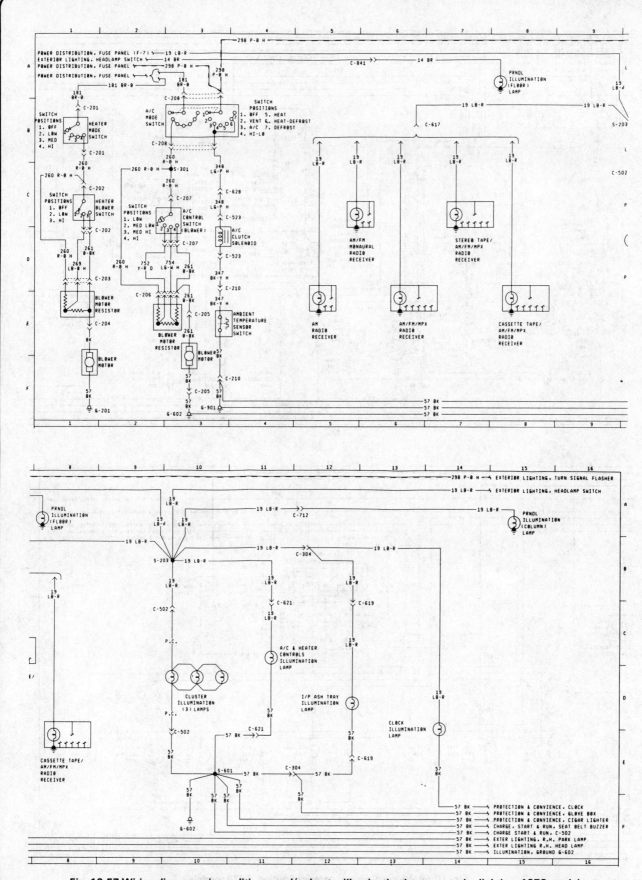

Fig. 10.57 Wiring diagram, air conditioner and/or heater illumination lamps, exterior lighting, 1978 models

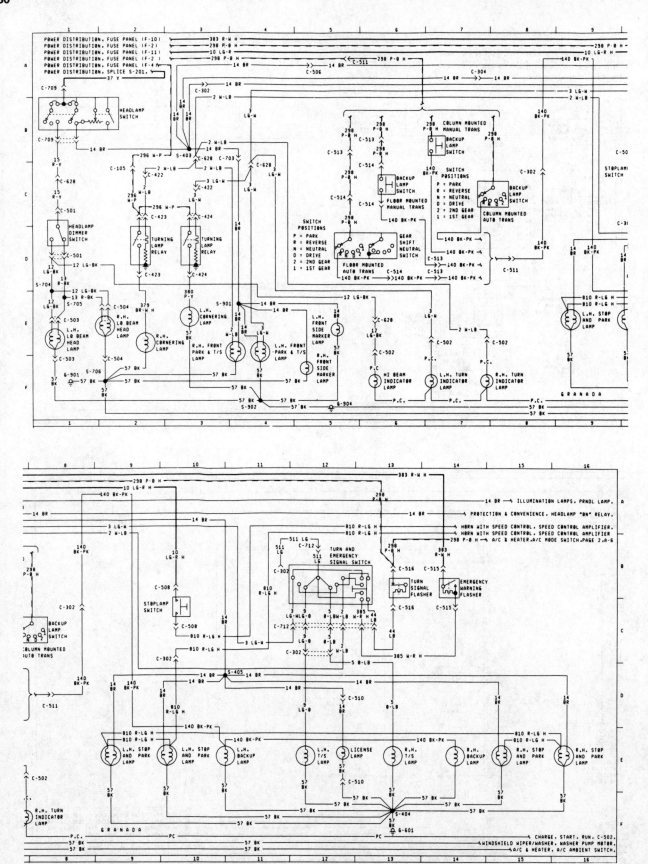

Fig. 10.58 Wiring diagram, exterior lighting, 1978 models

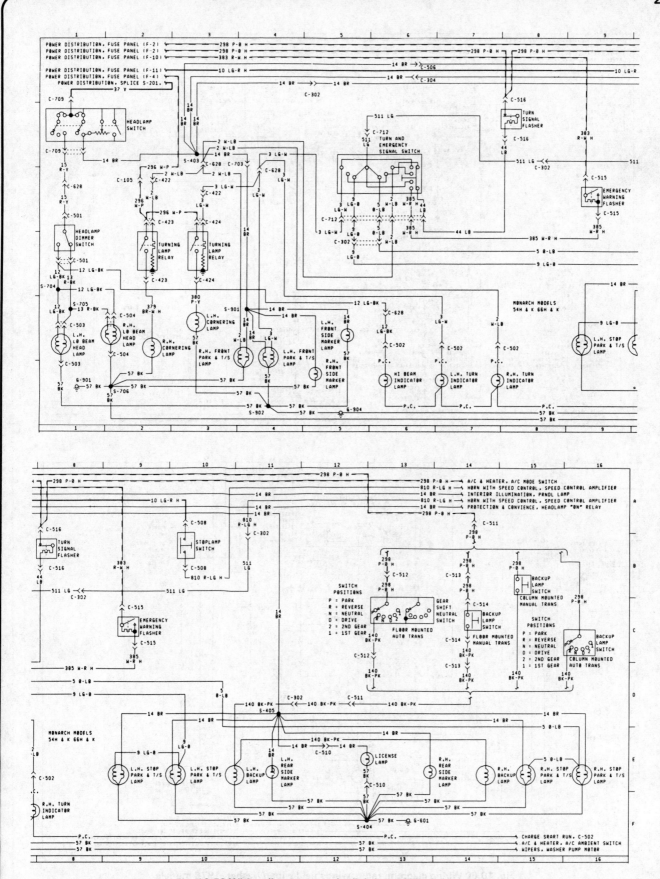

Fig. 10.59 Wiring diagram, exterior lighting, 1978 models (cont.)

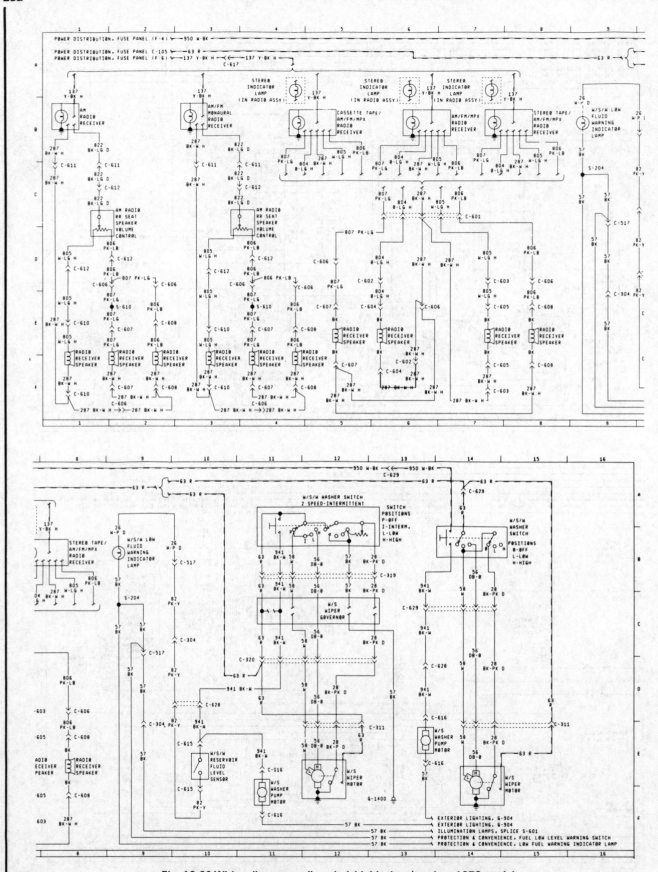

Fig. 10.60 Wiring diagram, radio, windshield wiper/washer, 1978 models

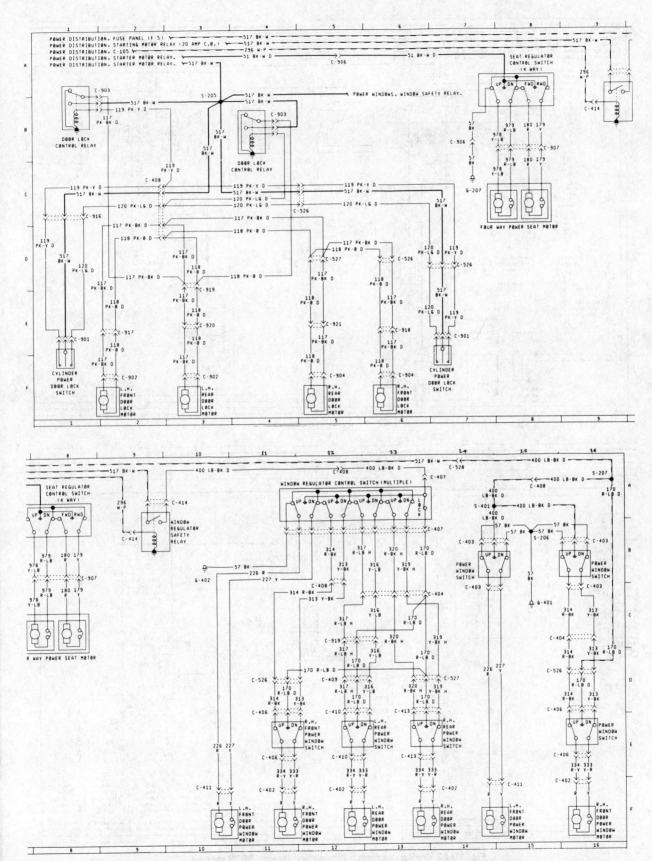

Fig. 10.61 Wiring diagram, power door locks, seats, windows, 1978 models

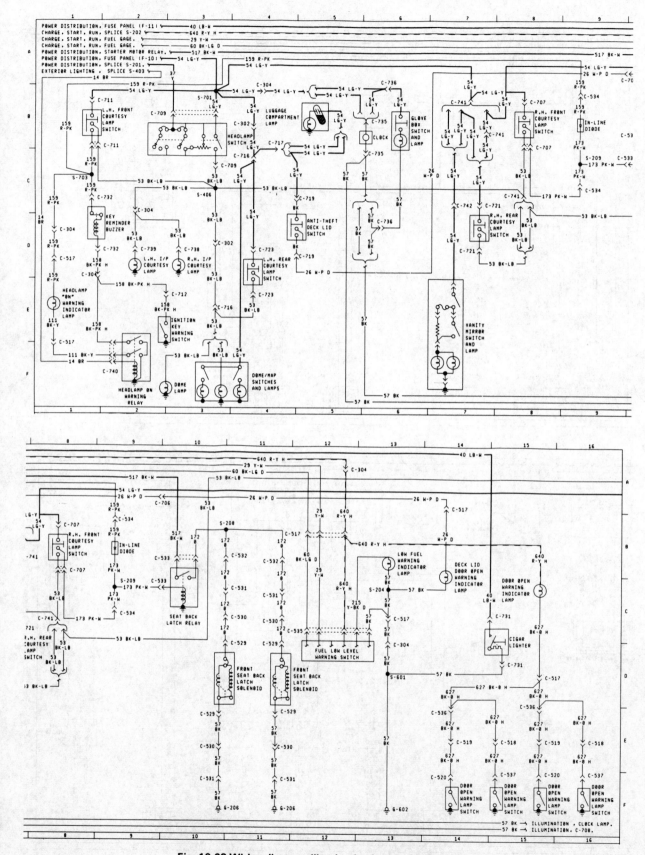

Fig. 10.62 Wiring diagram, illumination lamps, 1978 models

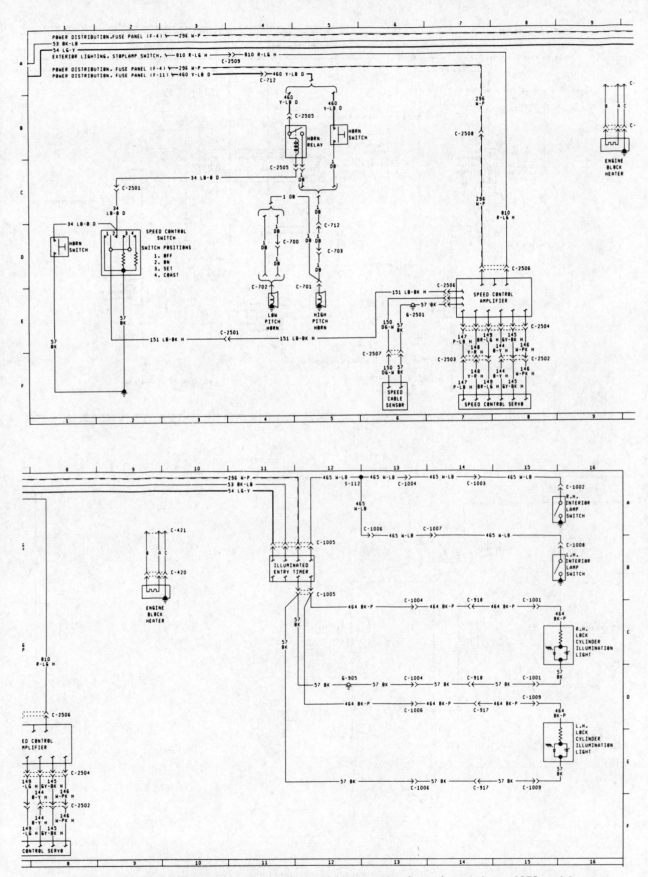

Fig. 10.63 Wiring diagram, horn with speed control, heater, protection and convenience, 1978 models

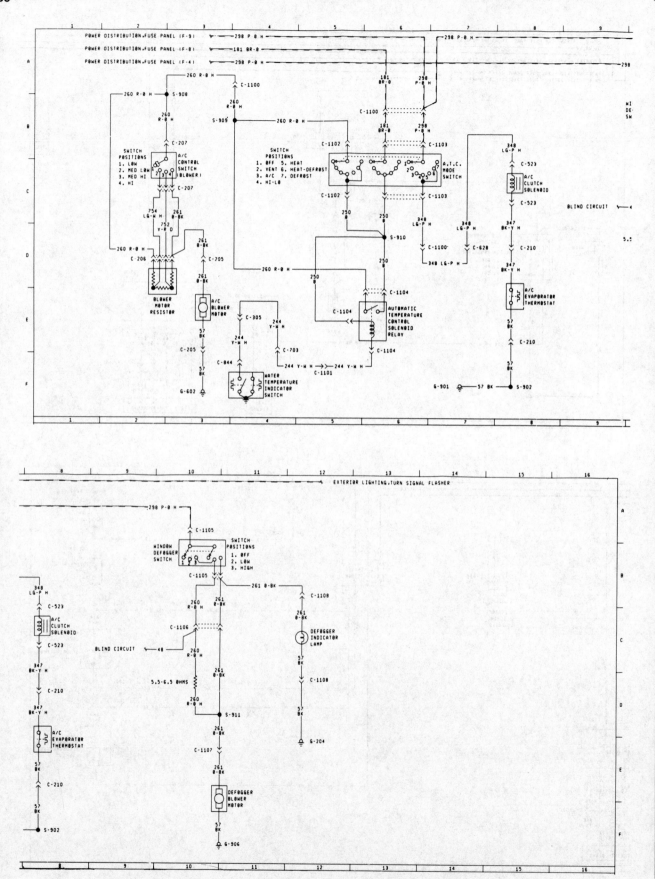

Fig. 10.64 Wiring diagram, air conditioning and/or heater, rear window defogger, 1978 models

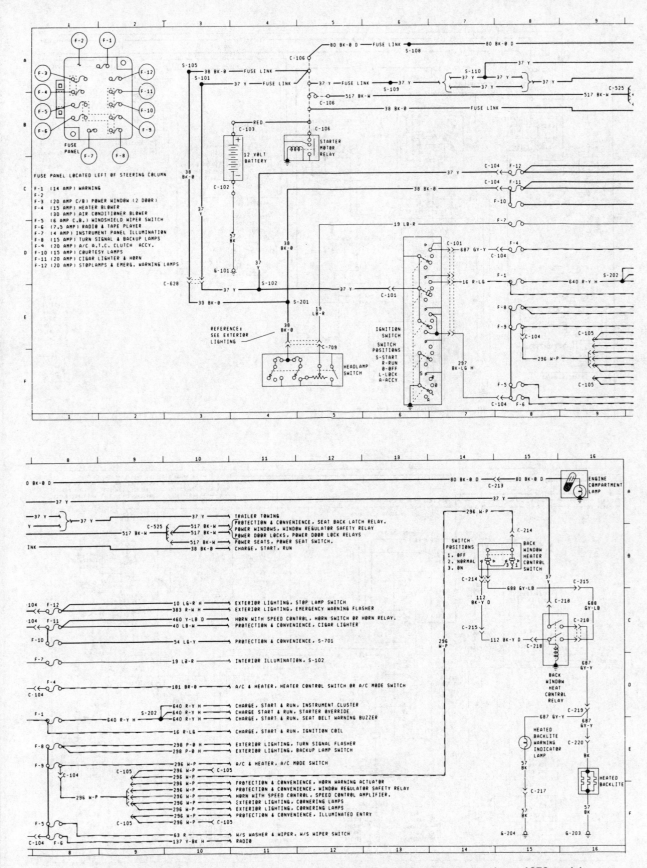

Fig. 10.65 Wiring diagram, power distribution, heated backlite, engine compartment lamp, 1979 models

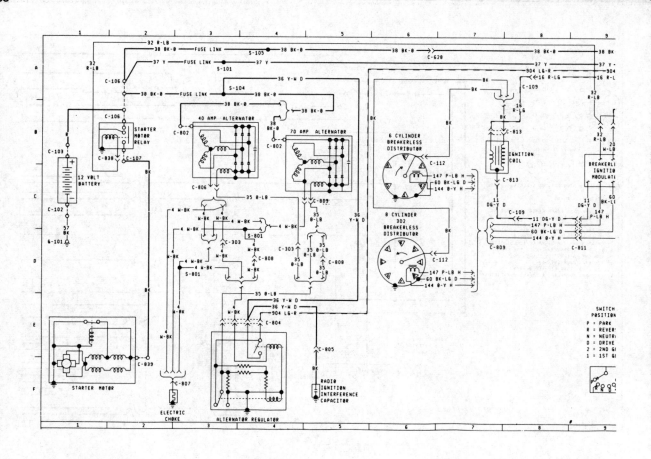

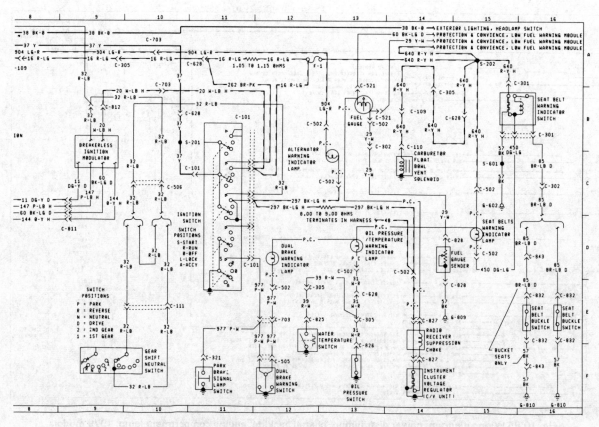

Fig. 10.66 Wiring diagram, charge, start, run, 1979 models

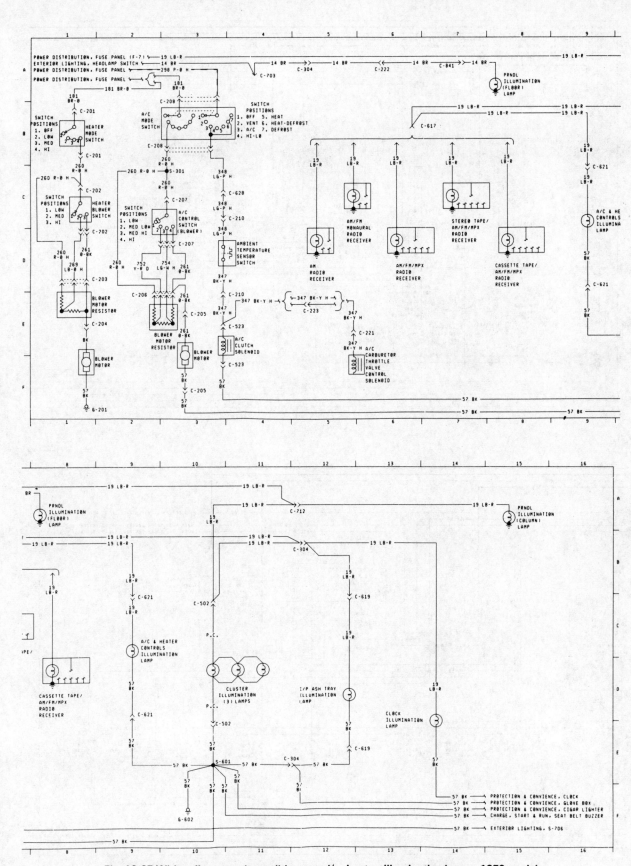

Fig. 10.67 Wiring diagram, air conditioner and/or heater, illumination lamps, 1979 models

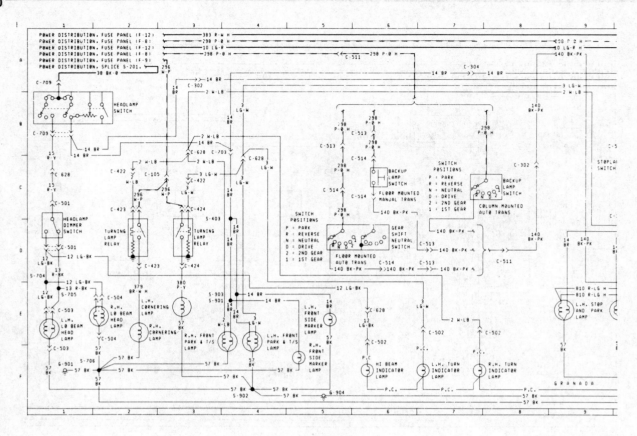

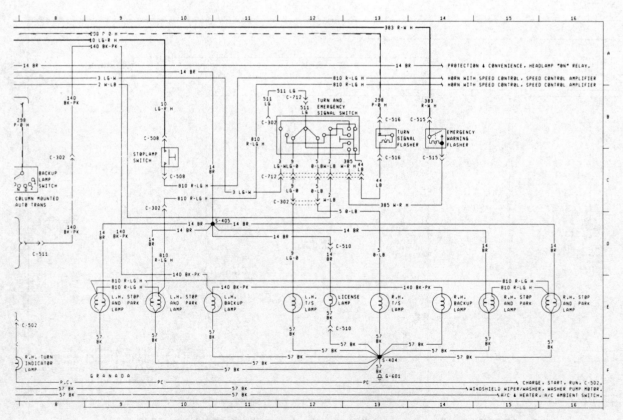

Fig. 10.68 Wiring diagram, exterior lighting, 1979 models

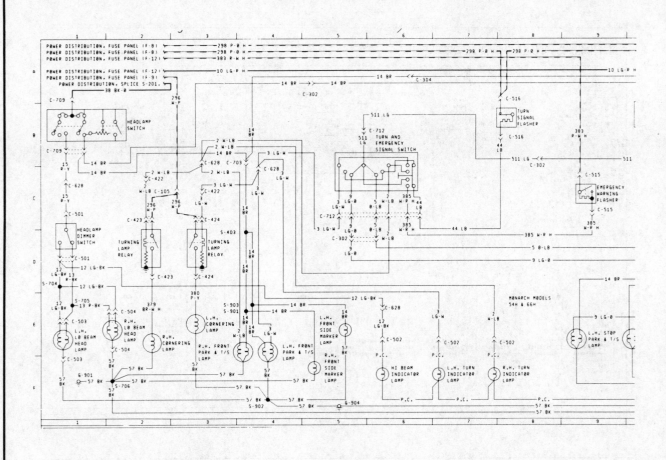

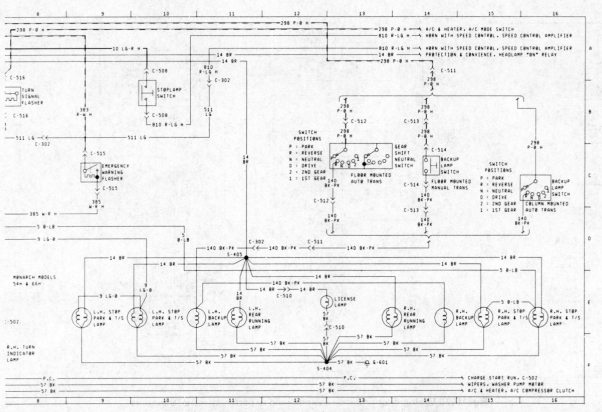

Fig. 10.69 Wiring diagram, exterior lighting, 1979 models

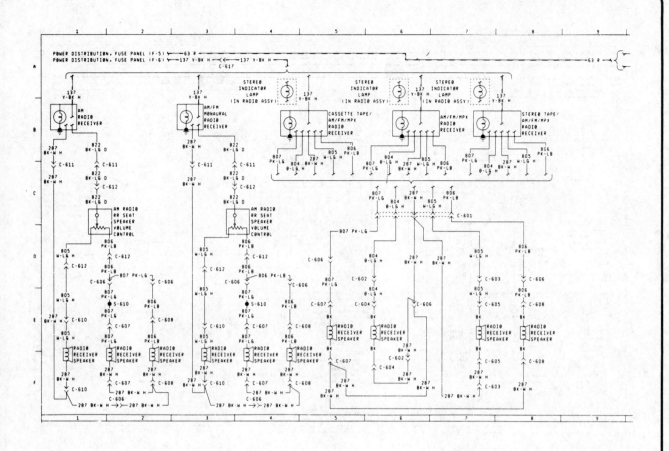

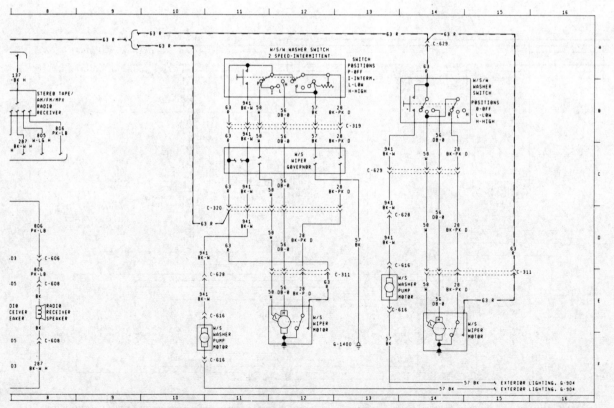

Fig. 10.70 Wiring diagram, radio, windshield wiper/washer 1979 models

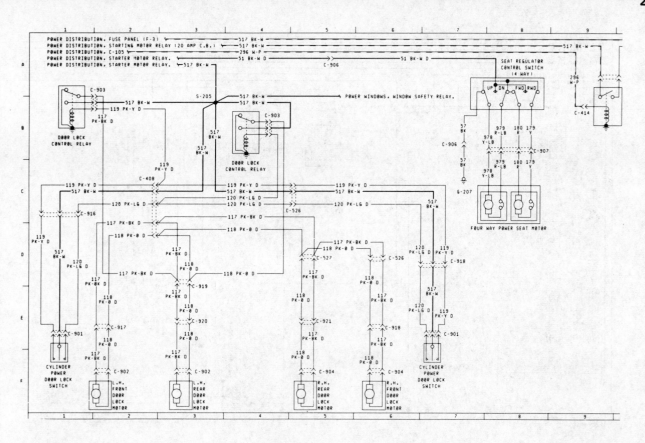

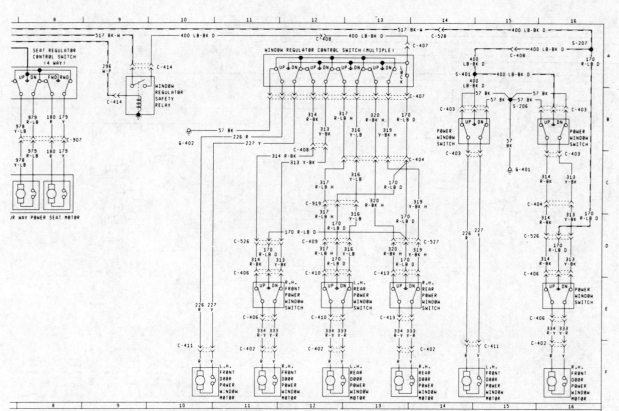

Fig. 10.71 Wiring diagram, power windows, seats, windows, 1979 models

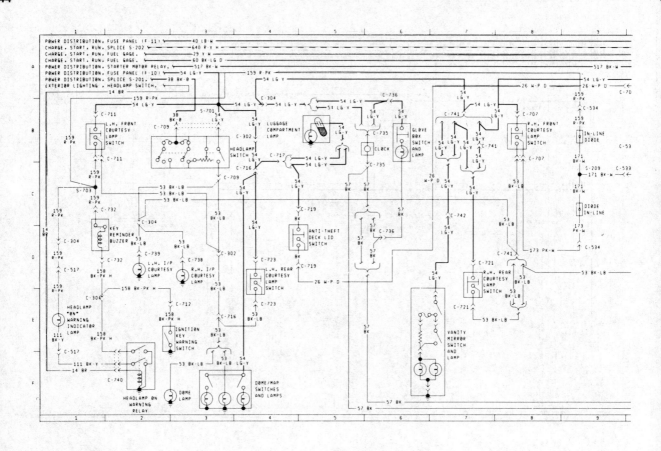

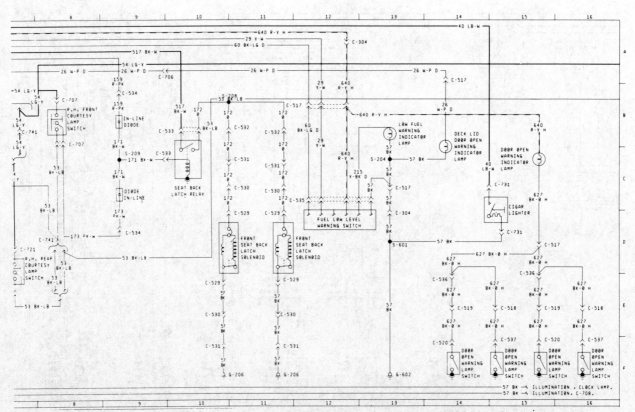

Fig. 10.72 Wiring diagram, illumination lamps, protection and convenience, 1979 models

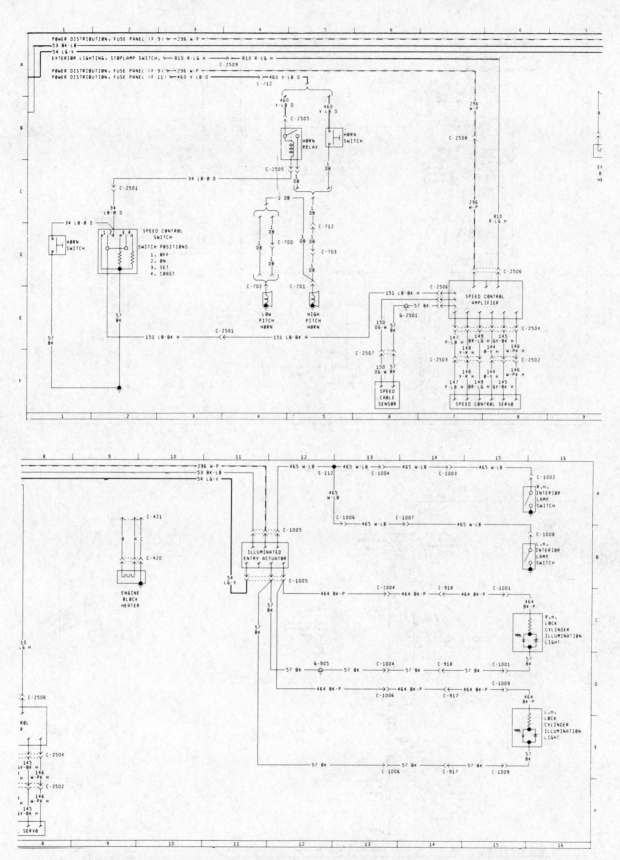

Fig. 10.73 Wiring diagram, horn with speed control, heater, protection and convenience, 1979 models

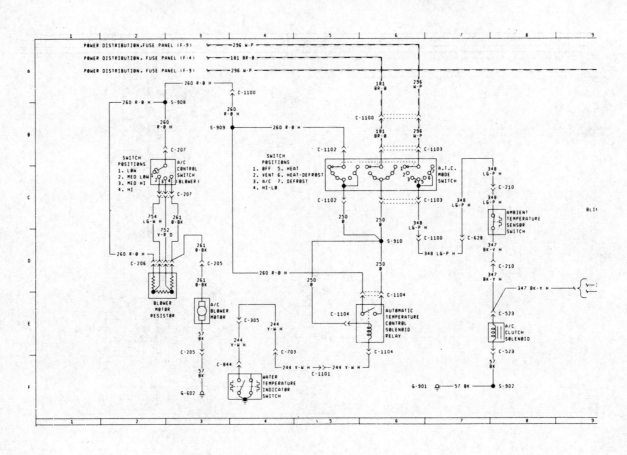

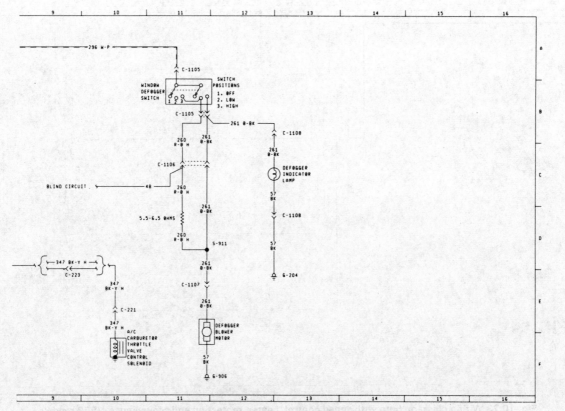

Fig. 10.74 Wiring diagram, automatic temperature control, rear window defogger, 1979

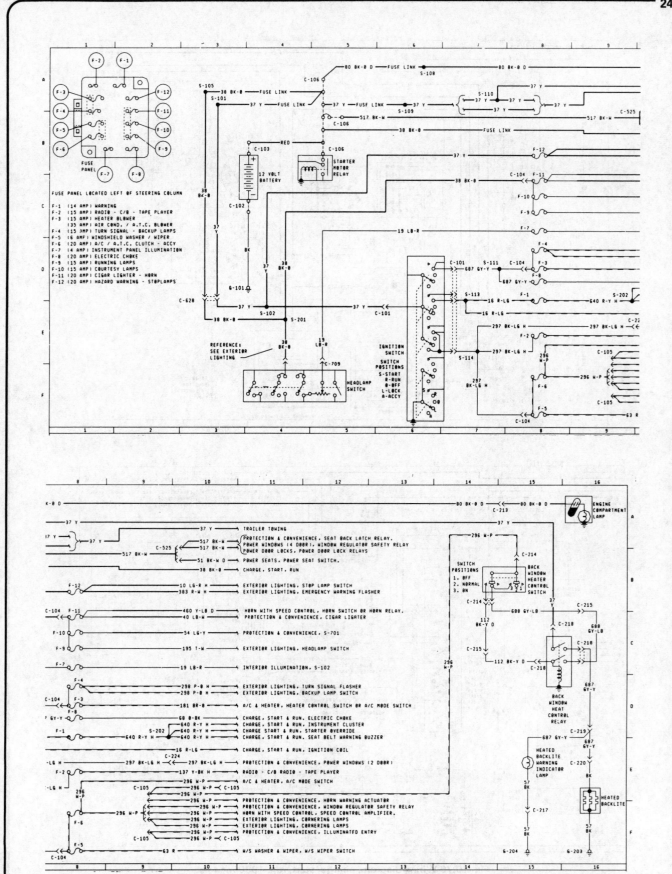

Fig. 10.75 Wiring diagram, power distribution, heated backlite engine compartment lamp, 1980 models

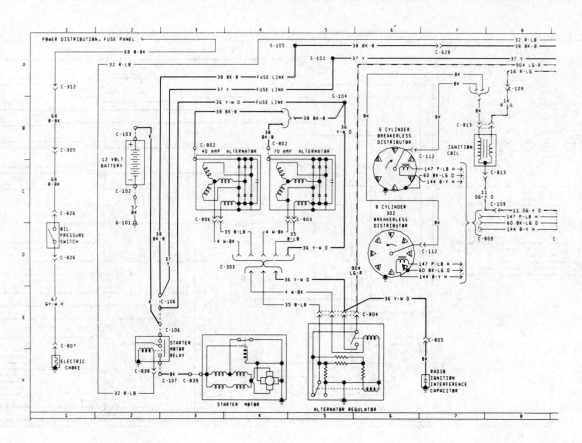

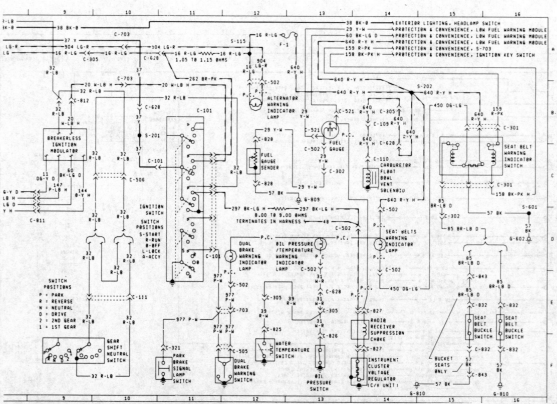

Fig. 10.76 Wiring diagram, charge, start, run, 1980 models

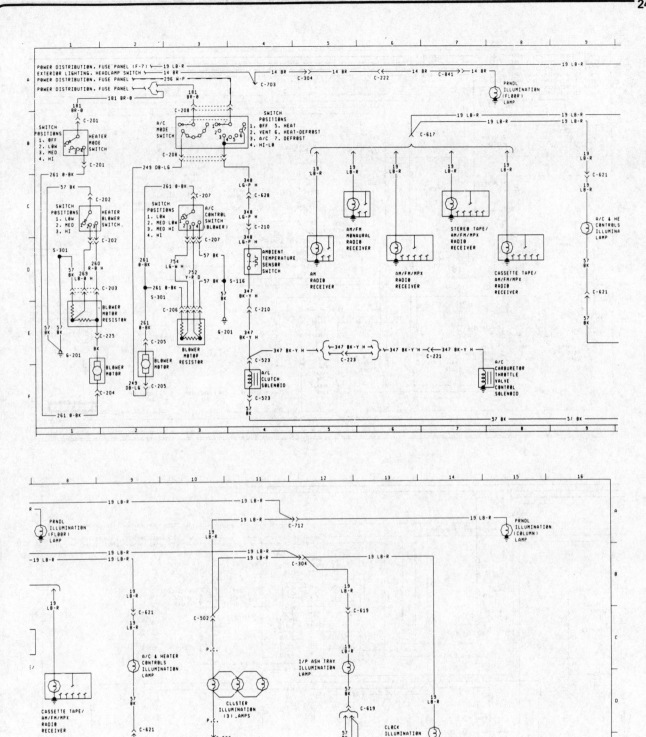

Fig. 10.77 Wiring diagram, air conditioner and/or heater illumination lamps, 1980 models

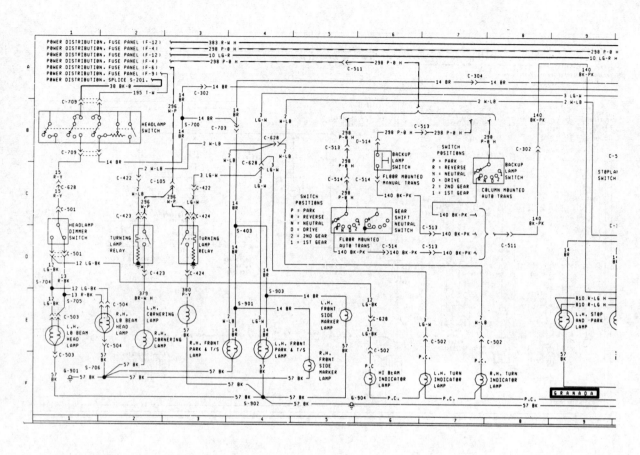

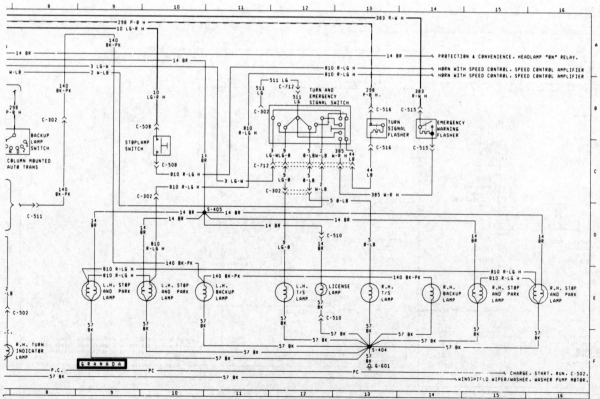

Fig. 10.78 Wiring diagram, exterior lighting, 1980 models

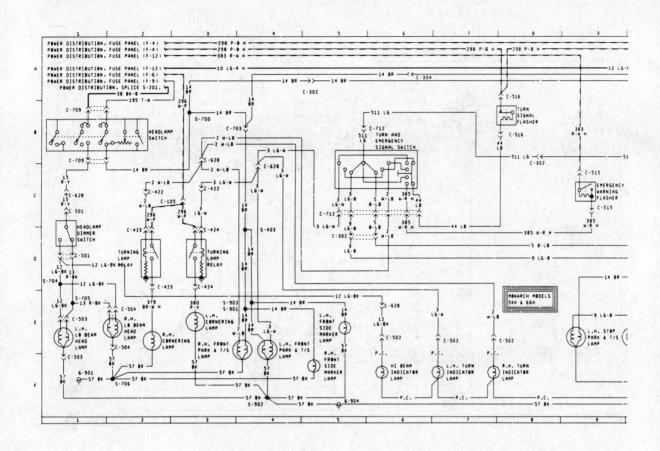

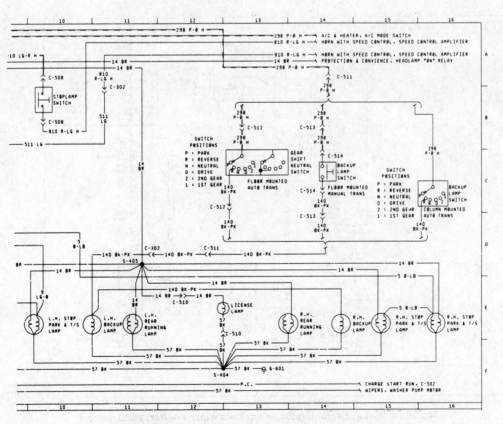

Fig. 10.79 Wiring diagram, exterior lighting, 1980 models

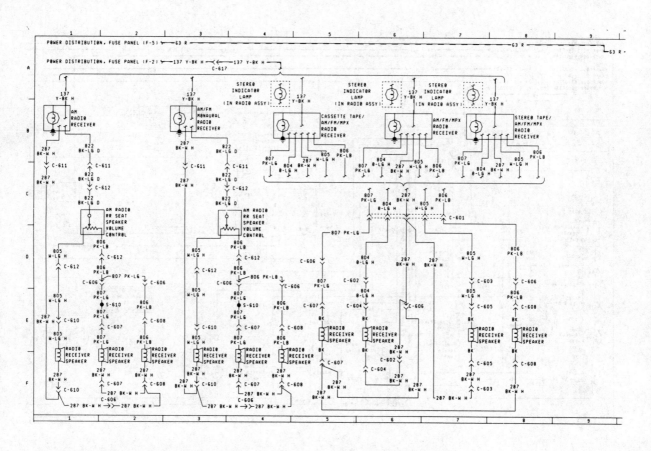

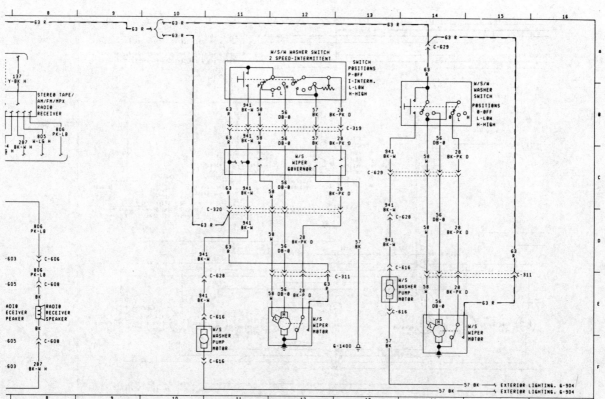

Fig. 10.80 Wiring diagram, radio, windshield wiper/washer, 1980 models

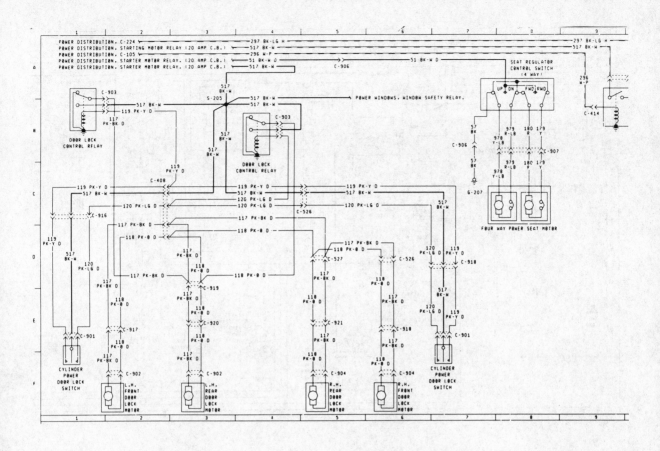

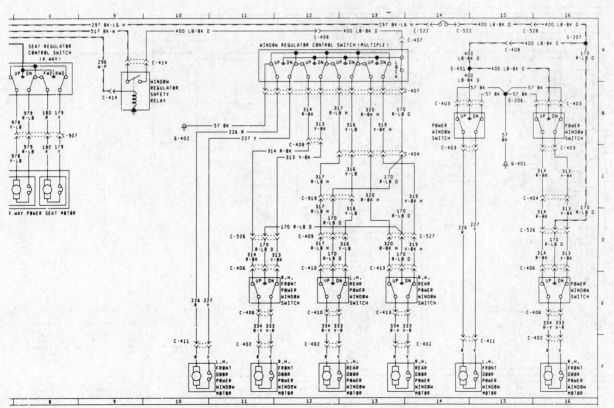

Fig. 10.81 Wiring diagram, power door locks, seats, windows, 1980 models

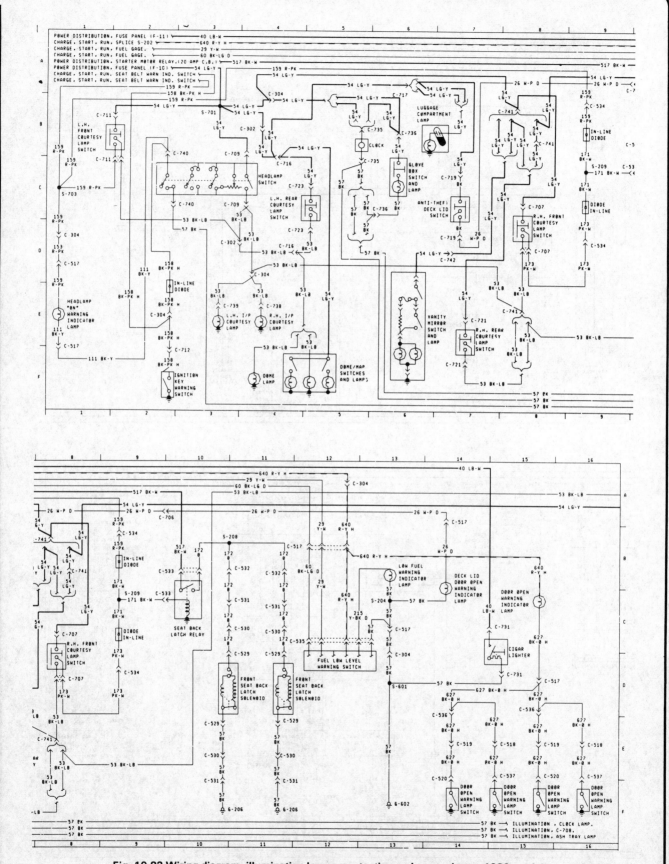

Fig. 10.82 Wiring diagram, illumination lamps, protection and convenience, 1980 models

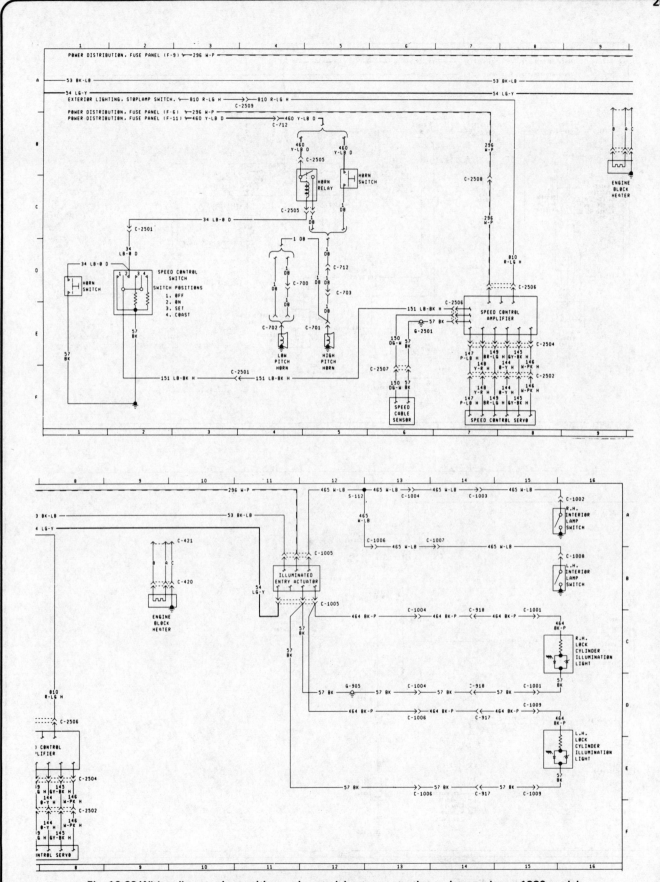

Fig. 10.83 Wiring diagram, horn with speed control, heater, protection and convenience, 1980 models

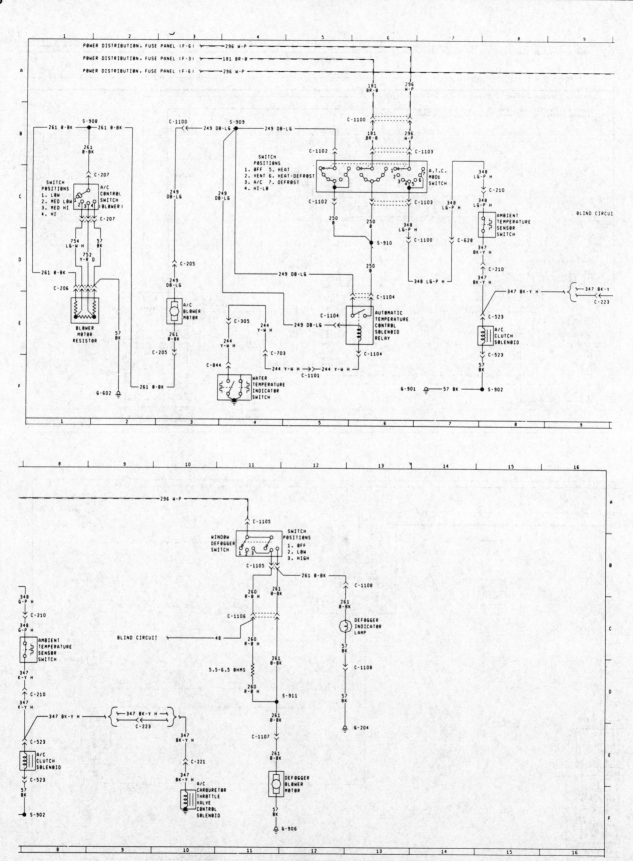

Fig. 10.84 Wiring diagram, automatic temperature control, rear window defogger, 1980 models

Chapter 11 Suspension and steering

Contents

Specifications

Front suspension
Type	Spring on upper arm
Toe-in	$\frac{1}{8}$ in
Caster	$+ \frac{1}{4}°$
Camber	$- \frac{1}{2}°$

Rear suspension
Type	Leaf springs and telescoping shock absorbers

Steering
Type	Recirculating ball, optional power assist
Lubricant type	ESW-M1C87-A or equivalent
Capacity	0.070 lb
Power steering pump capacity	3.6 US pints

Tires
Size	Refer to decal on left door pillar

Torque specifications

	Ft-lb	Nm
Front suspension		
Shock absorber-to-spring seat	8 to 12	11 to 16
Shock absorber upper attachment	10 to 16	14 to 21
Shock absorber upper bracket	32 to 48	44 to 65
Upper suspension arm-to-body		
1975 thru 1977	85 to 100	115 to 138
1978 thru 1980	110 to 130	150 to 176
Spring seat-to-upper arm	24 to 40	34 to 54
Balljoint-to-spindle	75 to 95	102 to 122
Strut-to-lower arm	90 to 115	123 to 155
Lower arm-to-underbody	85 to 100	115 to 135
Stabilizer bar mounting bracket-to-underbody	6 to 12	9 to 16
Strut-to-underbody nut	70 to 80	95 to 108
Sway bar-to-lower arm	6 to 12	9 to 16
Brake caliper-to-spindle	90 to 120	123 to 162

Rear suspension

Spring shackle	14 to 22	19 to 29
Shock absorber upper mount	45 to 65	62 to 88
Shock absorber lower mount	14 to 26	19 to 35
Axle U-bolt nut	30 to 45	41 to 61
Spring front hanger bolt	80 to 120	109 to 162

Steering

Pitman arm-to-sector shaft	200 to 225	276 to 311
Steering gear-to-frame	60 to 65	81 to 88
Steering shaft flexible coupling nut	20 to 30	27 to 39
Steering wheel attaching nut	30 to 40	39 to 54
Steering column stud nuts	20 to 37	27 to 50
Steering column adjustment bracket nuts	20 to 37	27 to 50
Steering power cylinder-to-center link	43 to 47	59 to 63
Power cylinder-to-bracket	18 to 24	25 to 32

1 General information

The front suspension on all models is of the spring-on-upper-arm type. This is comprised of a spindle which is mounted by balljoints to the upper and lower suspension arms which pivot at their inner ends and are located by a forward-facing lower strut. The spring and shock absorber are mounted between the spring seat on the upper arm and the top of the spring tower.

The rear suspension consists of two leaf-type springs mounted to the rear axle by U-bolts. Shock absorbers are attached at their upper ends to brackets on the chassis and their lower ends to studs on the U-bolt plates.

Steering is of the recirculating ball type with power assistance optional. The steering wheel is connected to the gear through a collapsible shaft and flexible coupling.

2 Sway bar and insulators – removal and installation

1   Raise the vehicle and support it securely on jack stands.
2   Disconnect the links at both ends of the sway bar.
3   Unbolt both of the attachment brackets and remove the bar assembly.
4   Lubricate the insulators and contacting parts of the sway bar with rubber lubricant. Slide the new insulators into place on the bar.

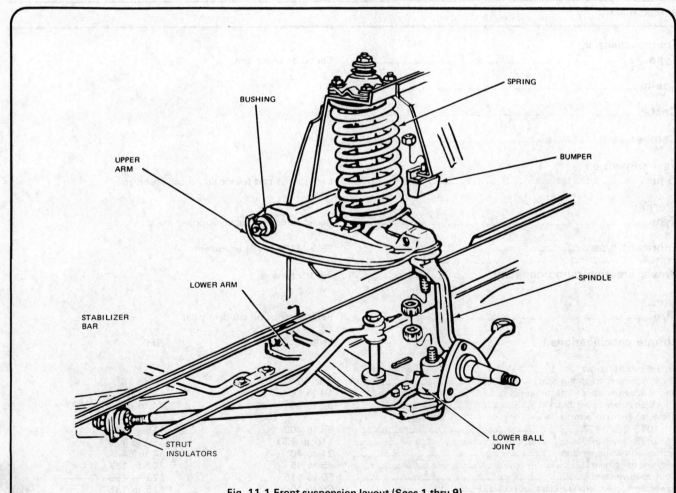

Fig. 11.1 Front suspension layout (Secs 1 thru 9)

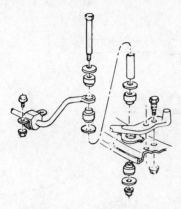

Fig. 11.2 Sway bar end link components (Sec 3)

5   Install the brackets and tighten the bolts to specification.
6   Reconnect the sway bar end links.
7   Lower the vehicle.

3   Sway bar link bushings – removal and installaiton

1   Raise the vehicle and support it securely on jack stands.
2   Remove the nuts, washers from the sway bar end link bolt and remove the bolt.
3   Assemble the cup-type washer and the new insulator bushing.
4   Install the end link through the sway bar end and install the spacer, cup washers and new bushings, referring to the accompanying figure.
5   Install the bolt with the bolt head at the top and tighten to specification.
6   Lower the vehicle.

4   Front coil spring – removal and installation

1   Install wood blocks under the upper suspension arm as shown in the accompanying figure.
2   Remove the front shock absorbers as described in Section 9.
3   Raise the vehicle and support it securely on jack stands.
4   Remove the front wheels, brake caliper and disc as described in Chapter 9.
5   Use a spring compressor tool to compress the spring.
6   Remove the two nuts attaching the upper suspension arm to the spring tower and swing away from the tower.
7   Slowly and carefully release the spring compressor tension and remove the tool from the spring. Remove the spring.
8   To install, position the upper insulator on the spring and secure it with tape.
9   Place the spring in position in the spring tower and compress it with the tool.
10 Swing the upepr suspension arm into position, install the bolts and nuts and tighten to specification.
11 Slowly release the compressor tool tension and guide the spring into position in the upper spring seat. The tail end must be within $\frac{1}{2}$ in (13 mm) of the tab on the spring as shown in the accompanying figure.
12 Remove the spring compressor.
13 Install the brake caliper, disc and shock absorber.
14 Remove the blocks from the upper suspension arm, install the wheels and lower the vehicle.

5   Lower strut – removal and installation

1   Position wood blocks under the upper suspension arm.
2   Raise the vehicle and support it securely on jack stands.
3   Remove the nut at the front end of the strut.
4   Remove the two strut-to-lower arm nuts. Tap on the strut in an upward direction to release the bolts from the serrations. Remove the strut from the lower suspension arm.

Fig. 11.3 Wood block installed between upper suspension arm and base of spring tower (Secs 4 thru 9)

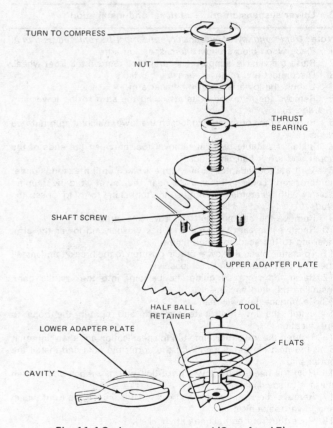

Fig. 11.4 Spring compressor tool (Secs 4 and 7)

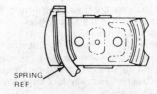

Fig. 11.5 Proper location of front spring upper end (Secs 4 and 7)

Fig. 11.6 Front strut installation at crossmember (Sec 5)

5   Use two pry bars at the rear of the front washer to pry forward to separate the inner and outer sleeves. Remove the components, referring to the accompanying figure.

6   To install, position the strut into the front crossmember and onto the lower suspension arm. Install the strut-to-arm nuts and bolts and tighten to specification.

7   Install the strut-to-crossmember components, referring to the figure, and tighten the nut to specification.

8   Remove the blocks from the upper arm and lower the vehicle.

Note: *The caster and camber must be checked after strut removal and/or replacement.*

6   Lower suspension arm – removal and installation

Note: *Upper and lower suspension arms must be replaced as a unit.*

1   Place wood blocks under the suspension arm.

2   Raise the vehicle, support it securely and remove the front wheel.

3   Disconnect and remove the sway bar links.

4   Unbolt the lower strut at the lower arm.

5   Remove the nuts and bolts attaching the strut to the lower arm (Section 5).

6   Remove the cotter pin and loosen the lower balljoint stud nut two turns.

7   Install a suitable balljoint removal tool between the ends of the upper and lower balljoint studs.

8   Turn the tool adaptor screw with a wrench until the stud is under compression. Loosen the spindle near the lower stud by tapping sharply with a hammer. Do not use the tool alone to try to loosen the stud.

9   Remove the balljoint stud and lower the arm.

10 Remove the cam bolt, nut and lock washer and lower the arm, referring to the accompanying figure.

11 To install, place the lower arm in position to the bracket and install the cam bolt, washer and nut, loosely.

12 Raise the arm and guide the balljoint into the spindle bore, installing the stud nut loosely.

13 Reconnect the sway bar.

14 Install the lower strut to the arm and tighten the bolts to specification.

15 Tighten the lower balljoint stud to specification and then tighten it until the next slot is aligned with the cotter pin hole and install the cotter pin.

16 Hold the head of the lower pivot bolt with a wrench and tighten the nut to specification.

17 Remove the wood blocks and jack stands, install the front wheel and lower the vehicle.

18 Have the front end alignment checked.

7   Upper suspension arm – removal and installation

Note: *Upper and lower suspension arm should be replaced as a set.*

1   Position blocks under the upper suspension arm. Raise the vehicle, support it securely and remove the front wheel.

2   Remove the shock absorbers (Sec 9).

3   Compress the spring with a spring compressor tool (Sec 4).

4   Place a jack stand under the lower arm, remove the cotter pin from the upper balljoint stud and loosen the nut two turns.

5   Seat a suitable balljoint remover tool between the ends of the upper and lower balljoint studs.

6   Use a wrench to turn the tool until the studs are under pressure.

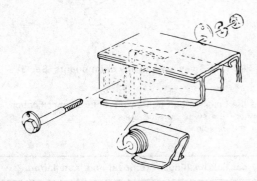

Fig. 11.7 Lower suspension arm bolt installation (Sec 6)

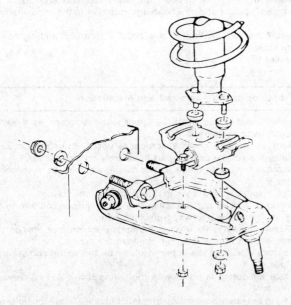

Fig. 11.8 Upper suspension components (Secs 7 and 9)

Fig. 11.9 Spindle installation (Sec 8)

Strike sharply with a hammer near the upper stud to release it. A combination of tool pressure and loosening with a hammer, not just the tool alone must be used.

7   Remove the nut and lift the stud from the spindle.

8   From inside the engine compartment, remove the upper inner shaft attaching nuts and remove the upper arm.

9   Clean the grease and loose dirt from the upper arm suspension parts.

10   To install, place the upper arm and spring seat assembly in position on the spring tower and install the attaching nuts.

11   Install the upper balljoint stud in the top of the spindle and tighten the nut to specification. Tighten the nut further so that the cotter pin hole lines up and install the cotter pin.

12   Release and remove the spring compressor tool.

13   Install the shock absorber, brake assembly and front wheel.

14   Remove the wood blocks and lower the vehicle.

15   Check the front end alignment.

8   Spindle – removal and installation

1   Place wood blocks under the front suspension arm.

2   Raise the vehicle, support it securely and remove the front wheel.

3   Remove the front hub and brake assembly as described in Chapter 9.

4   Disconnect the tie rod end, using a 'pickle fork' type wedge tool or a bearing puller.

5   Remove the balljoint stud cotter pins and loosen the nuts two turns.

6   Install a suitable balljoint removal tool between the upper and lower balljoint studs and turn the tool with a wrench so that considerable pressure is exerted at the studs.

7   Strike the spindle sharply with a hammer near the studs to break them loose.

8   Place a jack under the lower suspension arm.

9   Remove the balljoint stud nuts and lower the jack to remove the spindle.

10   To install, place the spindle onto the lower stud and install the nut to specification. Tighten the nut further if necessary to install the cotter pin.

11   Use the jack to raise the lower arm, guiding the upper balljont stud into the spindle. Install the nut to specification and remove the jack.

12   Re-connect the tie rod end and install the nut and cotter pin.

13   Install the brake assembly wheel.

14   Remove the wood blocks from the upper suspension arm and lower the vehicle.

15   Check the front end alignment.

9   Front shock absorber – removal and installation

1   From inside the engine compartment, remove the three shock absorber upper attaching nuts, referring to the accompanying figure.

2   Place wood blocks under the upper suspension arm to support it.

3   Raise the vehicle and support it securely.

4   Remove the nuts attaching the lower end of the shock absorber to the lower suspension arm.

5   The shock absorber can now be lifted from the spring tower.

6   Remove the bracket and insulators from the spring assembly.

7   Install the mounting brackets and insulators on the new shock absorber.

8   Lower the shock absorber into the spring tower, seating the studs into the pivot plate holes.

9   Install the attaching nuts and brackets, referring to the accompanying figures and tighten to specification.

10   Remove the wood blocks and lower the vehicle.

10   Rear leaf spring – removal and installation

1   Raise the vehicle and support it securely.

2   Remove the rear wheels.

3   Place a jack under the axle housing and raise it sufficiently to remove the weight from the spring.

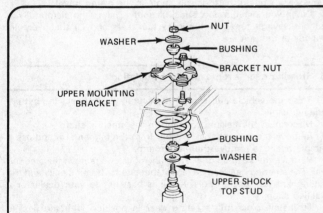

Fig. 11.10 Front shock absorber upper attachment (Sec 9)

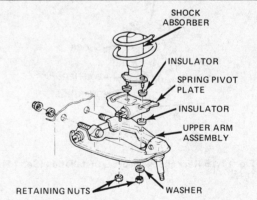

Fig. 11.11 Front shock absorber lower attachment (Sec 9)

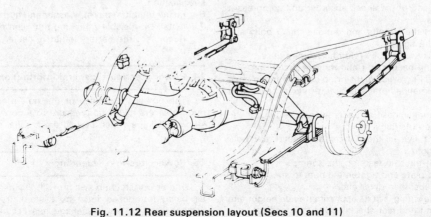

Fig. 11.12 Rear suspension layout (Secs 10 and 11)

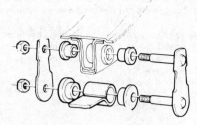

Fig. 11.13 Shackle components (Sec 10)

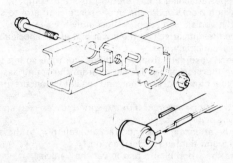

Fig. 11.14 Leaf spring front hanger components (Sec 10)

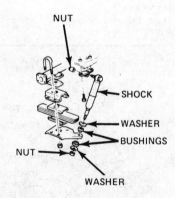

Fig. 11.15 Rear shock absorber installation (Sec 11)

4   Disconnect the lower end of the shock absorber and compress it upward and out of the way.
5   Remove the nuts from the U-bolts and remove the U-bolts and spring plate, referring to the figures.
6   Remove the rear shackle assembly, referring to the figure.
7   Remove the front spring hanger bolt and remove the spring.
8   If the bushings in the spring eyes are distorted or worn and in need of replacement, it is recommended that this be left to your dealer or a properly equipped shop.
9   To install, place the spring in position under the axle and install the shackle assembly, with the nuts finger tight.
10   Place the spring front eye in the hanger and insert the bolt, tightening the nut finger tight.
11   Lower the jack so that the axle rests on the spring.
12   Install the U-bolts and plate and tighten the nuts to specification.
13   Reconnect the shock absorber lower end.
14   Lower the axle until the spring is at its approximate ride height and tighten the front hanger nut and rear shackle bolts to specification.
15   Remove the jack and lower the vehicle.

11   Rear shock absorber – removal and installation

1   Raise the rear of the vehicle, support it securely and remove the rear wheels.
2   Remove the lower shock absorber nut and compress the shock upward.
3   Remove the upper nut and withdraw the shock absorber from the vehicle.
4   Install the new shock absorber on the upper mounting and install the nut finger tight.
5   Extend the shock absorber and insert it through the U-bolt plate with the washers and bushings in the order shown in the figure. Install the nut and tighten to specification.
6   Tighten the upper nut to specification.
7   Install the wheels and lower the vehicle.

12   Shock absorbers – inspection

1   The most common test of the shock absorber's damping is simply to bounce the rear corners of the vehicle several times and observe whether or not the car stops bouncing once the action is stopped by you. A slight rebound and settling indicates good damping, but if the vehicle continues to bounce several times, the shock absorbers must be replaced.
2   If your shock absorbers stand up to the bounce test, crawl beneath your car and visually inspect the shock body for signs of fluid leakage, punctures or deep dents in the metal of the body, and that the shock absorber is straight from several engines. If the piston rod is bent, you will not be able to see that it is. A bend in the shock body or signs of the upper portion of the shock body rubbing on the lower section will let you know. Replace any shock absorber which is leaking or damaged, in spite of proper damping indicated in the bounce test.
3   When you have removed a shock absorber, pull the piston rod out and push it back in several times to check for smooth operation throughout the travel of the piston rod. Replace the shock absorber if it gives any signs of hard or soft spots in the piston travel.
4   When you install a new shock absorber, pump the piston fully in and out several times to lubricate the seals and fill the hydraulic sections of the unit.

13   Steering gear – removal and installation

1   Raise the vehicle and support it securely. Disconnect the battery negative cable.
2   Disconnect the flexible coupling to the steering shaft.
3   Remove the nut and lock washer from the pitman arm and use a suitable puller to remove the pitman arm.
4   Remove the steering gear attaching bolts and remove the steering gear. The steering gear can be rebuilt, but due to its complexity and the requirement for special tools, repair is best left to your dealer or a qualified shop.
5   To install, place the steering gear in position with the flexible coupling on the steering shaft, install the attaching bolts and tighten to specification.
6   Install the pitman arm, washer and nut, tightening to specification.
7   Install the flexible attaching nuts and tighten to specification.
8   Reconnect the battery negative cable.

14   Power steering – general information

The power steering is of the non-integral type. A pulley driven pump delivers hydraulic pressure to a power cylinder mounted in the steering linkage which assists the manual steering gear.

15   Power steering – bleeding

1   The power steering system will only need bleeding in the event of air being introduced into the system, ie, where pipes have been disconnected or where leakage has occurred. To bleed the system proceed as described in the following paragraphs.

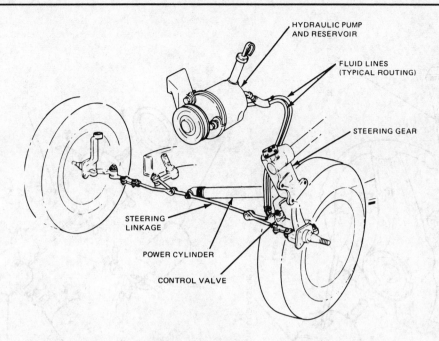

Fig. 11.16 Typical steering layout (Secs 13 and 14)

HYDRAULIC PUMP
AND RESERVOIR

FLUID LINES
(TYPICAL ROUTING)

STEERING GEAR

STEERING
LINKAGE

POWER CYLINDER

CONTROL VALVE

2   Open the hood and check the fluid level in the fluid reservoir. Top up if necessary using the specified type of fluid.

3   If fluid is added, allow two minutes then run the engine at approximately 1500 rpm. Slowly turn the steering wheel from lock-to-lock, while checking and topping-up fluid level until the level remains steady, and no more bubbles appear in the reservoir. Do not hold the steering wheel in the far right or left positions.

4   Clean and refit the reservoir cap, and close the hood.

16 Power steering pump – removal and installation

1   Loosen the pump adjusting bolt and retaining bolts.

2   Push the pump in toward the engine, and remove the drivebelt.

3   Disconnect the power system fluid lines from the pump and drain the fluid into a suitable container.

4   Plug, or tape over, the end of the lines to prevent dirt ingress.

5   If necessary, remove the alternator drivebelt(s) as described in Chapter 2.

6   Remove the bolts attaching the pump to the engine bracket and remove the pump. **Note**: *On some engine installations it may be necessary to remove the pump complete with bracket.*

7   Installation is a direct reversal of the removal procedure. Ensure that the fluid lines are tightened to the specified torque, top-up the system with an approved fluid, adjust the alternator drivebelt tension.

17 Steering wheel – removal and installation

1   Disconnect the battery negative cable.

2   Remove the horn cover attaching screws from the underside of the steering wheel.

3   Lift off the horn cover and disconnect the horn terminals.

4   Remove the steering wheel attaching nut.

5   With the steering wheel in the straight ahead position, use a suitable steering wheel puller to remove the wheel. **Note**: *Do not strike the end of the steering shaft or use a knock-off type puller.*

6   Install the wheel, making sure that the front wheels and the steering wheel are in the corresponding straight ahead position.

7   Install the attaching nut and tighten to specification.

8   Install the horn cover and screws.

9   Connect the battery negative cable and check for proper operation.

18 Steering column – removal and installation

1   Disconenct the battery negative cable.

2   Remove the steering wheel (Sec 17).

3   Remove the column trim shrouds and the instrument panel below the steering wheel.

4   Disconnect the automatic transmission column shaft indicator cable (if equipped).

5   Disconnect the turn signal and backup lamp switch wiring.

6   Disconnect the automatic transmission shift cable (if equipped).

7   Disengage the dust boot at the base of the steering column and remove the steering shaft flex coupling.

8   Remove the nuts securing the steering column to the brake pedal support.

9   Lower the steering column, disconnect the ignition switch wiring and carefully remove the steering column from under the dash panel.

10   Prior to installation, loosen the column adjustment brackets on the brake pedal support.

11   Insert the steering column lower shaft into the dash panel opening. Position the shaft flange against the flexible coupling and insert a $\frac{1}{4}$ in (6.35 mm) rod between the fabric and flange. Install the attaching nuts to specification, making sure that the flex coupling is installed flat. Use the pry bar to adjust the steering shaft up or down until the proper flatness is achieved.

12   Connect the ignition switch wiring.

13   Place the steering column over the pedal supports studs, install the attaching nuts and tighten to specification. Make sure the shift tube is centered on the steering tube to prevent rubbing.

14   Tighten the pedal support adjustment bracket nuts to specification.

15   Remove the rod from the flexible coupling.

16   On automatic transmission column shift models, connect and adjust the shift cable.

17   Install the dust boot on the dash panel, seating the lip of the boot into the panel opening.

18   Connect the turn signal and back up lamp switch wiring.

19   On column shift automatic transmission equipped vehicles, connect and adjust the indicator cable.

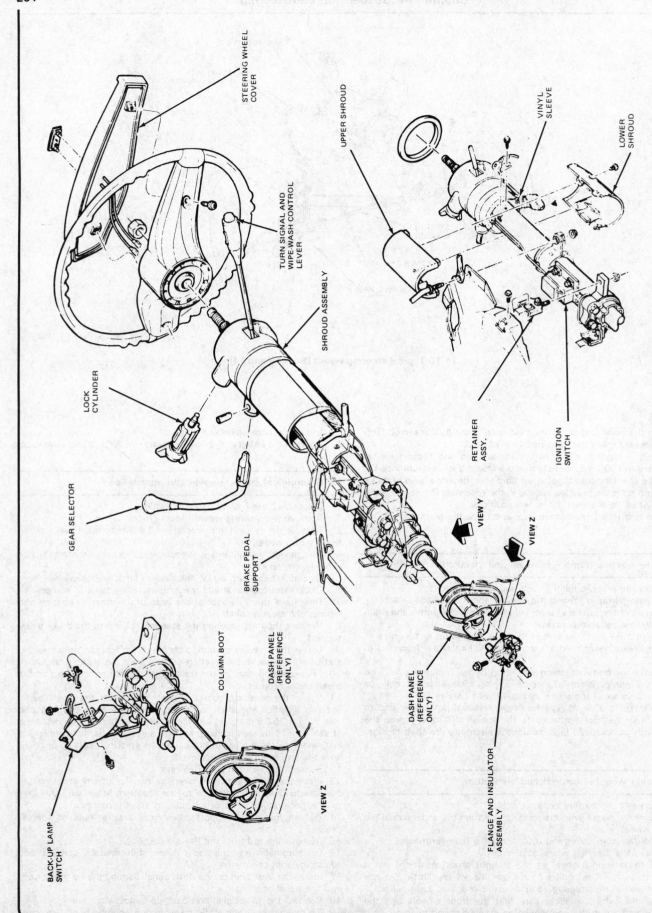

STEERING WHEEL COVER

UPPER SHROUD

VINYL SLEEVE

LOWER SHROUD

TURN SIGNAL AND WIPE-WASH CONTROL LEVER

SHROUD ASSEMBLY

RETAINER ASSY.

IGNITION SWITCH

LOCK CYLINDER

VIEW Y

GEAR SELECTOR

BRAKE PEDAL SUPPORT

VIEW Z

DASH PANEL (REFERENCE ONLY)

COLUMN BOOT

DASH PANEL (REFERENCE ONLY)

BACK-UP LAMP SWITCH

FLANGE AND INSULATOR ASSEMBLY

VIEW Z

Fig. 11.17 Steering column components (Sec 18)

20 Install the column trim shrouds and the lower instrument trim panel.
21 Install the steering wheel.
22 Connect the negative battery cable and check the steering column for proper operation.

19 Steering angles and front wheel alignment

1 Accurate front wheel alignment is essential for good steering and tire wear. Before considering the steering angle, check that the tires are correctly inflated, that the front wheels are not bent, the hub bearings are not worn or incorrectly adjusted and that the steering linkage is in good order, without looseness or wear at the joints.
2 Toe-in is the amount by which the distance between the front inside edges of the roadwheels (measured at hub height) is less than the distance measured between the rear inside edges.
3 Front wheel alignment (toe-in) checks are best carried out with modern setting equipment but a reasonably accurate alternative is by means of the following procedure.
4 Place the car on level ground with the wheels in the 'straight-ahead' position.
5 Obtain or make a toe-in gauge. One may easily be made from a length of rod or tubing, cranked to clear the sump or bellhousing and having a setscrew and lock nut at one end.
6 With the gauge, measure the distance between the two inner wheel rims at hub height at the front of the wheel.
7 Rotate the roadwheel through 180° (half a turn) by pushing or pulling the car and then measure the distance again at hub height between the inner wheel rims at the rear of the roadwheel. This measurement should either be the same as the one just taken or greater by not more than 0.28 in (7 mm).
8 Where the toe-in is found to be incorrect loosen the lock nuts on each trackrod, also the flexible bellows clips and rotate each trackrod by an equal amount until the correct toe-in is obtained. Tighten the trackrod-end lock nuts while the balljoints are held in the center of their arcs of travel. It is imperative that the lengths of the trackrods are always equal otherwise the wheel angles on turns will be incorrect. If new components have been fitted, set the roadwheels in the 'straight-ahead' position and also centralize the steering wheel. Now adjust the lengths of the trackrods by turning them so that the tie-rod end balljoint studs will drop easily into the eyes of the steering arms. Measure the distances between the centers of the balljoints and the grooves on the inner ends of the trackrods and adjust. If necessary, so that they are equal. This is an initial setting only and precise adjustment must be carried out by a properly equipped shop.

20 Wheels and tires

1 Check the tire pressures (cold) weekly.
2 Inspect the tire walls and treads for damage and remove any stones trapped in the tread pattern.
3 Never mix tires of different construction on the same axle.
4 Inspect the inner sides of the wheels periodically for rust or corrosion, particularly alloy wheels.
5 Check the wheel lug holes for rust, cracks or elongation.

Chapter 12 Bodywork

Contents

Specifications

Torque specifications

	ft-lb	Nm
Bumper-to-isolator bolts	33 to 50	48 to 67
Window glass regulator-to-inner panel screws	6 to 11	9 to 14
Guide-to-glass bracket	6 to 11	9 to 14
Power window motor drive attaching screws	4.4 to 7.4	5.6 to 9.6

1   General information

Models are available in 2-door and 4-door sedan body styles.

The body is of unitized, all-welded construction and certain components which are particularly vulnerable to accident damage can be replaced by unbolting them and installing replacement items. These include the fenders, inner fender skirts, radiator support panel, grille and bumpers.

2   Body exterior – maintenance

1   The condition of your vehicle's bodywork is of considerable importance as it is on this that the resale value will mainly depend. It is much more difficult to repair neglected bodywork than to replace mechanical assemblies. The hidden portions of the body, such as the wheel arches, fender skirts, the underframe and the engine compartment, are equally important, although obviously not requiring such frequent attention as the immediately visible paint.

2   Once a year or every 12 000 miles it is a sound idea to visit your local dealer and have the underside of the body steam cleaned. All traces of dirt and oil will have to be removed and the underside can then be inspected carefully for rust, damaged hydraulic pipes, frayed electrical wiring and similar trouble areas. The front suspension should be greased on completion of this job.

3   At the same time, clean the engine and the engine compartment either using a steam cleaner or a water-soluble cleaner.

4   The wheel arches and fender skirts should be given particular attention as undercoating can easily come away here and stones and dirt thrown up from the wheels can soon cause the paint to chip and flake, and so allow rust to set in. If rust is found, clean down to the bare metal and apply an anti-rust paint.

5   The bodywork should be washed once a week or when dirty. Thoroughly wet the vehicle to soften the dirt and then wash down with a soft sponge and plenty of clean water. If the surplus dirt is not washed off very gently, in time it will wear the paint down.

6   Spots of tar or bitumen coating thrown up from the road surfaces are best removed with a cloth soaked in a cleaner made especially for this purpose.

7   Once every six months, or more frequently depending on the weather conditions, give the bodywork and chrome trim a thoroughly good wax polish. If a chrome cleaner is used to remove rust on any of the vehicle's plated parts, remember that the cleaner can also remove part of the chrome, so use it sparingly.

3 Upholstery and carpets – maintenance

1   Remove the carpets or mats and thoroughly vacuum clean the interior of the vehicle every three months or more frequently if necessary.
2   Beat out the carpets and vacuum clean them if they are very dirty. If the upholstery is soiled apply an upholstery cleaner with a damp sponge and wipe off with a clean dry cloth.
3   Consult your local dealer or auto parts store for cleaners made especially for newer automotive upholstery fabric. Always test the cleaner in an inconspicuous place.

4 Roof covering – maintenance

Under no circumstances try to clean any external vinyl roof covering with detergents, caustic soap or petroleum based cleaners. Plain soap and water is all that is required, with a soft brush to clean dirt that may be ingrained. Wash the covering as frequently as the rest of the vehicle.

5 Body damage – minor repair

See photo sequences on pages 278 and 279.

Repair of minor scratches in the vehicle's bodywork

If the scratch is very superficial, and does not penetrate to the metal of the bodywork, repair is very simple. Lightly rub the area if the scratch with a paintwork renovator, or a very fine cutting paste, to remove loose paint from the scratch and to clear the surrounding bodywork of wax polish. Rinse the area with clean water.

Apply touch-up paint to the scratch using a thin paintbrush; continue to apply thin layers of paint until the surface of the paint in the scratch is level with the surrounding paintwork. Allow the new paint at least two weeks to harden: then blend it into the surrounding paintwork by rubbing the paintwork, in the scratch area, with a paintwork renovator or a very fine cutting paste. Finally, apply wax polish.

An alternative to painting over the scratch is to use a paint transfer. Use the same preparation for the affected area, then simply pick a patch of a suitable size to cover the scratch completely. Hold the patch against the scratch and burnish its backing paper; the paper will adhere to the paintwork, freeing itself from the backing paper at the same time. Polish the affected area to blend the patch into the surrounding paintwork.

Where the scratch has penetrated right through to the metal of the bodywork, causing the metal to rust, a different repair technique is required. Remove any loose rust from the bottom of the scratch with a penknife, then apply rust inhibiting paint to prevent the formation of rust in the future. Using a rubber or nylon applicator, fill the scratch with bodystopper paste. If required, this paste can be mixed with cellulose thinners to provide a very thin paste which is ideal for filling narrow scratches. Before the stopper paste in the scratch hardens, wrap a piece of smooth cotton rag around the top of a finger. Dip the finger in cellulose thinners and then quickly sweep it across the surface of the stopper-paste in the scratch; this will ensure that the surface of the stopper-paste is slightly hollowed. The scratch can now be painted over as described earlier in this Section.

Repair of dents in the vehicle's bodywork

When deep denting of the vehicle's bodywork has taken place, the first task is to pull the dent out, until the affected bodywork almost attains its original shape. There is little point in trying to restore the original shape completely, as the metal in the damaged area will have stretched on impact and cannot be reshaped fully to its original contour. It is better to bring the level of the dent up to a point which is about $\frac{1}{8}$-in (3 mm) below the level of the surrounding bodywork. In cases where the dent is very shallow anyway, it is not worth trying to pull it out at all.

If the underside of the dent is accessible, it can be hammered out gently from behind, using a mallet with a wooden or plastic head. While doing this, hold a suitable block of wood firmly against the impact from the hammer blows and thus prevent a large area of the bodywork from being 'belled-out'.

Should the dent be in a section of the bodywork which has double skin or some other factor making it inaccessible from behind, a different technique is called for. Drill several small holes through the metal inside the area – particularly in the deeper section. Then screw long self-tapping screws into the holes just sufficiently for them to gain a good purchase in the metal. Now the dent can be pulled out by pulling on the protruding heads of the screws with a pair of pliers.

The next stage of the repair is the removal of the paint from the damaged area, and from an inch or so of the surrounding 'sound' bodywork. This is accomplished most easily by using a wire brush or abrasive pad on a power drill, although it can be done just as effectively by hand, using sheets of sandpaper. To complete the preparation for filling, score the surface of the bare metal with a screwdriver or the tang of a file, or alternatively, drill small holes in the affected area. This will provide a really good 'key' for the filler paste.

To complete the repair see the Section on filling and re-spraying.

Repair of rust holes or gashes in the vehicle's bodywork

Remove all paint from the affected area and from an inch or so of the surrounding 'sound' bodywork, using an abrasive pad or a wire brush on a power drill. If these are not available a few sheets of sandpaper will do the job just as effectively. With the paint removed you will able to gauge the severity of the corrosion and therefore decide whether to renew the whole panel (if this is possible) or to repair the affected area. New body panels are not as expensive as most people think and it is often quicker and more satisfactory to fit a new panel than to attempt to repair large areas of corrosion.

Remove all fittings from the affected area except those which will act as a guide to the original shape of the damaged bodywork (eg headlamp shells etc.). Then, using tin snips of a hacksaw blade, remove all loose metal and any other metal badly affected by corrosion. Hammer the edges of the hole inward in order to create a slight depression for the filler paste.

Wire brush the affected area to remove the powdery rust from the surface of the remaining metal. Paint the affected area with rust inhibiting paint; if the back of the rusted area is accessible treat this also.

Before filling can take place it will be necessary to block the hole in some way. This can be achieved by the use of Zinc gauze or Aluminum tape.

Zinc gauze is probably the best meterial to use for a large hole. Cut a piece to the approximate size and shape of the hole to be filled, then position it in the hole so that its edges are below the level of the surrounding bodywork. It can be retained in position by several blobs of filler paste around its periphery.

Aluminum tape should be used for small or very narrow holes. Pull a piece off the roll and trim it to the approximate size and shape required, then pull off the backing paper (if used) and stick the tape over the hole; it can be overlapped if the thickness of one piece of insufficient. Burnish down the edges of the tape with the handle of a screwdriver or similar tool, to ensure that the tap is securely attached to the metal underneath.

Having blocked off the hole, the affected area must now be filled and sprayed – see Section on bodywork filling and re-spraying.

Bodywork repairs – filling and re-spraying

Before using this Section, see the Section on dents, deep scratches, rust holes and gash repairs.

Many types of bodyfiller are available, but generally speaking those proprietary kits which contain a tin of filler paste and a tube of resin hardener are best for this type of repair. A wide, flexible plastic or nylon applicator will be found invaluable for imparting a smooth and well contoured finish to the surface of the filler.

Mix up a little filler on a clean piece of card or board – measure the hardener carefully (follow the maker's instructions on the pack) otherwise the filler will set too rapidly or too slowly.

Using the applicator apply the filler paste to the prepared area; draw the applicator across the surface of the filler to achieve the correct contour and to level the filler surface. As soon as a contour that approximates the correct one is achieved, stop working the paste – if you carry on too long the paste will become sticky and begin to 'pick up' on the applicator. Continue to add thin layers of filler paste at twenty-minute intervals until the level of the filler is just proud of the surounding bodywork.

Once the filler has hardened, excess can be removed using a metal plane or file. From then on, progressively finer grades of sandpaper should be used, starting with a 40 grade production paper and finishing with 400 grade wet and dry paper. Always wraps the sandpaper around a flat rubber, cork or wooden block — otherwise the surface of the filler will not be completely flat. During the smoothing of the filler surface the wet and dry paper should be periodically rinsed in water. This will ensure that a very smooth finish is imparted to the filler at the final stage.

At this stage the repair area should be surrounded by a ring of bare metal, which in turn should be encircled by the finely 'feathered' edge of the good paintwork. Rinse the repair area wth clean water, until all of the dust produced by the rubbing down operation has gone.

Spray the whole repair area with a light coat of primer — this will show up any imperfections in the surface of the filler. Repair these imperfections with fresh filler paste or bodystopper, and once more smooth the surface with sandpaper. If bodystopper is used, it can be mixed with cellulose thinners to form a really thin paste which is ideal for filling small holes. Repeat this spray and repair procedure until you are satisfied that the surface of the filler, and the feathered edge of the paintwork are perfect. Clean the repair area with clean water and allow to dry fully.

The repair area is now ready for final spraying. Paint spraying must be carried out in warm, dry, windless and dust free atmosphere. These conditions can be created artificially if you have access to a large indoor working area but if you are forced to work in the open, you will have to pick your day very carefully. If you are working indoors, dousing the floor in the work area with clean water will help to settle the dust which would otherwise be in the atmosphere. If the repair area is confined to one body panel, mask off the surrounding panels; this will help to minimize the effects of a slight mismatch in paint colors. Bodywork fittings (eg chrome strips, door handles, etc.) will also need to be masked off. Use genuine masking tape and several thicknesses of newspaper for the masking operations.

Before commencing to spray, agitate the aerosol can thoroughly, then spray a test area (an old tin, or similar) until the technique is mastered. Cover the repair area with a thick coat of primer; the thickness should be built up using several thin layers of paint rather than one thick one. Using 400-grade wet-and-dry paper, rub down the surface of the primer until it is really smooth. While doing this, the work area should be thoroughly doused with water, and the wet-and-dry paper periodically rinsed in water. Allow to dry before spraying on more paint.

Spray on the top coat, again building up the thickness by using several thin layers of paint. Start spraying in the center of the repair area and then using a circular motion, work outwards until the whole repair area and about 2 inches of the surrounding original paintwork is covered. Remove all masking material 10 to 15 minutes after spraying on the final coat of paint. Allow the new paint at least two weeks to harden, then, using a paintwork renovator or a very fine cutting paste, blend the edge of the paint into the existing paintwork. Finally, apply wax polish.

6 Body damage – major repair

1　Major damage must be repaired by competent mechanics with the necessary welding and hydraulic straightening equipment.
2　If the damage has been serious it is vital that the body be checked for correct alignment as otherwise the handling of the vehicle will suffer and many other faults – such as excessive tire wear, and wear in the transmission and steering – may occur.
3　There is a special body jig which most body repair shops have and to ensure that all is correct it is important that this jig be used for all major repair work.

7 Maintenance – hinges and locks

Every 3000 miles (5000 km) or 3 months the door, hood and trunk hinges and locks should be lubricated with a few drops of oil. The door striker plates should also be given a thin smear of grease to reduce wear and ensure free movement.

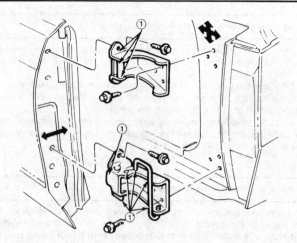

Fig. 12.1 Front door adjustment and lubrication points (numbered arrows) (Secs 8, 9 and 10)

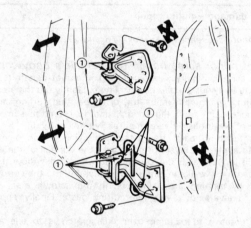

Fig. 12.2 Rear door adjustment and lubrication points (numbered arrows) (Secs, 8, 9 and 10)

8 Door – removal and installation

1　Use a pencil or scribe to mark the hinge location for ease of reinstallation.
2　With an assistant supporting the weight of the door, remove the upper and lower hinge retaining bolts. Lift the door away and stand it on an old blanket.
3　Installation is a reversal of removal, using the marks scribed around the hinges in step 1 as a guide. If it is necessary to realign the door, refer to Section 10.

9 Door hinges – removal and installation

1　Remove the door as described in Section 8.
2　Mark the location of the hinge on the door, remove the bolts and lift away the hinges.
3　Repeat this procedure for the body mounted hinges.
4　Installation is a reversal of removal. If new hinges are installed, it will probably be necessary to align the door as described in Section 10.

10 Door – alignment

1　The door hinge bolt holes are elongated or enlarged so that hinge and door alignment can be accomplished.

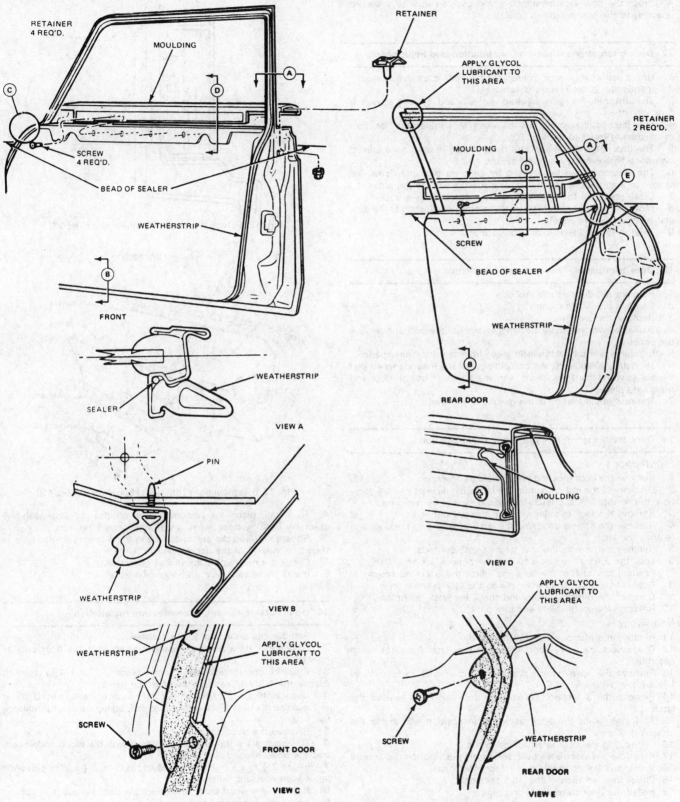

Fig. 12.3 Door weatherstripping installation (Sec 11)

2 Loosen the hinge bolts just enough so that the door can be moved with a padded pry bar.

3 After the door has been adjusted, tighten the hinge bolts and check the door fit.

4 Repeat this operation until the proper fit is obtained.

5 After the alignment is made, check the striker plate for proper closing.

11 Door weatherstripping – removal and installation

1 Remove the old weatherstripping by pulling it away from the door to break it loose from the adhesive.

2 Clean the old adhesive off the door.

3 Apply new adhesive to the door.

4   Press the new weatherstripping into position until it is secure, referring to the accompanying figure.

12 Door latch striker – removal, installation and adjustment

1   Use a pair of vise grips to unscrew the door latch striker stud.
2   Installation is the reverse of removal.
3   The striker stud may be adjusted vertically and laterally as well as fore-and-aft.
4   The latch striker must not be used to compensate for door misalignment (refer to Section 10).
5   The door latch striker can also be shimmed to obtain the correct clearance between the latch and striker.
6   The clearance can be checked by cleaning the latch jams and striker area and applying a thin layer of dark grease to the striker.
7   Close and open the door, noting the pattern of the grease.
8   Move the striker assembly laterally to provide a flush fit at the door and pillar or quarter panel.
9   Tighten the striker stud after adjustment.

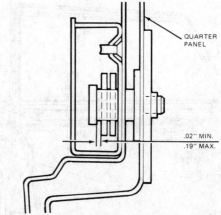

Fig. 12.4 Door latch striker adjustment (Sec 12)

13 Door trim panel – removal and installation

1   Remove the door handle and cup.
2   Remove the window crank.
3   Remove the armrest.
4   Use a screwdriver to pry the panel away from the door and remove the panel.
5   Carefully peel the watershield away from the door inner panel.
6   To install, position the watershield against the inner panel so that the adhesive on the back aligns with the adhesive on the door and press into place.
7   The rest of installation is the reverse of removal.

14 Door latch assembly – removal and installation

Front door
1   Remove the door trim and watershield as described in Section 13.
2   Disconnect the rod ends from the latch. Because of its configuration, the remote link and latch-to-lock rod cannot be removed.
3   Remove the lock cylinder rod from the cylinder lever.
4   Remove the screws attaching the latch assembly to the door and remove the latch.
5   Remove the remote link and latch-to-cylinder rods.
6   Lock the cylinder rod by installing the remote link and latch.
7   Position the latch in the door and install the attaching screws.
8   Connect the latch-to-cylinder rod to the lock cylinder lever.
9   Connect the remaining rods and check the latch operation.
10   Reinstall the watershield and trim panel.

Rear door
11   Remove the trim panel and watershield.
12   Disconnect the rear door latch actuating rod from the latch assembly.
13   Remove the screw which attaches the door latch bellcrank and remove the bellcrank.
14   Remove the 3 screws retaining the door latch and remove the latch.
15   To install, place the latch assembly in position and install the attaching screws.
16   Connecting the door latch actuating rod.
17   Assemble the door latch bellcrank to the push button rod control link and install the bellcrank to the door inner panel.
18   Check the operation of the latch assembly.
19   Install the door watershield and trim.

15 Door latch remote control – removal and installation

1   Remove the door trim panel and watershield.
2   Remove the 3 attaching nuts and disengage the control assembly.
3   To disengage the assembly from the diamond shaped slot in the inner door panel, squeeze the remote rod clip and then free the rod. Remove the assembly from the door panel.

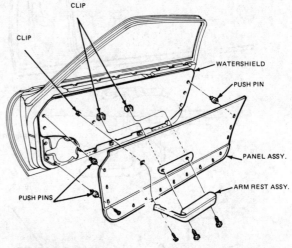

Fig. 12.5 Typical door trim panel installation (Sec 13)

4   To install, place the remote control on the rod and push the assembly into the door panel. Install the 3 attaching nuts.
5   Squeeze the rod clip and install it into the diamond-shaped hole as shown in View B of the accompanying figure.
6   Check the mechanism for proper operation.
7   Install the watershield and door trim panel.

16 Door outside handle – removal and installation

1   Remove the door trim and watershield.
2   Disconnect the door latch activating rod from the door outside handle.
3   Prop the door handle open with a piece of $\frac{1}{2}$ in x 4 in wood to expose the 2 blind rivets which retain the handle.
4   Use a drift punch to punch out the center of each rivet. Drill out the remainder of the rivet with a $\frac{1}{4}$ in drill, taking care not to enlarge the hole.
5   Remove the door handle.
6   To install, place the handle in position with the wood underneath and the holes aligned.
7   Install 2 $\frac{1}{4}$ in x $\frac{1}{2}$ in blind oval head rivets or 2 $\frac{1}{4}$ x 20 x $\frac{3}{4}$ in weld studs with nuts and washers.
8   Remove the wood block and check the door handle operation.
9   Install the trim panel and watershield.

17 Front door window glass – removal and installation

1   Remove the door trim panel and watershield.
2   Remove the screws attaching the glass stabilizers and remove the stabilizers.
3   Use a drift punch to remove the center pins of the rivets retaining

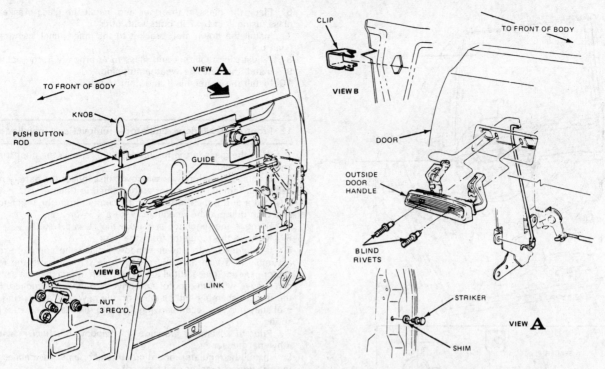

Fig. 12.6 Door latch assembly components and layout (Secs 14, 15 and 16)

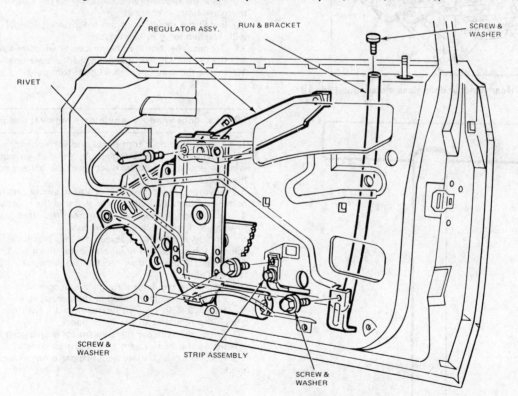

Fig. 12.7 Typical window regulator layout (Secs 17 and 18)

the glass. Drill out the remainder of the rivets using a $\frac{1}{4}$ in drill bit.
4   Push out the rivets and remove the glass.
5   To install, snap the plastic retainer and spacer assembly onto the glass with the metal retainer on the outside.
6   Place the glass in position to the bracket and install 3 $\frac{1}{4}$ inch rivets to fasten the glass to the bracket. As an alternative, $\frac{1}{4}$ in x 1 in bolts with nuts can be used in place of rivets.
7   Install the glass stabilizer and adjust the assembly.
8   Install the watershield and trim.

18 Rear door window glass – removal and installation

1   Remove the door trim and watershield.
2   Remove the 3 screws at the weatherstripping belt line.
3   Support the glass and remove the center of the attaching rivets with a punch, drilling out the remainder with a $\frac{1}{4}$ inch drill bit.
4   Remove the glass support and remove the glass.
5   Install the nylon glass protectors.

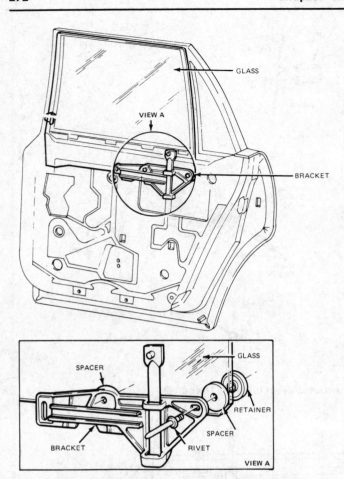

Fig. 12.8 Rear window door glass installation (Sec 18)

Fig. 12.9 T-bar tool used for window regulator spring removal
(Sec 19)

6   Place the glass in the door and install the glass bracket to the glass, using $\frac{1}{4}$ in by 1 in bolts with nuts.
7   Install the down stop bracket to the inner panel, using $\frac{1}{4}$ in hex head bolts.
8   Adjust the stabilizers and glass to fit properly in the opening.
9   Install the belt line weatherstripping.
10   Install the watershield and door trim panel.

19 Front door window regulator – removal and installation

1   With the glass in the full up position, remove the door trim panel and watershield.
2   If equipped with power windows, disconnect the battery negative cable and remove the motor as described in Chapter 10.
3   Use a drift punch to remove the centers from the regulator rivets and then drill out the remainder with a $\frac{1}{4}$ in drill bit.
4   Remove the regulator arm from the glass bracket.
5   Remove the regulator from the door.
6   If equipped with power windows, place the complete regulator assembly in a vise and drill a $\frac{5}{16}$ in hole through both the regulator sector gear and place. Intall a $\frac{1}{4}$ in bolt with nut so that the sector gear can't move when the motor and drive assembly is removed. Remove the motor assembly and install it on the new regulator, using a T-bar tool shown in the accompanying figure to release the counter balance spring.
7   Prior to assembly, lubricate the window mechanism with polyethylene grease.
8   Install the regulator mounting nut and retainer assemblies and the motor support bracket (if equipped).
9   Place the regulator in position on the door and insert the roller into the glass bracket channel.
10   Install the regulator to the inner panel, using $\frac{1}{4}$ in by 1 in screws with washers or $\frac{1}{4}$ in blind rivets.
11   Connect the motor wires on power window equipped models.
12   Check the window mechanism for proper operation.
13   Install the watershield and door trim panel.

20 Rear door window regulator – removal and installation

1   Remove the door trim panel and watershield.
2   Support the window glass in the full up position. On power window equipped models, disconnect the battery negative cable and the motor wires.
3   Drive out the center pin of the regulator retaining rivets with a punch and then drill out the remainder of the rivet with a $\frac{1}{4}$ in drill bit.
4   Disengage the regulator arm from the glass bracket and remove the regulator assembly from the door.
5   On power window equipped models, place the regulator in a vise, remove the motor and drive and install them on the new regulator.
6   Lubricate the window mechanism with polyethylene grease prior to installation.
7   Install the regulator through the access hole in the inner panel.
8   Place the regulator through the access hole in the inner panel.
9   Install 3 $\frac{1}{4}$ in by $\frac{1}{2}$ in hex head bolts with nuts and washers to attach the regulator to the inner panel.
10   Check the window mechanism for proper operation.
11   Install the watershield and door trim panel.
12   Reconnect the battery negative cable on power window equipped models.

21 Door window glass – adjustment

1   Remove the door trim panel and watershield.
2   For fore-and-aft adjustment, loosen the run and bracket assembly attaching screws and adjust the glass as necessary. Tighten the screws.
3   For in-and-out adjustment, lower the glass 2 inches and then loosen the lower guide screws. Move the top of the glass in or out until the proper position in the run is obtained and tighten the screws.
4   Install the watershield and trim panel.

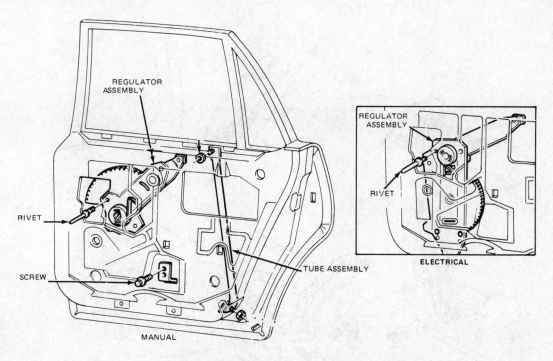

Fig. 12.10 Rear window regulator installation (Sec 20)

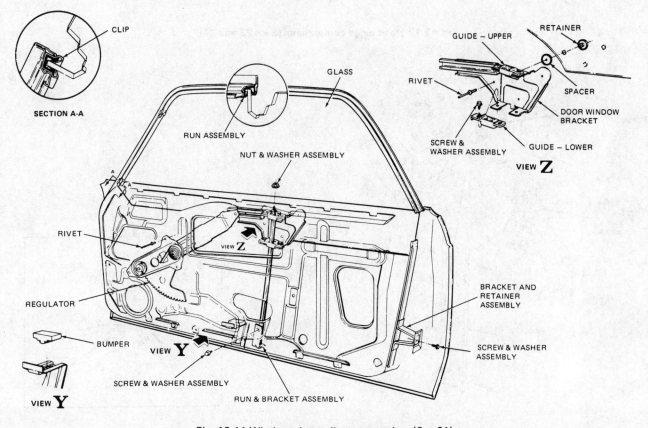

Fig. 12.11 Window glass adjustment points (Sec 21)

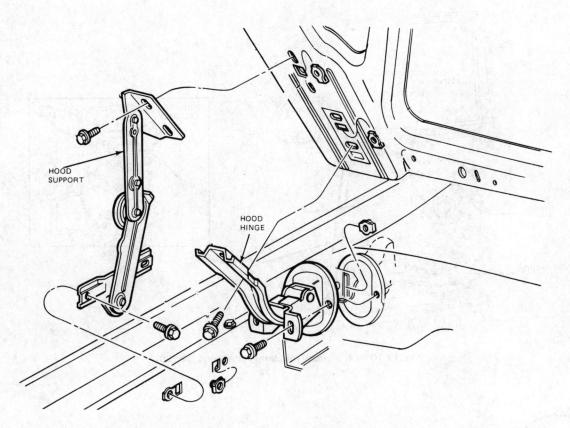

Fig. 12.12 Hood hinge components (Secs 23 and 24)

HOOD SUPPORT

HOOD HINGE

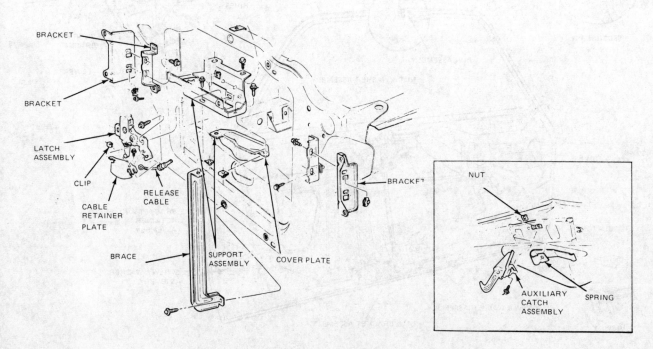

BRACKET

BRACKET

LATCH ASSEMBLY

CLIP

CABLE RETAINER PLATE

RELEASE CABLE

BRACE

SUPPORT ASSEMBLY

COVER PLATE

BRACKET

NUT

AUXILIARY CATCH ASSEMBLY

SPRING

Fig. 12.13 Hood latch assembly and components (Sec 25)

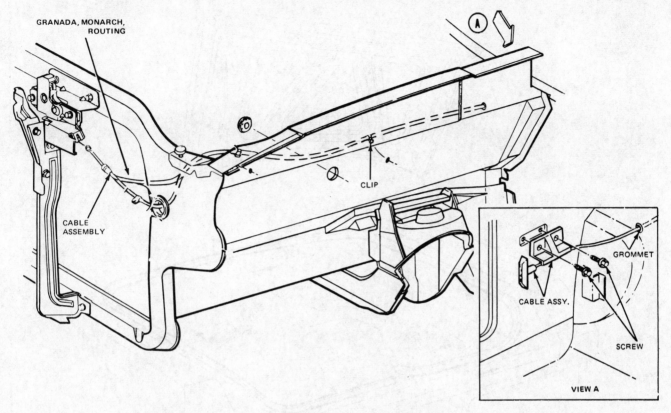

Fig. 12.14 Hood latch cable layout (Sec 26)

22 Windshield, stationary quarter window and rear glass – removal and installation

The windshield, stationary quarter window and rear glass on all models are sealed in place with a special butyl compound. Removal of the existing sealant requires the use of an electric knife specially made for the operation and glass replacement is a complex operation.

In view of this, it is not recommended that stationary glass removal be attempted by the home mechanic. If replacement is necessary due to breakage or leakage, the work should be referred to your dealer or a qualified glass or body shop.

23 Hood – removal and installation

1   Open the hood and support it in the open position.
2   Protect the fenders and cowl with suitable covering to prevent damage to the paint.
3   Scribe around the hinges for ease of reinstallation.
4   Have an assistant support the weight of the hood and remove the hinge-to-hood bolts.
5   Lift the hood over the front of the car.
6   Installation is a reversal of removal, taking care to align the hinges with the previously scribed marks.

24 Hood hinges – removal and installation

1   Open the hood and support it in the open position.
2   Remove the hood as described in Section 23.
3   Scribe around the hinge housing with a pencil for ease of installation.
4   Remove bolts and washers securing the hinge to the body and remove the hinge.
5   Installation is the reverse of removal.

25 Hood latch – removal, installation and adjustment

1   Open the hood and support it in the open position.
2   Remove the hood latch cable retainer plate and disengage the cable from the hood latch assembly.
3   Remove the latch attaching screws and remove the latch.
4   Installation is the reverse of removal. Do not fully tighten the latch screws until adjustment is made.
5   The hood latch can be adjusted from side-to-side to align it with the hood latch hook. It can also be adjusted up and down to obtain a flush fit between the hood and fenders.
6   Move the hood latch from side-to-side until it is properly aligned with the opening in the hood inner panel.
7   Loosen the hood bumper locknuts and lower the bumpers.
8   Move the latch up and down until the proper fit is obtained when the hood is pulled up. Tighten the hood latch screws.
9   Raise the hood bumpers to eliminate any hood looseness and then tighten the bumper locknuts.

26 Hood latch control cable – removal and installation

1   Prop the hood securely in the open position.
2   Remove the hood latch cable retainer screws, plate and cable clip.
3   Disengage the cable and ferrule from the latch assembly.
4   Remove the cable retaining clips.
5   From inside the vehicle, remove the bracket and screws and carefully pull the cable assembly through the retaining wall.
6   To install, insert the cable assembly through the retaining wall and seat the grommet securely.
7   Install the cable mounting bracket and screws.
8   Route the cable and install the retaining clips, referring to the accompanying figure.
9   Install the cable clip and hood latch retaining plate.
10 Prior to closing the hood, check the cable release for proper operation.

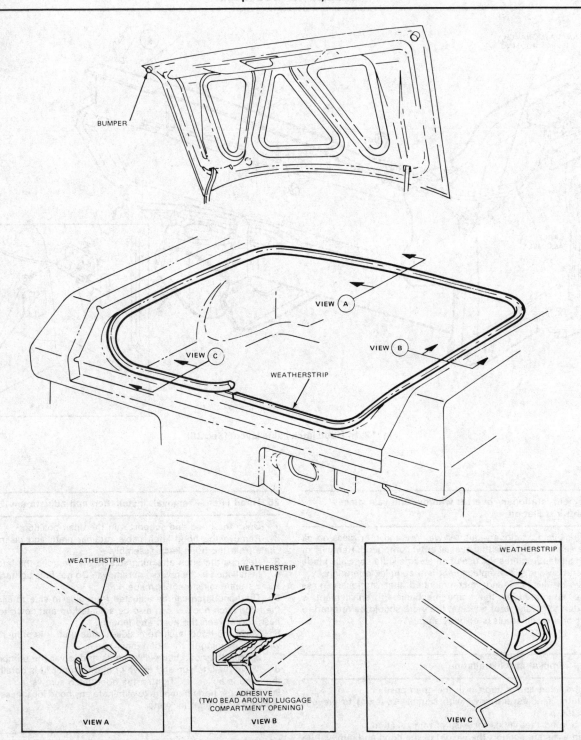

Fig. 12.15 Trunk weatherstripping installation (Sec 29)

27 Trunk lid – removal and installation

1 Support the trunk lid in the open position.
2 Remove the screws securing the hinges to the trunk lid.
3 With the help of an assistant, lift the trunk lid from the vehicle.
4 Installation is the reverse of removal. It may be necessary to adjust the position of the trunk lid after installation.

28 Trunk lid – adjustment

The trunk lid can be moved fore-and-aft by loosening the hinge-to-lid securing screws. The up-and-down adjustment is obtained by adding or subtracting shims between the hinge and lid.

29 Trunk lid weatherstrip – removal and installation

1 Open the trunk and carefully pull the old weatherstrip from around the opening.
2 Clean off any old adhesive from the weatherstrip mounting area.
3 Place the new weatherstrip in position and cut to required length, leaving 1 to 2 inches extra at one end.
4 Apply a bead of adhesive around the entire weatherstrip mounting area.

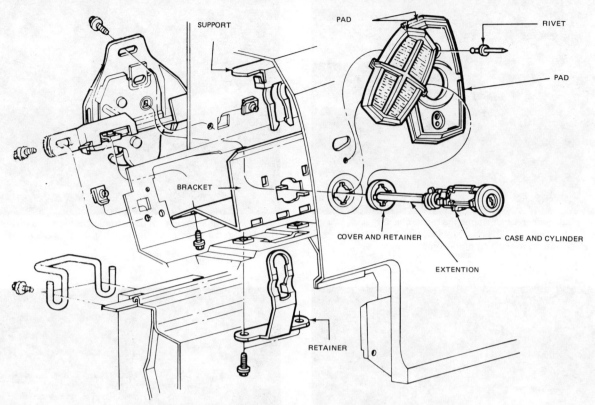

Fig. 12.16 Trunk latch and lock installation (Sec 30)

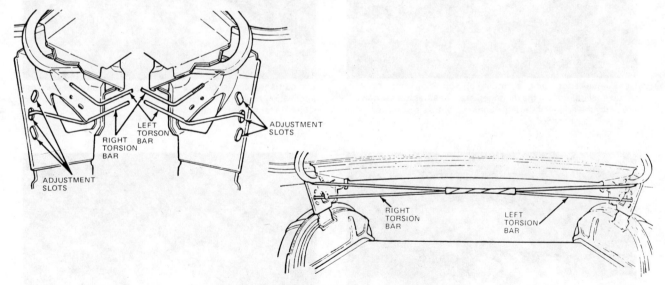

Fig. 12.17 Trunk lid torsion adjustment (Sec 31)

5   Fit the weatherstrip to the body opening with the joint at the rear center.
6   Close the trunk lid and leave closed until the adhesive has at least partially dried.

30 Trunk lid latch and lock – removal and installation

1   Open the trunk lid and scribe around any component which could affect adjustment, for ease of reinstallation.
2   Remove the lock cylinder retainer screws, rivets and retainer, referring to the accompanying figure.
3   Remove the latch attaching screws and latch.

4   Remove the lock cylinder cover and retainer and the lock cylinder.
5   Installation is the reverse of removal, taking care to align the latch components with the scribe marks made during removal.

31 Trunk lid torsion bar – adjustment

1   The trunk lid should pop open when the latch is released and if it doesn't, the torsion bar tension should be increased. If the lid opens with too much force, the torsion bar tension is excessive and must be decreased.
2   Prop the trunk lid open with a long piece of wood during torsion bar adjustment.

This photo sequence illustrates the repair of a dent and damaged paintwork. The procedure for the repair of a hole is similar. Refer to the text for more complete instructions

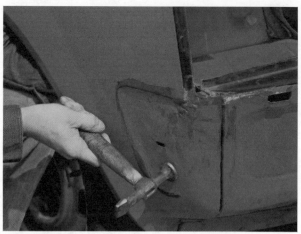

After removing any adjacent body trim, hammer the dent out. The damaged area should then be made slightly concave

Use coarse sandpaper or a sanding disc on a drill motor to remove all paint from the damaged area. Feather the sanded area into the edges of the surrounding paint, using progressively finer grades of sandpaper

The damaged area should be treated with rust remover prior to application of the body filler. In the case of a rust hole, all rusted sheet metal should be cut away

Carefully follow manufacturer's instructions when mixing the body filler so as to have the longest possible working time during application. Rust holes should be covered with fiberglass screen held in place with dabs of body filler prior to repair

Apply the filler with a flexible applicator in thin layers at 20 minute intervals. Use an applicator such as a wood spatula for confined areas. The filler should protrude slightly above the surrounding area

Shape the filler with a surform-type plane. Then, use water and progressively finer grades of sandpaper and a sanding block to wet-sand the area until it is smooth. Feather the edges of the repair area into the surrounding paint.

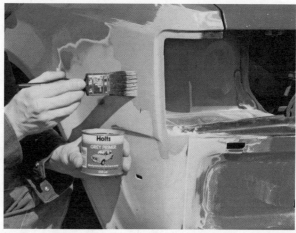

Use spray or brush applied primer to cover the entire repair area so that slight imperfections in the surface will be filled in. Prime at least one inch into the area surrounding the repair. Be careful of over-spray when using spray-type primer

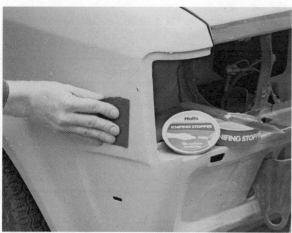

Wet-sand the primer with fine (approximately 400 grade) sandpaper until the area is smooth to the touch and blended into the surrounding paint. Use filler paste on minor imperfections

After the filler paste has dried, use rubbing compound to ensure that the surface of the primer is smooth. Prior to painting, the surface should be wiped down with a tack rag or lint-free cloth soaked in lacquer thinner

Choose a dry, warm, breeze-free area in which to paint and make sure that adjacent areas are protected from over-spray. Shake the spray paint can thoroughly and apply the top coat to the repair area, building it up by applying several coats, working from the center

After allowing at least two weeks for the paint to harden, use fine rubbing compound to blend the area into the original paint. Wax can now be applied

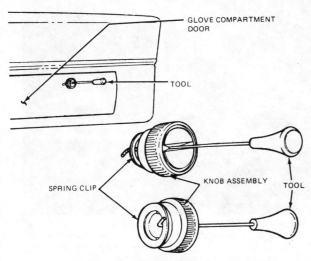

Fig. 12.18 Glove compartment knob removal (Sec 32)

3 Grasp the torsion bar near the adjustment slot with a suitable tool such as locking pliers and move it to the appropriate slot to increase or decrease tension. **Caution:** *Be extremely careful. The torsion bar is under considerable pressure.*
4 After adjusting one torsion bar, check the trunk lid operation before adjusting the other bar.
5 After adjustment, the difference between the right or left side torsion bar end should not be more than one slot.

32 Glove compartment lock and knob – removal and installation

1 Fabricate a tool from wire with a $\frac{1}{4}$ inch right angle bend as shown in the accompanying figure.

2 Unlock the glove compartment door and insert the tool through the key slot with the hook toward the drivers side. Engage the spring retainer and pull the knob from the lock assembly.
3 Remove the lock assembly screws and assembly.
4 Install the new lock assembly with the screws snug and push the knob in place.
5 Adjust the lock assembly for proper operation and tighten the screws.

33 Console – removal and installation

1 Open the console and remove the attaching screws, referring to the accompanying figure.
2 Disconnect any wiring connectors and remove the console assembly from the vehicle.
3 Installation is a reversal of removal, taking care to connect the wiring connectors.

34 Radiator grille – removal and installation

1 Remove the attaching screws and withdraw the grille assembly from the vehicle.
2 To install, position the grille to the opening and reinstall the 7 screws.

35 Front and rear bumpers – removal and installation

1 Scribe around the bumper isolator attaching bolts for ease of installation. Remove the bolts and with the help of an assistant remove the bumper, making sure to note the number and order of removal of the spacers.
2 If the bumper is to be replaced, transfer the bumper guards, pads and license plate bracket to the new bumper. To avoid damage to the license plate bracket tabs, squeeze them together during removal. On rear bumpers, remove the 2 license plate light screws and remove the

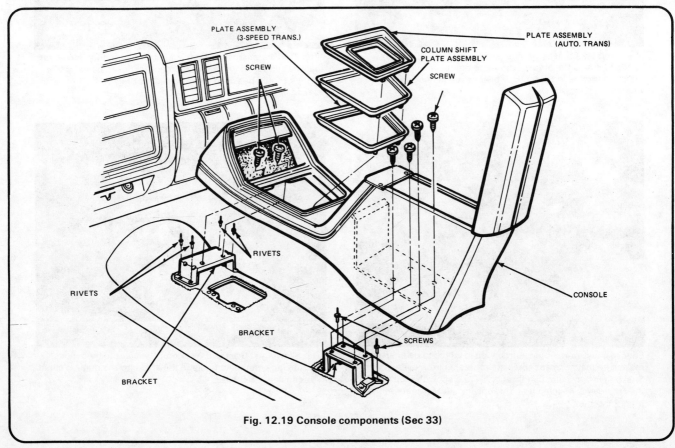

Fig. 12.19 Console components (Sec 33)

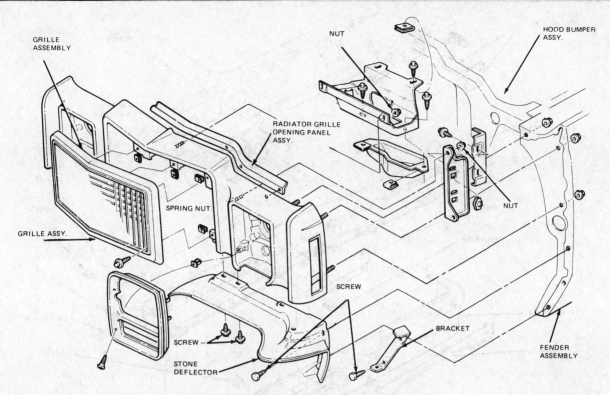

GRILLE
ASSEMBLY

NUT

HOOD BUMPER
ASSY.

RADIATOR GRILLE
OPENING PANEL
ASSY.

GRILLE ASSY.

SPRING NUT

NUT

SCREW

SCREW

BRACKET

SCREW

STONE
DEFLECTOR

FENDER
ASSEMBLY

Fig. 12.20 Radiator grille and components (Sec 34)

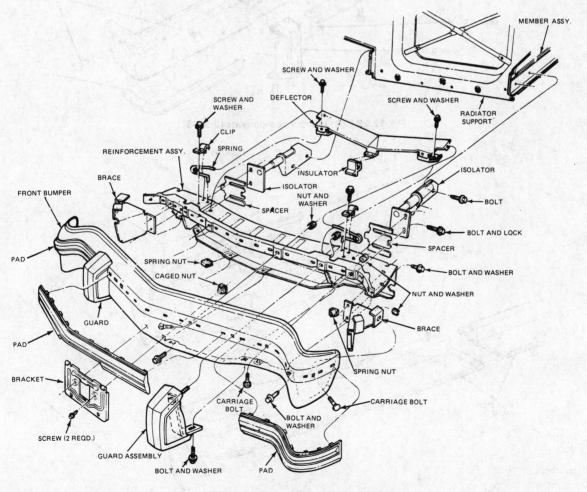

MEMBER ASSY.

SCREW AND WASHER

DEFLECTOR

SCREW AND WASHER

RADIATOR
SUPPORT

SCREW AND
WASHER

CLIP

SPRING

REINFORCEMENT ASSY.

BRACE

INSULATOR

ISOLATOR

ISOLATOR

NUT AND
WASHER

BOLT

FRONT BUMPER

SPACER

BOLT AND LOCK

PAD

SPRING NUT

SPACER

CAGED NUT

BOLT AND WASHER

NUT AND WASHER

GUARD

BRACE

PAD

SPRING NUT

BRACKET

CARRIAGE
BOLT

CARRIAGE BOLT

SCREW (2 REQD.)

BOLT AND
WASHER

GUARD ASSEMBLY

BOLT AND WASHER

PAD

Fig. 12.21 Front bumper installation (Sec 35)

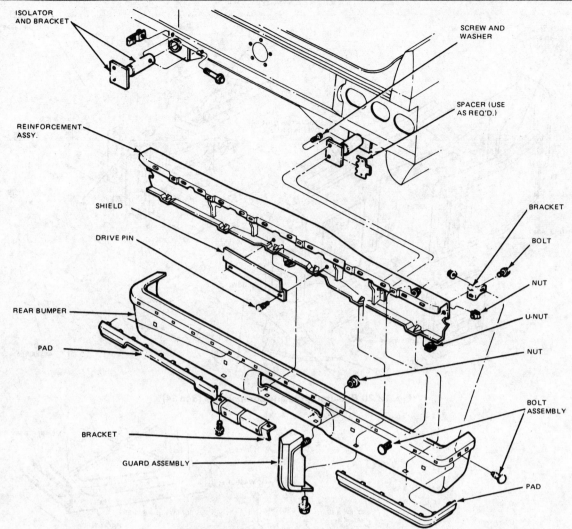

Fig. 12.22 Rear bumper components (Sec 35)

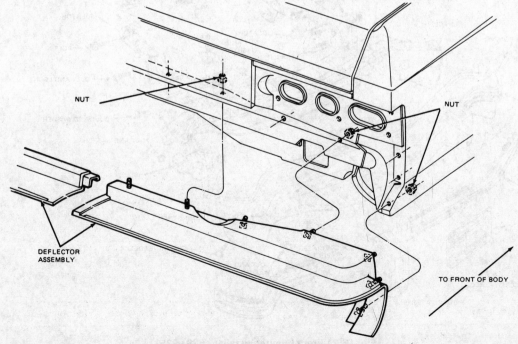

Fig. 12.23 Rear stone deflector installation (Sec 35)

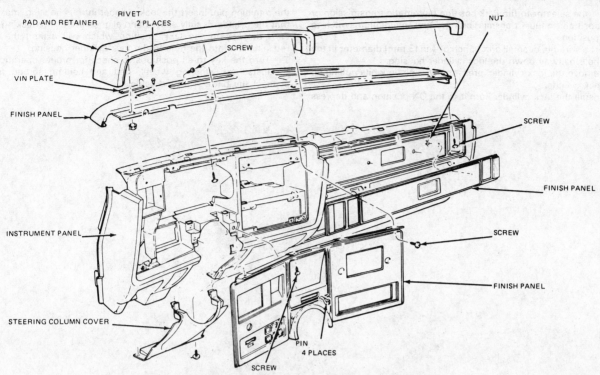

Fig. 12.24 Instrument panel pad and components (Sec 36)

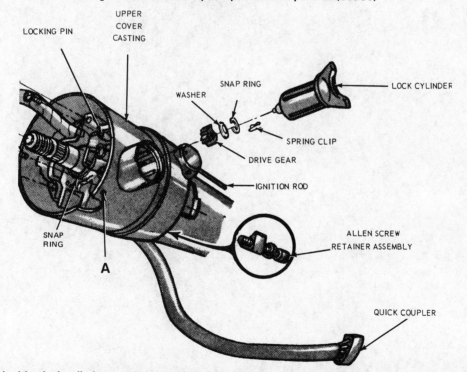

Fig. 12.25 Ignition lock cylinder removal showing hole at A for insertion of wire pin to release lock cylinder (Sec 37)

lights. On some models it may be necessary to remove the rear stone deflectors.
3   To install, with an assistant holding the bumper in place to the isolators, install the bolts and tighten to specification.

3   Pull the pad and upper finish panel toward the rear and withdraw them from the instrument panel.
4   To install, place the pad and upper finish panel in position on the instrument panel, align the screw holes and install the 8 screws.

---

36 Instrument panel trim pad – removal and installation

1   Remove the scrws from each defroster opening.
2   Along the lower edge of the pad, remove the 6 retaining screws, referring to the figure.

---

37 Ignition switch lock cylinder – removal and installation

1   Disconnect the battery negative cable.
2   Remove the horn pad, steering wheel and column trim pad (Chapter 11).

3   Move the selector to the Park position (automatic transmission or reverse position (manual transmission) and turn the ignition switch to the ON position.

4   Insert a wire pin or small drift punch of $\frac{1}{8}$ in (3 mm) diameter in the casting hole halfway down the lock cylinder housing.

5   To remove the lock cylinder, press the wire pin in while pulling up on the lock cylinder.

6   To install the lock cylinder, turn it to the ON position and depress the retaining pin. Insert the lock cylinder into its housing, making sure that the cylinder is fully seated and aligned in the interlocking washer. Turn the key to the OFF position which will extend the cylinder retaining pin into the hole in the lock cylinder housing.

7   Turn the key to all positions to check for proper operation.

8   Install the steering wheel, pad and column shroud trim and connect the battery ground cable.

Conversion factors

Length (distance)
Inches (in)	X	25.4	= Millimetres (mm)	X 0.0394	= Inches (in)
Feet (ft)	X	0.305	= Metres (m)	X 3.281	= Feet (ft)
Miles	X	1.609	= Kilometres (km)	X 0.621	= Miles

Volume (capacity)
Cubic inches (cu in; in³)	X	16.387	= Cubic centimetres (cc; cm³)	X 0.061	= Cubic inches (cu in; in³)
Imperial pints (Imp pt)	X	0.568	= Litres (l)	X 1.76	= Imperial pints (Imp pt)
Imperial quarts (Imp qt)	X	1.137	= Litres (l)	X 0.88	= Imperial quarts (Imp qt)
Imperial quarts (Imp qt)	X	1.201	= US quarts (US qt)	X 0.833	= Imperial quarts (Imp qt)
US quarts (US qt)	X	0.946	= Litres (l)	X 1.057	= US quarts (US qt)
Imperial gallons (Imp gal)	X	4.546	= Litres (l)	X 0.22	= Imperial gallons (Imp gal)
Imperial gallons (Imp gal)	X	1.201	= US gallons (US gal)	X 0.833	= Imperial gallons (Imp gal)
US gallons (US gal)	X	3.785	= Litres (l)	X 0.264	= US gallons (US gal)

Mass (weight)
Ounces (oz)	X	28.35	= Grams (g)	X 0.035	= Ounces (oz)
Pounds (lb)	X	0.454	= Kilograms (kg)	X 2.205	= Pounds (lb)

Force
Ounces-force (ozf; oz)	X	0.278	= Newtons (N)	X 3.6	= Ounces-force (ozf; oz)
Pounds-force (lbf; lb)	X	4.448	= Newtons (N)	X 0.225	= Pounds-force (lbf; lb)
Newtons (N)	X	0.1	= Kilograms-force (kgf; kg)	X 9.81	= Newtons (N)

Pressure
Pounds-force per square inch (psi; lbf/in²; lb/in²)	X	0.070	= Kilograms-force per square centimetre (kgf/cm²; kg/cm²)	X 14.223	= Pounds-force per square inch (psi; lbf/in²; lb/in²)
Pounds-force per square inch (psi; lbf/in²; lb/in²)	X	0.068	= Atmospheres (atm)	X 14.696	= Pounds-force per square inch (psi; lbf/in²; lb/in²)
Pounds-force per square inch (psi; lbf/in²; lb/in²)	X	0.069	= Bars	X 14.5	= Pounds-force per square inch (psi; lbf/in²; lb/in²)
Pounds-force per square inch (psi; lbf/in²; lb/in²)	X	6.895	= Kilopascals (kPa)	X 0.145	= Pounds-force per square inch (psi; lbf/in²; lb/in²)
Kilopascals (kPa)	X	0.01	= Kilograms-force per square centimetre (kgf/cm²; kg/cm²)	X 98.1	= Kilopascals (kPa)
Millibar (mbar)	X	100	= Pascals (Pa)	X 0.01	= Millibar (mbar)
Millibar (mbar)	X	0.0145	= Pounds-force per square inch (psi; lbf/in²; lb/in²)	X 68.947	= Millibar (mbar)
Millibar (mbar)	X	0.75	= Millimetres of mercury (mmHg)	X 1.333	= Millibar (mbar)
Millibar (mbar)	X	0.401	= Inches of water (inH₂O)	X 2.491	= Millibar (mbar)
Millimetres of mercury (mmHg)	X	0.535	= Inches of water (inH₂O)	X 1.868	= Millimetres of mercury (mmHg)
Inches of water (inH₂O)	X	0.036	= Pounds-force per square inch (psi; lbf/in²; lb/in²)	X 27.68	= Inches of water (inH₂O)

Torque (moment of force)
Pounds-force inches (lbf in; lb in)	X	1.152	= Kilograms-force centimetre (kgf cm; kg cm)	X 0.868	= Pounds-force inches (lbf in; lb in)
Pounds-force inches (lbf in; lb in)	X	0.113	= Newton metres (Nm)	X 8.85	= Pounds-force inches (lbf in; lb in)
Pounds-force inches (lbf in; lb in)	X	0.083	= Pounds-force feet (lbf ft; lb ft)	X 12	= Pounds-force inches (lbf in; lb in)
Pounds-force feet (lbf ft; lb ft)	X	0.138	= Kilograms-force metres (kgf m; kg m)	X 7.233	= Pounds-force feet (lbf ft; lb ft)
Pounds-force feet (lbf ft; lb ft)	X	1.356	= Newton metres (Nm)	X 0.738	= Pounds-force feet (lbf ft; lb ft)
Newton metres (Nm)	X	0.102	= Kilograms-force metres (kgf m; kg m)	X 9.804	= Newton metres (Nm)

Power
Horsepower (hp)	X	745.7	= Watts (W)	X 0.0013	= Horsepower (hp)

Velocity (speed)
Miles per hour (miles/hr; mph)	X	1.609	= Kilometres per hour (km/hr; kph)	X 0.621	= Miles per hour (miles/hr; mph)

Fuel consumption*
Miles per gallon, Imperial (mpg)	X	0.354	= Kilometres per litre (km/l)	X 2.825	= Miles per gallon, Imperial (mpg)
Miles per gallon, US (mpg)	X	0.425	= Kilometres per litre (km/l)	X 2.352	= Miles per gallon, US (mpg)

Temperature

Degrees Fahrenheit = (°C x 1.8) + 32   Degrees Celsius (Degrees Centigrade; °C) = (°F - 32) x 0.56

*It is common practice to convert from miles per gallon (mpg) to litres/100 kilometres (l/100km),
where mpg (Imperial) x l/100 km = 282 and mpg (US) x l/100 km = 235

Index

HAYNES AUTOMOTIVE MANUALS

NOTE: New manuals are added to this list on a periodic basis. If you do not see a listing for your vehicle, consult your local Haynes dealer for the latest product information.

ALFA-ROMEO
531 **Alfa Romeo Sedan & Coupe** '73 thru '80

AMC
Jeep CJ – see JEEP (412)
694 **Mid-size models,** Concord, Hornet, Gremlin & Spirit '70 thru '83
934 **(Renault) Alliance & Encore** all models '83 thru '87

AUDI
615 **4000** all models '80 thru '87
428 **5000** all models '77 thru '83
1117 **5000** all models '84 thru '88
207 **Fox** all models '73 thru '79

AUSTIN
049 **Healey 100/6 & 3000** Roadster '56 thru '68
Healey Sprite – see MG Midget Roadster (265)

BLMC
260 **1100, 1300 & Austin America** '62 thru '74
527 **Mini** all models '59 thru '69
*646 **Mini** all models '69 thru '88

BMW
276 **320i** all 4 cyl models '75 thru '83
632 **528i & 530i** all models '75 thru '80
240 **1500 thru 2002** all models except Turbo '59 thru '77
348 **2500, 2800, 3.0 & Bavaria** '69 thru '76

BUICK
Century (front wheel drive) – see GENERAL MOTORS A-Cars (829)
*1627 **Buick, Oldsmobile & Pontiac Full-size (Front wheel drive)** all models '85 thru '90
Buick Electra, LeSabre and Park Avenue; **Oldsmobile** Delta 88 Royale, Ninety Eight and Regency; **Pontiac** Bonneville
*1551 **Buick Oldsmobile & Pontiac Full-size (Rear wheel drive)**
Buick Electra '70 thru '84, Estate '70 thru '90, LeSabre '70 thru '79
Oldsmobile Custom Cruiser '70 thru '90, Delta 88 '70 thru '85, Ninety-eight '70 thru '84
Pontiac Bonneville '70 thru '86, Catalina '70 thru '81, Grandville '70 thru '75, Parisienne '84 thru '86
627 **Mid-size** all rear-drive **Regal & Century** models with V6, V8 and Turbo '74 thru '87
Regal – see GENERAL MOTORS (1671)
Skyhawk – see GENERAL MOTORS J-Cars (766)
552 **Skylark** all X-car models '80 thru '85

CADILLAC
*751 **Cadillac Rear Wheel Drive** all gasoline models '70 thru '90
Cimarron – see GENERAL MOTORS J-Cars (766)

CAPRI
296 **2000 MK I Coupe** all models '71 thru '75
283 **2300 MK II Coupe** all models '74 thru '78
205 **2600 & 2800 V6 Coupe** '71 thru '75
375 **2800 Mk II V6 Coupe** '75 thru '82
Mercury Capri – see FORD Mustang (654)

CHEVROLET
*1477 **Astro & GMC Safari Mini-vans** all models '85 thru '90
554 **Camaro** V8 all models '70 thru '81
*866 **Camaro** all models '82 thru '90
Cavalier – see GENERAL MOTORS J-Cars (766)
Celebrity – see GENERAL MOTORS A-Cars (829)
625 **Chevelle, Malibu & El Camino** all V6 & V8 models '69 thru '87

449 **Chevette & Pontiac T1000** all models '76 thru '87
550 **Citation** all models '80 thru '85
*1628 **Corsica/Beretta** all models '87 thru '90
274 **Corvette** all V8 models '68 thru '82
*1336 **Corvette** all models '84 thru '89
704 **Full-size Sedans** Caprice, Impala, Biscayne, Bel Air & Wagons, all V6 & V8 models '69 thru '90
Lumina – see GENERAL MOTORS (1671)
319 **Luv Pick-up** all 2WD & 4WD models '72 thru '82
626 **Monte Carlo** all V6, V8 & Turbo models '70 thru '88
241 **Nova** all V8 models '69 thru '79
*1642 **Nova and Geo Prizm** all front wheel drive models, '85 thru '90
*420 **Pick-ups '67 thru '87** – Chevrolet & GMC, all V8 & in-line 6 cyl 2WD & 4WD models '67 thru '87
*1664 **Pick-ups '88 thru '90** – Chevrolet & GMC all full-size (C and K) models, '88 thru '90
*1727 **Sprint & Geo Metro** '85 thru '91
*831 **S-10 & GMC S-15 Pick-ups** all models '82 thru '90
*345 **Vans** – Chevrolet & GMC, V8 & in-line 6 cyl models '68 thru '89
208 **Vega** all models except Cosworth '70 thru '77

CHRYSLER
*1337 **Chrysler & Plymouth Mid-size** front wheel drive '82 thru '89
K-Cars – see DODGE Aries (723)
Laser – see DODGE Daytona (1140)

DATSUN
402 **200SX** all models '77 thru '79
647 **200SX** all models '80 thru '83
228 **B-210** all models '73 thru '78
525 **210** all models '78 thru '82
206 **240Z, 260Z & 280Z** Coupe & 2+2 '70 thru '78
563 **280ZX** Coupe & 2+2 '79 thru '83
300ZX – see NISSAN (1137)
679 **310** all models '78 thru '82
123 **510 & PL521 Pick-up** '68 thru '73
430 **510** all models '78 thru '81
372 **610** all models '72 thru '76
277 **620 Series Pick-up** all models '73 thru '79
720 Series Pick-up – see NISSAN Pick-ups (771)
376 **810/Maxima** all gasoline models '77 thru '84
124 **1200** all models '70 thru '73
368 **F10** all models '76 thru '79
Pulsar – see NISSAN (876)
Sentra – see NISSAN (982)
Stanza – see NISSAN (981)

DODGE
*723 **Aries & Plymouth Reliant** all models '81 thru '89
*1231 **Caravan & Plymouth Voyager** Mini-Vans all models '84 thru '89
699 **Challenger & Plymouth Saporro** all models '78 thru '83
236 **Colt** all models '71 thru '77
419 **Colt (rear wheel drive)** all models '77 thru '80
610 **Colt & Plymouth Champ (front wheel drive)** all models '78 thru '87
*556 **D50 & Plymouth Arrow Pick-ups** '79 thru '88
*1668 **Dakota Pick-up** all models '87 thru '90
234 **Dart & Plymouth Valiant** all 6 cyl models '67 thru '76
*1140 **Daytona & Chrysler Laser** all models '84 thru '89
*545 **Omni & Plymouth Horizon** all models '78 thru '90
*912 **Pick-ups** all full-size models '74 thru '90
*349 **Vans** – Dodge & Plymouth V8 & 6 cyl models '71 thru '89

FIAT
080 **124 Sedan & Wagon** all ohv & dohc models '66 thru '75
094 **124 Sport Coupe & Spider** '68 thru '78
310 **131 & Brava** all models '75 thru '81
479 **Strada** all models '79 thru '82
273 **X1/9** all models '74 thru '80

FORD
*1476 **Aerostar Mini-vans** all models '86 thru '90
788 **Bronco and Pick-ups** '73 thru '79
*880 **Bronco and Pick-ups** '80 thru '90
014 **Cortina MK II** all models except Lotus '66 thru '70
295 **Cortina MK III** 1600 & 2000 ohc '70 thru '76
268 **Courier Pick-up** all models '72 thru '82
789 **Escort & Mercury Lynx** all models '81 thru '90
560 **Fairmont & Mercury Zephyr** all in-line & V8 models '78 thru '83
334 **Fiesta** all models '77 thru '80
754 **Ford & Mercury Full-size,** Ford LTD & Mercury Marquis ('75 thru '82); Ford Custom 500, Country Squire, Crown Victoria & Mercury Colony Park ('75 thru '87); Ford LTD Crown Victoria & Mercury Gran Marquis ('83 thru '87)
359 **Granada & Mercury Monarch** all in-line, 6 cyl & V8 models '75 thru '80
773 **Ford & Mercury Mid-size,** Ford Thunderbird & Mercury Cougar ('75 thru '82); Ford LTD & Mercury Marquis ('83 thru '86); Ford Torino, Gran Torino, Elite, Ranchero pick-up, LTD II, Mercury Montego, Comet, XR-7 & Lincoln Versailles ('75 thru '86)
*654 **Mustang & Mercury Capri** all models including Turbo '79 thru '90
357 **Mustang V8** all models '64-1/2 thru '73
231 **Mustang II** all 4 cyl, V6 & V8 models '74 thru '78
204 **Pinto** all models '70 thru '74
649 **Pinto & Mercury Bobcat** all models '75 thru '80
*1026 **Ranger & Bronco II** all gasoline models '83 thru '89
*1421 **Taurus & Mercury Sable** '86 thru '90
*1418 **Tempo & Mercury Topaz** all gasoline models '84 thru '89
1338 **Thunderbird & Mercury Cougar/XR7** '83 thru '88
*1725 **Thunderbird & Mercury Cougar** '89 and '90
*344 **Vans** all V8 Econoline models '69 thru '90

GENERAL MOTORS
*829 **A-Cars** – Chevrolet Celebrity, Buick Century, Pontiac 6000 & Oldsmobile Cutlass Ciera all models '82 thru '89
*766 **J-Cars** – Chevrolet Cavalier, Pontiac J-2000, Oldsmobile Firenza, Buick Skyhawk & Cadillac Cimarron all models '82 thru '90
*1420 **N-Cars** – Buick Somerset '85 thru '87; Pontiac Grand Am and Oldsmobile Calais '85 thru '90; Buick Skylark '86 thru '90
*1671 **GM: Buick** Regal, **Chevrolet** Lumina, **Oldsmobile** Cutlass Supreme, **Pontiac** Grand Prix, all front wheel drive models '88 thru '90

GEO
Metro – see CHEVROLET Sprint (1727)
Tracker – see SUZUKI Samurai (1626)
Prizm – see CHEVROLET Nova (1642)

GMC
Safari – see CHEVROLET ASTRO (1477)
Vans & Pick-ups – see CHEVROLET (420, 831, 345, 1664)

(continued on next page)

* Listings shown with an asterisk (*) indicate model coverage as of this printing. These titles will be periodically updated to include later model years — consult your Haynes dealer for more information.

Haynes Publications Inc., P.O. Box 978, Newbury Park, CA 91320 • (818) 889-5400 • (805) 498-6703

HAYNES AUTOMOTIVE MANUALS (continued from previous page)

(continued from previous page)

NOTE: New manuals are added to this list on a periodic basis. If you do not see a listing for your vehicle, consult your local Haynes dealer for the latest product information.

HONDA
138 360, 600 & Z Coupe all models '67 thru '75
351 Accord CVCC all models '76 thru '83
*1221 Accord all models '84 thru '89
160 Civic 1200 all models '73 thru '79
633 Civic 1300 & 1500 CVCC all models '80 thru '83
297 Civic 1500 CVCC all models '75 thru '79
*1227 Civic all models '84 thru '90
*601 Prelude CVCC all models '79 thru '89

HYUNDAI
*1552 Excel all models '86 thru '89

ISUZU
*1641 Trooper & Pick-up, all gasoline models '81 thru '90

JAGUAR
098 MK I & II, 240 & 340 Sedans '55 thru '69
*242 XJ6 all 6 cyl models '68 thru '86
*478 XJ12 & XJS all 12 cyl models '72 thru '85
140 XK-E 3.8 & 4.2 all 6 cyl models '61 thru '72

JEEP
*1553 Cherokee, Comanche & Wagoneer Limited all models '84 thru '89
412 CJ all models '49 thru '86

LADA
*413 1200, 1300. 1500 & 1600 all models including Riva '74 thru '86

LAND ROVER
314 Series II, IIA, & III all 4 cyl gasoline models '58 thru '86
529 Diesel all models '58 thru '80

MAZDA
648 626 Sedan & Coupe (rear wheel drive) all models '79 thru '82
*1082 626 & MX-6 (front wheel drive) all models '83 thru '90
*267 B1600, B1800 & B2000 Pick-ups '72 thru '90
370 GLC Hatchback (rear wheel drive) all models '77 thru '83
757 GLC (front wheel drive) all models '81 thru '86
109 RX2 all models '71 thru '75
096 RX3 all models '72 thru '76
460 RX-7 all models '79 thru '85
*1419 RX-7 all models '86 thru '89

MERCEDES-BENZ
*1643 190 Series all four-cylinder gasoline models, '84 thru '88
346 230, 250 & 280 Sedan, Coupe & Roadster all 6 cyl sohc models '68 thru '72
983 280 123 Series all gasoline models '77 thru '81
698 350 & 450 Sedan, Coupe & Roadster all models '71 thru '80
697 Diesel 123 Series 200D, 220D, 240D, 240TD, 300D, 300CD, 300TD, 4- & 5-cyl incl. Turbo '76 thru '85

MERCURY
See FORD Listing

MG
475 MGA all models '56 thru '62
111 MGB Roadster & GT Coupe all models '62 thru '80
265 MG Midget & Austin Healey Sprite Roadster '58 thru '80

MITSUBISHI
*1669 Cordia, Tredia, Galant, Precis & Mirage '83 thru '90
Pick-up – see Dodge D-50 (556)

MORRIS
074 (Austin) Marina 1.8 all models '71 thru '80
024 Minor 1000 sedan & wagon '56 thru '71

NISSAN
1137 300ZX all Turbo & non-Turbo models '84 thru '89
*1341 Maxima all models '85 thru '89
*771 Pick-ups/Pathfinder gas models '80 thru '88
*876 Pulsar all models '83 thru '86
*982 Sentra all models '82 thru '90
*981 Stanza all models '82 thru '90

OLDSMOBILE
Custom Cruiser – see BUICK Full-size (1551)
658 Cutlass all standard gasoline V6 & V8 models '74 thru '88
Cutlass Ciera – see GENERAL MOTORS A-Cars (829)
Cutlass Supreme – see GENERAL MOTORS (1671)
Firenza – see GENERAL MOTORS J-Cars (766)
Ninety-eight – see BUICK Full-size (1551)
Omega – see PONTIAC Phoenix & Omega (551)

PEUGEOT
161 504 all gasoline models '68 thru '79
663 504 all diesel models '74 thru '83

PLYMOUTH
425 Arrow all models '76 thru '80
For all other PLYMOUTH titles, see DODGE listing.

PONTIAC
T1000 – see CHEVROLET Chevette (449)
J-2000 – see GENERAL MOTORS J-Cars (766)
6000 – see GENERAL MOTORS A-Cars (829)
1232 Fiero all models '84 thru '88
555 Firebird all V8 models except Turbo '70 thru '81
*867 Firebird all models '82 thru '89
Full-size Rear Wheel Drive – see Buick, Oldsmobile, Pontiac Full-size (1551)
Grand Prix – see GENERAL MOTORS (1671)
551 Phoenix & Oldsmobile Omega all X-car models '80 thru '84

PORSCHE
*264 911 all Coupe & Targa models except Turbo & Carrera 4 '65 thru '89
239 914 all 4 cyl models '69 thru '76
397 924 all models including Turbo '76 thru '82
*1027 944 all models including Turbo '83 thru '89

RENAULT
141 5 Le Car all models '76 thru '83
079 8 & 10 all models with 58.4 cu in engines '62 thru '72
097 12 Saloon & Estate all models 1289 cc engines '70 thru '80
768 15 & 17 all models '73 thru '79
081 16 all models 89.7 cu in & 95.5 cu in engines '65 thru '72
598 18i & Sportwagon all models '81 thru '86
Alliance & Encore – see AMC (934)
984 Fuego all models '82 thru '85

ROVER
085 3500 & 3500S Sedan 215 cu in engines '68 thru '76
*365 3500 SDI V8 all models '76 thru '85

SAAB
198 95 & 96 V4 all models '66 thru '75
247 99 all models including Turbo '69 thru '80
*980 900 all models including Turbo '79 thru '88

SUBARU
237 1100, 1300, 1400 & 1600 all models '71 thru '79
*681 1600 & 1800 2WD & 4WD all models '80 thru '89

SUZUKI
*1626 Samurai/Sidekick and Geo Tracker all models '86 thru '89

TOYOTA
*1023 Camry all models '83 thru '90
150 Carina Sedan all models '71 thru '74
229 Celica ST, GT & liftback all models '71 thru '77
437 Celica all models '78 thru '81
*935 Celica all models except front-wheel drive and Supra '82 thru '85
680 Celica Supra all models '79 thru '81
1139 Celica Supra all in-line 6-cylinder models '82 thru '86
361 Corolla all models '75 thru '79
961 Corolla all models (rear wheel drive) '80 thru '87
*1025 Corolla all models (front wheel drive) '84 thru '91
*636 Corolla Tercel all models '80 thru '82
230 Corona & MK II all 4 cyl sohc models '69 thru '74
360 Corona all models '74 thru '82
*532 Cressida all models '78 thru '82
313 Land Cruiser all models '68 thru '82
200 MK II all 6 cyl models '72 thru '76
*1339 MR2 all models '85 thru '87
304 Pick-up all models '69 thru '78
*656 Pick-up all models '79 thru '90

TRIUMPH
112 GT6 & Vitesse all models '62 thru '74
113 Spitfire all models '62 thru '81
028 TR2, 3, 3A, & 4A Roadsters '52 thru '67
031 TR250 & 6 Roadsters '67 thru '76
322 TR7 all models '75 thru '81

VW
091 411 & 412 all 103 cu in models '68 thru '73
159 Beetle & Karmann Ghia all models '54 thru '79
238 Dasher all gasoline models '74 thru '81
*884 Rabbit, Jetta, Scirocco, & Pick-up all gasoline models '74 thru '89 & Convertible '80 thru '89
451 Rabbit, Jetta & Pick-up all diesel models '77 thru '84
082 Transporter 1600 all models '68 thru '79
226 Transporter 1700, 1800 & 2000 all models '72 thru '79
084 Type 3 1500 & 1600 all models '63 thru '73
1029 Vanagon all air-cooled models '80 thru '83

VOLVO
203 120, 130 Series & 1800 Sports '61 thru '73
129 140 Series all models '66 thru '74
244 164 all models '68 thru '75
*270 240 Series all models '74 thru '90
400 260 Series all models '75 thru '82
*1550 740 & 760 Series all models '82 thru '88

SPECIAL MANUALS
1479 Automotive Body Repair & Painting Manual
1654 Automotive Electrical Manual
1480 Automotive Heating & Air Conditioning Manual
1763 Ford Engine Overhaul Manual
482 Fuel Injection Manual
1666 Small Engine Repair Manual
299 SU Carburetors thru '88
393 Weber Carburetors thru '79
300 Zenith/Stromberg CD Carburetors thru '76

See your dealer for other available titles

4-1-91

* Listings shown with an asterisk (*) indicate model coverage as of this printing. These titles will be periodically updated to include later model years — consult your Haynes dealer for more information.

Over 100 Haynes motorcycle manuals also available

Haynes Publications Inc., P.O. Box 978, Newbury Park, CA 91320 ● (818) 889–5400 ● (805) 498–6703

Printed by
J H Haynes & Co Ltd
Sparkford Nr Yeovil
Somerset BA22 7JJ England